CHAPTER 7: Identity and Difference in Organizational Life

RX FOR SALES: RECRUIT CHEERLEADERS! Are good looks and a perky personality the most important qualifications for female sales representatives? Analyze the trend of hiring former NCAA female cheerleaders as pharmaceutical sales reps in light of your understanding of gendered identity performance. **228**

CHAPTER 8: Teams and Networks: Collaboration in the Workplace

THE NETWORKED UNIVERSITY: Universities have traditionally been closely associated with their geographic settings. In the digital age, however, universities are transcending their physical locations through online courses. If you were a reporter, how would you describe the changing landscape of higher education? **271**

THE NETWORKED COMMUNITY: Using your understanding of networks and teams to navigate existing community organizations and create new ones, help make one typical American city a better place to live. **272**

CHAPTER 9: Communicating Leadership

THE STYMIED CEO: Use what you have learned about leadership and communication to help Paula Santoro lead her regional health care system through a turbulent time while developing and executing a new vision for the organization. **307**

CHAPTER 10: Organizational Alignment: Managing the Total Enterprises

ADVERTISING AND THE AMERICAN WAY OF LIFE: Public space for noncommercial messages is diminishing in our media-saturated society. As part of a nonprofit, how would you build public awareness of social issues? **339**

HACKED OFF: Computers undoubtedly facilitate industry, but they also expose businesses to security risks. One of the challenges now facing organizations is how to create a fair policy on technology use in the workplace. How do you balance an organization's right to protect itself against an employee's need for access to technology? **340**

CHAPTER 11: Working with Integrity: Organizational Communication as Disciplined Practice

KING DICK **354** / MISS ELIZABETH **355** PHONE RAGE **356** / WHISTLE WHILE YOU WORK? **358** In each of these "caselets," taken directly from the authors' own consulting work, you are presented with a difficult workplace scenario and then given the challenge, "It's Monday morning. What do you do?"

FIFTH EDITION

ORGANIZATIONAL COMMUNICATION

Balancing Creativity and Constraint

ERIC M. EISENBERG
University of South Florida

H. L. GOODALL JR.
Arizona State University

ANGELA TRETHEWEY
Arizona State University

Bedford / St. Martin's
Boston ◆ *New York*

For Bedford/St. Martin's

Executive Editor: Erika Gutierrez
Developmental Editor: Karen Schultz
Editorial Assistant: Matthew Burgess
Production Supervisor: Andrew Ensor
Marketing Manager: Rachel Falk
Text Design: Books By Design, Inc.
Project Management: Books By Design, Inc.
Cover Design: Donna L. Dennison
Cover Art: *Tahkt-I-Sulayman Variation II*, by Frank Stella. Acrylic on canvas.
The Minneapolis Institute of Arts, Gift of funds from Bruce B. Dayton.
© 2006 Frank Stella / Artists Rights Society (ARS), New York.
Composition: Books By Design, Inc.
Printing and Binding: RR Donnelley & Sons, Inc.

President: Joan E. Feinberg
Editorial Director: Denise B. Wydra
Director of Marketing: Karen Melton Soeltz
Director of Editing, Design, and Production: Marcia Cohen
Manager, Publishing Services: Emily Berleth

Library of Congress Control Number: 2006920125

Copyright © 2007 by Bedford/St. Martin's

All rights reserved. No part of this book may be reproduced, stored in a retrieval system, or transmitted in any form or by any means, electronic, mechanical, photocopying, recording, or otherwise, except as may be expressly permitted by the applicable copyright statutes or in writing by the Publisher.

Manufactured in the United States of America.

2 1 0 9 8
f e

For information, write:
Bedford/St. Martin's, 75 Arlington Street, Boston, MA 02116   (617-399-4000)

ISBN-10: 0-312-44239-4
ISBN-13: 978-0-312-44239-2

Acknowledgments

Acknowledgments and copyrights appear at the back of the book on pages 405–7, which constitute an extension of the copyright page.

To those who remind us
of the necessity of the search for,
and the joy of creating,
"balanced" lives

Preface

These are strange times for organizational communication. As we set out to write this latest edition of our textbook, many of the natural and social systems we have taken for granted for decades seem headed for crises. The reality of global warming hit home along with the most urgent call yet for a planetary response. Soaring fuel prices put into doubt the long-term viability of many airlines and auto companies. The United States is engaged in what now seems destined to be a protracted war against a series of loosely connected networks of ill-defined enemies in the Middle East. And the horrific ethical missteps by corporations such as Enron continue to haunt the current business environment, as a series of denials and plea deals made by key executives in these cases makes the potential for real change unlikely.

Understanding this bleak and fragmented social context is important because we are each born into a world of dynamic but imperfect institutions and organizations. Like a set of Russian dolls, our identities sit inside relationships, families, communities, businesses, societies, and nations, each of which shapes how we think of ourselves and live in the world. As teachers, we believe that helping our students think critically about the state of organizations — from the university level to the national level — can generate profound conversations inside and outside the classroom and serve as an impetus for positive change. We trust that effective communication is the key requirement for creating and sustaining a truly democratic society.

This book, therefore, distills what we have learned about the role and importance of organizational communication within today's rapidly evolving social context, and we proudly share it with you. From its inception to this fifth edition, our text has evolved to meet the demands of the field and the organizational communication classroom. But it has remained unchanged in two important ways: its model and its goal. We emphasize balancing creativity and constraint, the ability to simultaneously consider the enabling and constraining aspects of communication. Striking this balance helps people to achieve their professional and personal goals. As humans we struggle to be individualistic and heroic (assert our creativity) yet still belong to a group (respond to social and institutional constraints). Our model examines this struggle through the lens of everyday communication practices as they play out in the workplace.

Likewise, our aim for this text has always been to help students bridge the gap between what they learn in school and what they experience at work. Toward this end, we have devised numerous case studies—many new to this edition—with thought-provoking assignments at the conclusion of each chapter. Our "What Would You Do?" boxes, included in every chapter, challenge students to resolve various ethical dilemmas they might face in today's business world. Based in fact and relevant to the ideas discussed in each chapter, the scenarios posed in the case studies and ethics boxes truly place the concepts of organizational communication in the context of the workplace. Finally, to assist students in recognizing and recalling them, we have placed all key concepts in bold-faced type.

NEW TO THIS EDITION

Whenever we approach a new edition of *Organizational Communication* we are guided by our colleagues' suggestions as well as a desire to provide our readers with the most current and relevant research available. In support of this goal, we added a superb new coauthor, Angela Trethewey. Angela brings a fresh critical voice to the book, focusing on numerous contemporary issues such as employee health, work/life balance, new communication technology, and identity and difference in the workplace.

We also care a great deal about finding new and innovative ways to offer students practical applications of organizational communication's theories and concepts. To this end, we are excited to introduce a new feature, "Everyday Organizational Communication," that enables students to recognize the ways they already use—or potentially could use—ideas from the text in daily life.

Organizational Communication, fifth edition, also boasts two new chapters and two refocused, significantly revised chapters:

- **A thoroughly revised Chapter 6.** "Critical Approaches to Organizations and Communication" utilizes compelling examples to provide students with an accessible introduction to critical concepts such as ideology, hegemony, concertive control, and discipline to better understand and critique commonly accepted organizing practices.
- **A new Chapter 7.** "Identity and Difference in Organizational Life" draws on feminist and critical theories to help students understand how differences, including gender, race, and class, are created and reproduced, particularly in relation to work/life balance, and enables students to explore how their own identities are already shaped by organizational communication.
- **A refocused Chapter 8.** "Teams and Networks: Collaboration in the Workplace" helps students understand and apply principles of democratic participation to the global workplace where collaboration on team projects, in

mediated groups, and across networks as well as within industries and cultures are the expectation.

- **A new Chapter 9.** "Communicating Leadership" examines the nature of effective leadership today and its heavy emphasis on communication. With a look at the vast body of work on leadership effectiveness, this new chapter identifies key practices of accomplished leaders across a range of settings.

An improved *Instructor's Manual* has been prepared by Marianne LeGreco to supplement the fifth edition of the text. This new manual contains clear and concise lecture notes, lists of key terms, essay/discussion questions, on-line resources, and lists of feature films, documentaries, and television shows that are useful in the classroom.

OVERVIEW OF THE BOOK

Part I of the text, "Approaching Organizational Communication," includes two chapters that provide readers with an overview of the discipline and the concepts they'll need to master the ideas and methods presented throughout the rest of the text. Chapter 1, "Communication and the Changing World of Work," introduces the idea of organizational communication, provides reasons for its study, and describes in detail the nature of the work today. Chapter 2, "Defining Organizational Communication," examines four definitions of the concept and offers the notion of organizational dialogues as a productive way to think about communication at work.

Part II of the text, "Theories of Organizational Communication," covers five distinct theoretical perspectives on organizational communication that motivate research and practice. Chapter 3, "Three Early Perspectives on Organizations and Communication," reviews classical organizational theory and explores its implications for communication. Chapters 4 and 5 address what are perhaps the two leading perspectives on organizations today: systems and cultures. More specifically, Chapter 4, "The Systems Perspective on Organizations and Communication," applies various forms of systems theories and demonstrates how they are useful for thinking about communicating and organizing. Chapter 5, "Cultural Studies of Organizations and Communication," uses a metaphor borrowed from anthropology and adopted by many organizations to examine the role of communication in the creation, maintenance, and transformation of organizational reality. Finally, Chapter 6, "Critical Approaches to Organizations and Communication," takes a different approach altogether, starting with the premise that research should be directed at illuminating and correcting inequalities at work. Particular attention is paid to how privilege is distributed unevenly across race, gender, and class differences.

Part III of the text, "Contexts for Organizational Communication," explores the various practical settings in which the theories described above can be applied. It starts with Chapter 7, "Identity and Difference in Organizational Life," which recasts organizations as the site of multiple and intersecting identifications and explores multiple ways of organizing difference. Chapter 8, "Teams and Networks: Collaboration in the Workplace," takes a specific look at incremental and more radical attempts to organize through the use of teams and networks, along with a review of those factors that most influence their success. Chapter 9, "Communicating Leadership," reframes leadership as a communicative activity, reviews relevant research, and presents a summary of practical forms of effective leader communication. Chapter 10, "Organizational Alignment: Managing the Total Enterprise," argues that for an organization to be truly effective, good communication must be accompanied by many other changes to an organization's current alignment.

Finally, Part IV, "Applications," is comprised of one chapter. Chapter 11, "Working with Integrity: Organizational Communication as Disciplined Practice," is the capstone of the text, bringing a semester's worth of experiences and learning to bear on the realities of organizational life in the workplace. The book concludes with an appendix, "A Field Guide to Studying Organizational Communication," that provides students and instructors with a helpful step-by-step process for planning, researching, participating in, and writing a qualitative account of an organization's communication practices.

ACKNOWLEDGMENTS

Textbooks are published with the authors' names listed on the cover but are in every way a team effort. We are especially grateful for the strong support this edition of *Organizational Communication: Balancing Creativity and Constraint* has received from Bedford/St. Martin's. In particular, we want to thank Erika Gutierrez, executive editor; Karen Schultz, our development editor; Matthew Burgess, editorial assistant; Emily Berleth, manager of publishing services; and Herb Nolan at Books By Design. All of these fine professionals contributed to this project in ways that have made the fifth edition of this text the best book it could have been.

We also want to thank our colleagues and friends at other universities and colleges who reviewed the fifth edition and offered insightful suggestions for improvement: Julian Scholl, Texas Tech University; AJ Critchfield, George Washington University; Alexandra Murphy, DePaul University; Kathleen Golden, Edinboro University of Pennsylvania; Linda Dickerhoof, George Mason University; Thomas Downard, Northeastern University; Steven Madden, Clemson University; Tammy Shapiro, Ithaca College; Joann Keyton, University of Kansas; and Ellen Bonaguro, Western Kentucky University.

In addition, we are personally and professionally indebted to a number of colleagues, students, and staff members for their support in this project: Pete Kellett of the University of North Carolina at Greensboro; Patricia Riley of the University of Southern California; Jay Baglia of the San Jose State University; and Bruce Hyde of St. Cloud State University. Thanks also to Marianne LeGreco at Arizona State University for her fine work on the *Instructor's Manual* for this edition.

Finally, we could not have written this edition without the enthusiastic and loving support of members of our immediate families—Lori Roscoe, Evan and Joel Eisenberg, Sandra and Nic Goodall, and Jeff and Anna Brown. We are also grateful for our extended families—especially Clarence and Martha Bray and Karner, Candy, and Allyson Trethewey—and our close friends.

As always, we are grateful to those individuals who, despite the intellectual, social, political, economic, and spiritual turmoil of our time, remain committed to continuing the dialogue.

Eric M. Eisenberg
University of South Florida

H. L. Goodall Jr.
Arizona State University, Tempe

Angela Trethewey
Arizona State University, Tempe

Contents

About the Authors

Eric M. Eisenberg first learned about the field of communication from his father, Abne Eisenberg, a communication professor at Queens College. Abne enlisted Eric's help in grading exams and papers, and over the next fifteen years, despite numerous detours (e.g., microbiology, poetry, and pre-med), Eric kept returning to his first love. He graduated Phi Beta Kappa with a bachelor's degree in communication from Rutgers University.

When selecting graduate schools, Eisenberg went in search of quality training in communication research methods to complement his fine education in communication theory at Rutgers. Michigan State University was purported to be a methodological Mecca, so Eisenberg packed up his old yellow Ford Fairlane 500 (with no heater!) and headed west. It was at MSU that he discovered that the research that interested him most had a decidedly practical bent. He received his master's degree in communication working with Dr. Cassandra Book on an experiment evaluating the most effective uses of simulations and games in the classroom. Dr. Book was a superb mentor and master teacher who encouraged Eisenberg to complete a second master's degree in education in 1980. Book also gave him his first taste of organizational research—they conducted a needs assessment and communication network analysis of the American Dietetic Association. He got rid of the freezing Ford the first winter in Michigan.

Having been raised in a household with no links to corporate America, Eisenberg was intrigued by the possibility of learning about the "real world" of organizational communication. Determined to become fluent in both management and communication, and under the expert guidance of Dr. Peter Monge, he immersed himself in management theory and practice, publishing work on organizational communication networks and superior-subordinate communication. Eisenberg received his doctorate in communication from Michigan State University in 1982. He now owned two suits.

The city boy had learned to love the Midwest, but it was time to head east again. Intrigued by the original and expansive writings of Dr. Art Bochner (who had spent a fortuitous semester at MSU), Eisenberg took his first academic position in the Department of Speech at Temple University in Philadelphia. It was there that he wrote his award-winning paper on the strategic uses of ambiguity in organizations, and with the support of his colleagues at Temple, turned his attention more closely to the uses of language and symbols in organizational life. He stayed connected to business practice by launching and directing the applied communication master's program at Temple and teaching at the downtown campus. During this period, he married Lori Roscoe (whom he had met at Michigan State) and they started building a life together.

In 1984, Eisenberg left Philadelphia to join the communication faculty at the University of Southern California. Over the next decade, he was promoted to associate professor with tenure, published numerous studies of organizational communication and culture, and received recognition as University Scholar and Outstanding Teacher. His paper "Jamming: Transcendence through Organizing" received the NCA research award for the best publication in organizational communication in 1990. At the same time, Eisenberg worked closely with Dr. Patricia Riley on numerous grants and contracts aimed at applying cutting-edge knowledge about communication to organizational practice across a variety of industries (e.g., aerospace, health care, electronics, manufacturing). Meanwhile, Evan and Joel were born at Good Samaritan Hospital in downtown Los Angeles. Eisenberg published his bittersweet poems from this period in a collection called *Fiction and Social Research: By Ice or Fire* (A. Banks and S. Banks, eds.).

USC was a world-class institution, but Los Angeles was a hard place to raise a family. Eisenberg took a position as full professor at the University of South Florida in 1994, staying true to his lifelong pledge to remain within driving distance of a Disney amusement park. He was attracted to USF for its extraordinary faculty, the energy of a young school with a new doctoral program in communication, and his old friend Art Bochner. Immediately he knew he had found his home—an eccentric but winning department where experience and philosophy were privileged over theory and method. More publications followed, including his first textbook (this one!) and other strange forays into the world of communication and organizational change.

Once in Florida, Eisenberg's consulting work shifted toward the hospitality and health-care industries. In 1996, Eisenberg was elected chair of the Department of Communication at USF, where he recently completed his second five-year term. In addition to this version of his textbook, Eisenberg recently completed a "greatest hits" collection of his writings entitled *Strategic Ambiguities*, to be published by Sage later this year. Eisenberg and his family love the Tampa Bay area and he is grateful for the opportunities to teach and learn from exceptional people whenever and wherever he finds them.

Harold Lloyd (Bud) Goodall Jr. has been both a subject and a student of organizations since his birth, in King's Daughters Hospital, in Martinsburg, West Virginia, in 1952. Reared in a traditional family; educated in public and private schools and universities; employed by large and small businesses in occupations/professions as diverse as short order cook, college professor, rhythm guitarist in a rock band, organizational detective, account executive for a broadcasting company, and member of a counter-terrorism group; participant and volunteer in community and political activities; co-owner of a publishing house; and partner in a consulting firm. All of these organizational experiences have shaped his approach to studying, writing about, and living his many and varied organizational lives.

He first became interested in researching and writing about organizational communication while a new faculty member at the University of Alabama in Huntsville. As a resident "communication specialist," he was asked to develop training sessions in "effective communication" for scientific and engineering firms that supported NASA's Space Shuttle, the U.S. Army's Redstone Arsenal, and the federal government's Star Wars project. Later, as his interest in organizations grew from training to consulting and his scholarly interests shifted from traditional social science to interpretive forms of inquiry, he applied detective methods to various high-technology firms and government agencies. These interpretive methods included his going undercover in the organizations to experience firsthand the lives that were lived there. The result of those years of study and writing were captured in his first two organizational ethnographies, *Casing a Promised Land: The Autobiography of an Organizational Detective as Cultural Ethnographer* (1989) and *Living in the Rock n Roll Mystery: Reading Context, Self, and Others as Clues* (1991).

Goodall received his B.A. from Shepherd College in 1973, his M.A. from the University of North Carolina at Chapel Hill in 1974, and his doctorate in speech communication from Pennsylvania State University in 1980. He has taught at the University of Alabama in Huntsville, the University of Utah, Clemson University, and the University of North Carolina at Greensboro, and currently serves as Professor and Director of the Hugh Downs School of Human Communication at Arizona State University. In four of his academic positions—UAH, Clemson, UNCG, and ASU—he applied his understanding of organizational and learning theories to lead communication departments and curricula in which vision, mission, values, and course work are strategically aligned and students are better served. His work in the academic community was honored with the Gerald M. Phillips award for Distinguished Scholarship in Applied Communication by the National Communication Association.

Goodall's primary scholarly mission has been to change the way texts about organizations and communication are written in an effort to make them more accessible, more representative of everyday life, and more creatively engaging. His ethnographies have received laudatory reviews and awards from both academic and nonacademic sources, and over two hundred colleges and universities worldwide have adopted his textbooks. He has been consistently featured in the popular press and media from coast to coast for his trade books. Most recently he authored *A Need to Know: The Clandestine History of a CIA Family* (Left Coast Press, 2006), a work that combines personal narrative with Cold War history and an organizational study of secrecy, power, and family during an "enduring war." As a member of ASU's Consortium on Strategic Communication, he is also actively involved in analyzing message strategies deployed in the current global War on Terror. Overall, he is the author or coauthor of nineteen textbook, trade, and scholarly volumes and over one hundred journal articles, book chapters, and scholarly presentations. He is listed in *Contemporary Authors, Dictionary of American Scholars*, and *Who's Who International*.

"Dr. Bud" is married to Sandra Goodall, who received her advanced training in communication at the University of Utah. She is a private organizational consultant and Feng Shui master with a passion for organizing workplaces and home spaces as sources of balance and harmony in people's lives. Together they have a son, Nicolas Saylor Goodall, who already lives a life full of rock 'n' roll, fencing, computers, and good friends. They make their home in Chandler, Arizona.

As a critical communication scholar, **Angela Trethewey** believes she is a discursive production of several intertwining and sometimes contradictory cultural, institutional, organizational, familial, and relational narratives. Trethewey was born into a long line of strong women in Washington State in 1965, during the early days of the second wave of the feminist movement. Her great-grandmother, an immigrant homesteader, spent her life working the family farm. Her grandmother defied the conventions of both her immigrant parents and the social mores of the day by moving off the farm and into the big city (Seattle), where she eventually supported her husband and three daughters as a jazz pianist. She instilled in her daughters a love of music and books and modeled self-sufficiency in an era that did not encourage women to combine work outside the home and family, let alone "balance" those two worlds. Trethewey's research on women's struggles to negotiate effective and efficacious identities in the workplace is both a homage to and a continuation of her foremothers' trailblazing, but very different, lives.

Trethewey spent her childhood in a small town in Northern California in a family in which education was understood to be life's work—both literally and figuratively. She was raised by two public school teachers who embodied the sheer joy and the practical utility of continuous, lifelong learning. Neither her mother nor her father told her that education was inextricably linked to living a rich, full, interesting and productive life; that message was simply evident in all that they did. Today, Trethewey strives to model that same message for her students at Arizona State University. That teaching philosophy was honored when she received the Master Teacher Award from the Western States Communication Association.

Trethewey received her undergraduate and master's degrees from California State University, Chico. She earned her doctoral degree in organizational communication at Purdue University, where she had the good fortune to work with two of the brightest minds in the field—Dr. Linda Putnam and Dr. Dennis Mumby. She was first introduced to the field of communication in an undergraduate gender and communication course. She was so intrigued by the subject matter that she changed her major from business administration to communication. It was in that same course that she first encountered her future husband, Jeff Brown. Nearly twenty years later, she continues to delight in exploring the complexities and organization of gendered communication—both in her research and in her marriage.

Trethewey is currently an associate professor and the associate director of the Hugh Downs School of Human Communication at Arizona State University, where she teaches classes in organizational communication, communication theory, and critical research methods. She has published over twenty articles and book chapters, one of which received the Organization for the Study of Women and Language's Article of the Year Award. She is involved in the Project for Wellness and Work-Life at ASU, a working group of scholars, including Drs. Sarah Tracy and Jess Alberts, whose mission is to conduct research and inspire policy and practice that enable employees to experience richer, fuller, and healthier work/lives.

Trethewey can trace the impact of her narrative roots as she continues to craft her current story in her everyday life. Today, her own work/life is often complicated by, but always joyful as a result of, her relationship with her delightful daughter, seven-year-old Anna Trethewey Brown. Each day, Trethewey lives the sometimes energizing, sometimes draining, identity of a working mother in contemporary organizational and family life. She uses those experiences to help her reflect on and ultimately change the ways that our culture, organizations, and even family systems, however unwittingly, constrain women's and men's ability to live their lives to their fullest potential.

At end of the day and at the end of her career, Trethewey hopes to leave Anna with new versions of the narrative gifts she has inherited from her mothers—resiliency, intellectual curiosity, gratitude, laughter, joie de vivre, and, of course, a rich, productive and empowering communicative repertoire! It is in that same spirit that she embraced the writing of this book.

PART I

APPROACHING ORGANIZATIONAL COMMUNICATION

CHAPTER 1

Communication and the Changing World of Work

From the moment we are born we are surrounded by people. With few instincts, human beings need each other for survival. As we seek to understand the people on whom we rely most, we learn many related things at once—a language, a culture, and, most important, a sense of self. We discover who we are through our communication with others.

Although each of us goes through this discovery process, no two people come out the same. Even small differences in genetics or upbringing result in marked variations in character and perception. Over time, we each develop habitual ways of seeing the world—called **worldviews** or perceptual sets—that reflect our inclinations and experiences. Tall or short, male or female, manager or employee, African or Eastern European, people perceive the world differently in accord with their worldview, and no two are exactly alike.

Where do these worldviews come from? Which life experiences are most influential in shaping who we become? We spend our lives as members of numerous social groups: family, church, school, business, and country. Our membership in these groups shapes our sense of self. At the same time, participation in these groups requires interaction with others who are often different from us. To both have a self and be a functioning member of a society, we must learn how to communicate with diverse others. In primitive times, humans banded together to hunt, gather, and grow food, as well as to propagate the species. Human survival has always hinged on our ability to work together. The history of human civilization is fundamentally a history of organizing.

While collaborating with diverse others is unavoidable, it is by no means easy. What makes organizing so challenging? Let's start by recognizing that some tasks are easier than others. In sports, for example, where there are clearly defined rules, roles, and goals, coordination is relatively unproblematic. Simple bank transactions, mail delivery, and traffic patterns on an interstate are other examples of continuous coordination around clearly defined rules that are not open to interpretation. In each of these instances, people know what they want and have a well-defined notion of what it will take to get it.

Unfortunately, many organizing challenges are far more complex and ambiguous. For example, how does one build a successful business? What is the best structure for local government? What kind of communication characterizes successful work-life balance? We are on very different ground here: Goals, rules, and roles are negotiable and open to interpretation. Particularly in contemporary societies (as opposed to traditional ones), there are few givens in social life — most everything is negotiable.

In school, the dreaded group project provides an emotionally charged example of the challenges inherent in organizing. On the surface, the assignment seems straightforward, and we tend to assume that our fellow group members have ideas similar to ours. In time, however, it becomes clear to us that people have different goals, values, motivations, and worldviews. For each group member who seeks perfection, there is someone who has no problem settling for a C; for every person who likes to get work done in advance, there is someone who prefers to wait to finish the project the night before it is due. Organizing people in business is equally challenging. The quick fix seldom works. For example, redefining how people work together by grouping a bunch of people who are accustomed to working in isolation and calling them a "team" is misleading and does more damage than good. In any setting, organizing takes work, and the special challenge of organizing is to collaborate in ways that both acknowledge and bridge differing worldviews.

The interaction required to direct a group toward a set of common goals is called **organizational communication**. Nothing about this process is automatic or easy; certain knowledge and skills are required to succeed. Moreover, as we go about our lives we enter into one interaction after another, always in the shadow of multiple large organizations, whether at a school, a hospital, or a local restaurant. In each of these interactions, we are occasionally satisfied, but more often we are frustrated by incompetence, insensitivity, lack of coordination, and red tape, all of which result from ineffective organizational communication. A deeper understanding of communication permits us to better comprehend the factors that contribute to successful organizing. We designed this book to help you to develop this deeper understanding.

◪ THE CHANGING WORLD OF WORK

What kinds of communication are required for survival in the world of work? To answer this, we must first understand how this world has evolved and the conditions to which we must adapt and respond to be successful. These conditions have changed significantly in recent years, so it is important that we reexamine our assumptions about what is most likely to be effective as we strive to create a successful work life.

☐ Questions, Not Answers

Students embarking on careers often harbor misconceptions about the world of work. Many expect their first "real" job to be far more serious and orderly than it turns out to be. Likewise, they expect competent and fair managers. They are often disappointed. Once on the job, they may expect a stable career with a company, only to be surprised by the steady stream of mergers, acquisitions, and joint ventures that change their job duties and add to their workload. The near universal feeling of continuous change is disturbing to many people, and each of us, regardless of industry, is challenged to find ways to deal with it. Even at the university, many long-time teachers are highly frustrated with what they see as changing priorities of the institution, which include a greater emphasis of fund-raising and funded research.

How can we deal with constant change in the world of work? There are no easy answers. Even seemingly straightforward questions like "What is the best way to supervise employees?" or "How does one attract and keep customers?" don't permit a simple response. As a result, the definition of effective communication necessarily varies by company and industry, the particular people involved, and the culture.

Put another way, answers to questions about organizational communication are highly situated and perishable. By "situated," we mean that communication that works well for an on-line T-shirt distributor like Digital Gravel may be inappropriate for a mature film-production company like Paramount Pictures. By "perishable," we mean that patterns of interaction that were effective last year may be outdated today due to changes in customer tastes and technology. Companies that fail to recognize the need for change may perish. One example from our experience involves a machine shop in California. The general manager, a Marine Corps veteran, modeled the shop's management systems and structures on the military. Although this approach may have been effective for selected industries in the past, it did not work for this machine shop. Neither the managers nor the employees were comfortable with the rigid hierarchy and the intimidating management style. Eventually, employee resistance turned into open hostility, and the general manager was ousted by the board of directors and replaced by an outsider with a more participative approach.

The rapid changes taking place in today's world demand speedy, flexible responses. Flexibility is not characteristic of the traditional military model. In a historic company-wide restructuring in the 1980s, IBM escaped obsolescence by creating numerous independent business units to meet the demand for greater flexibility. Similarly, in the 1990s, General Electric reconsidered the wisdom of an autocratic management style, moving from a top-down approach to the current structure, in which employees are regularly given opportunities ("Workouts") to talk back to managers and to question the status quo. Most recently, Apple Computer put potential employees through numerous rounds of interviews aimed at identifying those candidates who will fit best with its challenging, dynamic corporate culture.

When we first taught classes in organizational communication over twenty-five years ago, the banking, air transportation, and fast-food industries were considered to be relatively placid. Competition was weak, and there was room for many players in each industry. Today, these are among the most highly competitive industries in the world. Rapid change also means that the nature of organizational communication in the business world of even five years ago no longer applies. Moreover, what we believe to be true today may have limited relevance in the future. For this reason, our focus here is on enabling you to ask good questions about organizations, the answers to which may change over time.

As a successful executive, consultant, researcher, manager, or employee you must have a talent for asking good questions about organizational communication situations. Over time, your actions will be guided by how you see and make sense of such situations, by keeping an open mind to the various interpretations, and by remaining committed to a lifetime of learning. Flexibility enables you to manage diversity more effectively and to adapt more readily to a turbulent business environment. You will be able to reinvent yourself and your organization both in response to and in anticipation of changing times.

☐ New Developments in the World of Work

In the space of just a few years, tragic world events transformed how Americans think and feel about organizations. The terrorist attacks on New York, Madrid, and London revealed the depth of animosity harbored by at least some of the world's citizens against capitalism and its most visible associations. In the 1990s, we were faced with shocking news concerning massive financial misconduct by trusted executive officers and their accountants (e.g., Enron, WorldCom, Tyco, Arthur Andersen), and the more we learn about the actions of these corporate executives, the more cynical we become. The ensuing dramatic decline of the stock market was only one symptom of the pain caused by these events; many thousands of layoffs provide further bleak testimony. Americans were left to wonder "How could these things happen?" and "What next?" The current attitude toward organizations in the United States could well be characterized as one of deep skepticism, if not anger.

Moreover, the intensity of these feelings shows no sign of subsiding. The war in Iraq continues to claim many lives and has polarized American citizens, as evidenced in the 2004 U.S. presidential elections. Politically aware, well-intentioned individuals disagree strongly about the meaning of American actions in the world today. In the meantime, prisoner abuse in Iraq has caused many people to question both the intentions and the competence of their government. Taken together, we are witnessing a fantastic breakdown in public confidence in governance of all kinds, both federal and corporate. All of the old structures designed to provide order, oversight, and, above all, control, are no longer effective and have in some cases led to staggering abuses of power.

But alongside these hopeless feelings there is also some slim sense of a possible rebirth, of a desire to rediscover and recommit to the things that matter most: our core values and beliefs. At a superficial level, most corporate and government leaders have rewritten their public addresses to emphasize the importance of ethics and integrity. But regaining public confidence will not be easy, nor will these leaders reestablish credibility any time soon. For this to happen, these new claims to integrity must be tested repeatedly on a global economic stage that continues to reward ruthlessness, exploitation, and expediency.

One ray of hope in the search for value-driven work lies in the proliferation and increasing sophistication of not-for-profit organizations (Eisenberg & Eschenfelder, 2006). Although these types of agencies were traditionally founded to address specific social problems, governments are relying on them more than ever to provide both needed social services and broader social advocacy for important elements of the common good. Two notable examples are homeless services and environmental advocacy. In the Tampa Bay area, not-for-profit agencies like the Mustard Seed receive federal and state funding to provide services to the homeless population. Less formally, concerned citizens formed the Hillsborough River Greenways Task Force as a not-for-profit whose mission is to ensure a positive future for the river (Andrews, 2000). While neither organization operates for profit, both provide advocacy for important issues and direct public service. In this way, not-for-profits serve by emphasizing the importance of community within our increasingly individualist, capitalist society.

The massive changes in the realities of organizing in the twenty-first century can be characterized using three critical dimensions: space, time, and loyalty. In the remainder of this chapter, we discuss each dimension and provide examples of how it has changed the nature and meaning of organizational communication.

☐ Beyond Space: The Global Economy

Toward the end of the twentieth century, remarkable changes in global politics — the end of the Cold War, the breakup of the Soviet Union, the destruction of the Berlin Wall in Germany, and the forging of a unified European Community — altered or dissolved divisions that once seemed insurmountable. Many saw in the collapse of old structures the promise of new alliances striving to end poverty and suffering worldwide, and the potential to adopt a universal, indeed, planetary code of human rights. This is one version of the dream of **globalization**, defined as:

> the closer integration of the countries and peoples of the world which has been brought about by the enormous reduction of costs of transportation and communication, and the breaking down of artificial barriers to the flows of goods, services, capital, knowledge and (to a lesser extent) people across borders. (Stiglitz, 2002, p. 9)

Many aspects of globalization, such as artistic exchange and easier access to medical care, are almost universally welcome. More controversial have been the economic issues, specifically the policies, agenda, and effectiveness of the international institutions that have emerged to regulate the global economy: the World Bank, the International Monetary Fund (IMF), and the World Trade Organization (WTO). Both the World Bank and the IMF were formed in 1944 to rebuild a war-torn Europe and prevent future international economic depressions. (Note the focus on Europe: Many of today's so-called Third World countries were colonies of European nations at the time, and their development was clearly a secondary concern.) The same 1944 agreement called for the formation of a facilitating body that would encourage the free flow of goods through measures such as lowering tariffs. More than fifty years later, the World Trade Organization finally came into being, and its conferences have become a lightning rod for those protesting the negative economic effects of globalization on the environment and the world's poor. Violent protests accompanying WTO meetings (in Washington, D.C.; Seattle; and Genoa, Italy, during 2001 and 2002) highlighted for the first time the widespread opposition to aspects of economic globalization.

There is growing recognition among social commentators that the institutions promoting a global economy have made a number of serious errors. The most critical mistakes have been those involving the pace at which it is possible or desirable for a country to make the transition to a market economy where prices and wages are determined mainly by the laws of supply and demand, rather than being regulated by the government. An unreasonably optimistic belief in the self-regulating power of a market economy has led the IMF in particular to force nations needing its help to privatize their industries and open their markets before adequate regulatory frameworks are in place. Such changes have brought disastrous results in some countries. For example, in Russia, the poor are in many ways worse off under market capitalism than they were under their prior socialist regime. A second problem with the current approach has been the failure to recognize that there are multiple models for a market economy and that other versions — for example, the Japanese, German, and Swedish models — have advantages that may be more useful (and a better fit than the American model) for developing countries. On a more hopeful note, those countries that have not relied on the magic of self-regulation but have recognized the role government could play in the transition to markets (e.g., Thailand, Indonesia) have been more successful (Stiglitz, 2002).

Amidst this struggle, the number of organizations that operate globally has grown exponentially. As of 2004, more than half of all U.S. companies conduct business internationally, which includes having foreign customers, suppliers, and employees. While half of Xerox's 110,000 employees work overseas, half of Sony's employees are not Japanese. The United States enjoys imported music, and American music, films, and television command large markets abroad. In China, foreign investors in 2004 alone invested $57 billion and started 40,000 new companies.

Three regions will dominate the global marketplace during the next few decades: the Pacific Rim (China, in particular), North America (Canada especially), and the European Union (EU). Although globalization gives the United States an expanded market for its products and services, it also threatens to erode U.S. business because of increased foreign competition. At one time, U.S. consumers could respond meaningfully to these challenges by "buying American," but the globalization of business has made this slogan almost meaningless. For example, in October 2002 VF Corporation—the largest apparel firm in the world—shut down its only remaining American plant. Many new automobile buyers who want to remain loyal to American brands have discovered that their supposedly American cars are manufactured or assembled in foreign countries. Similarly, it is harder to define precisely what is foreign. Consider that Jaguar, once a British manufacturer, is now a Ford subsidiary, as is Volvo, which was once a Swedish company.

But globalization has provided far more challenges to our way of thinking and working than simply complicating how we define the origin of a particular product or service. It has also brought new issues concerning questionable labor practices, multicultural management, and communication technology.

Questionable Labor Practices

The emergence of a new world labor pool has encouraged businesses to search the globe for the lowest possible labor costs and move jobs wherever cheap labor can be found, a practice known as **outsourcing**. Although such practices have a long and checkered history in textiles and manufacturing, they were confined almost exclusively to blue-collar jobs. Today, white-collar jobs in most industries are also affected by this trend. For example, most U.S. software designers employ engineering and call-center staffs in India and the Philippines. It is even likely that the final manuscript for this textbook was prepared by keyboarders in Asia.

Not all outsourcing of work leads to the loss of U.S. jobs, however. In some cases, European and Asian companies have set up operations in the United States. As of 2004 foreign companies employed 6.4 million workers in the United States. Many of these jobs—like those at the BMW plant in South Carolina and the Honda plants in Ohio—pay higher wages than the many jobs that are outsourced to other countries.

The potential consequences of U.S. jobs being moved overseas were at the center of the debate over the North American Free Trade Agreement (NAFTA), an

EVERYDAY ORGANIZATIONAL COMMUNICATION

Globalization and You!

Although many of us as consumers are uncomfortable with some of the more damaging and controversial effects that globalization has had on the environment, communities, and employees (both domestic and international), we feel overwhelmed and are unsure about how to respond productively. After all, how can one person have an impact on such a massive international challenge? Luckily, several organizations have begun campaigns to involve average citizens, from college students to CEOs and retired grandparents, in the cause to counter the negative effects of globalization.

Oxfam America, an international development and relief agency, has developed a student action group that offers "young people a wide range of opportunities to become better educated and join the fight against global poverty and injustice around the world" (Oxfam America, 2006). Such education is achieved through workshops and training aimed at students, and also through the publication of campus action guides that offer specific plans, such as fighting for fair-trade coffee on campus, for combating problems associated with globalization. The organization also highlights stories of everyday people who are attempting to have a positive impact on the world. Consider the story of a six-year-old boy who went door-to-door passing out brochures on world hunger to educate his neighbors and the students at Cornell University who organized a fair-trade carnival featuring such games as "bowl for subsidies" and pin the tail on the CAFTA (Central American Free Trade Agreement) to call attention to important global issues (Oxfam America, 2006). The point behind these strategies and stories remains consistent: You can make a difference on a daily basis by educating yourself about the effects of globalization, sharing this information with friends and colleagues, and committing to small but positive lifestyle changes (such as supporting a local, independent grocery store).

Several Web sites offer additional strategies that individuals can pursue to curb the negative consequences produced by globalization. Point your browser to a few of the following Web sites and consider their suggested actions.

- http://www.ethicalconsumer.org/aboutec/tentips.htm
- http://www.usft.org/
- http://www.unionlabel.org/
- http://www.howtobuyamerican.com/
- http://www.globalexchange.org/campaigns/sweatshops/
- http://www.oxfamamerica.org/whatyoucando/act_now

DISCUSSION QUESTIONS

1. Generate a list of strategies recommended by antiglobalization advocates (e.g., participating in Adbusters' Buy Nothing Day campaign, asking for fair-trade coffee at Starbucks, buying local, recycling, urging your campus decision makers to contract with fair-trade suppliers). Which strategies would you be willing to participate in on a regular basis?
2. Which strategies, if any, do you think have the greatest potential to enact positive social change? Why?
3. Can you envision any unintended negative consequences that may result from these suggested actions?
4. Do you think that the efforts of individuals or activist groups can make a difference in the way multinational organizations operate? Why or why not?

attempt to reduce restrictions on trade between the United States, Canada, and Mexico. On the one hand, an expanded labor pool makes U.S. companies more competitive by allowing them to hold down costs. By hiring people from less developed countries (thereby putting money in their pockets), U.S. companies gain new consumers for their products and services. On the other hand, sending work elsewhere may lead to the destruction of U.S. communities that are unable to withstand plant closings or massive job losses. Furthermore, the low wages paid to workers in less developed countries—as little as 10 to 15 percent of U.S. wages—raise questions about exploitation.

But exploitation is not limited to offshore ventures. One domestic statistic neatly reflects the nature of management-labor relations in the United States today. Between 1980 and 2000, the average pay of regular working people increased just 66 percent, while CEO pay grew a whopping 1,996 percent. According to *Business Week*'s 54th Annual Executive Compensation Survey (published in 2004) the gap in pay between average workers and large company CEOs surpassed 300-to-1 in 2003 (Lavelle, "Executive Pay," April 19, 2004). (To compare working people's salaries with those of CEOs, visit http://www.aflcio.org/corporatewatch/paywatch/.) In 2000, the United States became the Western industrial nation with the largest percentage of the world's rich and the biggest gap between rich and poor (Phillips, 2002).

Many workers in the new global economy do not operate with the safeguards that American organizations often provide, including fair wages, health benefits, and safe working conditions. Immigrants in America, both legal and illegal, often work in subpar conditions for considerably less than minimum wage as piece-rate workers in the garment industry or as farm laborers who follow the harvest across the country, all the while living in cramped, unair-conditioned, and inhospitable camps. The American economy could not function without these underpaid and undervalued employees who come to this country in search of a better life. In fact, most middle-class Americans can scarcely get through a day without consuming the fruit of the working poor's labor, whether it be in the grocery store buying vegetables or at the mall purchasing the latest clothes or shoes (Shipler, 2004).

Another particularly troubling trend is the expanding sex trafficking industry across the globe, and particularly in Southeast Asia. Trafficking refers to the illegal trade of human beings across borders. The United Nations estimates that over 2 million people are trafficked each year, and most of these are women and children who are sold into the sex trade. Many vulnerable and poor women and children are lured by traffickers who offer promises of a better life, legitimate work, or an education, while others are sold by family members or friends for a profit. These young women and girls often end up working in brothels where the need for money "overpowers basic human rights" (Flamm, 2003, para. 3). Victims of trafficking are physically confined, their travel or identity documents are taken away, their families are threatened if they do not cooperate, and they are made dependent on their traffickers for basic needs such as food and shelter. While the United Nations and others are working to curb the illegal trafficking of women and children, it continues to be a significant problem in our increasingly global world.

Multicultural Management

Yet another challenge associated with globalization involves the **multicultural management** of customers, suppliers, and employees. Multicultural management is the ability to adapt one's leadership style to both respond to and make the most of pervasive cultural differences in values and practices among a diverse employee population. Globalization does not eliminate differences in language and culture. When expanding business across cultures, it is essential to introduce a product or service that is an identifiable example of the brand but still reflects local tastes and tolerances. McDonald's, for example, has many locations in India, where cows are sacred. In a great example of flexibility, the company's "Maharaja Macs" are made with mutton.

Success across national boundaries requires highly sophisticated, global communication skills (Dalton, Ernst, Deal, & Leslie, 2002). At a minimum, this means that employees must speak the language of their customers and suppliers and, preferably, understand the subtleties of the other cultures. Finland has relied on export markets throughout much of its history, and consequently many Finns speak four or more languages. Similarly, Western countries doing business with Japan have learned much about the Asian tendency to spend what westerners perceive as an inordinately long time planning and developing relationships.

An infamous example of botched multicultural management is Disneyland Paris (formerly Euro Disney). After achieving outstanding success with Disneyland in

Japan, where the meticulously designed theme park was consistent with the local culture, Disney opened a park in France. In this case, however, the park ignored important aspects of French culture and climate. For instance, the American-style hotels built around Disneyland Paris with rooms that cost $300 a night were not practical for the typical French family, which takes a three- to six-week vacation. In addition, when the park first opened, it did not serve alcohol, which conflicted with the French custom of drinking wine at lunchtime (this policy was soon changed). More recently, it appears that Disney has learned its lesson; the appointment of a French citizen to run Disneyland Paris and the serving of alcoholic beverages on the property have noticeably eased tensions.

Starbucks' experience expanding into Asia further illustrates the complexity of multicultural management. When seeking to open his first store in Japan, Star-bucks founder Howard Schultz was strongly cautioned by market researchers that the Japanese would not accept European-style coffee, that they preferred their cof-fee light and sweet. Schultz refused to budge, insisting that once they had experi-enced his product, the Japanese would enjoy it. After initial success in marketing the Starbucks product to the Japanese (it is pronounced STAH-buks-zu), customer acceptance of the new product declined. While sales for 2002 were up 22 percent, profits dropped 55 percent the following year due to rising import and expansion costs combined with dampening enthusiasm for its once-popular coffee. But lately there has been a resurgence of interest, as the company continues to expand and adapt to local habits and tastes.

With the acquisition of global markets, businesses have no choice but to ac-quire a more culturally diverse workforce. At Sheraton's Vistana Resort, an award-winning resort hotel in Orlando, Florida, the company's environmental services department meets regularly to address communication issues pertinent to the multi-ethnic staff, which is mainly Latino, Anglo, and Haitian. At computer hardware supplier Kyocera America in San Diego, California, a Japanese management team struggles to communicate effectively with the mostly male African American super-visors and mostly female Filipino employees on the line. As these examples show, effective organizational communication today must address a host of multicultural and multinational concerns.

An increasingly important element of diversity in the workplace is religion. In the United States, organizations regularly struggle to define the line between work and personal beliefs, understanding that people with dramatically different world-views must work side by side. Some institutions only select and promote employees with certain belief systems (Ehrenreich, 2005). In some cases, rules concerning the "right" beliefs are stated overtly, but more often they are subtle and covert. For ex-ample, a colleague of ours reports on her difficulties in getting tenure at a university with a unique religious affiliation. While no one ever said outright that she had to be a practicing member of the sect to be promoted, she was frequently asked by admin-istrators about her church attendance and her personal religious beliefs. Although the subject has not yet received much research attention, we predict that the role of religion at work will be a hot topic in the near future.

Being able to manage across cultures can be useful even within the same country. In one case, software managers at Lucent Technologies (the high-technology company that spun off from AT&T in 1996) were challenged to create the most complex product in their company's history, using five hundred engineers scattered over three continents and thirteen time zones. The product was a fiber-optic phone switch called the Bandwidth Manager. The work process was called "distributed development," and the managers found that the technology was the easy part. The hard part was agreeing on the meanings of basic words, like *test*, and reaching consensus on procedures and protocols, since each location had its own culture and traditions. Personality tests revealed that New Jersey employees, who were mostly former professors, exhibited a highly rational style of thinking. In contrast, Massachusetts employees (who were mostly manufacturing engineers) were more in tune with values and the human impact of decisions. In the end, the managers' ability to work with these differences and across these vast distances paid off handsomely, with the switch shipping on schedule, within budget, and technically superior to what was expected. The project is now described as a success story showing the potential of distributed development.

The Center for Creative Leadership, a research and development firm in North Carolina, studied the factors that lead global managers to succeed and identified four pivotal skills: (1) international business knowledge; (2) cultural adaptability; (3) ability to take the perspective of others; and (4) ability to play the role of innovator (Dalton, Ernst, Deal, and Leslie, 2002). The thread connecting these capabilities is effective communication, the ability to forge relationships with others in an open, informed way.

Communication Technology

Although we will detail the role of communication technology in contemporary organizations later in this text, it is important to say at the outset that the global business community — and the global markets, economy, and joint ventures that we have been describing — is in large part made possible by recent advances in **communication technology**. By communication technology we mean any type of electronic tool or device that may be used to enhance or enable information sharing or person-to-person interaction.

Globalization requires companies to communicate in ways that transcend space and time. Computerized communication networks — ranging from those operating over short distances (such as *intranets*) to those that span the globe (such as the *Internet*) — allow companies to coordinate production, take and service orders, schedule work, recruit employees, and market their services. Microsoft executive Bill Gates (1999) called this emerging configuration of point-to-point (or place-to-place)

Religious Differences in the Classroom

One of the most challenging issues facing organizations today is how to best honor and accommodate religious differences among their members. In a recent (2005) meeting of the Hillsborough County School Board in Tampa, Florida, a proposal by Muslim citizens to add their religious holidays (as days off) to the school calendar was met with resistance. A committee of the Board advanced a counterproposal eliminating all religious holidays, granting students "personal days" instead that they could make use of however they wished. But this proposal also met with resistance. As our societies/schools/organizations diversify, to what degree must they adapt to the religious beliefs of their members?

Another good example of the rising challenge of religious diversity occurred recently between a communication professor and her student at a state university in the southern United States. The student refused to purchase the required text for her "Women and Communication" class because she objected to the coarse language in the book title (a feminist critique of characterizations of women, it is called *Bitches, Bimbos and Ballbreakers: The Guerrilla Girls' Illustrated Guide to Female Stereotypes*). She continued, "I am a pastor's daughter. I don't swear and I don't expose myself to this kind of material. And I won't be seen around town purchasing or carrying a book with that title."

DISCUSSION QUESTIONS

1. To what extent are organizations of all kinds responsible for creating an environment that supports the religious diversity of their members? Is there a difference between accommodating, tolerating, and encouraging religious differences?
2. Have you experienced a time when your own religious beliefs came into conflict with those of an institution in which you were a member? What did you do about it, if anything, and why?
3. What should the instructor's response be to this student? What are the trade-offs between validating individual belief systems and standing up for the value of a more secular and critical approach to education?
4. How might your response to question 3 be translated into policy and practice in a broader range of noneducational organizations? What problems would you anticipate and how might you address them?

connectivity a company's "digital nervous system." Indeed, some of the most ingen-
ious applications of new communication technology have been in software manufacturing. Software and hardware manufacturer Texas Instruments has operations
in Texas, Ireland, and Indonesia that allow it to conduct business continuously. Before the workday ends in Indonesia, employees forward their work electronically to
employees in Ireland, who are just starting the workday. The employees in Ireland,
in turn, transmit their work to those in Texas before they sign off for the day.

Communication technologies also both require and invite organizations to
use information in new and often complex ways. In an increasingly dynamic environment, organizations are challenged to not only discover what they know, but
also to catalog, package and utilize their knowledge productively. **Knowledge
management** refers to the ways organizations make use of knowledge as a resource
and commodity. There are two broad approaches to knowledge management,
information-based and people- or interaction-based (Iverson & McPhee, 2002).
Information-based knowledge management is concerned with tracking, cataloging,
managing, and displaying knowledge products, which might include organizational
documents and records, speech ("this call may be recorded for quality assurance
purposes"), and behaviors. People-based knowledge management assumes that
organizational knowledge is not comprised of "information," but of networks of
"knowers" who transform data into knowledge by making it meaningful and sharing it with relevant others in a larger social context. To be truly successful, organizations must link the information-based "know how" with people-based "know
who" or knowledge of who knows what within the organization (Dooley, Corman,
& Mcphee, 2002). New communication technologies are helping organizations to
do just that.

Communication technology also enables businesses to structure themselves in
novel ways. Some observers credit the development of the telephone with the creation of the modern skyscraper, which would have been impractical and unsafe
without the ability to communicate quickly between floors. Advances in communication technology both promote global business and create new sites for work, such
as offices in cyberspace. As a billboard for telecommunications giant AT&T pro-
claims, "The office of the future has no office."

A profound impact of new communication technology on organizations within
the last decade has been the emergence of electronic commerce as a viable way of
doing business. Today, an enormous number of consumer products and services are
available for purchase over the World Wide Web, and for those products and services that cannot be purchased that way, the Web often enables the consumer to
learn about and preview the product. A study by DaimlerChrysler showed that the
vast majority of the carmaker's customers coming to their dealerships had already
visited the company Web site for information about models and available options.
Consumer hesitation associated with security and privacy are no match for the con-
venience of on-line shopping. One consequence of this shift is that *store* (along with

bank, and, soon, *library*) does not necessarily refer to a physical place. Reverberations of this are also being felt in colleges and universities; nearly one hundred educational institutions now offer virtual degree programs that can be completed anywhere. The relationships and interactions that constitute organizing can now occur without regard to physical distance or geography.

Naturally, all of this easy access to information comes at a significant risk. You have likely heard about the phenomenon of **identity theft**, whereby someone steals your identifying information and impersonates you in transactions with various stores and institutions. Universities are in the process of taking extraordinary precautions to secure student information; recently at the University of South Florida, all student I.D. numbers were changed from Social Security numbers to better protect students' identities. In 2005 alone, there were twelve instances in which large financial institutions (e.g., Citigroup, Bank of America) "lost" private data of millions of customers to hackers who infiltrated their databases. The threat posed by such thefts puts significant pressure on corporations to secure access and use of customer information.

□ Beyond Time: Competition and the Urgent Organization

Profound changes have also taken place with regard to time. In fact, we see most businesses today as **urgent organizations**, companies whose main challenge is to shorten the time in which they develop new products and respond to customer demands.

A trend that began with fast food, fax, and overnight mail continues today with the proliferation of automated teller machines, virtual libraries, and customer service call centers that are open twenty-four hours a day, seven days a week. The main motivation for all this emphasis on speed is increased competitiveness. Customers now expect to get exactly what they want, exactly when they want it (Gleick, 2000). The volume of calls to 911 has prompted some communities to create 912 numbers for serious conditions, reserving 911 for real emergencies. If *quality* was the watchword of the last decade, *velocity* is ruling the early years of this one (Gates, 1999).

Speed conveys a number of advantages to one company over another (Stalk, 1998). Consider three examples. First, companies vie to see how quickly they can bring a new product or service to market. Often, the first company to release a new product has an edge and, in computers and electronics, can sometimes set the standard by which future products are measured. Second, businesses today compete over who can provide the quickest response time to customer inquiries and concerns. In the personal computer industry, Dell has made an enormous investment in next-day, on-site service if needed, but most problems can be resolved over the phone through a customer service representative. Finally, companies today strive to shorten delivery times so that the product or service is available to you as close to the moment of purchase as possible. In the past, it was common for delivery to take six to eight weeks for a simple order; today people are demanding that customized products be both assembled and shipped within a few days at most.

One impact of organizations viewing time as a competitive advantage is greatly increased pressure on managers and employees to work faster and to be available around the clock to keep their customers, and ultimately, their jobs. Technology makes this easier all the time. At a recent executive development program we attended, senior leaders split their attention between the invited speakers and the messages on their Blackberry PDAs (personal digital assistants) for the full two days of the meeting (revealing why some call them "Crackberries" to reflect their addictive nature). While 24/7 access to employees has a clear upside for customers, its downside is the toll it may take on the health of employees and their relationships.

One useful way of thinking about how organizations are changing their relationship with time and space is to introduce the concept of an organization's environment. An organization's environment is defined as the sum total of people, institutions, and activities that exist outside of the organization's boundaries but exert actual or potential influence over the company's internal operations. The character and complexity of **organizational environment** are influenced by customers, competitors, suppliers, relevant governments, and the physical setting. From a biological perspective, we typically think of successful organisms as effectively adapting to changes in their environment. The same can be said for organizations—only in this case the changes could be happening anytime, anywhere in the world. Who could have predicted the struggles of Levi Strauss, an otherwise superb organization, when millions of young people abandoned classic "501" jeans for hip-hop inspired brands and styles. Often, companies don't know the extent of the changes brewing in their environments until a crisis reveals it to them.

The classic analysis of organizational environments employed a weather metaphor to describe variations in speed and complexity (Emery & Trist, 1965). At one extreme is the so-called turbulent environment—dense, complicated, and hard to predict. An organization in such an environment is in constant fear of environmental jolts (unexpected events that can negatively affect its business) and has difficulty forecasting the consequences of its actions (such as a new marketing strategy, distribution policy, or product feature). At the other extreme is the placid environment—uncomplicated, calm, and predictable. A company in a placid environment need not fear unexpected events and is better able to predict the consequences of its actions. Unfortunately, placid environments no longer exist outside of our grandparents' memories. Turbulence is the order of the day.

The unpredictable nature of a turbulent organizational environment has led some companies to focus on rapid retrieval of information about environmental conditions. This can involve such traditional methods as market research and customer focus groups or more innovative scanning approaches using the Internet. Recently, many companies have increased their environmental scanning efforts, but most firms still have not taken full advantage of the available wealth of information.

Perhaps the simplest, although often overlooked, way to keep in touch with environmental conditions is through **boundary spanners**, company employees who have direct contact with the public (Adams, 1980). Bank tellers, telephone receptionists, repair technicians, market researchers, salespeople, and customer service representatives can provide important information about the outside world. Boundary spanners serve at least three functions: (1) They can access the opinions of people outside of the organization and use that information to guide organizational decision making; (2) their awareness of subtle trends in the environment can serve as a warning system for environmental jolts; and (3) they serve as important representatives of the organization to its environment (Adams, 1980).

An interesting tension emerges from the twin pressures to provide responsive service, on the one hand, and to remain speedy and flexible as a company, on the other. The ability to provide instantaneous, customized responses — or what one observer calls "just-in-time, just-for-me" service — requires an enormous investment in people, training, and technology. As a result, only very large companies with sufficient financial resources have the ability to compete. Since size is itself an obstacle to flexibility and innovation, these large firms are seeking to provide more responsive service through consolidation — by purchasing smaller companies with proven technologies and a loyal customer base. One consequence of this pattern is that it is nearly impossible to compete in any industry today as a midsize company. Midsize companies have neither the entrepreneurial swiftness of the small companies nor the megacapital and reputation of the big firms to sustain them. Although we do not necessarily welcome this change, it seems inevitable that in most industries we will soon have three or four major players that control the vast majority of the market.

□ Beyond Loyalty: The New Social Contract

Over the last hundred years, people have left their homes, farms, and communities to work for large companies in exchange for wages. Many worked all their lives for a single company and were rewarded with job security and a decent pension. The old social contract stipulated that acceptable performance and good behavior would be rewarded with lifetime employment. At the close of the twentieth century, this relationship between organizations and employees became obsolete, both in the United States and abroad. With global competition came plant closings, downsizing, and cutbacks. As economies picked up, people were rehired under different terms, either as temporary or short-term contract employees. This change is having a dramatic impact in Japan, where individual identity is closely tied to corporate membership; layoffs there have caused stress levels to skyrocket and an increase in the suicide rate.

Today, few employees believe that their employer will remain loyal to them, and, indeed, the feeling is mutual. The **new social contract** is a different kind of employment relationship wherein "job security" is fleeting and tied expressly to whether one's skills fit the organization's needs at that time. Owners jump at the possibility of selling out for a tidy profit, and employees are always on the lookout for a better opportunity. Many business schools teach their students to think of themselves as a small business, and to see their careers as a series of finite contracts with corporations. In this new environment, employees must engage in continual learning to remain in demand; at the same time, businesses must strive to attract and retain the best talent. In this spirit, one of Warner-Lambert Company's (now a part of Pfizer) senior human resources managers is now director of "talent management," with the job of continually "re-recruiting" the best employees, making sure that they are challenged, satisfied, and likely to stay with the firm.

Perhaps the greatest challenge to employee loyalty in recent years has been the extraordinary number of corporate officers (e.g., CEOs, CFOs), corporate directors, and corporate accountants who are either being investigated for or have been indicted for criminal behavior. Fueled by an arrogance and sense of invulnerability not seen since the robber barons of the 1920s, these individuals are accused of a range of self-serving behaviors aimed at adding to their fortunes at the expense of average employees. A partial list of prominent indictments from the past decade includes:

- CEO, WorldCom, for hiding $3.9 billion in expenses as a way of boosting profit numbers
- CEO, Tyco International, for tax evasion and evidence tampering
- CEO, ImClone Systems, for insider trading — that is, tipping off friends and family to sell stock
- CEO, Enron Corporation, for creating a maze of off-the-book partnerships to hide catastrophic losses
- CEO, Arthur Andersen LLP, for obstruction of justice by shredding documents providing evidence of willful wrongdoing

The most storied of these cases is Enron, now synonymous with grievous ethics violations. In 2001 as the company was clearly moving toward bankruptcy, it paid out $681 million in cash and stock to its 140 most senior managers (nearly $5 million per manager), while most of Enron's former employees received a maximum of only $13,500 in severance pay ("Managing to make money," 2002). The recent documentary film *Enron: The Smartest Guys in the Room* (2005) chronicles one perspective on the spectacular rise and fall of the ENRON Corporation, foreshadowing the trials of Enron's most senior leaders (Ken Lay and Jeff Skilling) that resulted in their convictions.

Shifting Power Bases

In nineteenth-century America, power was measured by a person's tangible assets: land, equipment, oil, and even slaves. Not surprisingly, those in control of these resources wielded the greatest power. By the second half of the twentieth century, information resources replaced tangible resources as a measure of power. By the year 2000, more than half of the U.S. labor force was involved in the transfer, reprocessing, or transmittal of information, a figure that is predicted to increase significantly by 2010 (U.S. Department of Labor, 2002). A growing number of people can be classified as "knowledge workers," and those with the best access to information are the most likely to succeed. Indeed, a company such as American Airlines cites the information aspects of their business (computerized travel reservations) as its greatest financial success (Davis & Davidson, 1992).

However, some observers argue that having the right information is not sufficient for achieving and maintaining power. According to Kanter (1989), informal **communication networks**—relationships with trusted co-workers characterized by quick, verbal communication—are the most dynamic source of power in contemporary organizations because of the role they play in responding to a turbulent business environment. In this challenging environment, the formal reporting relationships specified by the organizational chart (for those companies that still have organizational charts!) are far too limiting to be effective. Informal relationships allow employees to get things done across functions within organizations, across organizations, and among business, government, and other stakeholders. Under the new social contract, loyalty is limited to those trusted colleagues who can be relied on in a pinch.

Finally, under the new social contract the career ladder (an expectation that one's career will follow an orderly progression of increasingly responsible jobs in the hierarchy) has been replaced by the opportunity to work on an expanding set of challenges to hone one's own skills and the strategic application of those skills through a web of work opportunities and projects. Since careers no longer follow predictable paths, personal connections and interpersonal relationships have become essential for success.

New Values and Priorities

At the same time that competition has increased and managers demand more from employees, new values and priorities about home and family have emerged. The desire for balance between work and family is increasing among many workers (Hall, 1986); at the same time, people seek more meaningful, involving work experiences. In short, many American workers are changing their definition of success to include not only a career, but also family and community (Bellah, Madsen, Sullivan, Swidler, & Tipton, 1985).

Two primary factors have contributed to this shifting of priorities. First, with fewer high-paying, unionized manufacturing jobs available in the United States, two-career families are prevalent. According to the latest census figures, more than 67 percent of the workforce consists of dual-earner couples. Second, because grandparents and other members of extended families rarely live nearby, child care is in high demand. As a result, family issues have become a big part of the national political agenda.

It was not that long ago that the model American employee came to work early, stayed late, and was willing to travel anywhere at a moment's notice. Being a success meant putting one's job ahead of almost everything else, leading many to become "workaholics" (see *What Would You Do?* on p. 23). Today's men and women are seeking to redefine the work ethic of the past. Although some are willing to work as hard as needed to get ahead, others seek more balanced lives. Some businesses are moving to accommodate these needs by providing child care, flexible hours, and parental leave (Moskowitz & Townsend, 1991; Zedeck & Mosier, 1990). While flexible working programs have been hailed as a low-cost means of recruiting and retaining employees and enhancing productivity, recent trends reveal a surprising pattern. Organizations are offering fewer flextime schedules today than they were just a few years ago. One study conducted by the Society for Human Resource Management reports that 64 percent of organizations offered flextime in 2002. In 2005, that number has dropped to 54 percent. Analysts suggest that the current labor market does not require employers to offer flextime and other work-life programs in order to attract employees. Moreover, many employees are hesitant to ask for or demand flexible schedules because they believe it may signal a lack of commitment to the organization that could put their careers in jeopardy.

In sum, today's organizations acknowledge the importance of employee **quality of life**. Broadly speaking, an employee's quality of life is overall satisfaction with his or her work experience in the context of other life experiences, constraints, and aspirations. This value, however, is easier to espouse than to enact given varying definitions and priorities among employees. For example, an unmarried colleague of ours confided that he resents "family-friendly" company policies because they favor the personal lives of families over those of singles (Kirby & Krone, 2002). On-site day care is seen as a boon by many but is resisted by some who see it as further encroachment by business into employees' personal lives. In the end, probably the best any organization can do is to treat employees as whole people while maintaining a great deal of latitude in how particular individuals seek to establish balance in their own lives.

The Meaning of Work

Some of the values being espoused today about work signal not a retreat from it but a transformation of its meaning—from drudgery to a source of personal significance and fulfillment. Employees want to feel that the work they do is worthwhile, not just a way to draw a paycheck. This trend is increasingly pervasive. For example, while white-collar workers and college students tend to view blue-collar workers as being motivated primarily by money, job security, and benefits, the most important incentives for workers at all levels include positive relationships with co-workers and managers. Also important are opportunities to participate in organizational decision making. Without these major determinants of job satisfaction, worker stress and burnout may occur. Work has considerable social significance for Americans, who, despite increased concerns for balance, as a rule spend more time on the job than they do with their families.

WHAT WOULD YOU DO?

Organizational Structure and Employee Well-Being

Workaholic is a term used to describe a person who is unnaturally preoccupied with work. Typically, a workaholic spends long hours at work, including nights and weekends. Family relationships and friendships are often abandoned in favor of relationships with co-workers or other workaholics. Some workaholics truly enjoy their work, but most worry obsessively about getting unfinished work done. Workaholics are often viewed as people who choose to dedicate themselves to their work at the expense of their health, family, and friends. Some organizations consider the behavior of workaholics desirable—a sign of the employee's dedication to the job and the company and a source of increased productivity.

Several organizational theorists propose a new interpretation of workaholism as a disease, a condition brought about by the profound influences that organizations have over how people define themselves through their work (Alvesson, 1993; Deetz, 1991; Karasek, 1979). In this view, organizational power structures may destabilize the employee's personality and produce an unhealthy level of dependency.

The causes and symptoms of workaholism are, in a sense, ethical problems. As organizational theorist Stan Deetz argues, "It is wrong to knowingly do physical or psychological harm to others" (1991, p. 38). This raises several ethical questions:

DISCUSSION QUESTIONS

1. To what extent do organizations intentionally reward unhealthy but productive behavior as a way of maximizing employee output?
2. As a manager in a company that rewards workaholic behavior, how would you counteract the problem? What questions would you ask? Who in the company would you consult?
3. As an employee of a company that rewards workaholic behavior, how would you address the problem? Who would you discuss it with?
4. As an employee or manager, would you have an ethical obligation to help a co-worker who is a workaholic? Explain why or why not.
5. Can a student be a workaholic? What might this term mean in an educational environment? Do you know anyone who fits the description?

Who Can Afford to Prioritize?

For many people, prioritizing work, family, and other needs is a luxury. "Sure," they say, "I want all those things—more meaningful work, more time for myself, more time with family and friends. But most of all I really need this job to survive!"

Any discussion of the quality of work life must take into account the millions of U.S. workers who are either unemployed or underemployed and live below the poverty line. As we struggle to make work more meaningful, we must also seek to improve the education, living standards, and working conditions of those at the bottom of the economic ladder by setting priorities that include everyone. More specifically, we must recognize that traditionally disadvantaged groups—for example, people of color and women—are disproportionately represented among the working poor. This awareness must lead us to redouble our efforts to fight both racism and sexism on the way to establishing economic parity.

SUMMARY

Defining organizational communication for the twenty-first century requires the identification of important social trends and the repositioning of communication practices in an ever-changing landscape. In the present turbulent environment, traditional ways of doing business—and of communicating—are no longer effective. Instead, new principles of effective organizational communication must be developed to reflect the new environment—principles that transcend time and space and that acknowledge the formation of a new social contract between owners and employees. Dissatisfaction with current forms of economic globalization and corporate corruption on an unprecedented scale has created conditions for a new activism around the nature of work.

As we stated at the outset, the history of humanity is the history of organizing, which is in turn accomplished through communication. In the next chapters we will consider more specifically the theories and definitions that will guide us toward a better understanding of organizational communication today.

QUESTIONS FOR REVIEW AND DISCUSSION

1. Explain what is meant by the idea that organizing in business always entails bridging diverse perspectives. How is this idea directly related to the study and practice of communication at work?

2. What do we mean by the statement "Answers to questions about organizational communication are highly situated and perishable"? How is the answer to this question directly related to the idea that there are no hard-and-fast rules for effective communication?

3. Why is it more important to learn how to ask good questions than it is to have pat answers about communication in organizations?

4. Describe how the global economy, changing management practices, and information technologies have reshaped the world of work. Then explain how each of these changes has affected the study and practice of communication in organizations.

5. Describe the concept of the urgent organization. Explain how this concept relates to the idea of today's business being done in a "turbulent environment."

6. What is meant by the "new social contract"? What social changes have helped create it?

7. How can studying organizational communication prepare you for the world of work, regardless of your future professional plans?

Key Terms

Boundary spanner, p. 19
Communication network, p. 21
Communication technology, p. 14
Globalization, p. 8
Identity theft, p. 17
Knowledge management, p. 16
Multicultural management, p. 12

New social contract, p. 19
Organizational communication, p. 4
Organizational environment, p. 18
Outsourcing, p. 9
Quality of life, p. 22
Urgent organizations, p. 17
Worldview, p. 3

CASE STUDY

The Case of the Corporate Peacemakers

Darshan Rao is an assistant professor of management who specializes in management communication, corporate ethics, and global economics. Born in New Delhi, India, he came to the United States for college and never left. He became a U.S. citizen in 1995 and three years later took a faculty position at Rutgers University in New Jersey.

In 2001, Professor Rao was visiting family in New Delhi when India and Pakistan's long-standing conflict over the Kashmir region flared up. He was never physically in danger, but war rhetoric from both sides brought back terrible memories; his father had fought in two wars with Pakistan over the same issue, and he was angry that peace seemed so elusive. The fact that both countries had nuclear weapons only added to his anxiety, and, for a time, they seemed on the brink of using them. Darshan thought about changing his plane ticket so that he could be with his parents in case things got any worse. Then, in June 2001, the sabre-rattling suddenly stopped. Parties on both sides were surprised and confused about what had led to the sudden de-escalation. Further investigation by Darshan turned up some amazing information.

He knew, of course, that Indian companies provided critical support to some of the world's biggest companies, including Dell, Reebok, VF, Avis, Sony, and American Express. He also discovered that General Electric's largest research center is in Bangalore, a city with over 1,700 engineers and scientists. When the U.S. State Department had advised Americans to leave India because war prospects with Pakistan had risen to serious levels, information technology ministers from every Indian state approached the government and warned them about the economic chaos that would be caused by a disruption of this magnitude. One American journalist even concluded: "The cease-fire is brought to you by GE—and all its friends here in Bangalore" (Friedman, 2002, p. 8A) .

Professor Rao has mixed feelings about this situation. As one of his best students, you hope to understand his thoughts and feelings and perhaps even provide some counsel.

ASSIGNMENT

1. What are the social, political, and economic conditions that made this scenario possible?
2. Why is Professor Rao feeling conflicted over corporate influence in government matters?
3. What aspects of globalization are highlighted by this case, and how might they be applied to other situations?
4. What should be the relationship, if any, between multinational corporations and nation-states? Explain your answer.

CHAPTER 2

Defining Organizational Communication

As stated in the last chapter, so long as there have been humans there has been organizing, and with organizing comes a concern about how to do better, whether the task is hunting, coaching a sports team, or running a multinational corporation. Unfortunately, those with practical interest in organizational communication have not as a rule ascribed to the same definitions and assumptions. For example, when engineers speak of the importance of communication, they often (but not always) refer to its role in promoting clarity and consensus. In contrast, a group of clergy calling for improved communication would likely focus on the evocative and emotional power of discourse. In this chapter, we describe some common approaches to organizational communication, beginning with models of communication as information transfer, transactional process, strategic control, and a balance of creativity and constraint, and concluding with a model of communication as dialogue.

▧ APPROACHES TO ORGANIZATIONAL COMMUNICATION

Of the various conceptions of organizational communication, four have attracted the greatest number of adherents: (1) communication as information transfer, (2) communication as transactional process, (3) communication as strategic control, and (4) communication as a balance of creativity and constraint.

☐ Communication as Information Transfer

The **information-transfer** approach views communication as a metaphoric pipe-line through which information flows from one person to another. Managers thus communicate well when they transfer their knowledge to subordinates and others with minimal "spillage." According to Steven Axley (1984), this version of communication theory rests on the following assumptions:

1. Language is capable of transferring thoughts and feelings from one person to another person.
2. Speakers and writers insert thoughts and feelings into words.
3. Words contain those thoughts and feelings.
4. Listeners or readers extract those thoughts and feelings from the words.

The information-transfer approach sees communication as a tool that people use to accomplish their objectives. This view, popularized in the early to mid-1900s, compared human communication to the flow of information over a telegraph or telephone wire. During this period, clear, one-way communication was emphasized as a means of impressing and influencing others. Along these lines, communication is typically defined as "the exchange of information and the transmission of meaning" (Dessler, 1982, p. 94). It is further characterized as "information engineering," wherein information functions as a tool for accomplishing goals, but the process of transmission is not seen as problematic—that is, "If I say it and you can hear it, you ought to understand it" (Feldman & March, 1981). An analogy can be made to the classroom teacher who relies completely on lectures, never stopping to engage with students. The underlying belief is that since the professor said it, you should get it.

According to this perspective, miscommunication occurs only when no message is received or when the message that is received is not what the sender intended. Typical communication problems include information overload, distortion, and ambiguity. Information overload occurs when the receiver becomes overwhelmed by the information that must be processed. Three factors can contribute to information overload: (1) amount, or the absolute quantity of information to be processed; (2) rate, or the speed at which the information presents itself; and (3) complexity, or the amount of work it takes to interpret and process the information (Farace, Monge, & Russell, 1977). Information overload situations can vary in intensity and type. A government worker in a severely understaffed bureaucracy, for example, may have to deal with mountains of simple, steady work. In contrast, a police officer on patrol may be faced with varying amounts of complex information that presents itself at a fast rate.

Distortion refers to the effects of noise on the receiver's ability to process the message. Noise can be semantic (the message has different meanings for the sender and the receiver), physical (the sound of static on a telephone line or of a jet plane passing overhead), or contextual (the sender and the receiver have different perspectives that contribute to the miscommunication). A typical example would be trying to communicate with a co-worker who is experiencing a personal crisis; although you may be saying important things, the co-worker's emotional "noise" may prevent him or her from getting the message you intend to send.

Finally, ambiguity occurs when multiple interpretations of a message cloud the sender's intended meaning. Abstract language and differing connotations are common sources of ambiguity. When a manager asks two employees to work "a little harder," for instance, one might put in an extra half-hour a day, and the other might work all night.

David Berlo (1960) offered a communication model that reflects the information-engineering approach. According to his SMCR model, communication occurs when a sender (S) transmits a message (M) through a channel (C) to a receiver (R). The sender "encodes" an intended meaning into words, and the receiver "decodes" the message when it is received. The information-transfer model, while dated, remains a useful way to explain certain communication situations in organizations, such as the giving and receiving of technical instructions or e-mail exchanges among employees. To illustrate a more complex application of the information-transfer approach, let's assume that an advertising agency has just received a new account. The senior account representative calls a team meeting and gives assignments to the junior people. One of the team members, however, has difficulty with the assignment. He found the senior representative's presentation confusing, and was distracted by people coming in and out of the room during the team meeting. The deadline arrives, and his assignment is not complete. In this situation, communication is said to have broken down because the intended meaning of the sender (the senior representative) did not reach the receiver (the junior member).

Critics of the information-transfer approach argue that it is simplistic and incomplete, painting a picture of communication as a sequential process (i.e., "I throw you a message, then you throw one back"). In addition, the model assumes that the receiver remains passive and is uninvolved in constructing the meaning of the message. Finally, this theory is incomplete due to its inability to take into account important — and often ambiguous — nonverbal signals. People's facial expressions, for example, often carry significant information about one's degree of understanding and attitude toward the message.

☐ Communication as Transactional Process

Dissatisfaction with the information-transfer approach to communication led to the development of the **transactional-process** model. It asserts that in actual communication, clear distinctions are not made between senders and receivers. Rather, people play both roles simultaneously. "All persons are engaged in sending (encoding) and receiving (decoding) messages simultaneously. Each person is constantly sharing in the encoding and decoding processes, and each person is affecting the other" (Wenberg & Wilmot, 1973, p. 5). The transactional-process approach highlights the importance of feedback, or information about how a message is received, and particularly nonverbal feedback, which may accompany or substitute for verbal feedback. Consider, for example, the nonverbal messages that students send to instructors during a lecture to indicate their degree of attention and comprehension. While the members of one class may be on the edge of their seats and making consistent eye contact with the teacher, the members of another class may be slouching, fidgeting, and avoiding the instructor's gaze. Rightly or wrongly, most teachers will imbue these nonverbal behaviors with meaning and interpret the first class as more engaged and intelligent. The importance of nonverbal communication is captured by the famous axiom "You cannot not communicate" (Watzlawick, Beavin, & Jackson, 1967, p. 49). In other words, a person need not speak to communicate; nonverbal messages are conveyed through a person's silence, facial expressions, body posture, and gestures. As a result, then, any type of behavior is a potential message (Redding, 1972).

The transactional-process model differs from the information-transfer approach in terms of the presumed location of the meaning of the message. In the information-transfer model, the meaning of a message resides with the sender, and the challenge of communication is to transmit that meaning to others. The transactional-process model rejects this idea in favor of one in which meanings are in people, not words (Richards, 1936). It focuses on the person receiving the message and on how the receiver constructs the meaning of that message. As a result, says Steven Axley (1984), "Miscommunication is the normal state of affairs in human communication. . . . Miscommunication and unintentional communication are to be expected, for they are the norm" (p. 432).

One area to which the transactional-process model may be applied is leadership. Ideas about leadership have evolved from the simple belief that certain people are born with leadership skills to the acknowledgment that leadership involves a transaction between leaders and followers. Thus, successful leaders can shape the meanings that followers assign to what leaders say or do. In this sense, then, leadership is the transactional management of meaning between leaders and followers. Compare this to the information-transfer model, which gauges a leader's effectiveness solely on his or her ability to "put across" an inspirational message. In contrast, the transactional-process model predicts that a common understanding will emerge between a leader and his or her followers over time through communication.

Many experts criticize the transactional-process view for its emphasis on the creation of shared meaning through communication. This bias toward shared meaning may be based more on ideology than on empirical research. The degree of shared meaning between people can never be truly verified; all one ever has as proof is people's reports about what they mean, which can be manipulated and may be unreliable. Shared meaning implies consensus, and it is commonly observed that organizational communication is more typically characterized by ambiguity, conflict, and diverse viewpoints.

☐ Communication as Strategic Control

Unlike the transactional-process model, which assumes that effective communicators are clear and open in their efforts to promote understanding and shared meaning, the **strategic-control** perspective regards communication as a tool for controlling the environment (Parks, 1982). It recognizes that, due to personal, relational, and political factors, greater clarity is not always the main goal in interaction. The strategic-control perspective sees communicators as having multiple goals. For example, in a performance review, a supervisor might have two primary goals: to be understood and to preserve a positive working relationship. In this view, a competent communicator is one who chooses strategies that are appropriate for accomplishing multiple goals.

In addition, the strategic-control approach to communication recognizes that while people may have reasons for their behavior, they cannot be expected to communicate in ways that consistently maximize others' understanding. Communicative choices are socially, politically, and ethically motivated. We all recognize that others may violate the communicative expectations of clarity and honesty when they believe it is in their interest to do so.

The limits of general statements about what constitutes "effective" communication led to a focus on communication as goal attainment, as a means to accomplish one's ends through adaptation and saying what is appropriate for the situation. Communicators must be able to recognize the constraints of the situation and to adapt to multiple goals simultaneously, such as being clear, assertive, and respectful of the other person (Tracy & Eisenberg, 1991).

In organizational communication, **strategic ambiguity** is an important concept that describes the ways in which people may communicate unclearly but still accomplish their goals (Eisenberg, 1984). While common sense may dictate that effective communicators speak clearly, Eisenberg notes that clarity is not always, nor should it be, a primary communicative goal. Rather, there are several instances in organizational life when ambiguous messages may be productively deployed. Specifically, strategic ambiguity

- Promotes unified diversity
- Preserves privileged positions
- Is deniable
- Facilitates organizational change

First, strategic ambiguity takes advantage of the diverse meanings that different people can give to the same message. For example, the mission statement "Quality is job one" is sufficiently ambiguous to allow all Ford employees to read their own meanings into it. In contrast, the more specific statement "Quality through cutting-edge engineering" is less inclusive and less likely to inspire unity, particularly in the manufacturing and administrative ranks of the company.

Second, strategic ambiguity preserves privileged positions by shielding those with power from close scrutiny by others. A seasoned diplomat or a professor emeritus giving a speech, for example, is traditionally given the benefit of the doubt by supporters who may have to fill in some gaps in their understanding. Fans of seasoned performers often come to shows rooting for their heroes, willing to overlook what may seem to others as signs of weakness (e.g., a hoarse voice, eclectic song selection). Similarly, by being less than precise (e.g., in providing a lukewarm reference for a mediocre colleague), employees can protect confidentiality, avoid conflict, and conceal key information that may afford them a competitive advantage. In this sense, strategic ambiguity is said to be deniable; that is, the words seem to mean one thing, but under pressure they can seem to mean something else.

Finally, strategic ambiguity facilitates organizational change by allowing people the interpretive room to change their activities while appearing to keep those activities consistent. For example, with the advent of air travel, transatlantic ocean liner companies that provided overseas passage by ship were faced with a major challenge to their service. The firms that defined themselves as transportation companies did not survive, whereas those that interpreted their business more broadly (and ambiguously) as entertainment went on to develop vacation or leisure cruise businesses. An example of the pros and cons of strategic ambiguity appears in *What Would You Do?* on page 34.

Unlike other models of communication, the strategic-control approach opposes the idea of shared meaning as the primary basis or motivation for communication. Rather, it holds that shared meaning is an empirically unverifiable concept (Krippendorff, 1985) and that the primary goal of communication should be organized action (Donnellon, Gray, & Bougon, 1986). If we accept that the meaning one person creates may not correspond to the meaning that another person gives to the same communication, it is less important that the two people understand each other than it is that they act in mutually satisfying ways (Weick, 1995).

Although the strategic-control perspective advances our appreciation of the subtleties of communication, it is not without problems. First, it minimizes the importance of ethics. While strategic ambiguity is commonplace in organizations, it is often used to escape blame. Particularly when called upon to testify about their actions in a court of law, many if not most executives will make good use of the "wiggle room" afforded by vague or ambiguous language. That way, when they succeed they can claim credit, but when they fail they can quickly identify an interpretation of events that lets them off of the hook.

Another limitation of the strategic-control approach is its emphasis on the behavior of individuals (or on individuals controlling their environment through communication), often at the expense of the community. As such, it clouds issues related to cooperation, coordination, power and inequality, and the interdependent relationships of individuals and groups. The strategic control model suggests that the world is composed of independent communicators, each working to control his

WHAT WOULD YOU DO?

Sudden Flags: Organizational Ambiguity in Action

The strategic uses of ambiguity can have positive or negative influences on the quality of organizational life. Viewed positively, strategic ambiguity can encourage members of an institution to unite around common symbols (such as a college mascot or tradition) without requiring people to hold the same meanings for those symbols. Viewed negatively, strategic ambiguity can be used to mask and even suppress important differences between individuals.

An interesting example of this dynamic occurred in 2005 when the Florida state legislature voted to place American flags in every classroom in the state. The intent of the law was to remind people of their citizenship as part of their education. Nearly overnight, thousands of inexpensive flags mounted on plastic PVC pipes were affixed to the walls of classrooms at every level of education in Florida (preschool to postgraduate).

DISCUSSION QUESTIONS

1. Flags are a classic example of ambiguous symbols. If you were a student in one of these classrooms, how would you react to the appearance of the flag?
2. How would you react if you were the teacher?
3. How should teachers react to students who have varied views of the flag and may even oppose its presence in the classroom?
4. Outline a conversation that you might have with your class on the first day the flag appears. How would you solicit multiple interpretations of its meaning, and how would you handle strong differences in beliefs?

or her own environment, and that meaning exists only within people's minds. It thus overemphasizes the role and power of individuals in creating meaning through communication.

☐ Communication as a Balance of Creativity and Constraint

Since the late 1960s, the central focus of social theorists has been the relationship between individuals and society, which in our case translates to the relationship between employees and organizations. Two competing perspectives examine this relationship. The macro perspective sees individuals as being molded, controlled, ordered, and constrained by society and by social institutions. In contrast, the micro perspective sees individuals as creating society and its social systems. This dichotomy has obvious implications for organizational communication, depending on whether the emphasis is on how employees communicate to create and shape organizations or on the constraints organizations place on that communication. In other words, while we no doubt conform to social pressures, rules, laws, and standards for behavior, "we are rule and system users and rule and system breakers as well" (Wentworth, 1980, p. 40).

In their foundational text on the individual and society, *The Social Construction of Reality* (1967), Peter Berger and Thomas Luckmann argue that societies and organizations are constructed as people act in patterned ways; over time, people take those behavior patterns for granted as "reality." In other words, most of what we take for granted in organizations is created or constructed through people's choices and behavior. Over time, routines develop and members amass a general knowledge of "how things are done." What results is a tension between the need to maintain order and the need to promote change.

Although many writers have contributed significantly to this line of thought, Anthony Giddens's (1984) theory of structuration is especially relevant to students of organizational communication. In discussing the relationships between individual communication and social systems and structures, Giddens simultaneously focuses on the creative and constraining aspects of structure, or what he calls the duality of structure. In this view, the designer of a new product advertisement is both bound by the rules, norms, and expectations of the industry and open to the possibility of transcending those structures by designing a creative ad. In this sense, creativity is the design and modification of social systems through communication. The communication process is not viewed as what goes on inside organizations but as how people organize (Barnard, 1968; Farace, Monge, & Russell, 1977; Johnson, 1977). This does not mean that the process is always deliberate or rational; to the contrary, much of what is taken for granted as organizational reality is either unintentional or based on people's perceptions and assumptions (which may or may not be valid). People create social reality through communication in an ironic sense: They rarely get the reality they set out to create (Ortner, 1980). The process of designing a new retail store, for example, is necessarily a series of compromises among differing dreams and worldviews; rarely does one individual get to call all the shots. Both the physical design and the interpretations of that design are the result of overt and covert negotiation.

The theory of **structuration** thus sees human behavior as an unresolvable tension between creativity and constraint. William Wentworth (1980) acknowledges as much when he describes the conflict between under- and oversocialized images of people. For Wentworth, the idea that people are either inherently constrained

or inherently creative does not offer a complete characterization of the relationships between individuals and society. Instead, he argues, social life is a balance of
creativity and constraint—of constructing social reality and of being constrained
by those constructions—and it is through communication that the balance is
achieved.

Our definition of organizational communication in this text—as the **balance
of creativity and constraint**—is derived from the perspectives of Wentworth and
others. We believe that communication is the moment-to-moment working out of
the tension between individual creativity and organizational constraint. The phrase
"moment-to-moment working out of the tension" refers specifically to the balance
of creativity (as a strategic response to organizational constraints) and constraints (as
the constructions of reality that limit the individual's choice of strategic response).

As an example of how the tension between creativity and constraint is constructed through communication, we can cite the meetings we attended at a company that manufactures hydraulic lifts. These staff meetings were controlled by the
company president according to an agenda that he prepared. Most discussions were
marked by short briefings on various topics (such as new sales, personnel changes,
and capital equipment expenditures) and little actual decision making. Although
the executives in attendance were experienced decision makers, they knew that the
president viewed any opposing viewpoint as a sign of disloyalty. Nicknamed "Little
General," the president routinely embarrassed employees who disagreed with him
or who attempted independent action. Over time, employee nonconfrontation was
taken for granted, and what had started out as a human construction came to be accepted as an organizational reality (Berger & Luckmann, 1967). Despite the strong
constraints on communication and the norm of nonconfrontation at the company,
however, occasionally the urge to be creative emerged during meetings. An employee might, for instance, introduce a topic that was not on the president's agenda
or present new data that conflicted with data given by the president. By observing
communication in these ways, we saw both creativity and constraint in action, as
the company's norms were applied or challenged.

Notice that this balancing act stimulates creativity as a strategic response to organizational constraints. In our example, the staff members acted on information
they already had to guide their choices of when to speak and what to say. Unfortunately, however, the organizational reality of nonconfrontation limited their strategic choices and their ability to respond. Because the president seemed unable to
respond to their initiatives positively and because they were unable to alter his construction of reality, the balance was tipped toward constraint and away from creativity. It was this lack of balance that made the staff meetings relatively unproductive, one-sided affairs.

Fortunately, the balance does not always tip in favor of constraint, although
some degree of structure is always necessary. A great example of an organization
known for encouraging idiosyncratic behavior on the part of its employees is

EVERYDAY ORGANIZATIONAL COMMUNICATION

On-line Networking Profiles:
Balancing Creativity and Constraint

Balancing creativity and constraint, the metaphor we conceived of as an analytical framework, may also be used to make organizations and individuals more successful. Let's consider the usefulness of the metaphor in an arena that you may already be familiar with—that of successful on-line networking and self-promotion.

If you are a student who wants to meet new people on campus, an individual who wants to find a prospective dating partner, or a member of a new band that wants to be discovered, you may not need to look any further than today's on-line networking sites such as Facebook, Match.com, and MySpace. These sites allow groups and individuals to market themselves to a desired audience (whether a social group, a date, or a company) by posting on-line profiles that reveal personal and professional information. As individuals grow increasingly comfortable with the use of technology, however, more profiles appear on these sites (160,000 new accounts are created every day on MySpace), increasing the competition for "hits" and possible connections. As such, profiles have had to become increasingly unique to attract attention, while still offering the requisite information desired by would-be readers. The authors of successful profiles have to walk the line between creativity and constraint to market themselves appropriately and effectively.

In this chapter, we discussed Anthony Giddens's theory of structuration and offered the example of a designer of a new product advertisement. A successful advertisement must be bound by the rules and norms of a given industry while remaining open to the possibility of creatively transcending those structures. The same can be said for successful advertising and marketing in the virtual world. The developed norms of on-line networking pressure individuals to offer key pieces of information. Successful dating profiles, for example, typically offer the author's age, height, weight, hair color, profession, and a list of personal interests as well as desired traits in a prospective date. Without this information, a profile will be entirely overlooked or considered suspect for its glaring omissions.

Despite the constraint to offer this requisite personal information, dating experts agree that profiles that are too constrained, and lack creativity, are not likely to receive many hits. Or, as dating expert Evan Marc Katz states: "If you're writing a profile, you have one job and that is to sound different than everybody else" (qtd. in Dykstra, 2006). In other words, profile authors must go beyond offering the standard bits of information—they are not enough for success in and of themselves. Sites like Match.com do allow room for these spots of creativity. Catchy

(continued, On-line Networking Profiles)

profile titles attract visitors, as do personal photographs and open responses that allow the author — in his or her own words — to relate additional information from an explanation of a favorite hobby to a description of the ideal vacation.

Many bands have found a great deal of success by balancing creativity and constraint on-line, particularly on the MySpace networking site. With major record labels signing fewer acts and spending less money on marketing, MySpace allows artists to get their music out to the masses. Naturally, over time, rules, norms, and expectations developed for the types of profiles that bands create. Most successful profiles offer a photograph of the group, MP3 music files of recent performances, and a list of upcoming tour dates. Profiles also need to be found easily through MySpace's search engine, and therefore lists of music genre and influences tend to be fairly lengthy: They need to cast a wide enough net but not be so exhaustive that they're meaningless. And there is hardly a band that doesn't give plenty of kudos to other bands, in a quid pro quo system that has everyone advertising for everyone else.

But despite these constraining norms, there is plenty of room for creativity. Gavin DeGraw, a pop singer who writes earnest lyrics, has a black-and-white photo of himself smiling, a straightforward bio, and blog entries with comments like "just saying hello and letting you know that i'll be checking in frequently" and "thanks to all of y'all for the support." The Indie band Fletch hasn't recorded an album yet, but their profile does have (in true Indie spirit) a self-designed feature called "Help Us Decide," which asks viewers to pick which songs should go on their first album. The most popular profiles are widely different from one another, with each artist tailoring their pages to their personal tastes and individual styles.

DISCUSSION QUESTIONS

1. If you have an on-line profile or have ever viewed on-line profiles, consider which ones stand out the most. What characteristics do they share? In what ways are they different?
2. What are some of the other everyday contexts in which your life is organized through your own attempts to balance creativity and constraint? Consider the choices you make about your personal style of dress in various contexts (school, social events, work) or the way you interact in meetings (whether at work, a religious institution, or a campus organization).
3. In which organizational environments do you organize your self-presentation in ways that favor creativity? In which environments do you accommodate organizational constraints? Why do you make those choices?

Southwest Airlines. From its inception, Southwest has cultivated an organizational culture that values individual creativity and initiative, most keenly manifested in the employees' dress, informal attitude, and use of off-beat humor. To better understand the two approaches, reflect on the different classroom climates that you have experienced. More than likely, you will be able to place each on a continuum between those that emphasized constraint (strict rules, centralized control) and those that stressed creativity (flexible rules, tolerance for a range of acceptable behaviors).

The main advantage of this framework appears to be the ability to simultaneously consider the enabling and constraining aspects of communication. Occasionally, researchers and theorists lose this important point and lapse back to the information-transfer approach, suggesting that individuals create society, which then in turn constrains the individual. This is a serious misunderstanding of the theory. Finally, there are some who object to the use of the balance metaphor to characterize what happens between people and institutions, claiming that there is an implied norm of "good balance" that might not be in anyone's best interest. Researchers who study the interplay between home and work spheres, for example, frequently maintain that the decision to regard these arenas as separate and then seek balance between them both defines and perpetuates our current predicament (e.g., Jorgenson, Gregory, & Goodier, 1998). They argue instead for a view of work that sees experience as continuous across activities and settings, suggesting the need to study human "occupation" more generally and in ways that go well beyond paid work. Further study and discussion of these ideas is needed.

Having now reviewed the high points of organizational communication theory—communication as information transfer, transactional process, strategic control, and a balance of creativity and constraint—we use the best concepts from each perspective to develop our own model of organizations as dialogues. A summary of the perspectives appears in Table 2.1. A specific representation of the "balance" metaphor for understanding organizational communication is shown in Figure 2.1 (p. 42).

ORGANIZATIONS AS DIALOGUES

We are both social and private beings. As such, we establish a sense of self that is apart *from* the outside world (an identity) that engages in a lifelong conversation with another sense of self that is a part *of* the outside world (a member of a community). If we could somehow construct reality all on our own—as a monologue—we would then be totally alone. Conversely, if our contexts for interpretation came entirely from others, we would lose our unique identity. The critical issues, then, revolve around these concepts of identity and community, or self, other, and context.

TABLE 2.1

Organizational Communication: Preliminary Perspectives

Communication as Information Transfer	Communication as Transactional Process	Communication as Strategic Control	Communication as a Balance of Creativity and Constraint
Metaphor: Pipeline or conduit — sender transmits a message to receiver.	*Metaphor:* Process — communication is a process that creates relationships; "You cannot not communicate."	*Metaphor:* Control — individuals attempt to control their environments.	*Metaphor:* Balance — individuals attempt to develop distinct identities while participating in an organized community.
Assumptions: (1) Language transfers thoughts and feelings from person to person; (2) speakers and writers insert thoughts and feelings into words; (3) words contain the thoughts and feelings; (4) listeners or readers extract the thoughts and feelings from the words.	*Assumptions:* (1) There are rarely clear distinctions between senders and receivers; (2) nonverbal feedback accompanies or substitutes for verbal messages; (3) meanings are in people, not words.	*Assumptions:* Strategic ambiguity gains control because it (1) promotes unified diversity, (2) preserves privileged positions, (3) is deniable, and (4) facilitates organizational change.	*Assumptions:* All communication accomplishes two things at once: It reflects historical constraints of prior contexts, and it represents individuals' attempts to do something new and creative. This is the duality of social or organizational structure.
Description: Source transmits a message through a channel (air or light) to a receiver; communication is a tool people use to accomplish objectives.	*Description:* Person receiving the message constructs its meaning; the idea is for senders to adapt their messages to the needs and expectations of their listeners.	*Description:* Strategic ambiguity takes advantage of the diversity of meanings people often give to the same message; choices of what to say are socially, politically, and ethically motivated; strategies can be selected to accomplish multiple goals.	*Description:* Communication is the moment-to-moment working out of the tension between individual creativity and organizational constraint. Approaching organizations as constructed through communication requires simultaneous attention to the ways

TABLE 2.1 *(continued)*

Organizational Communication: Preliminary Perspectives

COMMUNICATION AS INFORMATION TRANSFER	COMMUNICATION AS TRANSACTIONAL PROCESS	COMMUNICATION AS STRATEGIC CONTROL	COMMUNICATION AS A BALANCE OF CREATIVITY AND CONSTRAINT
			in which groups of people both maintain order through their interactions, and allow individual actors the freedom to accomplish their goals.
Measure of effectiveness: Receiver of communication understands (or does) what the speaker intended.	*Measure of effectiveness:* Shared meaning.	*Measure of effectiveness:* Coordinated actions accomplished through diverse interpretations of meanings.	*Measure of effectiveness:* A balance between satisfied individuals and a coherent community.
Limitations: (1) Overly simplifies communication: Treats transmission of the message as linear and unproblematic; (2) sees the receiver as a passive receptor uninvolved with the construction of the meaning of the message; (3) does not account for differences in interpretation between speaker and listener.	*Limitations:* (1) Emphasis on shared meaning is problematic and ultimately unverifiable; (2) bias toward clarity and openness denies political realities; (3) does not account for ambiguity, deception, or diversity in points of view.	*Limitations:* (1) Can minimize the importance of ethics; (2) places strong emphasis on individuals over communities; (3) over-emphasizes the role and power of individuals to create meaning through communication.	*Limitations:* Can sometimes be difficult to identify what counts as a constraint; also tends to draw attention away from material economic realities that may threaten the system independent of member behaviors.

FIGURE 2.1

Communication as a Balance of Creativity and Constraint

Metaphor: Balance

Assumptions

1. The duality of structure: Individuals are molded, controlled, ordered, and shaped by society and social institutions; individuals also create society and social institutions.

2. Communication is the moment-to-moment working out of the tensions between the need to maintain order (constraint) and the need to promote change (creativity). As such, communication is the material manifestation of

   a. institutional constraints
   b. creative potential
   c. contexts of interpretation

Representative Model

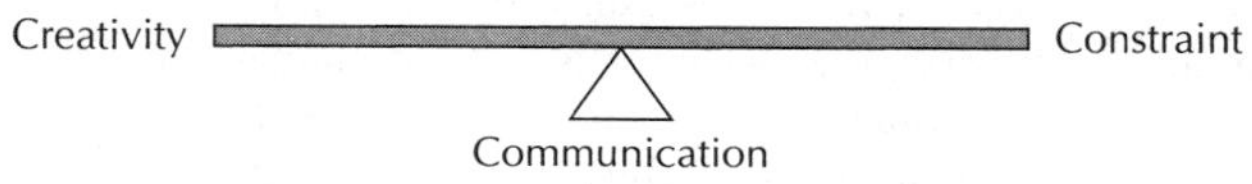

Creativity ▬▬▬▬▬▬▬△▬▬▬▬▬▬▬ Constraint
Communication

Description

Creativity	Communication	Constraints
Interpretations of meanings; all forms of initiative; new ways of organizing tasks and understanding relationships; resistance to institutional forms of dominance; uses of storytelling and dialogue to alter perceptions; uses of social constructions of reality to forge new agreements and to shape coordinated actions at work	Reveals interpretations of contexts; asks questions about resources for creativity and the presence of constraints; suggests the possibility of dialogue	Social and institutional forms, laws, rules, procedures, slogans, and management styles designed to gain compliance and limit dialogue at all costs; top-down decision making and problem solving

☐ Foundations of Dialogue: Self, Other, and Context

Our self-concept is formed in part from the social relationships we have with others and from others' responses to what we say and do (Bakhtin, 1981; Blumer, 1969; Jackson, 1989). According to George Herbert Mead (1934), the **self** consists of two interrelated "stories": (1) the story of "I," or the creative, relatively unpredictable part of a person that is usually kept private, and (2) the story of "me," or the socially constrained, relatively consistent part of a person that is more openly shared with others. The "I" is impulsive, whereas the "me" strives to fit into society's rules and norms. The creative aspect of the self (the "I") desires meaningful action with others. The constraining aspect of the self (the "me") guides this action by anticipating responses and applying social rules of behavior.

This definition of the self has important implications for interpreting organizational communication. Because the self is constructed out of our need to balance our own needs with those of others, the self is necessarily dialogic, or made in concert with others (Bakhtin, 1981). Whenever we interact with others, we engage in conversations that affect our perceptions of ourselves. We retell stories that were told to us by others, and we use and comment on others' opinions of who we are (Blumer, 1969; Laing, 1965). We make use of both real and imagined characters and relationships (Goodall, 1996). The voice of our experience, therefore, carries with it the perceptions, memories, stories, fantasies, and actions of the many people who shape our lives — co-workers, family members, friends, teachers, students, enemies, celebrities, heroes, and villains (Conquergood, 1991). In other words, our identity only makes sense in relation to others.

At the same time, we construct the **other** in relation to our conception of self. It is said that people who consistently speak badly about others often reveal their own negative self-concept. Conversely, people who generally speak well of others may have a positive self-concept. Our construction of others is not entirely of our own making. It is constrained by the self's culture, race, gender, and subconscious. How we learn to see and respond to the presence, actions, and meanings of others is shaped by many influences. In this sense, then, the self's symbolic construction of the other is also always complex and dialogic.

Especially interesting is the role of others in our understanding of organizations. As noted earlier in the chapter, the information-transfer, transactional process, and strategic-control models of communication focus on how the sender (the self) acts toward the receivers (others). The sender is usually viewed as a manager and the receiver as a subordinate, reflecting the managerial bias of these theories (Putnam, 1982). Employees are too often viewed as "others" to be acted upon, communicated to, ordered, and controlled, rather than as participants in an organizational dialogue. This concept of others as partners to the dialogue contains the important idea of plurality, which refers to the fact that the self and others mutually construct the meanings they have for each other. It also encompasses the idea that multiple interpretations of a relationship are possible and that neither the self nor the others alone can control those interpretations.

Context refers to where communication occurs (i.e., the physical setting) and the interpretive frameworks used to make sense of the communicative exchange. Context is vital to our understanding of organizational communication. For one thing, it shapes our interpretations. In addition, multiple contexts are always available for sense making, and the concept of context tells us much about organizational dialogue.

There can be no meaning without context (Bateson, 1972). If we think of a message as a text, the context is information that goes with and helps make sense of the text. For example, if you overhear a friend call someone you don't know a "loser," how would you make sense of the comment? You would need to know more about the relationship between your friend and the other person and about what happened just before your friend made the comment. You might even need to know where the comment was made. Relationship and situation, two basic aspects of context, would affect your interpretation. If your friend and the other person had been teasing each other all day, the comment might be interpreted as a sign of friendship.

The role of context is always complex. We cannot fully understand the meaning of a message without first examining the relationship, its history, and the immediate situation for clues. This is especially true in organizations, where lines of authority, personal relationships, politics, the business situation, and other factors affect the interpretation of communicative exchanges. Because it is impossible to communicate in isolation, people necessarily communicate in contexts. However, contexts are not stable. According to the *Oxford English Dictionary*, the word *context* originated as a verb meaning "to weave together, interweave, join together, compose." We favor this older definition because it highlights context as "a verbal process aimed at the manufacture of something . . . the seaming together of otherwise disparate elements, perceptions, fabrics or words, the piecing together of a whole out of the sum of its parts" (Goodall, 1991a, p. 64).

When we say that individuals communicate in contexts, we use that term to refer to both (1) how a person defines a situation at any given moment and (2) the process of altering that definition over time. Our definition of context reflects the duality of structure: People both create contexts through communication and are constrained by those contexts as they are created (e.g., one's creative decision to tell off one's boss will constrain future interactions with him or her). As Linda Putnam (1985) puts it, "People establish the context, use the context to interpret messages, and use the messages to change the context" (p. 152). Over time, what we define as context becomes the constructed reality that we take for granted. Therefore, when we say that individuals communicate in context, we mean that they communicate in accord with their constructions of reality, or with their interpretations of the evolving situation.

Notice that we are, in a way, redefining what it means to participate in an organization. Rather than viewing institutional members as the product of a particular organizational culture, we believe that a large part of working together is the interpretation of contexts. Although most obvious in white-collar jobs, this applies to blue-collar work and other kinds of organizations (e.g., religious institutions, sports clubs) as well. The performance of all organizational roles, whether pastor or accountant, soccer coach or college professor, is defined through interaction and collective sense making. How people think and talk about their role in the organization and how they feel about the relationships they maintain there have a significant impact on their behavior choices and, ultimately, on the effectiveness of the organization.

Suppose you are a supervisor at a local copy center and during lunchtime you discover one of your part-time employees sobbing in the rest room. What would you do or say? Your first challenge would be to interpret the situation and the context because human communication makes sense only in context. What do you know about this employee that could help you make sense of his behavior? Might personal problems or stress play a role? Recalling that the employee's mother had been ill, you inquire about the situation and discover that his mother's illness has become life threatening. This is the relevant context; it makes sense of the employee's behavior and allows you to offer an appropriate response. Furthermore, your interaction with the employee will affect your future interactions in ways that depend on how you and the employee interpret the situation. Thus, your relationship might become more aloof—or more friendly—as a result. Not only is context necessary to make sense of the initial communication, but that communication will, in turn, shape the context for making sense of future interactions.

☐ Dialogue and the Situated Individual

Multiple contexts exist for interpreting communication. What are multiple contexts? Consider this definition provided by Goran Ahrne (1990):

> From birth every human being is affiliated to a family and a nation-state. Children's first experiences of the exercise of power occur within the family. After some years all children will have to yield to the power of the nation-state in the form of school. Growing up, children will slowly get to know the world outside the family and the school. Gradually the everyday world will be larger, adolescence being the typical time for activities in groups or gangs of various kinds. . . . Having married and settled down and started to work, people fill their everyday lives with organizational affiliations. In the course of their lives individuals orient themselves within the existing organizations in the social landscape. Every individual attempts to establish a domain within this landscape, balancing between different organizational influences and leaving some unorganized space. (p. 72)

In other words, we grow up and learn about life in multiple contexts, each of which has its own constraints—or rules, norms, and expected understandings—that make it unique. These constraints play two roles: (1) They limit creativity and individual freedom, and (2) they suggest particular constructions of reality that assist in interpretation. For example, if a co-worker leans over and kisses you (against your wishes), it would be clear from the business context that such behavior is inappropriate and that a strong negative reaction on your part is warranted. If a family member does the same thing, the meaning would be entirely different, as would your likely response.

Consider also how interpretation is complicated by multiple contexts in the typical family business or when husband and wife work together in the same company. You can imagine the conversations: "Dad, you can talk to me that way at home, but not here in front of the other employees!" or "How could you, my own wife, vote against me at the faculty meeting!" Different contexts suggest different rules for action and interpretation. Even within a small organization, multiple contexts are always available for interpretation.

In conducting performance appraisals, how tough should supervisors be on marginal performers? Seen in the context of the business as a financial entity accountable primarily to shareholders, the supervisor should be direct and tough. In a context that emphasizes the supervisor-employee relationship, however, the supervisor could justify being more understanding. Interpreting and communicating in multiple contexts is the tough stuff of organizational life.

This brings us to our key point: All individuals are situated in multiple contexts. In a broad sense, this means that behavior is both guided and constrained by the types of organizations with which we affiliate, whether they be capitalist enterprises, voluntary associations, nation-states, or families. More specifically, all behavior is situated in smaller, or more local, contexts: The **situated individual** is a person who is conducting the everyday business of the maintenance and construction of the social realities in which we live.

> The situated individual is connected to others through a network of shared, mutually negotiated, and maintained meanings. These meanings provide location, identity, action, and purpose to the individual. They tell me where I am, who I am, what I am doing, how to do it, and why. . . . The network of meanings is not independent of the situated individual. It is the product of the interaction among situated individuals. (Anderson, 1987, p. 268)

Difficulty is encountered when the multiple contexts impinging on an individual suggest inconsistent or conflicting communication or behavior. A study of Disneyland's corporate culture provides a detailed example of multiple conflicting contexts for interpretation (Smith & Eisenberg, 1987). In the early days of the theme park, employees used two metaphors, "the show" and the Disney "family," which were keyed to larger contexts. The first metaphor — Disneyland as a show — suggested that employees were actors who played important roles. They could thus be told by the "director" to act in particular ways because of "box office concerns" (e.g., to smile more or to style their hair). The other metaphor — Disneyland as a family — however, suggested a different and sometimes opposing context in which management, like a concerned parent, took care of its employees and provided a nurturing environment. These conflicting contexts for interpretation had very different consequences for Disney policy, and in the mid-1980s, company employees actually called a strike in response to a pay cut that was being sold by management as a "sacrifice families are sometimes called upon to make." In fact, recent case studies suggest that the drama metaphor—so compatible with business—has in fact won out.

The situated-individual model of organizational communication may be summarized as follows:

1. The individual is an actor whose thoughts and actions are based on the interpretation of contexts.
2. More than one context always exists to guide the individual's actions and interpretations.
3. Communication is a practice that includes both interpretation and action; as such, it can reveal sources of creativity, constraint, meaning, interpretation, and context.

A final example can help clarify this notion of the situated individual. One of the authors of this textbook (Eric) became involved with a problem facing a customer service manager at a large travel agency. The manager (we'll call her Laura) sought to convince management of her need for a full-time accountant to manage the record keeping of customer service billings. Laura's initial request was met with assurances from her boss that an accountant would be hired, but then management decided suddenly to deny her request. The problem, then, was how to interpret the denial and what, if anything, to do about it. There were various possible ways to make sense of (or contextualize) the situation. From Laura's point of view, the problem centered on a lack of expertise in her department and the need to address it by hiring an accountant. The finance department saw the situation differently. Because it had sought for several years to hire its own accountant, it strongly resisted the idea that one might now be hired in customer service. As a result, rumors surfaced among the finance department staff about Laura's competency as a manager, suggesting that she would not need the new position if she were doing her job properly. Still another view of the situation came from the general manager of the travel agency. He resisted the new hiring simply because none of the companies he had worked for in the past had had an accountant in customer service. The board of directors based its disapproval on economic concerns. Any new hires in a recession would not please shareholders. Finally, Laura's peers perceived her as aloof and a loner, rather than as a team player. Consequently, no informal group within the company was inclined to support Laura's agenda to hire an accountant. Laura might not have faced this problem if she had been more involved in informal communication networks or if the company had ways of considering multiple interpretations side by side in conversation—that is, in some form of dialogue.

Keep in mind that this is a *simple* example of how multiple contexts can inform the interpretation of selves, others, and action. Although the facts remain the same—whether or not to hire an accountant in customer service—the meanings of those facts are constructed differently depending on which context is applied. Because no one individual has access to all potential contexts, each individual's interpretation is based on a limited understanding of the reality being constructed. The information drawn on to build a context for interpretation is varied, multiple, and always limited. All interpretations, therefore, are partial, partisan, and problematic (see Chapter 3). Fortunately, however, the limitations of one person's interpretations are usually offset by others' perspectives. Because sense making is a social activity, more than one person is always involved in the construction of reality. When individuals work to coordinate their contexts, interpretations, communication, and actions, they are said to be organizing. One way of viewing this organizing process is as dialogue.

◧ DEFINITIONS OF DIALOGUE

In our working definition of communication as a balance of creativity and constraint, we maintain that dialogue is balanced communication, or communication in which each individual has a chance to both speak and be heard. Dialogue has three levels representing an increasing degree of collaboration and respect for the other: dialogue as (1) equitable transaction, (2) empathic conversation, and (3) real meeting.

☐ Dialogue as Equitable Transaction

An **equitable transaction** from a communication perspective is one in which all participants have the ability to voice their opinions and perspectives. In defining dialogue this way, we call attention to the fact that not everyone in an organization has an equal say in making decisions or in interpreting events. In the traditional organization of the early twentieth century, people in low-level jobs were discouraged from "interact[ing] with anybody in the organization unless [they] got permission from the supervisor, and then he wanted to know what [they] were going to talk about. So there's this notion in an organization that talking to people is not what your job is, that talking to people [means] interfering with . . . productivity" (Evered & Tannenbaum, 1992, p. 48). Even in some of the most progressive companies, certain people's voices are valued more highly than others'. These people are said to have power because they can back up what they say with rewards or sanctions. The extent to which one person's remarks carry more weight than another's is not always obvious to the casual observer because a deeper exercise of power is applied to the shaping or defining of context. That is, determinations of whose voice counts most are either well established before the observer arrives on the scene or are created by those who define what is addressed. Numerous contextual factors—the structure of rooms, the arrangement of furniture, differences in dress and appearance, the length of time scheduled for meetings, who is invited (or not invited) to attend meetings, and norms derived from prior communication situations—affect how much weight is given to the points of view of certain people. Once we are in a situation we can try to speak as if from a position of power, but this is often difficult given the numerous contextual constraints already in place.

One way to learn about how individuals participate in organizational dialogues is to ask questions about voice (who does and does not get to speak on organizational issues) and to pay close attention to when, where, and for how long individuals speak. **Voice** manifests itself in the ability of an individual or group to participate in the ongoing organizational dialogue. In most organizations, a few voices are loud and clear (e.g., those of the owners or senior managers), while others are muted or suppressed (e.g., those of the janitorial and clerical staffs). In the literature on organizations, voice has a more specific meaning: It refers to an employee's decision to speak up against the status quo rather than keep quiet and stay or give up and leave (Hirschman, 1970). In an ideal world, voice is the preferred option because it raises important issues and encourages creativity and commitment. In most companies, however, many barriers to voice exist. The suppression of employee voice within organizations can lead to whistle-blowing, wherein frustrated employees take their concerns to the media, the courts, or others outside of the organization (Redding, 1985). In extreme cases of suppressed employee voice, the results may include sabotage and violence in the workplace (Goodall, 1995).

At a minimum, then, dialogue requires that communicators be afforded equitable opportunities to speak. While the notion of dialogue as equitable transaction is a good starting point for thinking about organizational communication, it does not explicitly address the quality of that communication.

☐ Dialogue as Empathic Conversation

In defining dialogue as **empathic conversation**, we refer to the ability to understand or imagine the world as another person understands or imagines it. Achieving empathy is difficult for people who believe that their view of reality is the only correct view and that others' perceptions are misinformed or misguided. Indeed, Western communication is largely based on assumptions of what is "right." As a result, it becomes much more difficult to accept the validity of a different perspective, especially a radically different one. However, empathy is crucial in organizations. It promotes understanding among different departments, makes managing diversity possible, and acknowledges that although individuals and groups have different perspectives on the organization, no single perspective is inherently better than others. In this way, we can focus on common problems without immediately turning those who have a different view of these problems into enemies. The challenge, of course, is in learning to appreciate differences in interpretation without feeling pressured to either demonize the other or to strive for complete agreement. Put differently: "Can I recognize the value of your [perspective] . . . without us having to somehow merge into something that's less rich than the community of differences?" (Evered & Tannenbaum, 1992, p. 52).

Researchers at the Massachusetts Institute of Technology (MIT) take a similar view of organizational dialogue in their efforts to create learning communities (Isaacs, 1999; Senge, 1991; Senge et al., 1994). Building on the work of physicist David Bohm, the researchers define dialogue as a kind of "collective mindfulness" in which the interactants are more concerned about group effectiveness than about individual ego or position. From this perspective, dialogue affords new opportunities for people in organizations to work together. Not merely a set of techniques, dialogue requires that people "learn how to think together — not just in the sense of analyzing a shared problem or creating new pieces of shared knowledge, but [also] in the sense of occupying a collective sensibility, in which the thoughts, emotions, and resulting actions belong not to one individual, but to all of them together" (Isaacs, 1999, p. 358). The MIT dialogue project has attracted the attention of business because it links the fate of whole systems of individuals (e.g., organizations, societies, species) with dialogue, flirting with the idea that our relationships with others can possess a spiritual quality.

We know that treating people like objects is inappropriate, but are understanding and empathy enough? These questions recall the work of contemporary philosophers Martin Buber and Mikhail Bakhtin, whose critique of empathy as the goal of dialogue leads us to yet another definition.

☐ Dialogue as Real Meeting

In defining dialogue as **real meeting**, we mean that through communication, a genuine communion can take place between people that transcends differences in role or perspective and that recognizes all parties' common humanity. John Stewart (2000) refers to this state as "letting others happen to you while holding your ground." The notion of dialogue as empathic conversation is insufficient because it assumes that one individual experiences the other as a kind of object, rather than as a fellow interpreter. In other words, even empathic communicators, once the conversation has ended, may continue to view the dialogue as mainly instrumental in accomplishing their personal and professional goals. Therefore, one's performance of empathy may be false or even a means to a personal strategic end.

Certain types of dialogue are valuable in and of themselves. Buber distinguishes between interhuman dialogue, which has inherent value, and social dialogue, which has value as a route to self-realization and fulfillment. According to Buber, "We are answerable neither to ourselves alone nor to society apart from ourselves but to that very bond between ourselves and others through which we again and again discover the direction in which we can authenticate our existence" (as cited in Friedman, 1992, p. 6). Consider also this quote from Bakhtin (1984):

> A single consciousness is a contradiction in terms. Consciousness is essentially multiple. . . . I am conscious of myself and become myself only when revealing myself for another, through another and with the help of another. . . . The very being of man [sic] is the deepest communion. (p. 287)

From this perspective, since life exists only in communion with other humans, dialogue is a fundamental human activity. How do meetings in organizations resemble Buber's ideal? Buber sees it as a relationship between "I and Thou," wherein two individuals acknowledge that each is an interpreter and that neither reduces the other to an object of interpretation within a context that has already been constructed. For example, we have seen senior managers who have struggled to understand each other deeply move to an even higher level of trust and coordination in which their respect and regard for the others appear as the foundation of each of their conversations. This respect for another's subjectivity and worldview is the key ingredient in real meeting.

Seeking dialogue because it has value for itself can often result in positive consequences for the organization:

> [Dialogue] is one of the richest activities that human beings can engage in. It is the thing that gives meaning to life, it's the sharing of humanity, it's creating something. And there is this magical thing in an organization, or in a team, or a group, where you get unrestricted interaction, unrestricted dialogue, and this synergy happening that results in more productivity, and satisfaction, and seemingly magical levels of output from a team. (Evered & Tannenbaum, 1992, p. 48)

This definition of dialogue combines the abstract or spiritual with the more practical aspects of how we communicate. Are we open to the voices of others? Do we recognize that all views are partial and that each of us has the right to speak? Are we open to the possibility of maintaining mutual respect and openness of spirit through organizational communication? Such questions are not easily answered by people in organizations today. Although people may desire to maintain an open dialogue, they are too often constrained by learned behaviors that guard against intimate disclosure, by the social, professional, and political consequences of those disclosures, and by the habit of separating emotions from work.

To establish dialogue as real meeting, we must learn to interpret communication as a dialogic process that occurs between and among individuals, rather than as something we do to one another. All parties are responsible for the dialogue as well as for the risks taken; only together can they make progress. We engage in dialogue to learn more about the self in context with others. Dialogue helps us attain new appreciations for the multilayered dimensions of every context: "The crucial point is to go into a dialogue with the stance that there is something that I don't already know, with a mutual openness to learn. Through dialogue we can learn, not merely receive information, but revise the way we see something. Something about the dialogue honors inquiry and learning from the inquiry" (Evered & Tannenbaum, 1992, p. 45).

Authentic dialogue also provides a practical communication skill that is invaluable: We learn to speak from experience and to listen for experience. By sharing and risking the truth of our experience, we discover important questions that can guide our interpretations of contexts, of others, and of ourselves. We gain access to the shaping forces of our own and others' experiences. These forces guide our individual and collective constructions of reality, teach us about what counts as knowledge as well as how to value it, and influence how we generate our evaluations of people and things.

Dialogue as real meeting is difficult to achieve, which is why it does not characterize most relationships inside or outside of organizations. Most organizations readily acknowledge the importance of equitable transactions and are pleased to create increased empathy across hierarchical levels and professional groups. Still, dialogue as real meeting is an important communicative goal because it can transform organizations into energetic and dynamic workplaces. Such organizations are both effective and enjoyable because they encourage the kinds of communication required for real human connection.

There are advantages and limitations associated with promoting dialogue in organizations. It can increase employee satisfaction and commitment, reduce turnover rates, and lead to greater innovation and flexibility within the organization. However, it is also time consuming, requiring that issues be screened in terms of the amount of dialogue they warrant. It is also necessary that certain people possess the power to decide which issues are most important in a turbulent business environment. In addition, promoting dialogue may lead communicators to assume that their ideas and opinions will be implemented. Although there may be an equitable distribution of power and voice in the group, within a capitalist system the owners and their agents make the final decisions. Recent moves to develop employee-owned companies are beginning to address this concern. Finally, dialogue may lead to a lack of closure or to the feeling that "no right answer" can be found. This problem is related in part to the nature of Western society, in which people expect definitive answers about science, medicine, politics, and technology. In organizational communication, it may be more appropriate to focus on practical guidelines for action.

We conclude this section with two important questions. First: Is dialogue possible in organizations? Our experiences lead us to believe that while dialogue is possible, it is exceedingly rare. More common is communication that creates barriers to real meeting by attempting to convince others that their perceptions are faulty: "Management shouldn't think that way," "That idea will never fly," and "I know my people aren't dissatisfied." Much may be gained by expanding the current interest in coordinating the diverse voices in business. In fact, critical organizational scholar Stan Deetz (2006) suggests that organizations can make dramatic improvements by initiating dialogical decision making only occasionally. Drawing a parallel to the Judeo-Christian tradition of tithing, Deetz argues that if organizations devoted a mere 10 percent of their time engaging employees in meaningful dialogue, these organizations would be more productive 90 percent of the time.

Our second question is more difficult: What role does the situated individual play in constructing organizational reality through communication? Some observers take exception with the concept of the situated individual. They argue that it simply restates the idea that a person has a political ideology in favor of free will and capitalism (Grossberg, 1991). In their view, most choices are so constrained that decisions are made for us, and what we believe to be free or motivated action is actually the force of the world acting through us. Other observers, however, are less willing to underestimate the experiences of the situated individual (Jackson, 1989). In this view, we are born into a society that expects us to act out a balance of individual and social responsibilities. We are expected to make decisions about ourselves and about how our actions may influence and be influenced by others. Ultimately, however, the responsibility for those actions is our own. If someone commits a serious crime, for example, society may be implicated, but it is the criminal who goes to jail.

SUMMARY

Researchers commonly encounter four definitions of organizational communication in the literature: communication as information transfer, transactional process, strategic control, and a balance of creativity and constraint. This list is roughly chronological and reveals an increased interest in feedback and two-way interaction as key to organizational sense making. Our own view of organizations as dialogues extends this trend.

Recasting organizations as dialogues (in contrast, say, with economic or political models) places our focus on the interplay between self and other in multiple, changing contexts and situations. Each of these foundational elements arises in relationship with the others, culminating in the idea that every individual is "situated" in flows of communication.

When situated individuals come together to organize, they may vary considerably in the sort of communication in which they engage. On one end of the spectrum is discussion, wherein people seek to dominate others. At the other end is dialogue. Writers on dialogue (Isaacs, 1999) have outlined what we categorize as three levels that increasingly reveal people with a fundamental respect for the subjectivity and differing worldview of the other. The three levels are dialogue as equitable transaction, dialogue as empathic conversation, and dialogue as real meeting. Although dialogue in contemporary organizations is rare, our experience suggests that some level of dialogue is indeed possible.

QUESTIONS FOR REVIEW AND DISCUSSION

1. What are the major approaches to communication discussed in this chapter? What insights does each approach provide?

2. Explain what we mean by our definition of organizational communication. What are the sources of individual creativity? Of organizational constraint?

3. How do the concepts of self, other, and context contribute to our understanding of organizational communication? How do these concepts help us understand the differences among the major approaches?

4. Strategic ambiguity is discussed as a way to encourage empowerment by allowing employees at different levels within the company to interpret the meaning of statements in relation to their own jobs. However, it doesn't always work out that way. What potential problems are associated with using strategic ambiguity?

5. What is dialogue? Of the types of dialogue described in this chapter, which ones do you believe are most likely to be available to organizational employees? Why?

6. How would you characterize the kinds of communication that are most prevalent in university life, both in and outside of the classroom? For example, do students of the humanities and the social sciences follow different definitions of communication than their counterparts in the natural sciences?

KEY TERMS

Balancing creativity and constraint, p. 36
Empathic conversation, p. 49
Equitable transaction, p. 48
Information transfer, p. 29
Real meeting, p. 50
Self, other, and context, p. 43–44

Situated individual, p. 46
Strategic ambiguity, p. 32
Strategic control, p. 32
Structuration, p. 35
Transactional process, p. 30
Voice, p. 49

The Many Robert Smiths

JASON, THE JANITOR

"Smith is a tidy man. I pass by his desk at night when I'm cleaning up, and his area is the only one that's perfect. Nothing is ever out of place. I've made a kind of study out of it. You know, paid lots of attention to it on account of it being so unusual. So I've noticed things.

"I'd say Smith must be a single man. There are no pictures of family on his desk or on the walls. Most people leave keys to their personal life in the office — photographs, items they picked up during vacations, stickers with funny sayings on them. But not Smith. In Smith's area, there is no trace of anything personal. Just some books and the computer. The books never change positions, which tells me he never has to look things up. So I think Smith must be a smart man, too.

"I've never met him. Or if I did, I never knew it. But I see him in my mind as a tall, thin guy with glasses who doesn't smile too often. He may be shy, too. Fastidious people are often shy. Maybe he's an accountant or a computer programmer. It's hard to say. But Smith makes my job interesting. I look at his desk every night to see if anything has changed."

CATHERINE, THE RECEPTIONIST

"Smith is okay, a little shy maybe. He says 'hello' to me every morning. Just a 'hello,' though — nothing more, not even my name. I didn't know his name for months. But then, I didn't say much to him either.

"Then one afternoon he had a visitor. It was a woman — a beautiful woman in her late twenties or early thirties. She asked to speak to Bobby. 'Bobby who?' I asked. She looked confused; then she smiled and said, 'Bobby Smith, I thought everyone knew.' Well, this was interesting. I mean, I suddenly realized Smith had a first name — Robert. I had never thought of him as anyone's 'Bobby' before.

"I paged Smith, and he came downstairs. When he saw the woman, his face turned white like he'd seen a ghost. She called his name, and he stood still. I thought he was about to cry or something, but instead he just shook his head, as if to say, 'No.' He didn't say anything. Just shook his head. Then he turned and walked back upstairs, slowly. The woman just watched him. Then she turned around and walked out. I never saw her again. I don't know if she was a girlfriend, sister, or friend. Smith never said anything about her.

"In this job, I meet all kinds of people. I've learned a lot about people while working here as a receptionist. But Smith is still a mystery to me. I don't know

(continued, The Many Robert Smiths)

much about him. All I know is that his first name is Robert but that some people call him Bobby, that he says 'hello' to me every morning like clockwork, and that there was once a beautiful woman in his life. Oh yeah, and he's about 5 feet, 7 inches tall, has short hair and a big mustache, wears an earring, and obviously works out a lot."

WILSON, THE BOSS

"Smith is a strange guy, but a good worker. He never misses a day and is even willing to work nights or weekends to get the job done. His work is always neat and well organized. Personally, I wish he would get rid of his earring and mustache, but that's just him, I guess.

"I hired him five years ago as an entry-level accountant. His work in that position was good. He was promoted to a senior accountant position very quickly, as if someone up there in the company ranks were watching out for him. Usually it takes the best accountant five to seven years to make it to senior status; Smith made it in three. Last fall I asked him to take charge of a major audit, and he's been diligently working on that project ever since.

"Smith never talks about his life outside of work. And I never ask him. He seems to like it that way. But from the way he is built, I'd say he spends a lot of time working out at a gym. He drives a vintage black sports car, a Speedster, and it is always clean. He leaves it open during the day with a pair of Ray-Bans on the dash, always in the same position.

"I figure he comes from a wealthy family. He graduated from Stanford. But he doesn't act like a Californian. I'd say he's from Pittsburgh. I don't know why I say that. Actually, to be honest, Smith scares me a little bit. I don't know anyone who's as calm and collected and perfect as Smith is. In movies it's always the mass murderer who's like that. Not that I think Smith is that way. But I wouldn't be surprised, either. I wish his starched shirts would just one time come back with a rip in them or something. I know that sounds small. I can't help it. Smith does that to me."

FELICIA, A CO-WORKER

"Robert is my good friend. He's a warm, sensitive person with a heart of gold. He and I have talked a lot over the past couple of years. Mostly about our dreams. We both want to work hard, save a lot of money, and be able to do something else with our lives while we are still young enough to enjoy it.

"Robert came from a poor family. He grew up moving around from town to town while his mother looked for work in construction. He had two brothers and a sister, all older. He was the baby. His father was killed in the Vietnam War. His older brothers are both in the military and don't have much in common with Robert, and his sister is a successful lawyer in Washington. Robert showed me a picture of her once; she's a beautiful woman. They had a big argument a while back. He wouldn't say much about it, except that he hasn't seen her since. His mother died of lung cancer two years ago.

"Robert worked hard in school but won an athletic scholarship to Stanford. He was a gymnast. Or still is, because he spends two or three nights a week working with underprivileged kids downtown, teaching them gymnastics. And he is big in Adult Children of Alcoholics, which I took him to. That's a whole story in itself. He has a lot of hobbies, which, when he does them, aren't exactly hobbies anymore. He is such a perfectionist! Like that car of his, for instance. He built it himself, out of a kit. And you should see his apartment."

Jenkins, the Retired CEO

"Robert Smith is one of the company's finest employees. And he is an exceptional young man. I recruited him at Stanford when I was teaching there right after I retired. Since then, I've followed his career. I asked him not to say much about our relationship because a lot of people might get the wrong idea. I want him to make it on his own, which he has. I put in a good word for him here and there, but never anything too pushy.

"I knew his father in Vietnam. He served in my command and was a good soldier. He was due to be shipped home later in the week when he was killed. It was sad. I wrote the letter to his family myself. When I got out of the Army, I moved into the private sector. You can imagine how odd it was for me to walk into that accounting class at Stanford and see Robert Smith, who looks just like his dad except for the mustache and earring, sitting in the front row. I couldn't believe it. Still can't.

"In a way, I feel related to Robert. He still comes to visit us on the holidays. I like that."

Assignment

1. You are the executive recruiter (or headhunter) who compiled the preceding information about Smith from interviews with his colleagues. You also have Smith's résumé and performance appraisal reports to supplement the interviews. Your job is to prepare a personality profile of Smith for a firm that may

(continued, The Many Robert Smiths)

be interested in hiring him. What would you write? How would you explain the different perspectives on Smith? If you were Robert Smith, what would you say about the interview statements?

2. We live complex (and often contradictory) lives as situated individuals in organizations. This should make us sensitive to the various ways in which meanings are constructed through communication. Construct an investigation of yourself, using interview statements by others describing who you are. Supplement these statements with your own résumé. What do the statements tell you about yourself? About your construction of others? About yourself as a situated individual in an organization? About the complexities of interpreting meaning?

3. As a student of communication, you are interested in finding ways to improve your own and others' interpretations of meanings. Review the case study as if you were the communication consultant working with the executive recruiter. Your job is to help the headhunter construct better follow-up questions and produce a complete report on Smith. What questions would help explain the different views of Smith?

PART II

Theories of Organizational Communication

Three Early Perspectives on Organizations and Communication

We have so far discussed the pervasiveness of organizational communication in society and provided you with some definitions for thinking about the nature and process of communication in general. In this chapter, we hone in on the organizational context and discuss in some detail three early theories of organizations that were not written with a communication focus, although they do have implications for communication. Instead, they had more of a business focus, but we must begin with these early theories because the ways they defined (or failed to define) communication have had enormous impact on organizational practice and continue to inform our practice today. The three organizational perspectives are classical management, human relations, and human resources. Before we start, however, we want to make sure that you have a thorough understanding of what is meant by theory.

◻ WHY THEORY?

Theories of human behavior run the gamut from simple ideas to formal systems of hypotheses that aim to explain, predict, and control. All theories share two features: They are historical and metaphorical. Any theory of organizational communication is historical in that it is a product of the time in which it emerged, reflecting the concerns and interests of the culture that produced it. A **theory** is metaphorical in that it uses language to suggest enlightening comparisons between organizational communication and other processes. For example, scientific management theory, which we will discuss in this chapter, compares organizations to machines.

Our approach to the role of theories in understanding organizations is a practical one that recognizes both their uses and limitations. As students of organizational communication, we choose to participate in a particular discourse community, which in this case is made up of individuals who share an interest in organizations and communication. Communication and literary theorist Kenneth Burke (1989) likened participation in a discourse community to entering a room in which conversation is already in progress. We wander around for a while, listen, and occasionally join in the talk. Sooner or later, we find ourselves engaged in conversation that seems important. As time passes, we have many such conversations. Eventually, we notice that the hour is late and that it is time to leave, but the conversation continues without us. Here we recognize that participation in the discourse community requires detailed attention to the talk that *preceded* our entry into the room.

Theories function as resources or thinking tools in that they enhance our ability to explain and to act on a wide variety of practical issues, such as what motivates people to work. The way we talk about an issue or a problem influences the solutions we can propose. The more tools we have at our disposal, the more likely we are to craft appropriate and enabling responses to organizational communication dilemmas or opportunities. But theories are also historical narratives, goal-oriented stories told for the purpose of explanation. Theories may offer a creative integration of disparate issues (such as how organizations can be both pro-profit and pro-people or why communication and efficiency are linked), or they may provide a complete explication of a narrow topic (such as how to lead an effective decision-making group or to relieve employee stress). In either case, theories reflect unique historical circumstances and diverse cultural and political interests.

Because organizational communication theories are evolving episodes in an ongoing historical narrative, it is important that we not strive to choose one theory over another. Instead, we should learn to see each theory as a participant in a larger, ongoing dialogue where each conversational thread both reveals and conceals some aspect of organizational life and the larger social milieu in which organizations are located. Consequently, our interest in theories goes beyond what they help us to explain. We are also interested in the position of theories in the general stream of events, in their relationship to other theories, in their unique properties, in their strengths and limitations, in the interests they represent or exclude, and in the effects of retelling them on our conversation and the world.

ORGANIZATIONAL COMMUNICATION THEORIES AS HISTORICAL NARRATIVES: THE THREE *P*'S

The three *P*'s of historical writing — that such writing is partial, partisan, and problematic — provide an important perspective on communication and reveal the limitations of any account. All talk is partial, partisan, and problematic, and theories are no exception. The kinds of questions we raise about our reading of theory add to our understanding of organizational communication.

☐ Theories Are Partial

An argument could be made that any attempt to trace the history of organizational communication is necessarily incomplete and therefore misleading. Obviously, we have chosen to write this chapter anyway. Our primary condition is **partiality**: Our account tells only part of the story. However, the inability to articulate a complete account of the history of organizational communication is not unique to our field, nor is it disabling. As French philosopher Jacques Derrida (1972) notes, all thought is inscribed in language, and language is rooted in an inescapable paradox: There is no point of absolute meaning outside of language from which to view—or to prescribe—the truth of the world. Furthermore, it is logically impossible to say everything about anything; new perspectives are always possible, now and into the future. Because all language is partial (regardless of length!), there can be no absolute history, no full account, no complete story of organizational communication. Therefore, from this perspective, our account is necessarily partial, as are the theories themselves.

☐ Theories Are Partisan

We write this chapter, and indeed this book, under the limitation of **partisanship**: The story we tell is one that we favor. The history of organizational communication typically emphasizes the interpretations of dominant white males in Western culture, with little attention given to how members of oppressed, marginalized, or subjugated groups like women and minorities would tell the story.

Compare, for example, how a Native American might interpret the nineteenth-century expansion of railroads, mining, and manufacturing interests across the Great Plains with the account given in many U.S. history textbooks. Depending on one's interests, or partisanship, this story can be seen as one of tragedy or opportunity. Notice that although there may be disagreement about how the story gets told and who should tell it, there is likely to be agreement on at least some of the story's events and characters. Everyone agrees that Native Americans considered the Great Plains their natural hunting grounds and that westward expansion by white settlers took place. Partisanship, then, is not so much about identifying facts as it is about interpreting their meanings.

All thought is partisan. Knowledge is shaped by the theories and interpretations we use to make sense of the world, or to create what we call a worldview. If we think of each theory as a kind of mini-worldview, then we see clearly that one theory cannot explain everything. No one partisan view can comprehend all the interests of all people over all time. When we read about theories, then, it is useful to think of each theory as telling a particular story. Because each story represents the interests of the storyteller, it is a partisan perspective on broader, more complex stories about the world. In this sense, many theories contribute to the complex story of organizational communication.

This principle can be directly applied to routine episodes of communication at work. For example, let's assume that Deon makes the following announcement at a team meeting: "I just talked to Beth about our project, and she thinks we ought to go with the approach I suggested last week." His comment may be viewed as partisan on several accounts. The other team members might consider whether Deon's interpretation of his conversation with Beth was influenced by what he wants to happen. Alternatively, perhaps Deon influenced Beth's opinion. The key point here is not that Deon has intentionally misrepresented Beth's opinion at the team meeting, but that all talk is partisan. When we speak, we tend to represent our views of situations in ways that favor our interests and goals, and theorists are no different.

☐ Theories Are Problematic

Finally, we write this chapter knowing that the story itself will be **problematic**: Our account asks more questions than it can answer, and the answers it does provide are based on what is currently known rather than on all that could be known. Theorists who generated the theories we take up were operating under similar constraints. In admitting the problematic nature of our narrative, we also invite dialogue, asking our readers to bring to our account their experiences and understandings.

Consider how this concept can inform our understanding of everyday organizational communication. Rather than making ultimate statements, it encourages us to ask more questions and to invite others into the dialogue. Rather than assuming that we know the whole truth about any issue, it urges us to ask for the input of others who may hold different perspectives. This is very much in line with our philosophy and conception of this text—not as a book of answers, but rather as a way of thinking that produces good questions across multiple contexts and situations. Now that you have a clearer understanding of our perspective on theories, it is time to examine some specific theoretical perspectives on organizations with implications for communication.

◣ CLASSICAL MANAGEMENT APPROACHES

Classical management approaches are represented by a collection of theories that share the underlying metaphor of organizations modeled after efficient machines. This section shows the evolution of this idea from the eighteenth century to more recent times, beginning with the nature of preindustrial organizations and concluding with the apex of the classical approaches, the Industrial Revolution.

☐ From Empire to Hierarchy

From the eighteenth century to the early twentieth century, organizations functioned much like empires. Corporations were viewed as extensions of governments; they expanded trade, provided employment for the masses, and contributed to economic and social development (Rose, 1989). Cities in the New World (North America) were even mapped according to the appropriation of territories by organizations.

Today, we can still see the close relationship between homes and factories in some regions, and we can also see how wealth and status allow a family to move farther away from the site of production. The closer a house is to a factory, the less material power and social status the family living in that dwelling tends to have. Thus, social control is effectively produced in part by the relationship between the location of industry and neighborhoods.

In the mid-eighteenth century, Benjamin Franklin (1706–90) popularized some early notions of empire and pragmatism in his *Poor Richard's Almanac*. It is primarily a collection of parables and quotations that elevate hard work (called "industry"), independence (the accumulation of wealth on individual, corporate, and national levels), and the virtues of planning, organizing, and controlling one's life through work. Here are some sample axioms from Franklin's almanac (1970):

- Industry need not wish — There are no Gains without Pains.
- God gives all things to industry.
- God helps them that help themselves.
- Sloth makes all things difficult, but industry all easy.
- Early to Bed, early to rise, makes a Man healthy, wealthy, and wise.

Although Franklin was not the only writer to express these ideas (similar sentiments are found in Japanese and Chinese proverbs, the Old Testament, and the Talmud), he was the first to popularize them as the foundation for an American work culture. Moreover, the proverbs were influential precisely because they fit neatly into the wisdom of older narratives used in churches, schools, and business.

During this same period, Frederick the Great (1712–86), King of Prussia, organized his armies on the principles of mechanics: ranks, uniforms, regulations, task specialization, standardized equipment, command language, and drill instruction (Morgan, 1986). His success served as a model for organizational action, one based on the division of labor and machinelike efficiency. Given this historical background, it is perhaps no surprise that inventor Eli Whitney's (1765–1825) groundbreaking demonstration of mass production in 1801 was based on the production of guns, whose purpose was to maintain order and extend the power of empires.

Adam Smith (1723–90), a philosopher of economics and politics, published *Wealth of Nations* in 1776, which praised the divisions of labor evident in factory production. As Karl Marx (1818–83) would demonstrate in the mid-nineteenth century, division of labor was essential to organizing corporations and societies along class lines. By 1832, a blueprint for such an organizational form had emerged. Characterized by strict divisions of labor and hierarchy, it would later be called the "classical theory of management." Notice in Figure 3.1 that the classic bureaucratic organization privileges a top-down or management-oriented approach. Two assumptions of this perspective are worth noting. First, the emphasis on developing scientific methods for production is politically and socially linked to providing that information only to managers and supervisors, who in turn use it to organize and control workers. Second, the model endorses the need to foster a passive audience in the workplace. In other words, workers are viewed as silent receptors of management information, incapable of responding, interpreting, arguing, or counteracting this subtle but persuasive form of control. Thus, effective communication in the nineteenth century meant giving orders and emphasized the downward transmission of information. Managerial authority and the presumption that there was "one best way" of doing things (which, of course, only managers knew) effectively stifled any upward communication. Despite its considerable drawbacks, we continue to see significant remnants of this sort of chart (and of this management philosophy!) in some organizations today.

The top-down flow of information in hierarchies also led to the emergence of *domination narratives*, which ascribed particular readings of how truth, power, and control were constituted in everyday conversation. The next section discusses these narratives.

☐ From Resistance to Domination

The rapid expansion of industrialization in nineteenth-century northern Europe and North America created the need to organize and manage labor in ways that mirrored dominant social and political values. In the United States, slavery both supplied the laborers for agricultural work in the South and mirrored a view of hierarchy that was based on the racial divisions sanctioned by white slaveholders. One result of the deep divisions between ways of organizing labor and the social values that supported them was the Civil War (1861–65). The outcome of that war is an interesting, but often overlooked, part of the history of organizations and communication in this country. It can be viewed as a struggle between social values that coincided with the hierarchical division of organized labor and the different interpretations of how hierarchies should be established. Whereas the South supported a racial hierarchy, the increasingly industrial North favored one governed by social class. This accounts for the observation on the part of some freed slaves that the hidden "slavery" of the northern factories was in many ways as bad as or worse than the overt slavery practiced by plantation owners in the South.

Where differences exist in the type of work that people do, there will also be differences in how that work is done, evaluated, valued, and compensated. Those in power control the interpretation of such differences; the story they tell clearly favors their interests. For white slaveholders in the South, slavery was justified on economic and moral grounds. They believed they had a right to a cheap source of

FIGURE 3.1

Organization Chart Illustrating the Principles of Classical Management Theory and Bureaucratic Organization

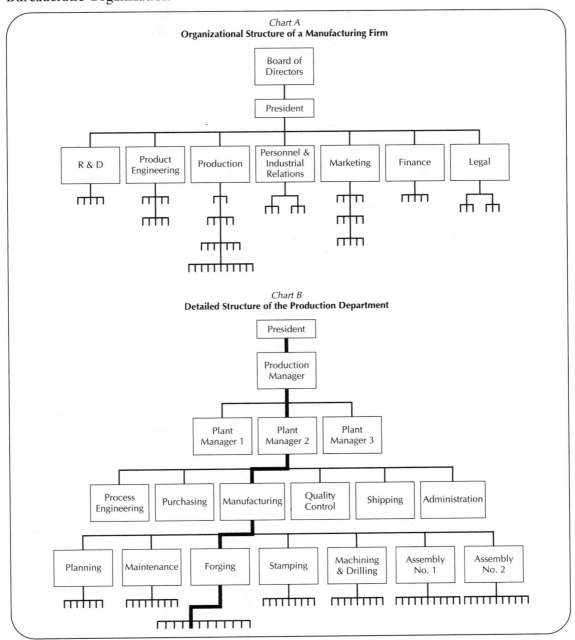

Source: Gareth Morgan, *Images of Organization* (Newbury Park, Calif.: Sage, 1986). Reprinted by permission of Sage Publications, Inc.

labor to farm their lands and that their accumulation of wealth was at the heart of Calvinist moral advancement (Raban, 1991). From their perspective, slavery was necessary for the productive accomplishment of work that would grant them entry to a Protestant heaven. This partisan view of racial division and moral order gave slaveholders the power to control both the daily lives of slaves and the means of resolving conflict. Thus, any slave attempt to challenge white authority was viewed as a challenge to the moral order. As a result, communication between slaveholder and slave was one-sided, strongly favoring the slaveholder's interests.

One feature of societal dialogue, **resistance to domination**, helps us understand organizational dialogue. Resistance to domination is defined as any action on the part of oppressed individuals to lessen the constraints placed on them by those in power. Such resistance takes many forms. In addition to the domination narratives discussed earlier in the chapter, all societies have narratives of resistance. These are the narratives of the less powerful and the powerless, of those who ordinarily have little or no voice in organizational and societal dialogue. They provide different accounts of events and the meanings those events had for the participants (Freire, 1968). Unless the domination is eventually overturned, these stories only rarely make it into textbooks. Slave narratives are an example of an elaborate set of stories from a particular point of view that almost never appears in the historical accounts of the period.

James Scott (1990) points out how the accounts of the powerless can function as **hidden transcripts** of the other side of the story. Hidden transcripts include themes and arguments that are well known by members of the oppressed group but kept out of the public eye for fear of reprisal from those in power. One kind of hidden transcript is the resistance narrative, like those that gave slaves a way to express their outrage among others who were caught in the same situation. Their stories reversed the order of things, placing slaveholders in inferior intellectual, moral, and performance positions. In this "world turned upside down" (Scott, 1990; Stallybrass & White, 1986), those without power could take control of the story and use it as a "performative space for the full-throated acting out of everything that must be choked back in public" (Conquergood, 1992, p. 91). By looking at the dominant narrative alongside the slave narrative, we get a sense of the potential dialogue that might have occurred between the two groups. Unfortunately, however, that dialogue remained mostly implicit because the dominant group's narrative was told in public and the slave's narrative in private.

In addition to slave narratives, other forms of resistance to domination came with the slave songs, ditties, and dirges that would later become known as "the blues." This, in turn, would lead to two other musical forms of resistance to domination: rock and roll and rap music (Goodall, 1991a). Similarly, there are accounts of resistance to domination from those who were once among the dominant and powerful. Perhaps the best known of these accounts is the gospel hymn "Amazing Grace," which combines the rhythms and sensibilities of a slave song with words penned by a former slave trader turned English minister, John Newton (1798):

Amazing Grace, how sweet the sound,
That saved a wretch like me.
I once was lost, but now I'm found,
Was blind, but now I see.

Newton's diaries also contain evidence of the values of hierarchy and empire in the operation of slave ships (Moyers, 1989). Dramatic testimony is found in Newton's drawings of how chained slaves were "scientifically organized" for the long voyage between Africa and the New World (Figure 3.2). Like cattle or dry goods, slaves were kept in tight, straight lines to minimize wasted space in the ship's hull. Meager food and water were dispensed according to a rigid schedule. Management took the form of absolute tyranny and utilized scientific principles of cost efficiency and production.

Although in later decades many economic and technical advances would attest to the benefits of rational approaches to organization, the scientific management that was applied to slave ships shows how it can be abused in the service of absolute power. In the twentieth century, the Holocaust provides yet another example of the abuse of classical principles of organization. Unfortunately, abuses of power based on hierarchically ordered systems of domination continue to persist in areas under severe political and military occupation as well as in illegal sweatshops employing immigrant laborers the world over. One study suggests that in 2005 at least 12.3 million people worldwide were made to endure some form of forced servitude, including such activities as brick-making, logging, sewing, and prostitution ("Millions," 2004). In some cases the abuses are fostered by criminals working outside of the law, while in others they are perpetrated by employers or governments. Examples of the different forms of slavery still practiced in 2005 include the following:

ALBANIA: Teenage girls are tricked into sex slavery and trafficked by organized crime rings.

BRAZIL: Lured into the rainforest, families are forced at gunpoint to burn trees for valuable heating charcoal.

BURMA: The ruling military junta enslaves its own people to build infrastructure projects, some of which benefit U.S. corporations.

DOMINICAN REPUBLIC: Haitians are rounded up at random, taken across the border, and forced to cut cane in sugar plantations.

GHANA: Families repent for sins by giving daughters as slaves to fetish priests.

INDIA: Children trapped in debt bondage roll beedi cigarettes fourteen hours a day.

IVORY COAST: Child slaves are forced to work on cocoa plantations.

MAURITANIA: Arab-Berbers buy and sell black Africans as inheritable property.

PAKISTAN: Children with nimble fingers are forced to weave carpets in looms.

SUDAN: Arab militias from the north take southern Sudanese women and children in slave raids.

THAILAND: Women and children become sex slaves for tourists.

FIGURE 3.2

Diagram Showing How Slaves Were Stowed on Ships

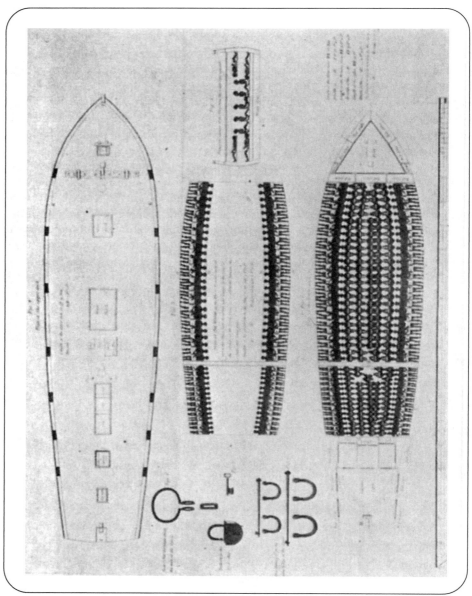

Source: Reproduced from George Francis Dow, *Slave Ships and Slaving* (1969), p. 159.

United Arab Emirates: Bangladeshi boys are transported and exploited as
jockeys for camel racing.
United States: The CIA estimates that fifty thousand people are trafficked
each year as sex slaves, domestics, garment workers, and agricultural slaves.
(American Anti-Slavery Group, 2005, p. 2)

☐ The Industrial Revolution

Although organizations and communication existed before the steamboat, railroad,
and cotton gin, it was not until the Industrial Revolution that modern machinery
and methods of production emerged, with the rise of the factory bureaucracy (Perrow, 1986).

The rise of the modern factory during the industrial period was an extension
of a social (and racial) class structure that sought to stabilize power relations among
people by controlling the means of production and consumption in society (Foucault, 1972, 1979). This period also marked an important shift. Before the Industrial Revolution, only rarely did anyone work for someone else in exchange for
wages. In the mid-1980s, in contrast, only about 15 percent of our working population was able to get by without working for someone else (Perrow, 1986). (As
we discuss in Chapter 8, this trend may now be reversing, as businesses downsize,
restructure, or move operations overseas and more people are becoming self-
employed providers of goods and services.)

The organization of work and communication in the early factories was highly
influenced by the then-emerging concepts of division of labor and hierarchy. **Division of labor** refers to the separation of tasks into discrete units; **hierarchy** refers
to the vertical arrangement of power and authority that distinguishes managers
from employees. These concepts, which form the foundation of the modern organization, originated in an affluent, class-conscious view of social control in which
the rise of the middle class was seen as a threat to the upper class. The rationale was
that the work institution should mirror the organization of the ideal society. (This
may help explain why prisons and factories were modeled on the same architectural
principles and why the behavior of inmates and workers was monitored and controlled in similar ways.) Another clue about why organization and order were
linked to hierarchy may be found in Kenneth Burke's work on purposive (i.e.,
rhetorical) language. Burke (1989) states that people are symbol users moved to a
sense of order. From his perspective, language is a hierarchical and symbolic construction of order that we use to attempt to "perfect" nature. In our construction of
language-based realities, we create rules for organizing sentences (grammar) and
arguments (logic) and for cooperating with audiences through symbols (rhetoric).
It can be argued, then, that hierarchical forms of organization mirror the hierarchical nature of language.

The relationships among class-consciousness, purposive language, and social control developed simultaneously with the rise of science. With science came much more than a highly ordered method of explaining phenomena: From explanation emerged the ability to predict, and from the ability to predict came the potential to control. Thus, the underlying theme of the classical management approach to organization is the scientific rationalization of control. Organizations are viewed as the primary vehicle through which our lives are rationalized—"planned, articulated, scientized, made more efficient and orderly, and managed by experts" (Scott, 1981, p. 5).

☐ Scientific Management

The years 1880 to 1920 were characterized by both significant racial and class prejudice and unprecedented economic expansion in the United States. With massive industrialization came the ruthless treatment of workers by owners who subscribed to a "survival of the fittest" mentality. Those employees who succeeded were deemed to be morally strong; those who failed were deemed to be unworthy of success (Bendix, 1956).

Born in this era was the middle-class engineer Frederick Taylor (1856–1915), a pioneer in the development of **scientific management**. His book *The Principles of Scientific Management* (1913) is based on the assumption that management is a true science resting on clearly defined laws, rules, and principles. Taylor's time and motion studies led to improved organizational efficiency through the mechanization of labor and the authority of the clock. Work was divided into discrete units that were measured by how long it took a competent worker to accomplish them. This principle was then used to plan factory outcomes, to evaluate worker efficiency, and to train less-skilled workers. The production system thus required divisions of labor, carefully developed chains of command, and communication limited to orders and instructions.

Taylor's goal was to transform the nature of both work and management. He hoped that cooperation between managers and employees would bring a new era of industrial peace: "Under scientific management, arbitrary power, arbitrary dictation, ceases; and every single subject, large and small, becomes the question for scientific investigation, for reduction to law" (Taylor, 1947, p. 211). But things didn't work out that way. Instead of industrial peace, scientific management led to increased conflict because it reinforced hierarchical distinctions and further objectified the already downtrodden worker. Although Taylor claimed that he was developing his ideas to help the working person, by the end of his life he was cursed by labor unions as "the enemy of the working man" (Morgan, 1986). Even so, Taylor's work ushered in a new focus on the relationship between managers and employees as a key to organizational productivity, and remains a bedrock principle of contemporary management theory (Braverman, 1979).

More specifically, Taylor's model ushered in a systematic approach to the division of labor that has gone far beyond the design of work for which it was originally developed. Scientific management created a firm division between managers — whose task was to plan and control the design of work — and employees — whose job was to implement those plans. In short, scientific management assumed that some employees are better suited to "thinking" work and some to "doing" work, thus laying the groundwork for the class-based distinction between white-collar and blue-collar employees that we know today. Other divisions would follow. Male employees (who were also white and middle-class) were believed to be better managers because they were more "rational" and less "emotional" than their female counterparts. Men also came to be seen as better suited to the demands of public work because they were not burdened with private domestic responsibilities.

Women, who were largely written out of Taylor's theory (and out of formal organizational life), soon appropriated scientific management for use in the domestic realm. The emphasis on science and mechanization, the production of new household technologies and so-called conveniences, and the "cult of domesticity" combined to create a scientific management approach to home life at the turn of the century. In 1913, Christine Frederick, an editor for the popular magazine *The Ladies' Home Journal*, wrote a "how-to" book for women called *The New Housekeeping*. In it, she outlined the twelve principles of scientific efficiency that applied to the home, including ideals (or "the one best way" to complete a task), standardized operation, and scheduling. Further, she encouraged women to adopt the correct attitude toward efficiency because not only the household but also the mind must be "managed" and "organized." She admonished:

> First of all, the efficient attitude of mind for the housewife and homemaker is to realize that no matter how difficult and trying are the household tasks and burdens she finds placed upon her, there positively are ways to meet and conquer them efficiently — if she approaches these problems vigorously, hopefully, and patiently. Second, that far from being dull drudgery, homemaking in all its details is fascinating and stimulating if a woman applies to it her best intelligence and culture. Third, that no matter how good a housekeeper and homemaker a woman may already be, she will be eager not only to TRY, but to persistently and intelligently keep on trying, to apply in her home the scientific methods of work and management already proved and tried in shop and office throughout the world. (para. 50–52)

While they may not use the label, many working families today adopt a scientific management approach in their efforts to give order to their busy lives. Consider the working mother who checks her PDA to scan her color-coded itinerary of work (blue), family (yellow), and volunteer (pink) commitments as she leaves work to pick up her children from school before depositing them at their various activities. Her constant desire to find the most efficient way to control her work and personal lives extends Taylor's theory into the present era.

EVERYDAY ORGANIZATIONAL COMMUNICATION

Scientific Management at the Gym

For many people, exercise is a therapeutic means of escaping the daily grind and a way to work out stress on the job and in life. We often hear students vocalizing the need to hit the gym during finals week as a way of dealing with the pressure and anxiety! Increasingly, however, gyms and exercise routines are becoming as carefully managed or as "Taylorized" as many work environments. This is not to say that exercise is becoming less enjoyable or relaxing, but rather that gyms and fitness instructors are becoming increasingly savvy about utilizing and marketing a key attribute of scientific management: looking for the most effective way to complete a task (getting fit or losing weight) in the shortest amount of time while conserving the most energy.

Consider the example of Curves, a women's gym established as a franchise in 1995. Curves is known for its "30-minute workout" that includes "all five necessary [exercise] components: Warm-up, Aerobic exercise, Strength training, Cool down, and Stretching" (Curves, 2006). Women work out in a circuit on machines and aerobic exercise mats performing exercises that target different areas of the body: "You move from machine to mat, where you walk, jog, jump, dance, or move in place in any way for another 30 seconds to keep up your heart rate. The entire rotation through the circle of machines and mats takes place in these 30-minute intervals. The idea is to go through the circuit twice, with stretching afterwards." ("A Gym," 2004, para. 8). The ultimate goal of this routine is, of course, to offer maximum benefit in a minimal amount of time—especially as would-be gym members often cite "lack of time" for their decision not to commit to regular exercise.

The appeal of scientific management has also affected the very machines that you come across at your local gym. An increasingly popular machine in the fitness world, the pilates reformer, takes the stretching exercises and breathing techniques made famous by Joseph Pilates in a new direction with a system of strings, pulleys, and moveable carriages that help to ensure proper body alignment and, therefore, increased effectiveness during exercise. Similarly, weight-lifting machines are purposefully designed for users to practice the "one best way" to do an exercise with maximum benefit, and stair-climbers, treadmills, and stationary bicycles display the number of calories burned per hour, offering the user the chance to track and improve his or her efficiency in ways that would have made Taylor himself proud.

DISCUSSION QUESTIONS

1. With these examples in mind, what do you feel are the benefits and burdens of a Taylorized approach to fitness?
2. If you work out, do the principles of scientific management influence your workouts? What steps do you take to ensure maximum benefit with minimal time commitment?
3. If you do not currently work out, are you attracted to the idea of scientific management at the gym? Would a scientifically managed approach to fitness inspire you to exercise more regularly or make you less likely to work out? Why?
4. Consider other ways in which scientific management plays out in your life. Have you held a professional or volunteer position that stressed maximum benefit in minimal time? What ways did you benefit from such a system and in what ways did you find it frustrating? What were the pros and cons for the organization or company that employed you?

Scientific management, then, is a management-oriented, production-centered view of organizations and communication. Its ideal, the efficient machine, holds that humans function as components or parts. It also assumes a fundamental distinction between managers and employees: Managers think, workers work (Morgan, 1986). The ideal of scientific management is best realized in straightforward task situations that require no flexibility in responding to contingencies and that offer no opportunities for initiative. This description of an organization does not take into account human motivations for working, personal work relationships, and the flexibility required by the turbulent nature of organizational environments. Moreover, efforts to improve efficiency by raising production levels often alienate workers, as in Henry Ford's automobile plant, which experienced a turnover rate of 280 percent annually under scientific management (Morgan, 1986).

☐ Fayol's Classical Management

At roughly the same time Taylor was working on scientific management in the United States, the French industrialist Henri Fayol (1949) was developing his influential theory of "administrative science," or classical management. Fayol was a highly successful director of a French mining company, and his management principles became popular in the United States and elsewhere in the late 1940s. He is perhaps best known for articulating the five elements of classical management: planning, organizing, commanding (goal setting), coordinating, and controlling (evaluating). He was even more specific in detailing how this work ought to be done.

Katherine Miller (1995) groups Fayol's principles into four categories: structure, power, reward, and attitude. Regarding structure, Fayol prescribed a strict hierarchy with a clear vertical chain of command; he called this the "scalar principle." He believed that each employee should have only one boss and should be accountable to only one plan. Like Taylor, Fayol advocated division of labor through departmentalization (the grouping of similar activities together). The resulting organizational structure is the classic hierarchical pyramid.

In terms of power, Fayol advocated the centralization of decision making and respect for authority. He held that authority accrues from a person's position and character and that discipline and obedience could be expected only if both were present. Moreover, he viewed discipline as a respect for agreed-upon rules, and not solely a respect for position.

Mirroring Taylor's view of rewards, Fayol advocated fair remuneration for well-directed efforts, foreshadowing the potential of profit sharing as a compensation system (Tompkins, 1984). Most concerned about the employee's perception of equity in pay and other issues, Fayol believed in the value of a stable workforce. He was thus a proponent of stable tenure for employees as a means of avoiding high turnover rates and recruitment costs.

Finally, regarding organizational attitude, Fayol held that employees should subordinate their personal interests to those of the organization. He also saw rational enforcement of agreements through fair supervision as the method for ensuring this organizational attitude. At the same time, Fayol encouraged employee initiative, or the capacity to see a plan through to completion, and believed that supervisors should work hard to build positive employee morale.

Fayol intended to develop a set of guidelines for organizational administration that would be useful across a variety of situations. Some of his principles, most notably those related to unity of command and centralization, are especially relevant for students of communication (Tompkins, 1984). However, as Fayol cautioned, "There is nothing rigid or absolute in management affairs, it is all a question of proportion. Seldom do we have to apply the same principle twice in identical conditions; allowances must be made for different changing circumstances" (1949, p. 19).

☐ Bureaucracy

A final piece of the classical approach fell into place with the development of the idea of bureaucracy. In the harsh working conditions of the early 1900s, job security did not exist, young children worked long hours for meager wages, and workers were hired and fired for reasons that had to do with their race, religion, sex, attitude, or relationship to the boss. This method of dealing with employees, called **particularism**, was expedient for owners and managers but had dire consequences for employees. Particularism also presented an ideological conflict in the United States: "On the one hand, democracy stressed liberty and equality for all. On the other hand, large masses of workers and nonsalaried personnel had to submit to apparently arbitrary authority, backed up by local and national police forces and legal powers, for ten to twelve hours a day, six days a week" (Perrow, 1986, p. 53).

It was this conflict between ideology and practice that gave rise to a system that protected employees better than particularism. We now call that system **bureaucracy**. According to W. Richard Scott (1981), organizational bureaucracy has the following characteristics:

1. A fixed division of labor among participants
2. A hierarchy of offices
3. A set of general rules that govern performances
4. A rigid separation of personal life from work life
5. The selection of personnel on the basis of technical qualifications and equal treatment of all employees
6. Participants' view of employment as a career; tenure protecting against unfair arbitrary dismissal

Although the well-known German scholar Max Weber (1864–1920) was not a blind advocate of bureaucracy (he feared that its sole focus on instrumental rationality would drive out mystery and enchantment from the world), he saw it as technically superior to all other forms of organization. Furthermore, he was a strong advocate for universalism, or equal treatment according to ability. Most people today associate bureaucracy with the red tape and inflexibility of public agencies. However, these may not be necessary results of a bureaucratic approach. In his famous defense of bureaucracy, Charles Perrow (1986) argues that the machine itself ought not be blamed, but rather the people who misuse it to further their own interests.

It is useful to examine bureaucracy in terms of both what came before it — particularism — and Weber's goal of universalism, which sought to introduce standards of fair treatment in the workplace. Even today, managers struggle to hold on to the powers to hire, fire, promote, and discipline employees at will. In addition, prebureaucratic decision making is viewed by managers as easier and more expedient than decision making in a bureaucracy. The latter makes decisions harder to implement at the same time that it protects employees from abuse.

The ideal bureaucracy cannot be fully realized for several reasons: (1) It is not possible to rid organizations of all extraorganizational influences on member behavior; (2) bureaucracy does not deal well with nonroutine tasks; and (3) people vary in terms of rationality (Perrow, 1986). These inadequacies of bureaucracy were the impetus for other theories. Alternative forms of organizing were proposed that loosened the rigid assumptions of classical management theory, thus paving the way for new insights into human organization.

☐ Implications for Organizational Communication

Classical management approaches view communication as unproblematic. They posit that in organizations communication is simply a tool for issuing orders, coordinating work efforts, and gaining employee compliance. Moreover, in a hierarchical world, the primary function of communication is the transfer of information through the proper channels. In the classical management approach, any attempt at achieving a balance between individual creativity and organizational constraint through dialogue will tilt in favor of constraint. This approach raises several ethical questions, some of which are addressed in *What Would You Do?* on page 79.

It is important to recognize, however, that many of the tenets of the classical approach to management are alive and well in organizations today. The military still maintains strict divisions of labor and a scalar, chain-of-command hierarchy, and Taylor's ideas about designing jobs scientifically, making work routine, and hiring people fit to accomplish a specific task can be found in contemporary corporate concerns with organizational efficiency. In applications ranging from software design to fast-food sales to the creation of computerized accounting systems, the goal of reducing the number of steps involved to reliably produce a quality result is still paramount (Miller, 2003). Additionally, the classical management objective of fitting the right person to the right job is now called "individualizing the organization" (Lawler & Finegold, 2000), wherein physical criteria have been replaced by psychological profiles that focus on individual differences in abilities, needs, and career aspirations. In the next section we will explore the origins of many of these challenges to, and modifications of, the classical approach.

◪ THE HUMAN RELATIONS APPROACH

Noted communication theorist Kenneth Burke was once asked how he became interested in the study of human communication. Burke replied, "People weren't treating each other very well. I wanted to help find a way to make relationships better" (as cited in Goodall, 1984, p. 134). Burke's comment was made during a time of unparalleled economic depression when models of bureaucracy were questioned and theories of human relations first emerged.

☐ Historical and Cultural Background

Three major events—the Great Depression, World War II, and a new way of understanding human behavior—came at a time when the perceived limitations of scientific management were at their peak. The Great Depression created economic and social hardships for millions of people and led to major changes in government policies regarding Social Security, public assistance, and the funding of

Rank Has Its Privileges:
Influences of the Bureaucratic Organization on Home and Family Life

Among the world's largest bureaucracies is the U.S. military. Characterized by principles of scientific rationality, the military is organized according to hierarchies or ranks and relies on standardized procedures for behavioral control. It seeks to operate as an efficient machine.

Often neglected in studies of bureaucracy is its influence on employees' home and family life. How do those who work for bureaucracies make the daily transition from a highly controlled work life to a more loosely organized home life? Does the bureaucracy have an effect on home and family management?

In the following excerpt from Mary Truscott's *Brats: Children of the American Military Speak Out* (1989), the narrator explains how growing up in the military deeply affected her childhood and family life.

I learned to snap off a salute before I learned to ride a bike. There were plenty of role models for me to imitate; people who were always saluting my father. It didn't seem unusual. Some men saluted, and others were saluted.

The military jargon that was so pervasive on the post and in our household included many rank-related qualifiers. The size and location of our houses were based on rank. We lived on "Colonel's Row" in stately three story duplexes with full maid's quarters in the basement, but we had done our time in apartments before my father made colonel. . . . My mother came home from the Officers' Wives Club functions and frequently told my father about the "little captain's wife" or "little major's wife" she had met. Too young to remember when my father had been a lowly major, I developed a mental image of a community of Lilliputian people, captains and majors and their families, inhabiting the smaller and, I knew, inferior housing on the other side of the post.

The ascending rank was always part of a family name. I answered the telephone with "Colonel Truscott's quarters, Mary speaking." I addressed all adults with their surname and current rank. I never knew many men who were "mister," with the exception of school principals.

We lived on the post for the most part, only minutes away from my father's office, but I had no idea of what my father did at work. . . . In his study at home he had a framed poster from a lecture he had given that had his picture on it and the caption "the nation's foremost expert on radioactive fallout." Whatever it was that my dad did at work, I felt certain that if we were bombed and fallout came raining out of the sky, my father would lead us to the designated fallout shelters on the post and we would survive, no matter how awful the blast, because he was "The Nation's Foremost Expert."

(continued, Rank Has Its Privileges)

We visited my father's office a few times, and it was remarkably devoid of any sign or indication of his work. The walls in his office were pale green, with perhaps a flag and a strictly functional map or two to break the monotony. . . .

Rank truly had its privileges. The written and unwritten rules that established the chain of command for the men in uniform also applied to their families. Rank created a virtual caste system, and life on a military post had no uncertainties. There were stripes and insignia on uniforms, stickers on cars, and name-plates on houses. Families were segregated, by rank, in separate and not necessarily equal enclaves, and there were separate club facilities for officers and enlisted men. Post housing was the most obvious indicator of rank. . . .

Regardless of who the father was and what he did, rank was either a source of pride and status or an embarrassing label that put the military brat on the wrong side of the tracks. And all military brats, no matter where their father had fit in the hierarchy of rank, emphasized, over and over, that rank was pervasive and clearly defined.

DISCUSSION QUESTIONS

Ethical questions can be thought of as sources of creativity or constraint. On the basis of the preceding narrative, how would you respond to the following questions?

1. What ethical issues surround the notion that rank has its privileges? Is it ever appropriate for those privileges to extend beyond the duties and responsibilities of work? Why or why not?
2. How does hierarchical thinking influence the narrator's view of the world? How does this type of thinking contribute to your own understanding of social divisions in class, race, age, and gender?
3. Is the integration of home and work as described by the narrator necessary to the survival of all bureaucracies or only the military? Explain.

public improvement projects. The Depression also contributed to major migrations of workers—from the drought-ridden central farming states to the West Coast, and from the impoverished rural South to northern cities—as people went in search of jobs. A surplus of available workers and a lack of employment opportunities meant keen competition for work and widespread abuse of workers by employers. It is not surprising, then, that this period was also marked by the expansion of powerful labor unions. These organizations advocated human rights, fair wages, and improved working conditions.

While divisions between managers and workers had existed since the Industrial Revolution, they became more intense during the Depression. Demands for improved working conditions were accommodated only when the improvements increased productivity and profits. Wages were determined by factory output, but increased output tended to increase the number of incidences of work-related injury, illness, or death. In addition, the typical twelve-hour workday, six days a week, with one half-hour break for a meal, contributed to the strained relationship between workers and managers.

With World War II, however, came an enormous expansion of new jobs in both the military and the private sector. The war also placed academic researchers, managers, and military personnel in direct communication with one another for the first time. W. Charles Redding (1985), a pioneer of organizational communication and one of its leading historians, refers to this threesome as the "Triple Alliance." He argues that through the alliance, managers and military officers benefited from new ideas about organizing work and developing trust among workers, while academic researchers benefited from their access to industrial plants and their involvement in training workers, military personnel, and managers. The effects of this war-formed alliance would have a lasting impact, particularly on the subdiscipline that was created out of that alliance: organizational communication (Redding, 1985).

Finally, the period was marked by a new approach to understanding human relationships and behavior, which Herbert Blumer (1900–1987) would later call "symbolic interactionism." Symbolic interactionism draws on the pragmatism of social philosophers Charles Peirce, William James, and John Dewey; the writings of George Herbert Mead; and the Freudian interpretation of the symbolic realms of experience. According to Blumer (1969), symbolic interactionism is a simple but revolutionary alternative to behaviorism: *Humans respond to the meanings they have for things* (Figure 3.3). A meaning-centered, rather than behavior-centered, approach to understanding human action was thus born.

FIGURE 3.3

Behaviorism versus Symbolic Interactionism

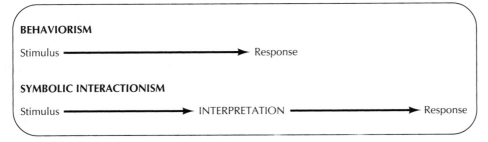

☐ What Is Human Relations?

Although Frederick Taylor had hoped to emphasize the importance of cooperative relationships between managers and employees, his methods did little to contribute to the quality of those interactions in the early twentieth century. It was not until the 1920s–1930s that Mary Parker Follett, Elton Mayo, and Chester Barnard would examine the employee-manager relationship in an entirely new way. Their work would provide the foundation for the **human relations** approach and would become a precursor of contemporary thinking about management and leadership. Human relations thinking emphasized the interpersonal and social needs of individuals and marked a clean break from earlier points of view. The human relations approach starts with the assumption that all people "want to feel united, tied, bound to something, some cause, bigger than they, commanding them yet worthy of them, summoning them to significance in living" (Bendix, 1956, p. 296).

Mary Parker Follett (1868–1933), whom Peter Drucker called "the brightest star in the management firmament of her time" (1997, p. 24), was a Boston social worker who used her experience running vocational guidance centers to develop new ideas about leadership, communication, social processes, and community, which she expressed in a controversial series of articles, books, and lectures on management that were far ahead of their time. In contrast to the dominant scientific management preoccupation with efficiency and strict divisions of labor and decision making, Follett was a democratic pragmatist who believed that only cooperation among people working together in groups under visionary leadership produced excellence in the workplace, the neighborhood, or the community (Dixon, 1996; McLarney & Rhyno, 1999). She advocated what we would consider today a feminist view of management that focused on empowering workers by sharing information with them, emphasizing cooperation to solve problems, and organizing teams to accomplish tasks. She believed that "genuine power can only be grown . . . for genuine power is not coercive control but coactive control" (cited in Hurst, 1992, p. 57), and that workers at all levels in any organization were sources of creativity whose loyalty "is awakened . . . by the very process that creates the group" (cited in Hurst, 1992, p. 58). The democratic ideal, she believed, was achieved by integrating organizations, neighborhoods, and communities through teamwork and by encouraging individuals to live their lives fully. These ideas, considered radical in their time, marked the start of a new way of thinking about leadership, groups, communication, and relationships between managers and workers that still holds sway today (Graham, 1997).

Elton Mayo, a Harvard professor, also set out to critique and extend scientific management. Like Follett, Mayo did not share Taylor's view of organizations as comprising wage-maximizing individuals. Instead, Mayo stressed the limits of individual rationality and the importance of interpersonal relations. In contrast to scientific management, Mayo (1945) held that

1. society comprises groups, not isolated individuals;
2. individuals are swayed by group norms and do not act alone in accord with self-interests; and
3. individual decisions are not entirely rational, but are also influenced by emotions.

Chester Barnard, a chief executive at Bell Telephone in New Jersey, the author of the influential book *The Functions of the Executive* (1938), and a man very much influenced by Mary Parker Follett, asserted the importance of cooperation in organizations: "Organizations by their very nature are cooperative systems and cannot fail to be so" (Perrow, 1986, p. 63). The key to cooperation, he argued, lay in persuading individuals to accept a common purpose, from which all else would follow. Unlike Taylor's emphasis on economic inducements, for Barnard the role of management was largely communicative and persuasive. Effective managers thus strived to communicate in ways that encouraged workers to identify with the organization. Barnard also valued the contributions of informal contacts to overall organizational effectiveness. For the first time, then, the purpose of management was seen as more interpersonal than economic.

☐ The Hawthorne Studies

While Barnard was running New Jersey Bell, a landmark event was taking place at another subsidiary of AT&T, the Hawthorne plant of Western Electric in Cicero, Illinois. Mayo and F. J. Roethlisberger (also a Harvard professor) were called into the Hawthorne plant by W. J. Dickson, a manager and industrial engineer concerned about widespread employee dissatisfaction, high turnover rates, and reduced plant efficiency. Previous efforts to correct these problems by using principles of scientific management had failed. Perrow (1986) picks up the story:

> The researchers at Western Electric took two groups of workers doing the same kinds of jobs, put them in separate rooms, and kept careful records of their productivity. One group (the test group) had the intensity of its lighting increased. Its productivity went up. For the other group (the control group), there was no change in lighting. But, to the amazement of the researchers, its productivity went up also. Even more puzzling, when the degree of illumination in the test group was gradually lowered back to the original level, it was found that output still continued to go up. Output also continued to increase in the control group. The researchers continued to drop the illumination of the test group, but it was not until the workers were working under conditions of bright moonlight that productivity stopped rising and fell off sharply. (pp. 79–80)

Over time, Mayo and his colleagues realized that the productivity improvements they had measured had little to do with the degree of illumination or other physical conditions in the plant. Instead, they found that the increased attention given to the workers by management and researchers was the key to increased productivity.

This finding—that increased attention raises productivity—has come to be known as the **Hawthorne effect**.

Further research supported Mayo's critique of scientific management. A prominent finding of the Hawthorne studies was drawn from an experiment in the bank-wiring observation room, where it was found that even under poor working conditions, supportive informal group norms could have a positive effect on productivity. For the first time, then, it was shown that individual workers were complex beings, sensitive to group norms and possessing multiple motives, values, and emotions. Studies after Hawthorne have been greatly influenced both by its sociopsychological model of human motivation (it's not always about money) and its description of the informal organization.

□ Reflections on Human Relations

It is difficult to criticize the primary goal of the human relations approach: to restore whole human beings and quality interpersonal relationships to their rightful place in what had become an overly rational view of organizations. In this spirit, the work of Chris Argyris has been influential. According to Argyris (1957), the principles of formal organization, such as hierarchy and task specialization, are incongruent with the developmental needs of healthy adults. But do real alternatives exist? Critics have labeled Argyris and others who share his views "romantics," arguing that alienation is an inherent part of organizational life (Drucker, 1974; Tompkins, 1984).

Indeed, there is little empirical evidence to support the effectiveness of the human relations approach, particularly the claim that positive employee morale fosters productivity (Miller & Form, 1951). Nevertheless, the approach, reflecting the romantic ideals of the time, has played an important role in further research on organizational behavior. (Table 3.1 summarizes the move from classical management to human relations in the study of organizations and communication.) Generally, however, research that applies human relations thinking to the relationship between management and organizational effectiveness has been inconclusive and disappointing. Its underlying ideology has been interpreted as an unacceptable willingness to trade profitability for employee well-being. William Whyte (1969), in his classic critique, criticizes the human relations approach for attempting to replace the Protestant work ethic and entrepreneurialism with a social ethic of complacency that emphasizes dressing well, acting nice, and "fitting in." Another critic has referred to human relations as "cow sociology": "Just as contented cows [are] alleged to produce more milk, satisfied workers [are] expected to produce more output" (Scott, 1981, p. 90). Likewise, another claims that human relations is nothing more than "the maintenance crew of the human machinery" (Braverman, 1979, p. 87), adjusting the mind to demands made on the worker's body.

A similar critique of a simplistic connection between good feeling and organizational effectiveness has been offered by communication scholars (Eisenberg &

TABLE 3.1

Summary of Historical and Cultural Influences on the Classical Management and Human Relations Approaches to Organizations and Communication

CLASSICAL MANAGEMENT	HUMAN RELATIONS
Theme: Scientific rationality leads to improved efficiency and productivity	*Theme:* Improved human relations leads to improved efficiency and productivity
Enlightenment ideals	Romantic ideals
Industrial Revolution	Development of psychology
Scientific methods	Social scientific methods
Dominant metaphor: Organization as an efficient machine	*Dominant metaphor:* Organization as the sum of relationships
Supporting principles: *Ideal form of society* is authoritarian and values hierarchical organization	*Supporting principles:* *Ideal form of society* is democratic and values open and honest relationships
Divisions of labor/social classes/races/sexes/nations; if "the rules" were applied equally to everyone, individuals who worked hard and obeyed instructions could better themselves	*Divisions* of labor/management honored; negotiation of differences through open communication valued
Conflict based on divisions; dialectical relationships between management and labor based on power and money	*Conflict* based on lack of shared understanding; dialogic model of relationships between management and labor based on trust, openness, honesty, and power
Application of the principles of mechanics to organizations and communication led to operationalizing the machine metaphor (e.g., "This business runs like clockwork.")	*Application* of humanistic and behavioral psychology to organizations and communication led to operationalizing "relational metaphors" (e.g., "This business is like family.")
Communication — top-down and procedurally oriented; following "the rules" is valued, and opposing them calls into question the whole moral order	*Communication* — relational and needs-oriented; self-actualization is valued if it occurs through work

TABLE 3.1 *(continued)*

**Summary of Historical and Cultural Influences on the
Classical Management and Human Relations Approaches
to Organizations and Communication**

CLASSICAL MANAGEMENT	HUMAN RELATIONS
Dominant form of organizing: Bureaucracy	*Dominant form of organizing:* Teams or groups within bureaucracies
Stability best obtained through adherence to procedural forms of order	Stability best obtained through relational and personal happiness
Limitations: Too constraining; encourages mindless adherence to details and procedures and discourages creativity	*Limitations:* False openness, abuse of trust and/or honesty; equation of employee happiness with efficiency or productivity

Witten, 1987). Although we would all like to believe that openness, self-disclosure, and supportive relationships have positive effects on organizational productivity, research does not support that contention. Instead, models of employee motivation have become increasingly complex, causing us to revise what is meant by good leadership and the conditions under which a focus on interpersonal relations may be desirable. However, the applicability of these contingency models is limited to specific situations, resulting in a body of research with no clear implications for practice.

Finally, an emerging line of historically based research asks how much of human relations theory—and of Maslow's work specifically—is best understood as a manifestation of the Cold War mentality? The Cold War (circa 1947–1991) was a time of high tension (underscored by the threat of nuclear war) among the former Soviet Union, China, and the West. It was characterized not only by a widespread fear of nuclear annihilation and a war in Southeast Asia, but also by a preoccupation with psychological assessments of identity, anxiety, relationships, leadership, and hierarchy, particularly as these concepts related to decision making and emotional states. As we noted earlier, theories are as much a product of the times in which they were produced as they are the "natural" extensions of existing lines of scientific research. Hence, the resurgence of national interest in common human relations themes—identity, anxiety, relationships, and leadership—in post-9/11, "War on Terror" discourse about organizations and society deserves assessment with its historical predecessor, the Cold War. It also begs the question: What topics would seem important to us today about communication in organizations if the Cold War and the War on Terror had *not* intervened to shape our thinking?

▨ THE HUMAN RESOURCES APPROACH

In retrospect, the human relations approach identified many important issues (e.g., that informal communication is important and that human decision making is emotional as well as rational), but fell short of truly valuing employee perceptions, worldview, and voice. Whereas human relations encouraged employee communication mainly to "blow off steam," it took another set of thinkers — whose work can be collectively characterized as the human resources approach — to fully assert the crucial role all employees can play in promoting organizational effectiveness. While incorporating most of the assumptions of human relations, the **human resources** approach is concerned with the total organizational climate as well as with how an organization can encourage employee participation and dialogue. Three theorists best capture the spirit of the original human resources movement: Abraham Maslow, Douglas McGregor, and Rensis Likert.

☐ Maslow's Hierarchy of Needs

According to Abraham **Maslow's hierarchy of needs**, people's basic needs for food, shelter, and belonging must be satisfied before they can move toward achieving their full human potential, which Maslow calls "self-actualization" (Figure 3.4). In Maslow's model, the lower-level needs cease to be motivating as soon as they are fulfilled. If, for example, someone is satiated, food will not serve as a motivating force. Self-actualization, however, continues to motivate even as the need is being satisfied.

In *Eupsychian Management* (1965), Maslow poses the question, "What kinds of management and what kinds of reward or pay will help human nature to grow healthily into its fuller and fullest stature?" He concludes that the conditions that foster individual health are often surprisingly good for the prosperity of the organization as well. He thus defines the problem of management as that of setting up social conditions in the organization so that the goals of the individual merge with those of the organization. A quick perusal of corporate Web sites reveals that many organizations recruit the best and brightest candidates by highlighting opportunities for personal growth, fulfillment, and possible self-actualization. For example:

- Nordstrom: "Nordstrom customers have come to expect the best possible service, selection, quality and value. It's also the place where employees build relationships, discover their potential, and reap the rewards." http://careers.nordstrom.com/connect.htm
- The Central Intelligence Agency: "The CIA offers exciting career opportunities and a dynamic environment. We're on the forefront of world-altering events — as they happen. So working here isn't just a job, it's a mindset and a lifestyle. You'll find a supportive environment to help you grow and excel

FIGURE 3.4

Maslow's Hierarchy of Needs

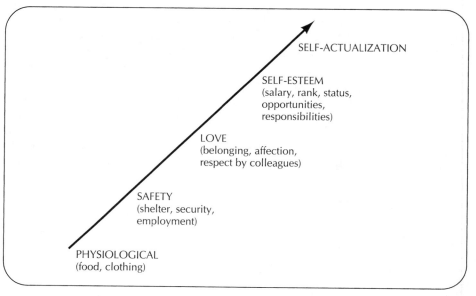

both professionally and personally. And a culture that expects you to do your personal best every day."
http://www.cia.gov/employment/life.html
- Microsoft: "Like-minded, intelligent and ambitious, our people want to be the best they can be."
http://www.microsoft.com/uk/careers/htm

Maslow's ideas permeate contemporary management theory and practice. Jim Collins (2001), one of the best-selling management authors today, argues that managers, entrepreneurs, and CEOs in great organizations are never satisfied with the status quo; rather, they yearn to be the best of the best. If designed correctly, the workplace becomes a site where individuals can realize their full potential and remain continually motivated to do so. Employees of award-winning organizations who work in rewarding and challenging positions may indeed find it possible to align their personal development goals with customer service, intelligence gathering, or software engineering. However, it is unlikely that all employees will have the opportunity to self-actualize. The maintenance crew, the cafeteria employees, and the mail room staff, for example, may find it difficult to "be all that they can be" while working monotonous, mindless, or otherwise unsatisfying jobs. Underlying

Maslow's theory, then, is an undercurrent of the same class-based divisions that characterized Taylor's thinking, namely the rather elitist notion that some members of society and organizations are more likely to become self-actualized than others. The tension between the "non-actualized masses and the actualized few" is one that permeates Maslow's work (Cooke, Mills, & Kelley, 2005, p. 134). In many ways, Maslow's work still has currency and paved the way for more recent theories of performance, including work on employee emotional intelligence (Sala, Drusket, & Mount, 2005).

☐ McGregor's Theory Y Management

Sharing Maslow's view that classical management theory fails to address important individual needs, Douglas McGregor (1960) argued that classical approaches are based in part on an assumption that the average employee dislikes work and avoids responsibility in the absence of external control. He calls the control-oriented, bureaucratic style of management "Theory X," which he summarizes as follows:

1. The average human being has an inherent dislike of work and will avoid it if he [or she] can.
2. Because of [their] . . . dislike of work, most people must be coerced, controlled, directed, [or] threatened with punishment to get them to put forth adequate effort toward the achievement of organizational objectives.
3. The average human being prefers to be directed, wishes to avoid responsibility, has relatively little ambition, and wants security above all. (pp. 33–34)

Although Theory X may seem quite limited, it helps identify some of the implicit and explicit assumptions of the traditional organization.

McGregor (1960) advances an alternative set of assumptions or principles in his **Theory Y**:

1. The expenditure of physical and mental effort in work is as natural as play or rest.
2. External control and threat of punishment are not the only means for bringing about effort toward organizational objectives. [People] will exercise self-direction and self-control in the service of objectives to which [they are] committed.
3. Commitment to objectives is a function of the rewards associated with their achievement (including the reward of self-actualization).
4. The average human being learns, under proper conditions, not only to accept but [also] to seek responsibility.
5. The capacity to exercise . . . relatively high degree[s] of imagination, ingenuity, and creativity in the solution of organizational problems is widely, not narrowly, distributed in the population.

6. Under the conditions of modern industrial life, the intellectual potential . . .
of the average [person is] only partially utilized. (pp. 47–48)

In Theory Y, McGregor builds on the best of the human relations approach to offer a fundamentally different view of employees and of their relationship with management. Employees are viewed as possessing a high capacity for autonomy, responsibility, and innovation. Unlike the Theory X manager, the Theory Y manager has a more participative and facilitative management style that treats employees as valued human resources. Optimistic about incorporating the individual's desires in an organizational framework, McGregor argues that "the essential task of management is to arrange things so people achieve their own goals by accomplishing those of the organization" (Perrow, 1986, p. 99). In contrast to the scalar principle of classical management, in which decision-making ability is centralized within management, McGregor offers the principle of integration, wherein employees are self-directed as a result of their commitment to organizational goals.

☐ Likert's Principle of Supportive Relationships

Continuing the trend toward employee participation in decision making, the work of University of Michigan professor Rensis Likert has contributed to our understanding of high-involvement organizations. Likert's (1961) **principle of supportive relationships** holds that all interactions within an organization should support individual self-worth and importance, with emphasis on the supportive relationships within work groups and open communication among them.

Likert divides organizations into four types, or "systems," based on degree of participation: System I — exploitative/authoritative; System II — benevolent/authoritative; System III — consultative; and System IV — participative. The principle of supportive relationships considers open communication to be among the most important aspects of management. It also favors general oversight to close supervision and emphasizes the role of the supportive peer group in fostering productivity. Therefore, Likert's principle supports System IV, participative management.

Research on Likert's systems has been inconclusive (Perrow, 1986). Many studies have shown that good classical changes in organizations (e.g., improved work procedures and plans) are as important as participation in increasing organizational effectiveness. The human resources approach continues the human relations tendency to treat all organizations as similar, which opponents in the institutional school and the cultural approach view as inappropriate (see Chapter 5). Moreover, while human resources emphasizes employee participation in organizational decision making, it does not explain the pragmatics or politics involved in establishing such a voice for employees. (See *What Would You Do?* on page 91 for an example of these complexities.) As a result, its prescriptions for participation tend to have limited use. Nevertheless, the quest for effective forms of participative decision making continues (Miller & Monge, 1986).

The Politics of Middle Management

A key assumption of the human resources approach is that happy employees are also productive employees. However, in the act of defining happiness, there is the potential for tyranny. Consider the following perspectives on happiness (Shorris, 1984, pp. 17–34):

1. The most insidious power is the power to define happiness. Happiness cannot be described, and what cannot be described cannot be attained. So it is that we create imagined happiness as the opposite of what we can describe—dissatisfaction.
2. All leaders must have the ability to define happiness. In the absence of absolute happiness, we content ourselves with relative happiness.
3. There are three ways in which capitalism and the bureaucratic society conspire to use happiness as a source of fear and reward:
   a. The merchant offers happiness in the immediate future. Commodity purchases offer material rewards; failure to consume commodities suggests material poverty and, therefore, a lack of relative happiness.
   b. The manager offers happiness in the future. According to human relations theory, his or her power is largely symbolic (kind words, generous deeds, a pat on the back). Because being in management is a source of symbolic attainment in our society, the manager represents what the rest of us aspire to. As such, the manager is the enforcer of our moral code.
   c. The despot offers happiness in the historical future. By making prophetic claims about the historical future, he or she is like a secular god and lacks only immortality to be a god. The despot combines displays of material and symbolic happiness and suggests that others may attain them only if they do as they are commanded.
4. When work becomes rationalized and bureaucratized, the resulting order symbolizes levels of happiness. The manager has the power to define happiness as the next step up the career ladder. The manager's definition of happiness creates the moral system in which white-collar workers and some managers live, but the despot's definition, with its ultimate promises and religious demands, has a greater effect on the middle manager's life. In return for happiness, middle managers agree to the abolition of their freedom, thereby becoming a part of the organization and accepting the notion that any sin against the organization may cast them out of heaven and into the limbo of the unemployed.

(continued, The Politics of Middle Management)

DISCUSSION QUESTIONS

Given these thoughts, consider how you would handle the following situations:

1. Your supervisor explains that you will be promoted if you can find ways to cut costs by one-third in your department. You know this will mean cuts in personnel, even though your boss never says so directly. However, you are already working with a limited staff, and stress is high among employees as a result of the heavy workload. In addition, you fear that any further reduction in staff may affect employee morale and lower productivity in your department. At the same time, you are personally heavily in debt and in need of the promotion to make ends meet. How will you handle the situation? Should you gain some happiness at the expense of others? Is the short-term gain of a promotion worth the long-term risks of negative morale and reduced productivity?

2. What role do teachers and professors play in shaping the happiness of their students? How do you respond to a teacher's encouragement to do something that may mean a lot to them (e.g., conducting extra research on a topic) but that you find uninteresting? Is there a hierarchy in higher education, and if so, how does it affect your experience as a student? What role does graduate or professional school play in this hierarchy?

SUMMARY

Three general approaches—classical management, human relations, and human resources—have had great impact on the development of communication theories and organizational practice historically and continue to shape current thinking. When striving to understand organizational communication, remember that all historical narratives and all human communication exhibit the three *P*'s: They are partial, partisan, and problematic.

The classical management approach emerged during the Industrial Revolution, a period characterized by a quest to adapt the lessons of science and technology to make perfect machines. These early organizations were built on the model of the efficient machine, and so-called "scientific management" was characterized by a machine-like dependence on hierarchy, divisions of labor, strict rules for communication between management and workers, and formal routines. The term *bureaucracy* is often used to describe the structure of these early organizations. In some industries, similar attempts to rationalize organizations continue today.

In the image of the ideal machine, communication happens *before* the machine is turned on, such as when a manager explains how to operate the machine to the workers responsible for the labor. Communication that occurs *during* work tends to slow down production; therefore, informal talk is considered unnecessary and costly. Morgan (1986) suggests that the machine metaphor is useful for organizing work that is straightforward and repetitive in nature and performed in a stable environment by compliant workers. He attributes the limitations of this approach to its narrow focus on efficiency: It does not adapt well to changing circumstances, and it can have a dehumanizing effect on employees. When opportunities for dialogue do not exist, employees' resentment may be expressed as resistance, leading to work slowdowns or even sabotage.

In the classical management approach, any attempt at achieving a balance between individual creativity and organizational constraint through dialogue will tilt in favor of constraint. The individual needs of workers are largely ignored, communication is limited to the giving of orders, and the strict imposition of rules and routines seeks to maintain order above all else. When such strict adherence to hierarchical power remains in place for too long, underground opposition or resistance is likely to emerge.

The human relations approach to organizations and communication emerged against the cultural and economic background of the Great Depression. Studies demonstrating a positive correlation between managers who paid attention to workers and improved productivity led to new theories about the role of communication at work. The balance in the organizational dialogue thus tipped back toward a concern for individual creativity and the satisfaction of needs. However, critics argued that the balance had tipped back too far and that making workers happy did not necessarily make them more productive. They saw the new social ethic as a threat to the Protestant work ethic with its emphasis on achievement and entrepreneurship.

Refinements in human relations theory led to the human resources approach. Through this approach, advances were made in our understanding of the relationship between individual needs for creativity and organizational structures. In the period following World War II, studies of leadership style, decision making, and organizations as institutions served to redefine the individual in organizations as socially situated and rational only within limits.

This highly contingent and dynamic view of the individual suggests a new role for communication: the construction of definitions of the situation and of decision premises that shape individual behavior. It also suggests a new view of employee motivation and performance: The employee's motivation is derived from his or her interests, which constitute the individual's definition of the situation. Hence, situations are symbolic constructions of reality that are individualized according to personal needs, desires, and interests. Many employees are motivated as much by symbolic rewards as they are by their paychecks.

The human resources movement is a precursor of many of today's most common management practices. Employees are given more freedom to construct organizational reality through opportunities for dialogue. Their increased involvement, however, also means greater responsibility and accountability for decisions and actions. Of all the approaches to management that we have observed in action, participative management is the most difficult to implement. However, when applied successfully, it fosters more satisfied, committed employees and more productive organizations.

Two extremes of thought on organization and management—tightly controlled formal bureaucracies versus a looser, more empathic view of employees as valuable human resources—are at the opposite ends of our theoretical continuum for understanding organizational communication. At the far right is bureaucracy, which holds that formal structure and communication that respect the chain of command ensure productivity and stability. At the far left is the human resources approach, which holds that open communication between managers and employees ensures creativity, adaptability to change, and satisfaction of the individual's needs and motivations. We have discussed the problems associated with an organizational dialogue that is tipped too far in favor of either approach. In the following chapters, we will examine new theories that propose solutions to these problems.

QUESTIONS FOR REVIEW AND DISCUSSION

1. Why do we need theory to study organizational communication? What do we mean by the idea that all theories are metaphors?

2. Why is all communication partial, partisan, and problematic?

3. What is the classical management approach? What does the machine metaphor imply about communication in organizations based on classical management? What is "scientific" about Henri Fayol's approach to decision making?

4. What is useful about the idea of resistance to domination when it is applied to classical management theories? Do you think this idea has relevance in today's organizations? If so, why and how?

5. Why do you think Mary Parker Follett's ideas about management were considered "radical" in her day? What specific influences of her work can you see in human relations and human resources theories?

6. What are the principles of the human relations and human resources approaches to organizational communication? What was the influence of the "Triple Alliance" on the historical development of organizational communication? Why do you think Elton Mayo's work had so much impact?

7. Why do you think Abraham Maslow's hierarchy of needs has had such far-ranging implications for the development of human resources approaches to management and communication? What are the fundamental differences between McGregor's Theory X and Theory Y when applied to human communication at work?

KEY TERMS

Bureaucracy, p. 77
Classical management, p. 64
Division of labor, p. 71
Hawthorne effect, p. 84
Hidden transcripts, p. 68
Hierarchy, p. 71
Human relations, p. 82
Human resources, p. 87
Maslow's hierarchy of needs, p. 87

Partial, p. 63
Particularism, p. 76
Partisan, p. 63
Principle of supportive relationships, p. 90
Problematic, p. 64
Resistance to domination, p. 68
Scientific management, p. 72
Theory, p. 61
Theory Y, p. 89

CASE STUDY

Riverside State Hospital

BACKGROUND

Riverside State Hospital is a five-hundred-bed, state-supported psychiatric facility located along the scenic banks of the Tennessee River. Admission to the facility requires a physician's order or court referral. The hospital staff consists of physicians, psychologists, psychiatrists, nurses, dietitians, pharmacists, therapists, technicians, and general housekeeping and groundskeeping personnel, all of whom are state employees. The hospital is run primarily as a bureaucracy, with levels of authority and salary based on seniority and rank.

All employees hold a government service (GS) rank, the lowest being GS-1 (groundskeeping trainee) and the highest GS-15 (administrator or CEO). In addition, within each rank are seven to ten steps, which are determined by seniority and achievement. Performance reviews are conducted annually, at which time promotions in steps or in GS rank may occur. Employees are given annual salary adjustments for inflation or cost-of-living increases. Full state benefits are provided to all workers.

Riverside employees work an eight-hour shift. Employees below rank GS-12 (head or chief) take a thirty-minute lunch break and two fifteen-minute breaks during their shift. Members of the professional staff (physicians, nurses, pharmacists, and the like) work on a three-shift schedule: 7 A.M. to 3 P.M., 3 P.M. to 11 P.M., and 11 P.M. to 7 A.M. The hospital operates year-round.

THE PROBLEM

A few days ago, a resident patient at Riverside State Hospital was killed when part of the wall next to his bed collapsed. Horris James Wilcox Jr. was fifty-six years old when he died. He had no family and had been a resident at the hospital for three years. He suffered from traumatic amnesia and scored in the borderline range on intelligence tests. He was otherwise in good health. He was also well liked and seemed to be responding to treatment.

In statements made to state investigators and the news media, hospital administrators called the accident a "tragedy." They explained, "There had been no indication that the wall was weak or that Wilcox was in any danger." You are the government investigator assigned to the Wilcox case. Your job is to determine whether any evidence exists that would make Riverside State Hospital liable for Wilcox's death.

THE INVESTIGATION

You learn from your investigation that Wilcox was a quiet man who tended to keep to himself, although he did join the other patients on the ward for scheduled games and activities. During these times, he talked a lot about current news events. Watching the cable news channel was his favorite source of entertainment. He was known among the staff as the most informed patient on the ward.

Your investigation also reveals that Wilcox's amnesia was complicated by his belief that he was directly affected by whatever he saw on television. News events — particularly family tragedies — affected him deeply. The hospital staff had tried reducing his television viewing time to prevent further complications, but he became depressed. His television privileges were restored as a result, and the staff tried instead to use the emotions he displayed about news shows in his therapy. Perhaps, they reasoned, some family tragedy had produced the traumatic amnesia.

In addition, for the past month Wilcox had repeatedly exclaimed, "The sky is falling," especially when he was confined to his bed at night and in the mornings upon awakening. He would also point at the ceiling and walls of his room and cry out, "There is trouble here, trouble from the sky." On several such occasions he had to be physically restrained and calmed with drugs. During this same month, an Air Force fighter plane had exploded in the sky during an air show, and videotaped replays of that event had appeared frequently on the television news. Given Wilcox's past history of responding emotionally to tragedies reported in the news, the staff linked his most recent behavior to the air show disaster. However, you think there may be more to it. Considering Wilcox's unwillingness to go to bed at night, his complaints about an impending tragedy may have had an altogether different meaning: Perhaps "the sky" was a reference to perceived structural defects in the walls and ceiling of his room. You wonder whether Wilcox was trying to direct attention to the actual physical deterioration of his room. Moreover, his psychiatric history may have led those in charge of his care to dismiss his allegations.

Upon further investigation, you learn that the walls and ceiling in Wilcox's room had been repainted three times during the past twelve months due to stains from a leaking water pipe. You think the leak may have seriously weakened the wall, and you feel that hospital personnel should have followed up on this warning. You also discover that state funding for maintenance had been cut back severely during the previous summer and that although there was structural damage to the wall, there was no indication that it was unsafe. From the hospital administrators' perspective, then, the culprits were an aging building and insufficient

(continued, Riverside State Hospital)

state funding to repair it. Even so, they maintain that the collapse of the wall was "an unforeseeable accident." You obtain copies of the building inspection reports for the past three years. You note that in the past year, state inspectors recorded the deteriorating condition of the wall and ceiling that eventually collapsed. These forms are signed by Hillary Hanks, the head of resident life.

In an interview with Hanks, you discover that although her name appears on the state inspection forms, she did not actually sign them. She explains that her secretary, Nancy Ellis, regularly signs her name on state forms to save time. She adds, "There are so many forms to sign that if I signed them all, I wouldn't get any real work done." When you speak to Ellis, she confirms Hanks's story. Furthermore, Ellis is annoyed because the man who delivered the forms to her was supposed to point out any problems that required attention. The problem with the walls and ceiling in Wilcox's room had not been reported verbally to Ellis, and therefore she didn't notify Hanks. Now Hanks is in trouble with her superior, and that means Ellis will lose her chance at a promotion. Any trouble for Hanks generally means trouble for Ellis, too. Ellis admits that she regularly avoids telling her boss any bad news for exactly that reason, but this time, Ellis claims, she was unaware of the bad news. You ask Ellis what she did with the inspection report. She points to the overstuffed filing cabinet behind her. "That's where I put it," she says, "along with all the other paperwork that never gets read around here."

You find out that the report was prepared by state inspector Blake Barrymore, who gave it to a groundskeeper for delivery to the appropriate hospital administrator because "it was raining that day, and I was late for another inspection." He adds that it is not his official responsibility to deliver the report himself or to follow up on it. You discover that the inspection report was delivered by Jack Handy, a reliable and well-liked groundskeeper, but you also discover that Handy is illiterate. He did not know what the forms contained because he could not read them. He did not report any problems with the walls or ceiling because Barrymore didn't tell him there were any problems. Besides, Handy added, "Nobody listens to a groundskeeper anyway. I could tell the administrators that there was a bomb in the hospital and because I'm just a groundskeeper, they'd let it pass. So I just do what I'm told to do."

You file your report. The insurance company claims that gross negligence on the part of Riverside State Hospital indirectly caused the death of Horris James Wilcox Jr. At a press conference, the hospital spokesperson places the blame for Wilcox's death on Nancy Ellis, claiming that it was her responsibility to report the problem to her superior, Hillary Hanks. He adds that Hanks has been "reassigned" to other duties and is unavailable for comment. In a final statement, the spokesman says, "The hospital deeply regrets this tragic accident, and reminds the state legislature that until the requested funds for structural repairs are made available, the hospital administration cannot be held accountable for structural defects that are beyond its control."

ASSIGNMENT

1. What management approach does Riverside State Hospital's style of management most resemble?
2. How does the management approach influence communication at the hospital?
3. Should Ellis be held responsible for Wilcox's death? Why or why not? In what ways did the hospital's organizational structure contribute to Wilcox's accidental death?
4. What recommendations would you propose to help Riverside State Hospital avoid similar occurrences in the future? How can organizational communication be improved?

Sala, F., Druskat, V., & Mount, G. (2005). *Linking emotional intelligence and performance at work: Current research with individuals and groups.* New York: Lawrence Erlbaum.

CHAPTER 4

The Systems Perspective on Organizations and Communication

In this and the following chapter we continue our story of organizations and communication by considering two prominent metaphors — systems and cultures — through which we seek to describe the contemporary world. According to one well-known observer of business, "The unhealthiness of our world today is in direct proportion to our inability to see it as a whole" (Senge, 1990, p. 168). By thinking in terms of systems and cultures, however, we find ways of thinking about wholes, and in so doing we may learn how to survive in an era of economic, political, and environmental limits. Unlike the machine metaphor of classical management theory, the focus of the systems and cultural approaches is not on individual parts or people but on relationships, on the pattern that connects (Bateson, 1972). As such, these approaches give supreme emphasis to communication — that is, to the development of meaning through human interaction.

We begin with the systems approach, one that broadens our way of looking at organizations by borrowing concepts from other, seemingly unrelated, areas of study, including engineering, biology, chemistry, physics, economics, and sociology. Associated with the nature of a system are such components as environment, interdependence, goals, feedback, and order. In addition, the systems approach has important implications for the situated individual striving to balance creativity and constraint.

◫ THE SYSTEMS PERSPECTIVE

A classic advertisement for BMW poses this question: "What makes the BMW the ultimate driving machine?" Is it the car's superb handling and braking? Aerodynamic design? Powerful engine? According to the advertisement, no single feature makes the BMW special; rather, the car is unique in the way that all of its qualities work together as a whole to create "the ultimate driving machine."

This advertisement nicely illustrates the **systems approach**, which emphasizes the important difference between a disconnected set of parts versus a collection of parts that work together to create a functional whole. That functional whole is called a "system," and in a system the whole is more than the sum of its parts. Sociologist Walter Buckley (1967) translates this expression as follows: "The 'more than' points to the fact of organization, which imparts to the aggregate characteristics that are not only different from, but [also] often not found in the components alone; and the 'sum of the parts' must be taken to mean, not their numerical addition, but their unorganized aggregation" (p. 42). In other words, organization makes a social system more than just its components. In a marriage, family, team, or business, the *relationships* that exist among people are what make the group a system.

Although it has come to be applied broadly to social systems, the systems approach has its roots in the sciences, notably physics, information theory, and biology. The impact of each is discussed in the following sections.

☐ The Origins of Systems Theory in the Sciences

Before the work of Albert Einstein, Isaac Newton's concepts of the universe prevailed. Space and time were viewed as distinct entities operating "in a fixed arena in which events took place, but which was not affected by what happened in it. . . . Bodies moved, forces attracted and repelled, but time and space simply continued, unaffected" (Hawking, 1988, p. 33). There is a parallel between this view of the physical world and classical approaches to organization. Scientific management, for example, relied heavily on time and motion studies (whose principles were drawn from Newtonian physics) to provide data to managers about worker productivity and efficiency.

Einstein's theory of relativity radically transformed how we saw our world. This new way of seeing brought new questions: What if time and space are not fixed but relative? If, as Einstein's general theory of relativity suggests, time runs slower nearer the earth due to the influence of its gravitational pull, does this imply that observations of what appears to be a fixed reality are skewed by the observer's position? For example, when seeing a commercial jetliner pass overhead it often appears to be floating, almost standing still, when in fact it is traveling at hundreds of miles an hour. Relativity theory explains what is wrong:

> Space and time are . . . dynamic quantities: when a body moves, or a force acts, it affects the curvature of space and time—and in turn the structure of space-time affects the way in which bodies move and forces act. Space and time not only affect but also are affected by everything that happens in the universe. (Hawking, 1988, p. 33)

In other words, rather than conceptualizing time and motion studies within the limited framework of a specific task, the interpretation of the task is expanded to include how it functions as part of a dynamic interdependent system. For example, a company can work hard to lower the cost of its product through more efficient production, but if it fails to closely monitor consumer tastes, it may end up failing anyway. Systems theory encourages us to explore how organizational effectiveness depends on the coordination of the total enterprise. Appropriate questions might include: What are the intended and unintended consequences of increased or decreased efficiency? How do pressures to reduce time and eliminate unnecessary motion affect employee morale, absenteeism, commitment, and turnover? How, in turn, do these factors affect productivity in important but potentially unexpected ways?

This shift in our understanding of the laws of the universe does more than simply call into question the rationality of time and motion studies. It also brings to our attention the idea of dynamic systems of interacting components, whose relationships and interactions point to a new kind of order based on pattern of interaction. The ideas of dynamic systems have been applied to atomic physics, navigational science, aerospace, and electronics, but it was not until World War II that a general systems paradigm emerged with applications to organizations. Indeed, today we don't have to look far to see the impact of systems theory on the field of communication. Consider some of the terms we routinely use to describe communication: sender, message, channel, receiver, and feedback. Before 1948, the vocabulary of communication developed by the ancient Greeks was still in use (e.g., speech, speaker, audience, ethos, pathos, and logos). Since then, our language about communication processes has been transformed by the information revolution. As Stuart Clegg (1990) puts it, "Systems ideas are now so much a part of the modernist consciousness that they barely require elaborate iteration" (p. 51).

In addition to the theoretical advances in physics, new technologies have been spawned by industries capitalizing on scientific advances. Primarily an outgrowth of transistors and, later, the microchip, communication technologies like television, satellites, and computers have contributed to the emergence of what Marshall McLuhan called the "global information society" (1964). McLuhan's idea is simple but profound. The instantaneous transfer of information across cultural boundaries means that our perceptions of reality, of cultural differences, of political and social events, and of what constitutes the news cease to be mediated by fixed notions of space or time. Because information now connects us in ways not possible before, the world has become — in McLuhan's famous phrase — a "global village."

☐ Biology and General Systems Theory

Within the broad context of the information revolution there emerged a more specific contributor to systems theory — the life sciences, and especially biology. It is easy to see why. A system is alive not because of any particular component or component process (e.g., a respiratory or digestive system), but because of the relationships and interchanges among processes. Within any system there are subsystems, and it is the *connections* between subsystems (e.g., how oxygen gets from the lungs into the blood, then into the muscles and synapses) that define the characteristics of biological or living organisms. To take a holistic approach means to consider the properties of systems that come out of the relationships among their subsystems or parts.

Biologists Ludwig von Bertalanffy (1968) and J. G. Miller (1978) are credited with advancing the study of living systems, and von Bertalanffy with pioneering the development of general systems theory in particular. **General systems theory** applies the properties of living systems, such as input, output, boundaries, homeostasis, and equifinality (the idea that there is more than one right way to accomplish the same goal), to a dazzling array of social phenomena. (Table 4.1 provides an overview of the hierarchy of general systems theory.) As biologist Lewis Thomas explains in his landmark work *The Lives of a Cell* (1975):

> Although we are by all odds the most social of all social animals — more interdependent, more attached to each other, more inseparable in our behavior than bees — we do not often feel our conjoined intelligence. Perhaps it is in this respect that language differs most sharply from biological systems for communication. Ambiguity seems to be an essential, indispensable element for the transfer of information from one place to another by words, where matters of real importance are concerned. It is often necessary, for meaning to come through, that there be an almost vague sense of strangeness and askewness. Speechless animals and cells cannot do this. . . . Only the human mind is designed to work this way, programmed to drift away in the presence of locked-on information, straying from each point in the hunt for a better, different point. (pp. 89–94)

In other words, the ambiguity of language makes the interdependencies between members of a social system (i.e., among people) looser than those found in biology or those that connect the parts of a car. Put another way: "social organizations, in contrast to physical or mechanical structures, are loosely coupled systems" (Scott, 1981, p. 103).

Thus, with the advent of relativity and the use of analogies between organic systems and human societies, the concept of dynamic systems was born, offering innovative ways of understanding the relationships among functioning components in space and time. However, applying systems theory to human language would prove to be challenging. The work of chemist Ilya Prigogine (1980) has helped to expand the potential application of systems thinking to social organization. By studying chemical reactions, Prigogine found that in open systems (defined as those systems that *must* interact with their environments to survive), a movement toward disorder often precedes the emergence of a new order. In contrast to the Newtonian vision of a universe constantly falling apart, Prigogine's findings suggest that both living and nonliving systems have the potential for self-organization or self-renewal in the face of environmental change, and that disorder is a natural part of the renewal process.

More recently, biological concepts and processes have gained greater prominence in organizational theory and practice. Most notably, manufacturing and information (computer) system designs are now being fashioned after robust biological systems. Abandoning the top-down, "central-processing" model implicit in classical approaches, all manner of new organizational structures and processes are being modeled after living systems, which tend to exhibit distributed intelligence. By **distributed intelligence** we mean that all members of the system—whether they be people or cells—play an important role in the system's ongoing self-organization. Imagine for a moment what life would be like under a central-processing model! What would happen if your brain had to "turn on" the rest of the body's systems each morning? Our tendency to equate rationality with intelligence has caused us to miss the very real (but non-linguistic) forms of intelligence that are distributed throughout our bodies.

The advantage of modeling organizations after living systems is that living systems—which exhibit distributed intelligence and seek to organize—are far more adaptive to a changing environment than are closed systems such as machines. Even theories of artificial intelligence have moved from centralized models to linked computers that share information in a web-like fashion. Echoing our earlier discussion of participation and voice, the tentative conclusion appears to be that people learn best in a complex environment when they are loosely connected and free to initiate action from anywhere in the organization.

☐ From Biology to Organizational Communication

Academic disciplines whose traditional focus had been on complex processes of information exchange embraced systems theory. Sociologist Albion Small (1905) used concepts of systems theory in his field-defining work at the University of Chicago, and other prominent social theorists, such as Talcott Parsons (1951) and George Homans (1961), followed suit. Similarly, the initial popularity of the systems approach to organizational communication studies was enormous. Daniel Katz and Robert Kahn's *The Social Psychology of Organizations* (1966), a landmark application of systems theory to organizations, argued that organizations are fundamentally open systems that require a constant flow of information to and from their environment. In the field of organizational communication, then, systems theory provided a new connection between communicating and organizing.

Following the collapse of the Berlin Wall in 1989 and the opening of the republics that comprised the former Soviet Union, new systems of PC-based communication combined with the new technology of powerful search engines created new business relationships and global markets via the Internet. One search engine in particular—Google—has as its corporate mission to "organize the world's information and make it universally accessible and useful." Never before has knowledge

TABLE 4.1

The Hierarchy of General Systems Theory

LEVEL	DESCRIPTION AND EXAMPLES	THEORY AND MODELS
Static structures	Atoms, molecules, crystals, biological structures from the electron microscope to the macroscope level	Structural formulas of chemistry; crystallography; anatomical descriptions
Clockworks	Clocks, conventional machines in general, solar systems	Conventional physics, such as the laws of mechanics (Newton and Einstein)
Control mechanisms	Thermostat, servomechanisms, homeostatic mechanism in organisms	Cybernetics; feedback and information theory
Open systems	Flame, cells, and organisms in general	Expansion of physical theory to systems maintaining themselves in flow of matter (metabolism); information storage in genetic code (DNA)
Lower organisms	Plantlike organisms: increasing differentiation of system (so-called division of labor in the organism); distinction of reproduction and functional individual ("germ track and soma")	Theory and models mostly lacking
Animals	Increasing importance of traffic in information (evolution of receptors, nervous systems); learning; beginnings of consciousness	Beginnings in automata theory (stimulus-response relations), feedback (regulatory phenomena), autonomous behavior (relaxation oscillations)
Humans	Symbolism; past and future, self and world, self-awareness as consequences; communication by language	Incipient theory of symbolism
Sociocultural systems	Populations of organisms (humans included); symbol-determined communities (cultures) in humans only	Statistical and possibly dynamic laws in population dynamics, sociology, economics, possibly history; beginnings of a cultural systems theory
Symbolic systems	Language, logic, mathematics, sciences, arts, morals	Algorithms of symbols (e.g., mathematics, grammar); "rules of the game," such as in visual arts and music

Source: Ludwig von Bertalanffy, *General Systems Theory* (New York: George Braziller, 1968), pp. 28–29.

of systems, and particularly of communication systems, been more highly prized worldwide.

◣ WHAT IS A SYSTEM?

As you can tell from the preceding discussion, a system may be defined as a complex set of relationships among interdependent components or parts. In the study of organizational communication, we are concerned both with the nature of those components in organizations and the relationships among them.

☐ Environment and Open Systems

According to systems theory, organizations do not exist as entities isolated from the rest of the world. Rather, organizations exist in increasingly turbulent environments that both provide inputs to the organization and receive outputs in the form of products and services. For a company to succeed, some of its members must spend a significant amount of time engaged in environmental scanning, the careful monitoring of competitors, suppliers, government legislation, global economics, new technologies, political developments, and consumer preferences. Failure to do so leaves an organization open to unexpected environmental jolts, which can have disastrous consequences. In most successful companies, environmental scanning is done by boundary spanners, employees who have regular opportunities for interaction with people outside of the company.

An organization's relationship with its environment, however, is not limited to scanning. As open systems, organizations must also work *with* their environments to be successful (e.g., by establishing joint ventures and strategic partnerships). This is a significant change from traditional "us-against-them" theories of competition. In today's world, it is difficult for companies to know who is a potential enemy or friend, so the best strategy is usually something called **coopetition**, a blend of cooperation and competition that tries to reap the best of both worlds (Brandenburger & Nalebuff, 1996). A landmark example of coopetition is SEMATECH, a semiconductor consortium formed by the U.S. federal government to improve the global competitiveness of the entire semiconductor industry (Browning & Shetler, 2000). At first, participating companies (e.g., Intel, HP, Motorola) were very uncomfortable sharing information with their "enemies"; they later came to the important realization that their individual competitiveness was enhanced, not hindered, by a certain level of cooperation.

This critical insight can be useful in the development of cross-functional collaboration within social networks and organizations. **Open systems** theory encourages individual members (whether they be people, departments, or organizations) to be mindful of the importance of the overall health of their industry "ecosystem" (Lewin, 1997). The analogy between organizations and living organisms helps to further explain the concept of open systems. Organisms are open systems in that they rely on exchanges with their environment to survive (human beings, for example, need food, air, and sunlight to live). Similarly, organizations rely on communication with their environments. As Walter Buckley (1967) explains, "That a system is open means, not simply that it engages in interchanges with the environment, but that this interchange is an essential factor underlying the system's viability, its reproductive ability or continuity, and its ability to change" (p. 50). Therefore, an open system that interacts productively with its environment tends to create structure or, more simply, to organize, whereas in a closed system there is little or no interaction with the environment and the organization may approach entropy or disorder.

☐ Interdependence

Another essential quality of a system, **interdependence**, refers both to the wholeness of the system and its environment and to the interrelationships of individuals within the system. These relationships can vary in terms of their degree of interdependence. For example, a student's refusal to acknowledge the legitimacy of a particular instructor would have a negative effect on the student's performance in the course but only a minimal effect on the instructor because of the lopsided nature of the student-teacher relationship: The student is dependent on the instructor, but the instructor is only minimally interdependent. In contrast, because most marriages are characterized by a high degree of interdependence, the decision of one partner to withdraw emotionally from the relationship puts the whole system at risk. In systems theory, then, the interdependent relationships between people not only give an organization its character, but are established and maintained through communication.

The failure to recognize interdependence in dynamic systems leads to what ecologist Garrett Hardin (1968) called the "Tragedy of the Commons." The tragedy (e.g., the destruction of rain forests, the exploitation of grazing land, the pollution of major waterways) occurs when a group of people (or organizations, or departments within organizations) with access to a common resource use it in ways that focus on personal needs rather than on the needs of the whole. While each individual's actions may make sense from his or her perspective, the failure to recognize the interdependency and consequences of one's actions can be devastating to both the individual and the system.

In organizations, division of labor can cloud peoples' perceptions of the interdependent nature of their work. For example, when we toured a company that manufactures high-technology radio transmitters, we asked employees to describe the various kinds of jobs available in the company and whether they had considered cross-training or moving to a different department. We found that most employees in the company were ignorant of the nature of their co-workers' jobs. Although familiar with the processes they controlled directly, they were not aware of the origin of their work materials or the destination of their finished products. Even employees within the same work group had little knowledge of each other's jobs, despite their daily contacts. One employee, who for fifteen years had been handing over his finished parts to a co-worker (through a small window in an interior wall), had no idea what the co-worker did with the parts. A worst-case scenario from a systems perspective, the company's employees did not see themselves as part of an interdependent system because of the strict division of labor. In an interdependent system, no part of the system can stand alone but instead relies on the other parts to do its job effectively. Breakdowns in communication anywhere in the system run the risk of negatively impacting the whole.

One recent example of such a breakdown is described in *The 9/11 Commission Report* (2004). Despite decades of warnings from military and intelligence sources and State Department officials, and even direct communication with the American people via television by the terrorists (such as Osama bin Laden's interview on ABC News), few Americans fully appreciated how the fateful interdependence of global economics, religion, technology, transportation, and ideology could result in terrorists flying hijacked jets into U.S. buildings. Even with the more recent expansion of knowledge about what made those tragic events possible, our ability to successfully combat global networks of terrorists depends on our ability to promote effective communication among increasingly complex and diverse stakeholders. Specifically, government agencies unaccustomed to sharing data and the analysis of it must learn to do so; governments, police departments, businesses, and religious organizations unaccustomed to sharing information must also learn to cooperate.

☐ Goals

Organizational **goals** are defined in various ways in theories of organization and communication. From a scientific management perspective, goals are central: Both individuals and organizations direct their activities toward goal attainment. From an institutional perspective, organizations and their members may espouse goals, but rarely do their goals guide their behavior (Scott, 1981). From the open-systems perspective, however, goals are negotiated among interdependent factions in the organization and are heavily influenced by its environment.

Michael Keeley (1980) makes an important distinction regarding organizational goals. Examining the traditional view of organizations as mobilized around common goals, he distinguishes between the goals *of* individuals, which are personal and highly variable, and the goals individuals have *for* their organization, which are more likely to be shared. Furthermore, Jim Collins (2004) reveals that big, hairy, audacious goals (BHADs) for the organization that are clearly articulated and broadly shared distinguish successful and enduring organizations from their less effective competitors.

Goals can differ across system levels. For example, a unit at one level within a large corporation may seek the goal of profitability. At the next level, however, the corporation may be under pressure from stakeholders to raise cash; this corporate goal may cause it to try to sell the business unit (a decision that is unfavorable to the unit). At the same time, the other unit's goal of profitability may conflict with the individual goals of workers or managers within the unit, who may advocate such goals as improving product quality or focusing on strategic products at the expense of others. Thus, systems theory emphasizes that what is good for one level of the system may or may not be good for the other levels.

☐ Processes and Feedback

A system is not simply an interdependent set of components; it is also an interdependent collection of processes that interact over time. For instance, the production of this textbook is the result of many rounds of development and revision. Editors respond to customer concerns and must somehow bring together the authors as well as the marketing and production teams. Moreover, these collaborative processes involve numerous handoffs the timing and quality of which will shape if not determine the nature of the finished product. Where classical theories directed our attention to the individual employee, systems approaches lead us to focus on core processes.

Suppose, however, that a student or instructor is dissatisfied with the textbook and calls to cancel future orders, or that he or she is generally pleased with the product but requests changes in its design. These are examples of **feedback**, which can be defined as a system of loops that connect communication and action. Individuals provide messages to others, who then respond to those messages in some way. The response closes the loop, providing communicators with information about how their messages were received. In other words, feedback contains information about the influence of a particular message or action, and it is usually expressed as a deviation from what the sender intended.

Feedback thus controls systems of communication by regulating the flow and interpretation of messages. In systems theory, there are two main types of feedback: negative and positive. Negative, or deviation-counteracting, feedback is illustrated by the customer's complaint about the textbook. The negative feedback seeks to reestablish the goals or quality levels that were initially established for the product. (This type of feedback is sometimes referred to as "cybernetic," after the Greek word for "steersman," or someone who used oars to stay on course.) The other type of feedback, positive, or deviation-amplifying, feedback, is illustrated by the consultant who suggests changes in product design. It seeks to find new avenues of growth and development. Positive feedback is often referred to generally as "second cybernetics" or "morphogenesis" (Maruyama, 1963).

In their work on learning organizations, Chris Argyris and Donald Schon (1978) assert that businesses need both deviation-counteracting and deviation-amplifying feedback to achieve success. While deviation-counteracting feedback encourages adherence to an established strategy or course of action, deviation-amplifying feedback ensures that alternative strategies or courses of action are considered. Argyris calls the latter practice "double-loop learning," or the ability to "learn how to learn" by using feedback to reexamine established assumptions and decision premises.

An intriguing contemporary application of this sort of complex thinking is found in organizational communication scholar Steve Corman's (in press) notion of "counternetworking." The term refers to "any approach that seeks to decrease performance of an adversary organization by identifying and seeking to modify its communication network." Corman's interest is in countering terrorist networks by using "reverse organizational science," which means turning around the usual advice given to business leaders about making their organizations more successful. In this way, counternetworking is a process for using a systems approach to create negative feedback, which is used to promote "un-learning" and chaos among terrorists. One example is the introduction of urgently needed but false information (e.g., the time of a scheduled rendezvous prior to a suicide bomber attack) through a credible source within the terrorist network. The misinformation would then travel throughout the network, the ability of the terrorist team to coordinate their work would be impaired, and one's ability to track the message backward through the network increases the likelihood of capturing the team members.

☐ Openness, Order, and Contingency

Systems theory evokes the image of a complex, interdependent organization that operates within a dynamic environment and is engaged in an ongoing struggle to create order in the face of unpredictability (Clegg, 1990; Thompson, 1967). In retrospect, it is indeed surprising that classical management theories paid so little attention to an organization's environment, focusing instead on treating organizations equally and directing management to conduct careful studies of the "one best way" to accomplish work within the boundaries of the organization. Ideas about environments or global economics were considered irrelevant or misplaced.

In contrast, today's open systems are less reassuring and more unpredictable. Environmental openness helps organizations see themselves as part of a dynamic system of intricate interdependencies and relationships. Openness in the organization-environment relationship also has implications for some of the more prescriptive aspects of organizational theory. The existence of diverse environments across industries, companies, and even geographic regions means that the same organizing principles and solutions cannot be applied in all situations; rather, they are contingent on various factors. In systems theory, the term **equifinality** means that the same goal may be reached in multiple ways. Jay Galbraith (1973) summarizes the two basic tenets of contingency theory as follows:

1. There is no one best way to organize.
2. All ways of organizing are not equally effective.

These principles imply not only that the forms of organizing that will work best depend on the environment, but also that the match between certain organizational approaches and specific environments should be explored because some approaches will work better than others. Organizations that exist in complex and highly turbulent environments require different forms of leadership, interpersonal communication, decision making, and organizational structure than those in relatively predictable environments (Lawrence & Lorsch, 1967; Weich & Sutcliffe, 2001).

For example, our post-9/11 world is highly complex and turbulent, which has caused most organizations to rethink how they deal with security issues. This is due in part to the fact that Al Queda and other terrorist networks promote small, mobile, task-specific cells to fight against large bureaucratic military organizations, corporations, and nations. These older bureaucratic structures have been slow to respond to this type of threat because they have great difficulty cooperating and are prone to policy shifts drawn from the influence of markets, media coverage, and political polls. For terrorists, a major method of communication between cells is the Internet, wherein embedded messages and instructions are lodged within images. Decision making, once the action order is given, is distributed and highly localized. Leadership of the network is derived from theocratic principles, inspirational speech-making, experience with violence, and connections to sources of funding (Howard & Sawyer, 2004). Trying to create a more secure environment for workers, politicians, military personnel, and citizens is therefore made far more difficult because of the effectiveness of semiautonomous cells.

◪ THE APPEAL OF SYSTEMS THEORY FOR ORGANIZATIONAL COMMUNICATION

Systems theory appeals to those who are interested in organizational communication because it highlights the importance of communication processes in organizing. In addition, it is theoretically capable of capturing much of the complexity of these processes. While experience teaches us that communication is complex and takes place over time, earlier theories were based on the overly simplistic idea that communication involved the sending and receiving of messages.

Research on systems theory has been disappointing. Researchers have had difficulty translating the concepts of systems theory into research designs. Scholars unable to create dynamic systems theories of communication often lack the methodological tools needed to analyze complex systems of communication and feedback. Systems theories are ideally tested using statistical methods that accommodate multiple factors interacting over time. Unfortunately, few people studying social systems are well trained in how to use these new statistics. As a result, studies of complex systems often apply the wrong analytic techniques or remain untested at the theoretical level. Because actual studies of complex social systems are rare, systems theory has been characterized as an appealing but abstract set of concepts with limited applicability to actual theory or research (Poole, 1996). Recently, however, efforts have been made to reinvigorate systems theory in ways that are compatible with organizational communication. We are referring specifically to the innovative theories of Peter Senge and Karl Weick, which we discuss next.

☐ Peter Senge's Learning Organization

Management theorist Peter Senge (1990) has succeeded at bringing systems thinking to those who manage corporations. He is both concerned with holism and inclined to use scientific terminology. However, Senge focuses on the distinction between what he calls "learning organizations" and organizations that have a learning disability or a lack of understanding about how they function as systems. **Learning organizations** exhibit five features:

1. *Systems thinking.* Combining holism and interdependence, systems thinking claims that for any one member to succeed, all members must succeed.
2. *Personal mastery.* All members share a personal commitment to learning and self-reflection.
3. *Flexible mental models.* Mental models are those patterns of belief that shape and limit an individual's interpretations and actions. In a learning organization, members engage in self-reflection, allowing them first to understand and then to change the mental models that tend to guide their thinking.
4. *A shared vision.* In learning organizations, tight hierarchical control is replaced by "concertive control" (Tompkins & Cheney, 1985), whereby members act in concert because they share a common organizational vision and understand how their own work helps to build on that shared vision.
5. *Team learning.* Team members in a learning organization communicate in ways that lead the team toward intelligent decisions, with an emphasis on dialogue as the key to team learning.

According to Senge (1990), developing a learning organization requires a major "shift of mind" toward a more participative and holistic notion of effective organizing. What one does with differences in mental models — and how one moves on to team learning — is critical to Senge's approach and our interest in it.

As mentioned in Chapter 2, Senge (1994) and his colleagues at the MIT Dialogue Project (Isaacs, 1999) build on the work of physicist David Bohm (1980) on the role of consciousness in communication problems. Bohm is critical of the human tendency to see ourselves as separate from the rest of the world. He argues that the result of such thinking is discussion, or "participative openness," wherein we feel free to advocate our opinions, but because we are unwilling to suspend our certainty about our own worldview, no real learning takes place. In contrast, dialogue, or "reflective openness," "starts with the willingness to challenge our own thinking, to recognize that any certainty we have is, at best, a hypothesis about the world" (Senge, 1990, p. 277). From this point, dialogue progresses through a combination of advocacy and inquiry, wherein we collectively offer and expose our ideas to tough scrutiny by others. The primary distinction between dialogue and the typical problem-solving meeting in business is that the former places more value on the communication process, and group members are thereby more willing to distance themselves from their own opinions and ideas.

☐ Karl Weick's Sense-Making Model

Karl Weick's exploration of sense making, developed in his books *The Social Psychology of Organizing* (1979) and *Sensemaking in Organizations* (1995), has greatly influenced the fields of organizational behavior and communication. In particular his work has reinvigorated systems theory by connecting it with issues of sense making, meaning, and communication, while also providing a bridge for the development of cultural studies of organizations (see Chapter 5).

According to Weick (1979), organizations exist in highly complex and unpredictable environments. The job of organizing involves making sense of the uncertainties in environments through interaction, a process that Weick calls "equivocality reduction." In the process of identifying the meaning of a given situation or event, the same facts can be interpreted in various ways by different observers. How the members of an organization communicate to make sense of equivocal situations is central to Weick's approach.

As illustrated in Figure 4.1, Weick's (1979) model of organizing has three parts: enactment, selection, and retention. In enactment, organizational members create environments through their actions and patterns of attention, and these environments can vary in terms of their perceived degree of equivocality or uncertainty. For example, college presidents and their staffs are struggling these days to decide what to include in their enacted environment. The usual list of students currently registered in courses and alumni is now being augmented by local communities, governments, senior citizens, and technology companies running virtual universities. School administrations vary greatly in the degree to which they pay attention to any of these forces.

Once an environment is enacted, the organizing process requires the participants to select the best explanation of the environment's meaning from a number of possible interpretations. In selection, then, collective sense making is accomplished through communication. In the case of higher education, some universities (like Portland State University, the University of North Carolina at Greensboro, and the University of Alabama at Birmingham) have chosen to interpret their purpose

FIGURE 4.1

Weick's Model of Organizing

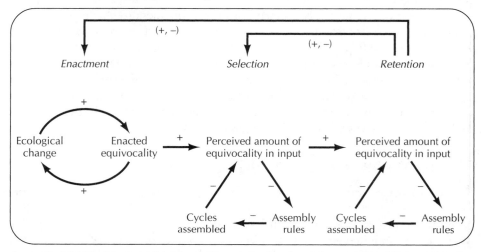

Source: Karl Weick, *The Social Psychology of Organizing* (Reading, Mass.: Addison-Wesley, 1979). Reprinted by permission.

and mission as in close partnership with the local community, and have even redesigned their reward systems to align with this interpretation. For example, the mission statement of UNCG begins with the words "The University of North Carolina at Greensboro is a student-centered university, linking the Piedmont Triad to the world through learning, discovery, and service" (*UNCG Undergraduate Bulletin*, 2002–2003, p. 9). As a result of establishing "learning, discovery, and service" connections to the Piedmont Triad (e.g., the communities of Greensboro, Winston-Salem, and High Point) as first and foremost in its mission, the faculty and administration also revised promotion standards to include a track based primarily on service to the Triad area. Additionally, the university's provost announced that one of UNCG's "Signature Programs" would be Service Learning, which means that each and every academic department is expected to develop core service learning opportunities for students within the Piedmont region and that academic departments will be evaluated, in part, based on the success of those community programs and initiatives.

Finally, in retention, successful interpretations are saved for future use. In the case of UNCG, time will tell what lessons are learned from their choice; success will not only reinforce their selection, but also allow others to see this as a legitimate option for their institutions. Retained interpretations also influence future selection processes, as indicated by the feedback arrow in Figure 4.1. Weick thus represents sense making as a set of interdependent processes that interact with and provide feedback to one another. In this sense, his model connects systems thinking with interpretation.

Perhaps Weick's (1979) most revolutionary concept is that of the enacted environment. Unlike theories of species evolution, in which degrees of environmental variation are determined objectively, in organizational environments people look for clues to threats or opportunities. Their perception is highly selective and dependent on their interests, motives, background, and behavior. Therefore, a company dominated by engineers would focus on changes in science and technology, whereas an organization made up mainly of accountants would focus on financial markets and global economic trends. This concept of the enacted environment is especially important in today's business world, wherein environmental scanning is crucial to an organization's survival. Among the most critical but often overlooked keys to organizational success involves keeping in touch with current issues through scanning relevant articles in newspapers and journals and maintaining contacts with others. Many times businesspeople overlook the importance of environmental scanning and miss information that has a direct bearing on their company. Because the enacted environment is always limited by subjective perception, organizational success requires an ongoing examination of current issues.

Weick extends his model of organizing through three important concepts: retrospective sense making, loose coupling, and partial inclusion.

Retrospective Sense Making

An underlying assumption of Weick's model is that decision making is largely **retrospective sense making**. In other words, although people in organizations think they plan first and then act according to a plan, Weick argues that people act first and later examine their actions in an attempt to explain their meaning. He sums this up in what he calls a "recipe": "How can I know what I think until I see what I say?" (1979). Weick (1995) goes on to identify seven "properties of sense making":

1. *Identity construction.* Who I am is indicated by how and what I think.
2. *Retrospection.* To learn what I think, I look back over what I said earlier.
3. *Enactment.* I create an object to be seen and inspected when I say or do something.
4. *Socialization.* What I say, single out, and conclude are determined by who socialized me and how I was socialized, as well as by the audience I anticipate will audit the conclusions I reach.
5. *Continuation.* My talking is spread across time, competes for attention with other ongoing projects, and is reflected on after it is finished (which means my interests may already have changed).
6. *Extracted cues.* The "what" that I single out and embellish as the content of the thought is only a small portion of the utterance that becomes salient because of the context and personal dispositions.

7. *Plausibility.* I need to know enough about what I think to get on with my projects, but no more, which means sufficiency and plausibility take precedence over accuracy. (pp. 61–62)

The seven properties also apply if we change the pronouns in the recipe to reflect collectively (e.g., "How can we know what we think until we see what we say?").

However, Weick's theory of retrospective sense making does not take into account that some people do act first and interpret later while others strive to act only in accordance with predetermined plans. Perhaps both processes are always at work. The important point in Weick's argument is that the balance between planned and unplanned behavior is often the reverse of what we assume it to be. Such challenges to commonsense beliefs have been called "counterrational" approaches to organizational theory. Weick pushes this position to the limit, even arguing that random decision-making processes may be superior to rational methods of decision making and planning. His work in this area further challenges the scientific approach to management, wherein communication serves only as a conduit for the one best way of doing things. In contrast, the manager in Weick's model is a manipulator of symbols who motivates employees to make sense of their work life. Interaction is thus emphasized over reflection, with an accompanying bias for action. According to Weick, employees do not need common goals to work well together, nor do they need to know precisely what decisions they will make before they make them. More important, according to Weick, is a willingness to engage in coordinated action aimed at reducing equivocality, which over time may lead employees to discover (in retrospect) the meaning of what they have done.

Loose Coupling

At the same time that Weick stresses the importance of communication at work, he points out that unlike the connections among biological systems, the communication connections among people in organizations vary in intensity and are often loose or weak. Weick's (1976) concept of **loosely coupled** systems has had a major impact on our understanding of organizations as communication systems.

Consider, for example, the typical college or university, in which a great deal of interaction occurs within departments but not across various fields of study. The activities of the history department have little effect on those of the engineering department. Similarly, loose or weak connections usually exist among the university's nonacademic units (staff, administration, and faculty). The university is a classic example of a loosely coupled system.

Whereas strictly rational approaches maintain that loose connections deter people from working together to achieve a common goal, Weick (1979) argues that such connections can sometimes be advantageous. The multiple goals of an organization can be coordinated without extensive communication or consensus (Eisenberg, 1984, 1986, 1990, 1995). In addition, a loosely coupled system is better able to withstand environmental jolts. In a system of close or tight connections, environmental jolts can affect the entire system, whereas in a loosely coupled system,

EVERYDAY ORGANIZATIONAL COMMUNICATION

Making Sense of Your Equivocal Past

Very often, there is a stark contrast between the tumultuous path we travel in life and the story we tell about the journey. As we discussed in this chapter, Karl Weick terms this phenomenon *retrospective sense making* and argues that people act first and later examine their actions in an attempt to explain their meaning. Have you ever considered how your own life story might be an attempt to come to terms with your equivocal past?

Consider the example of Steve Jobs, cofounder of Apple Computer and CEO of Pixar. At age eighteen, Jobs was a teenager who didn't know what he wanted to do with his life. Imagine his parents' reaction when he declared that the best decision for him to make was to drop out of Reed College! Although at the time this choice may have seemed rash, the benefit of hindsight allows Jobs to state that dropping out of school was one of the best decisions he ever made (Jobs, 2005, para. 5). And thank your iPod that he did—this was when Jobs joined up with Steve Wozniak to sell personal computers assembled in Jobs's garage. Despite the immediate consequences of Jobs's decision (sleeping on the floor in friends' dorm rooms and returning coke bottles for the 5¢ deposits to buy food), he became a multimillionaire less than ten years later (para. 6). Told retrospectively, it all makes sense.

Examples of retrospective sense making do not have to be as dramatic as Jobs's story. Even the way that you wound up in your current major is a story worth examining. For example, our editor's college roommate began her post-secondary education as biology major with a chemistry minor, intent on fulfilling a lifelong dream to become a pediatrician. Poor grades in a required physics course as well as a newfound passion for a general education course in literature caused her to switch her major to English. But what to do with nineteen years of interest in the sciences? How did those experiences enter into the story of her life? She indulged her various interests by studying medicine and illness in literature—and even the chemistry of illuminated manuscripts! Today she is a Ph.D. candidate in English, and looking back over her years of formal education, it makes sense that she arrived where she did.

For most of us, the lived experience of college and career is most often a series of happy accidents and opportunities. Told retrospectively, however, they are most often presented as a series of logical choices that led to an inevitable conclusion. Or as Steve Jobs says: "You can't connect the dots looking forward; you can only connect them looking backwards. So you have to trust that the dots will somehow connect in your future."*

*Stanford Commencement Address (para. #9), 6/12/05. <news-service.stanford.edu/news/2005/june15/jobs-061505.html>

(continued, Making Sense of Your Equivocal Past)

DISCUSSION QUESTIONS

1. Think back on how you arrived where you are today. How did you come to attend your current university? What factors led to your decision to declare your current major?
2. If you are currently employed, how does your job fit into your life story? For most people, jobs are primarily a source of income, but they often turn into steps on long-term career paths. Alternatively, an intense dislike of a particular job might lead one down a completely different path than expected. Have you experienced either scenario?
3. Conduct a brief informal interview with a successful person (face-to-face, by phone, or via e-mail) and ask them to recount to you the path they took to where they are today. Specifically ask, What were the crucial decisions or turning points in your life? Finally, find out the extent to which they were aware of their final destination when they were making those crucial decisions. The results should clearly reveal the difference between the experience of decision making and retrospective sense making of those decisions.

the whole is less affected because of the weak connections among units. Although it is subject to redundancy and inefficiency, a loosely coupled system may still be more effective in the long term.

Partial Inclusion

In analyzing the balance between work and other activities, Weick (1979) uses the theory of **partial inclusion** to explain why certain strategies for motivating employees are ineffective. He holds that employees are only partially included in the workplace; that is, at work we see some but not all of their behaviors. An unmotivated employee at work may be a church leader or a model parent, whereas the top performer at a company may engage in few outside activities. In either case, simple theories of organizational behavior are limited when they fail to consider the employee's activities, roles, and interests outside of the workplace. Every individual is a member of multiple systems, and this multiple membership shapes and limits their degree of commitment to any one in particular.

Weick (1979) mainly differentiates himself from those who value profitability above all else. He sees organizations as communities or social settings in which we choose to spend most of our adult lives. As such, organizations provide opportunities for storytelling and socializing; according to Weick, "they haven't anything else to give" (p. 264). A closer analysis of organizations as communities is the primary goal of the cultural approach, our focus in Chapter 5.

Surviving Hurricane Katrina

Following the devastation caused by Hurricane Katrina in late August 2005, many people questioned the effectiveness of local, state, and federal disaster preparedness and assistance planning. Below we reprint a posting from "The Armchair President" (formerly a blog) that asks important questions about the interoperability of systems of communication during a crisis — that is, the ability for people to talk across disciplines and jurisdictions via radio communications systems, exchanging voice and/or data with one another on demand, in real time, when needed. Read over the excerpt from the blog and construct a response to it based on your understanding of systems applications to communication challenges. What steps do you think should be taken to ensure better ethical communication in future crises?

In 2004, the U.S. Department of Homeland Security created SAFECOM. SAFECOM is managed by the Department of Homeland Security (DHS) Science and Technology (S&T) Directorate's Office for Interoperability and Compatibility (OIC). Its mission is to serve as the umbrella program within the federal government to help local, state, tribal, and federal public safety agencies improve public safety response through more effective and efficient interoperable wireless communications. On July 22, 2004, President Bush formally announced the RapidCom initiative, a program designed to ensure that a minimum level of public safety interoperability would be in place in ten high-threat urban areas by September 30, 2004. As part of the RapidCom team, SAFECOM worked closely with public safety leaders in Boston, Chicago, Houston, Jersey City, Los Angeles, Miami, New York, Philadelphia, San Francisco, and Washington to assess their cities' communications interoperability capacity and needs, and to identify and implement solutions. In keeping with the SAFECOM "bottom up" approach, local officials actively participated in the design and implementation of solutions in their jurisdictions.

Notice that New Orleans is not on the list of cities identified as high-threat urban areas. Yet, FEMA, an arm of the Department of Homeland Security identified a hurricane hitting New Orleans as one of the top three largest threats to prepare for. One has to wonder, if FEMA and numerous scientists felt a hurricane like Katrina was an imminent threat, why was New Orleans not added to the list?

Back to the SAFECOM website, scrolling through the FAQs, I came across the question we would all like to have answered. The answer was frankly as shocking as the images we are seeing on our televisions: According to the experts, in the most technologically rich nation in both brain trust and monetarily, it will take *20 years* to solve this problem. Can your city wait?

Source: http://www.safecomprogram.gov/SAFECOM/about/faq/#1132.

(continued, Surviving Hurricane Katrina)

How long will it take to achieve public safety communications interoperability? Given that Mike Brown, the Undersecretary for FEMA and Michael Chertoff, Secretary of Homeland Security, denied reports of food and water shortages, deaths, and the immensity of the tragedy for two days, despite the pleas from New Orleans Mayor Ray Nagin and the endless stream of information coming from CNN and other news stations, it would seem that communication needs to be a top priority for DHS and FEMA. Yes, let's improve cell phone communication. Let's get the technology to the cities so they can communicate in these types of disasters and get the help they need. But let's also look at the lack of communication between those at the highest level who should have been listening to those on the ground.

Summary

The broad term *systems approach* encompasses many theories with various assumptions and implications for action. In contrast to earlier organizational theories (many of which can be classified according to their underlying view of the goals of organizing and of workers), systems theory is more open-ended. Adopting a systems approach requires acknowledging the openness and complexity of social organizations as well as the importance of relationships among individuals over time. Table 4.2 provides an explicit comparison of scientific management and systems theories.

In practice, however, a systems approach can either help or hinder situated individuals. It can help individuals better understand overall workings of the organization. It can emphasize the importance of relationships and networks of contacts in allowing groups and organizations to achieve goals that are greater than those of the individual. A systems perspective can also reveal important interdependencies, particularly the connections with organizational environments that can affect an organization's survival. Despite its focus on communication and relationships, however, systems theory does not help to explain the meanings constructed by interactions. It can identify the potential participants in a productive organizational dialogue, but it cannot tell us about the content of that dialogue. It is in this area that Weick augments systems theory with issues related to sense making, arguably the central process of organizing.

Systems theory may also be applied in a way that elevates the whole and ignores or dehumanizes individuals. Any recognition of the role of whole systems must be accompanied by an understanding of how individuals create, refine, and

TABLE 4.2

Scientific Management and Systems Theories

SCIENTIFIC MANAGEMENT	SYSTEMS THEORIES
Metaphor: Machines.	*Metaphor:* Biological organisms.
Theme: Efficiency — a machine is the sum of its parts.	*Theme:* Complexity — a system is greater than the sum of its parts.
Influences: Industrial Revolution, modernity, capitalism, and empire; assembly-line production and management; division of labor, interchangeable parts, coordination of many small, skilled jobs.	*Influences:* Einstein's theory of relativity; McLuhan's global information society; Miller's biological systems; von Bertalanffy's general systems; information engineering model of communication.
Focus of management principles: "The only things that count are the finished product and the bottom line"; time and motion studies.	*Focus of management principles:* "Everything counts"; studies of interdependent processes, information flows and feedback, environments and contingencies.
Management of individuals as interchangeable parts	*Management of relationships* among components; focus on groups and networks
Planning the work, working the plan	*Planning* the work, using feedback to correct the plan
Motivation by fear and money	*Motivation* by needs and contingencies
Theory of communication:	*Theory of communication:*

S ——— M ——— C ——— R
e   e   h   e
n   s   a   c
d   s   n   e
e   a   n   i
r   g   e   v
        e   l   e
                        r

Sender—Message—Channel—Receiver

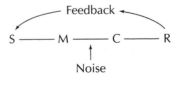

Sender—Message—Channel—Receiver
Noise

TABLE 2.1 *(continued)*

Scientific Management and Systems Theories

SCIENTIFIC MANAGEMENT	SYSTEMS THEORIES
Theory of leadership: Trait (tall, white males with blond hair and blue eyes, who come from strong moral backgrounds).	*Theory of leadership:* Adaptive (rhetorical contingency) — anyone can learn the skills of leading by attending to the requirements of behavioral flexibility.
Limitations: (1) Forgets that humans are more complex than machines; (2) encourages individual boredom and deep divisions between managers and employees; (3) discourages communication, individual needs, job initiative, task innovation, personal responsibility, and empowerment.	*Limitations:* (1) Forgets that humans are symbolic as well as biological; (2) encourages mathematical complexities that are difficult to put into every-day practices; (3) equates communication with information.

destroy them. All too often, system complexity can be used as an excuse for not recognizing individual rights or responsibilities.

Systems theory is likely to continue to exert significant influence on the field of organizational communication. Particularly in organizations that produce complex products or provide complex services, systems theory is evident in discussions of work-flow analysis, internal customers, and cross-functional work groups, as well as in the use of control charts and process maps. Businesses are increasingly recognizing the critical role of markets and environments in their survival. In Chapter 8, we return to the discussion of systems theory with application to the development of network forms of organizing.

QUESTIONS FOR REVIEW AND DISCUSSION

1. How has the information revolution influenced the development of systems theory?
2. How are biological systems and organizational communication systems similar? How are they different?
3. In what ways is organizational learning connected to the processes associated with systems thinking?
4. How has the sense-making model reinvigorated the application of systems theory to organizational communication?

5. Why do you think it has been difficult to operationalize systems thinking? In terms of doing systems research in an organization, what would you consider to be the major challenges?

KEY TERMS

Coopetition, p. 106
Distributed intelligence, p. 104
Equifinality, p. 110
Feedback, p. 109
General systems theory, p. 103
Goals, p. 108
Interdependence, p. 107

Learning organization, p. 112
Loose coupling, p. 112
Open systems, p. 116
Partial inclusion, p. 106
Retrospective sense making, p. 115
Systems approach, p. 101

CASE STUDY

Crisis in the Zion Emergency Room

Recently *U.S. News & World Report* declared the nation's emergency rooms (ERs) to be in crisis. Part of the problem is a lack of qualified nurses. Nurses everywhere are in short supply, and those who can work effectively in the emergency environment are even rarer. But there are other reasons for the widespread overcrowding of ERs. A large and growing population of people without insurance continue to make use of them for primary care needs. Emergency rooms, staffed primarily to serve the victims of trauma or acute illness, are increasingly overburdened by mothers and infants without adequate prenatal and pediatric care; the chronically ill and disabled; persons with HIV/AIDS; individuals with mental illnesses, including drug and alcohol addiction; and the homeless. The end result is excessive wait time, angry patients, and substandard care. The ER at Zion Hospital is no different.

On any given night, Zion's ER looks like a war zone. The halls of the ER are lined with twenty to twenty-five patients on gurneys, lying in limbo until one of the forty-five regular ER beds opens up; just walking through the ER can be tricky. The overcrowding of the ER creates a distinct lack of privacy, and, more important, it creates confusion about the location and status of patients, which increases the potential for serious errors. And more patients keep coming.

You have recently accepted the position of director of emergency medicine at Zion. Expectations are high that you will be able to do something quickly about the dreadful patient satisfaction ratings that have appeared in recent months. Your initial assessment of the situation, however, is discouraging. For the reasons just described, there appears to be an endless and growing stream of new patients into the ER, and the hospital financial committee looks unfavorably at turning people away. Meanwhile, all of your beds are taken, half of them by people who have already been admitted to Zion but have yet to be assigned a bed upstairs in one of the hospital wards/units. Your staff has to find a way of serving these bored and hungry patients while handling the more critical patients lined up in the hall.

Further investigation reveals that your patients are waiting for beds for a number of reasons: (1) Other units in the hospital, such as the heart center and the pediatric unit, have priority over the ER in getting beds; (2) all of the beds in the hospital are full, and those that are physically empty are locked in units that have been temporarily closed due to the lack of qualified nurses to staff them; and (3) there are long delays from the time a viable bed actually becomes empty to when housekeeping is able to clean the room for the next patient to when floor nurses can make themselves available to accept the new patient to their unit.

The situation is miserable and deteriorating. The nursing shortage is not going to end anytime soon, your current nurses are all threatening to quit, patients are furious, and hospital administration is urging you to "think outside the box" to find some relief.

ASSIGNMENT

Using what you know about systems theories of organization, answer the following questions.

1. How would you define the problem systemically? How does your choice of definition affect your likely course of action?
2. Using the language of systems theories, what "realities" in this case would be most difficult to change, and which are more malleable?
3. What role does communication play in perpetuating the current situation? How does your understanding of the systems approach help you identify specific communication issues?
4. Using your knowledge of systems, what kinds of communication might you use to address the situation? What obstacles would you expect to encounter, and how would you deal with them? Wouldn't dealing with those obstacles — in whatever way you choose to deal with them — also necessarily create new systemic issues? Given your choice of how to deal with the obstacles, what might these new issues be?
5. What role might communication technology play in developing a systems approach to your solution or solutions?

CHAPTER 5

Cultural Studies of Organizations and Communication

This chapter introduces the idea of organizations as cultures. The cultural approach departs from the more rational and formal approaches that preceded it (such as the systems approach) and brings a new focus on the language of the workplace, the performances of managers and employees, the formal and informal practices that mark an organization's character, such as rites and rituals, and the display of meaningful artifacts like architecture, interior design, posters, and furniture. Moreover, the cultural approach foregrounds the human desire to see organizational life as an opportunity to do something meaningful (Gendron, 1999). In this chapter, we trace the history of the cultural approach, explore the practical, methodological, and social reasons for its popularity, and look at some of the ways it has been applied by researchers and managers. Finally, we outline a communication view of organizational culture to show how an organization's unique patterns of interaction and sense making work together over time to create its culture.

◩ THE CULTURAL APPROACH

When you hear the term *culture*, you most likely think about it in a broad sense, such as the differences between American culture and French culture. A closer view, however, reveals that within every national culture there are thousands of smaller cultures based on religion, ethnicity, geography, and a myriad of other factors. Whenever people create groups or communities, a culture inevitably develops. The same is true for organizations. But what precisely do we mean by "culture"? How can one word serve to describe so many different kinds of social groups?

Anthropologist Marshall Sahlins (1976) defines culture as meaningful orders of persons and things. Thus, we learn about a culture not only by what its members say, but also by what they do on a regular basis (e.g., staff meetings, performance reviews, bowling leagues) and the things they choose to display in connection with their work. Clifford Geertz (1973) defines culture as "an historically transmitted pattern of meanings embodied in symbols, a system of inherited conceptions expressed in symbolic form by means of which men [*sic*] communicate, perpetuate, and develop their knowledge about and attitudes toward life" (p. 89). And Edgar Schein (1994) offers this variation: "An organizational culture is a pattern of shared basic assumptions that have been invented, discovered, and/or developed by a group as it learns to cope with problems of external adaptation and internal integration" (p. 247).

A culture is also something like a religion. According to T. S. Eliot (1949), "No culture has appeared or developed except together with a religion . . . [and] the culture will appear to be the product of the religion, or the religion the product of the culture" (p. 13). Put another way, a culture is like a religion in that both locate a set of common beliefs and values that prescribes a general view of order (the way things are) and explanation (why things are that way). The tie between religion and culture is important to organizational studies because it indicates how the search for order and explanation compels beliefs.

However, not all members of a culture accept or practice those beliefs in the same way. Culture is never so much about agreement as it is about a common recognition or intelligibility. Like religions, most cultures include various sects or subcultures that share the common order but whose ways of understanding or carrying out their beliefs differ. This point underscores the importance of understanding an organization's culture or cultures as a dialogue with many different voices.

☐ Cultures as Symbolic Constructions

To say that a word or thing is symbolic means that it stands for something other than itself. This is easy to see with words, which as symbols refer to ideas and things in the world (referents). But symbols also take other forms, such as office size and design, trophy displays, how managers and employees dress, and what hangs (or is absent from) the walls. For our purposes, then, the term **organizational culture** stands for the actions, ways of thinking, practices, stories, and artifacts that characterize a particular organization. We study the culture of an organization through close examination of its symbolic environment (e.g., the arrangement of parking lots, office cubicles, and conference rooms) as well as through its use of symbols (e.g., topics of conversation, key vocabulary and jargon, treasured accomplishments and awards). The study of organizational cultures thereby involves interpreting the meanings of these symbols.

Viewing organizations as symbolic requires several assumptions. First, all cultural studies begin with a focus on the centrality of language in shaping human perception. Consequently, a large part of any cultural analysis devotes considerable attention to the names of things and how these names are invoked in conversation. For example, from a cultural perspective it is very significant when an organization refers to its people as "human resources" or even more dramatically as "heads" to be added or cut. Relatedly, a company that speaks of facing their competition using the language of war is very different culturally from one that makes broad use of spiritual metaphors (Goodier & Eisenberg, 2006). In much the same way that we have come to appreciate the importance of nonsexist language in shaping basic assumptions, the terms organizational members use to describe their worlds are both crucial and largely unexamined. A cultural approach brings them into the light.

Another source of inspiration for viewing organizations as symbolic constructions involves defining human beings as symbol-using animals, as Kenneth Burke does in his classic essay "Definition of Man" (1966). Burke's view helps us understand why symbols both represent other things and evoke other symbolic possibilities. For example, an organizational chart simultaneously provides information about hierarchy and relationships (e.g., formal lines of communication; formal status relations) and suggests possibilities for future action (e.g., getting promoted). That is, symbols do not only stand for other things; they also shape our understandings of those things and help us to identify their meanings and uses. As such, symbols are instruments of human understanding and action. A company that anticipates being sold, for example, begins to "talk" differently to itself, and these new ways of communicating in turn affect action, as a culture of apathy or cynicism may develop. The culture of an organization induces its members to think, act, and behave in particular ways

☐ Cultural Elements

Organizational cultures emerge from organizational members' individual and collective symbol-using practices. These various symbolic expressions combine to create a "unique sense of place" that defines an organization's culture (Pacanowsky & O'Donnel-Trujillo, 1983). Scholars and practitioners often focus on one or more of those symbolic expressions, referred to here as *cultural elements*, to learn more about or to transform an organization's culture. Those elements include the following:

- *Metaphors*: **Metaphors** are figures of speech that define an unfamiliar experience in terms of another more familiar one. From a cultural perspective, when members describe their organization as a "family," a "machine," or a "ship" or compare their approach to decision making with "improv comedy" as the folks at Pixar do, they are not simply using flowery language; instead, they come to construct and experience their organizations in relation to those metaphors (Smith & Eisenberg, 1987).
- *Rituals*: **Rituals** "dramatize" a culture's basic values and can range in scope from personal, day-to-day routines for accomplishing tasks to annual organization-wide celebrations of top performers (Deal & Kennedy, 1982; Pacanowsky & O'Donnel-Trujillo, 1983). New product launches, office

birthday celebrations, sales conferences, and performance evaluations are all aimed at reinforcing organizational values. Nonprofit organizations have many of the same rituals plus regular events that involve fund-raising and the recruitment and development of volunteers.

- *Stories*: Storytelling is an important cultural activity because **stories** convey to members what and who is valued by the culture, how things are to be done, and the consequences for cultural compliance and/or deviation. Stories have been described as a particularly powerful means of creating and recreating cultures (Smith & Keyton, 2001). The Disney Corporation, for example, uses formal organizational texts, advertising, and informal channels to narrate a sense of community among its stakeholders.

- *Artifacts*: **Artifacts**, or the tangible and physical features of an organization, contribute to its culture. Office décor, spatial arrangements, corporate art, dress codes, and even graffiti are markers of culture (Scheibel, 2003). For example, the creativity and innovation that Pixar holds dear is evident in the fact that employees are permitted to decorate their office space any way that they choose.

- *Heroes and Heroines*: **Heroes and heroines** are members of an organization who are held up as role models. They embody and personify cultural values. Often heroic figures are organizational founders or hail from managerial ranks (Deal & Kennedy, 1982; Fairhurst, 1997). Apple Computer and Pixar CEO, Steve Jobs, who began his climb to the top when he and his partner created their first computer in his family's garage, is legendary as an innovative leader who embodies a passion for making technology accessible.

- *Performances*: Members often engage in dynamic, ongoing, and creative communication behaviors as they construct cultures. **Performances** center on rituals, passion, sociality (or organizational etiquette), politics, socialization of new members, and identity (Pacanowsky & O'Donnell-Trujillo, 1983). A great example of the performance of identity can be seen during hospital rounds, where less experienced physicians are called on to describe specific cases and receive immediate feedback regarding how well they are able to "talk like a doctor."

- *Values*: **Values** represent a (more or less) shared set of beliefs about appropriate organizational behaviors. They are often derived from charismatic leaders or founders or organizational traditions (Schein, 1991). For example, Southwest Airlines values a fun, casual work environment most, while General Electric values innovation above all else. These cultural value commitments can be very powerful in boosting employee loyalty and satisfaction as long as they are aligned with company goals.

These elements of culture are understood differently depending on the approach one takes. To understand the ways various scholars and practitioners unpack and make use of these cultural elements, we first turn to the historical and social trends out of which the cultural approach emerged.

◧ HISTORICAL AND CULTURAL BACKGROUND

The first known reference to organizational culture appeared in a 1979 article by Andrew Pettigrew published in *Administrative Science Quarterly*. The concept became immediately popular for a variety of reasons, including competitive pressures, the coming of age of interpretive research methods, and trends in the wider society. Each of these is discussed in turn in the following sections.

☐ Competitive Pressures

The business climate of the 1970s was characterized by a significant increase in global competition that highlighted productivity problems in the United States. Although for many years the United States had been the world leader in several industries, it suddenly found itself eclipsed by other nations, most notably Japan. In many industries, Japanese manufacturing techniques threatened to prevail, and many wondered what made them so successful.

Based on observations of management techniques that were commonly used by Japanese organizations in the 1970s, William Ouchi's Theory Z holds that the survival and prosperity of organizations depend heavily on their ability to adapt to their surrounding cultures. He uses the term *culture* to refer to national standards of organizational performance, and in comparing those standards in the United States and Japan, he found some major differences. For example, he contrasted the American emphasis on individual achievement with the Japanese emphasis on the performance and well-being of the collective. Ouchi thus proposed a Theory Z type of organization that would integrate individual achievement and advancement while also developing a sense of community in the workplace. A Theory Z organization, according to Ouchi, would be capable of reducing negative influences and segmented decision making by incorporating new cultural values into the work environment.

However, the economic troubles of Asia at the close of the twentieth century came as a surprise to most people and has caused many theorists to question the seemingly "magical" Japanese formulas. In hindsight, it appears that much of Japan's success was gained the old-fashioned way—through spectacular individual efforts, close informal contacts and partnerships, research and development of new products and services, and clever competitive tactics and strategy.

By the mid-1980s, many traditional organizations were failing financially or soon in danger of doing so. The old prescriptions—more hierarchy, bureaucracy, division of labor, and standardization—were no longer effective, and it became clear that radical changes were required for companies to remain competitive. As business leaders began speaking of organizational change—in attitudes, values, and practices—they also began thinking about a holistic transformation in terms of organizational culture. One of the authors of this textbook (Eisenberg) received a phone call in 1983 from a CEO in search of someone who could "install a new culture" at his company. Managers were attracted to the idea even without much knowledge of how culture develops, much less how it could be altered. Many questions remained: What types of cultures are most productive? What aspects of culture are most closely associated with business success?

☐ Interpretive Methodology

At the same time that practitioners were looking for new models of effective organizations, scholars were becoming disenchanted with the overly rational, mechanistic view of communication that characterized the field of organizational communication. As a result, research in organizational communication took an "interpretive turn" in the early 1980s (Putnam & Pacanowsky, 1983). Previously, the dominant vocabulary, derived from the fields of psychology, sociology, and management, covered such topics as performance, motivation, and rewards, as well as work units, hierarchies, and the outcomes of group problem solving, decision making, and leadership. Interpretive theorists became less concerned with these specific topics and became more interested in understanding the complex, dynamic nature of organizational life as it is experienced by members. The new focus on organizational cultures required a new vocabulary and new approaches for analyzing organizations and communication.

The anthropological vocabulary of the cultural approach gave organizational researchers, managers, and members new ways of viewing organizations, applying long-standing cultural concepts like values, rituals, and socialization (Table 5.1). Today, organization members themselves commonly use this language. It has both broadened the scope of what is considered important about organizations and communication and complicated our thinking about organizational communication processes. For example, the study of an organization's values is no longer limited to those stated in the company's formal publications; they may also be found in artifacts and cartoons, in the layout of work space, and even in the arrangement of cars in the employee parking lot (Goodall, 1989). Moreover, interpretive researchers are not interested in treating culture as simply another variable that the organization *has*; culture is not a variable that can be managed or manipulated by leaders. Rather, interpretive researchers are driven to treat culture as something an organization *is*. As a culture, an organization requires exceedingly detailed and nuanced observation of daily life to produce what Geertz called a "thick description" of the culture (Geertz, 1973). These highly descriptive accounts provide rich and complex portraits of members' organizational sense making experiences.

How does one analyze organizational culture in a systematic way? The most common methodology has its roots in anthropology and is called **ethnography** or the writing of culture (Clifford & Marcus, 1985). Because anthropologists have

TABLE 5.1

Cultural Terms Applied to Organizational Communication Studies

Symbols	Language	Metaphors
Words/actions	In-group speech 　Technical terms 　Jargon 　Jokes 　Gossip 　Rumors 　Gendered usage	Determined by use within the culture
Artifacts 　Objects 　Cartoons	Arrangement of the physical work space Personal meanings Humor in the workplace Social/political commentary	Power/status Irony/contrast Resistance to domination

Routines	Rituals/Rites	Communities
Repetitive behaviors	Individual performances Group performances New employee orientation Acceptance into group Promotions Annual celebrations Shunning/exclusion Retirement/layoffs	Continuity Acculturation Difference

Use of Objects	Employee Handbooks	Representation
Logos Awards	Company brochures Annual reports Identification Reward	 Symbolic unity Enhancement

long studied cultures, researchers sought to integrate anthropological research methods into cultural studies of organizations and communication (Goodall, 1989, 1991a; Van Maanen, 1979, 1988). Successful organizations (e.g., Xerox) hire ethnographers to review and evaluate their company cultures. In writing an ethnographic account of Disneyland, John Van Maanen (1991), a management professor at the

Massachusetts Institute of Technology with ties to anthropology and communication, relied on his recollections of working there while he was a student as well as his more recent observations of and interactions with employees and guests. Unlike traditional research methods in the social sciences, in which the researcher maintains distance from the group under study, ethnography requires the researcher to experience the culture firsthand. Van Maanen (1988) identifies three general types of ethnography: the *realist* tale, which conveys the basic elements of the culture in an objective way; the *impressionist* tale, which presents the research experience along with the findings, often in creative ways; and the *confessional* tale, which focuses on the emotional experience of the ethnographer in the cultural setting.

Organizational ethnography provides "thick" descriptions of organizational life, often capturing subtle points that are overlooked by traditional research methods. For example, consider the difference between a traditional written survey of patient satisfaction in a hospital and an ethnography of a hospital unit (Eisenberg, Baglia, & Pynes, 2006). Whereas the findings of the survey would likely be cut and dried and limited to the questions the researchers posed in advance, the ethnography—told in the form of a story—would reveal more about the communication and sense-making processes of all parties involved, including many observations and findings that might surprise the researcher. Ethnography is a stimulus for cultural dialogue as it exposes sources of power and resistance and reveals values and beliefs that might otherwise be taken for granted. Moreover, organizational ethnography encourages us to look beyond the managerial and profitability aspects of organizations and toward a definition of the workplace as a community. Office parties, softball games, provocative e-mail, rumors, and jokes can reveal much about the nature of an organization as a community

While there are many ways to conduct interpretive research, the best studies capture the spirit and diversity of an organization's values and practices through evocative vocabulary or metaphor. For example, Van Maanen (1991) uses the metaphor of a "smile factory" in his cultural study of Disneyland. The image of smiles (friendly, fun, courteous) being manufactured (e.g., the products of a rigid assembly-line factory) establishes the tensions of a cultural dialogue between Disney management and Disney employees. By using this language, Van Maanen delineates the interplays of a staged performance: Employees are "members of a cast" who wear "costumes," not uniforms, and who exhibit onstage, offstage, and backstage behaviors. He also uses the image of the factory to discuss the production of smiles: formal rules about informal behaviors, and the prevalence of supervisory spies who note every infraction. The result is an account of a strong culture whose everyday use of language constructs a metaphor that, in turn, becomes its unique sense of place.

Culture can also provide a unique sense of *identity*. In Goodall's (2004) study of the culture of Ferrari owners on Long Island, New York, he discovered a strong culture of exotic car enthusiasts whose privileged way of life shaped and informed their unique understanding of themselves in relation to the marque. He also revealed how important acquisition and displays of Ferrari baseball caps, tee shirts, coffee mugs, and other items were to their perceived place in the elite social order of "Ferraristi." Finally, his study emphasized the vital role of coming together in fun-filled organized events, particularly car rallies, wherein the risk to their automobiles far outweighs the value of the trinkets they win.

Organizational culture is the result of the cumulative learning of a group of people. This learning manifests itself as culture at a number of levels. According to Edgar Schein (1991), culture is defined by six formal properties: (1) shared basic assumptions that are (2) invented, discovered, or developed by a given group as it (3) learns to cope with its problems of external adaptation and internal integration in ways that (4) have worked well enough to be considered valid and, therefore, (5) can be taught to new members of the group as the (6) correct way to perceive, think, and feel in relation to those problems.

☐ Social Trends

The economic environment in the United States after World War II also contributed to the popularity of the cultural approach to organizations in the Western nations. As sociologist Todd Gitlin (1987) explains,

> By 1945, the United States found itself an economic lord set far above the destroyed powers, its once and future competitors among both Allies and Axis powers. Inflation was negligible, so the increase in available dollars was actually buying more goods. Natural resources seemed plentiful, their supplies stable. . . . The Depression was over. And so were the deprivations of World War II, which also brought relative blessings: While European and Japanese factories were being pulverized, new American factories were being built and old ones were back at work, shrinking unemployment to relatively negligible proportions. Once the war was over, consumer demand was a dynamo. Science was mobilized by industry, and capital was channeled by government as never before. The boom was on, and the cornucopia seemed all the more impressive because the miseries of the Depression and war were near enough to suffuse the present with a sense of relief. (p. 13)

As Gitlin goes on to point out, these sources of renewal and promise were balanced by powerful threats of nuclear holocaust in an atomic age. The tension created by these opposing influences helped shape the values of the new generation. Social, ethnic, racial, political, sexual, and economic tensions contributed to the complexity of the post–World War II climate, as did the new role of science in society, industry, and ideology. Since the Enlightenment, science had delivered on its promise of creating a more progressive and rational society. In the twentieth century, however, science demonstrated a new ability to create weapons that could destroy humanity. Although industry (since the Industrial Revolution) had delivered the products and services that made life easier and more humane, it also sanctioned inequalities between women and men and among ethnic and racial groups, and fierce competition for scarce natural resources and commodity markets contributed to worldwide tension. Similarly, new communication technologies like radios, stereos, televisions, and satellites made information more accessible as well as more open to commentary. Ideological battles among capitalism, socialism, and communism threatened world peace and led to the Cold War.

The political landscape was changing as well. The mid-1960s are commonly referred to by anthropologists, historians, and literary critics as the end of Western colonialism; European countries like England were forced to give up their colonies in Africa and elsewhere (Greenblatt, 1990; Said, 1978, 1984). With the end of colonialism came a redefinition of the role of Western interests in the political and economic subordination of Third World countries (Bhabha, 1990; Clifford & Marcus, 1985; Marcus & Fischer, 1986; Minh-Ha, 1991).

New global economic and political concerns also increased critical scrutiny of organizations. The emergence of multinational firms and a world economy dominated by capitalism and dependent on cheap labor in Third World countries exposed global problems and inequities, and the management of cultural differences in the workplace became important to firms doing business in other countries. Finding ways to improve cross-cultural understandings and communication skills was an integral component of the cultural approach to organizational communication.

In this turbulent social environment, new questions about organizations addressed such topics as power, participation, domination, and resistance in the workplace. For example, men exerted power over women by defining "real work" as that which was done outside of the home (by men) and "housework" as less worthy of compensation or respect. Housework was not valued for its major contributions to the ideals of family and society. As a result, housework brought women less status than men received for performing "real work." Furthermore, when women began to assert their right to work outside of the home and to assume positions of responsibility in the workforce (in secretarial, food preparation, elementary school teaching, and custodial jobs), they encountered widespread opposition by men.

Similarly, in the 1950s to 1970s, members of minority groups posed serious challenges to the Anglo elite that had long controlled their access to equality (the civil rights movement in the United States being a well-known example). These groups included people whose racial, ethnic, or religious heritage distinguished them from the dominant white majority, people with physical and mental disabilities, people who had served in the armed forces, and the elderly. They protested against unfair social and professional practices, discrimination, and oppression.

The social climate in which cultural studies of organizations emerged, then, was characterized by increased participation, globalization, diversity, and resistance to domination on the part of minority groups. The popularity of the cultural approach was thus tied to its focus on cultural differences within an organization or a society.

WHAT WOULD YOU DO?

The Politics of Interpreting Culture

Ethnographers (Conquergood, 1991; Thomas, 1993) often ask the question, Who gets to speak for whom? In studies of organizations, this question targets fundamental communication problems: Who owns the right to speak for a company's culture? Do employees own that right, and if so, at what level is the correct interpretation of meaning found? At the senior executive level? Middle manager? Staff? Customer and supplier? Some combination of these levels? Or does the right to speak for the culture reside with academic researchers and other outsiders?

Within these issues lie many challenges to researchers. Every act of communication is partial, partisan, and problematic; this is true of interpretation as well. The issues also speak to an ethical challenge: What are the consequences of making statements about an organization's culture? This challenge often divides researchers into two ideological camps. On the left are those who assert that Marxist, feminist, and critical theories of the production and consumption of culture provide the appropriate frameworks for the interpretations of cultures and hence are unwilling to accept the authority of traditional texts. On the right are those who assert that leftist critiques about production and consumption fail to recognize the transcendent value and importance of philosophical and artistic texts that have stood the test of time

While this debate rages on campuses and in academic journals, organizations struggle to survive in the increasingly competitive global marketplace. Academic studies of organizational culture, particularly those derived from liberal sympathies, often seem unnecessarily tedious. Although we have learned that culture is important to the success of a business, seldom do these studies present clear findings that can be applied to all organizations. As a result, the gulf between academic and business interests has widened.

Let's assume that you are interested in conducting a cultural analysis of an organization. For the purposes of self-reflection, let's assume this organization is either a political party or a religious foundation.

DISCUSSION QUESTIONS

1. What ethical issues would you address? How would your ideological commitments shape your study?
2. Why do a cultural analysis of an organization? Who would benefit? Who would you speak for?
3. How has culture itself affected your style of seeing, observing, talking about, writing about, and thinking about cultural issues? What directs your critical attention to particular interpretations of meanings?

◩ THREE VIEWS OF ORGANIZATIONAL CULTURE

As we have shown, competitive pressure, interpretive methodology, and social concerns contributed to the rise of the cultural approach. These concerns are more specifically reflected in three broad perspectives — practical, interpretive, and critical and postmodern — that characterize culture studies in organizations today.

☐ A Practical View

The **practical view** responds to managers' desires for practical advice and specific communication strategies for enhanced competitiveness and increased employee satisfaction. From this perspective, culture is an organizational feature, like technology or management style, that can be leveraged by managers to create more effective organizations. Adherents believe that quasi-causal relationships can be created between cultural elements, like stories or rituals, and organizational outcomes, like employee commitment. Two successful books, both sponsored by the McKinsey Corporation (a management consulting firm), provided the foundation for this view. The first, Terrence Deal and Allan Kennedy's *Corporate Cultures: The Rites and Rituals of Corporate Life* (1982), defined the elements of strong cultures as (1) a supportive business environment, (2) dedication to a shared vision and values, (3) well-known corporate heroes, (4) effective rites and rituals, and (5) formal and informal communication networks. The other book, *In Search of Excellence: Lessons from America's Best-Run Corporations* (1982) by Thomas Peters and Robert Waterman Jr., made the *New York Times* bestseller list for nonfiction. Its authors studied sixty-two financially successful companies and found eight common characteristics of their cultures:

1. *A bias for action.* Top-performing companies are characterized by active decision making; they are not characterized by thinking about decisions for long periods of time or relying on a lot of information to make decisions. If a change occurs in the business environment, they act.
2. *Close relations to the customer.* Top-performing companies never forget who makes them successful: their customers. One of the basics of excellence is to remember that service, reliability, innovation, and a constant concern for the customer are vital to any organization.
3. *Autonomy and entrepreneurship.* Top-performing companies empower their employees by encouraging risk taking, responsibility for the decisions they make and the actions they perform, and innovation. If an organization is too tightly controlled and the worker's performance is too tightly monitored, initiative, creativity, and willingness to take responsibility all tend to decay.
4. *Productivity through people.* A quality product depends on quality workers throughout the organization. Good customer relations depend on valuing

service throughout the organization. Top-performing companies recognize these factors and rally against we/them or management/labor divisions.

5. *Hands-on, value-driven.* Top-performing companies are characterized by strong core values that are widely shared among employees and by an overall vision—a management philosophy—that guides everyday practices. Achievement is dependent on performance, and performance is dependent on values.

6. *Stick to the knitting.* Top-performing companies tend to be strictly focused on their source of product and service excellence. They tend not to diversify by going into other product or service fields. They expand their organization and profits by sticking to what they do best.

7. *Simple form, lean staff.* Top-performing companies are characterized by a lack of complicated hierarchies and divisions of labor. None of the companies surveyed maintained a typical bureaucratic form of organizing. Many of them employed fewer than one hundred people.

8. *Simultaneous loose-tight properties.* Top-performing companies are difficult to categorize. They encourage individual action and responsibility and yet retain strong core values; they encourage individual and group decision making. They are neither centralized nor decentralized in management style because they adapt to new situations with whatever is needed to get the job done.

Over two decades later, this list of qualities remains a good reference point for the analysis of organizational cultures. Since the publication of *In Search of Excellence*, Peters has gone on to refine his thinking in a series of books, placing even more emphasis on customers and the need to manage amidst chaos. An interesting aside is that some of the companies that made Peters and Waterman's initial list have had difficulty sustaining their success, partly because they misread market trends and partly because a value-based system is difficult to sustain over a long period of time.

More recently, management theorists Jim Collins and Jerry Porras (2002) suggest that an organization's longevity can be sustained by a culture that preserves its core purpose and values while remaining open to change and opportunity in a dynamic world. This type of corporation creates a strong, "cult-like" culture, characterized by:

- *Fervently held ideology.* Cult-like cultures explicitly articulate their overriding goals and values and ensure that employee behavior is guided and consistent with the ideology. Nordstrom's core ideology, for example, centers on customer service and employees are expected and empowered to provide stellar service.

- *Indoctrination.* Cultism requires that organizations instill their core ideology through orientation programs, training, company newsletters and other publications, corporate songs, organizationally specific language, and socialization by peers into the culture. At Disney, "cast members" are steeped in

Disney's history, special language, mythology, wholesome image, and core ideology.

- *Tightness of fit.* Cult-like cultures employ an extensive screening process to ensure that those hired fit with the culture. They also have very clear norms of behavior. Those who fit with the culture are attracted to it and supportive of it; those who do not fit with the culture are penalized and are "ejected like a virus" (p. 121).
- *Elitism.* Belonging, specialness, superiority, and secrecy are the hallmarks of cult-like cultures. The elitism at Procter & Gamble is reinforced by its secretive culture. Employees are prevented from discussing work in public or working on airplanes where other travelers may see company information. One stock option plan even stipulated that if an employee revealed "unauthorized information" about the company, his or her stock options would be revoked.

Cultures built on these principles can be seen as effective or "strong" because they reproduce the core ideology for their members to see, feel, and internalize in very concrete, explicit, and purposeful ways. In all the examples above, culture is "a rational instrument designed by top management to shape the behavior of the employees in purposive ways" (Ouchi & Wilkins, 1985, p. 462). PepsiCo, Hyatt, McDonald's, Microsoft, and Disney, for example, are noted for their strong corporate cultures. Each invests tens of millions of dollars annually in the selection and indoctrination of employees into their company's way of doing things. Companies with strong corporate cultures tend to encourage a strong sense of commitment among their employees. However, such companies may require employees to give up significant freedoms (even in the area of personal appearance) in exchange for membership.

Strong corporate cultures can lead to positive or negative consequences for employees and other stakeholders. For example, many successful companies today are in the process of replacing top-down management processes with management that is driven by a vision of the future and a set of corporate values. Under this scenario, leadership's main role is to help employees understand and work according to the organization's vision and values (Deetz, Tracy, & Simpson, 2000; Eisenberg & Riley, 2001). When this approach succeeds, the result is an organizational culture characterized by attention to process improvement as well as employees' supervision of their own behavior. In a multisite study relating corporate culture to performance, John Kotter and James Heskett (1992) found that value consensus can enhance organizational performance, but only under the following circumstances:

1. When people agree on the importance of adapting to a changing environment (i.e., continuous learning or improvement);
2. When a strong entrepreneur is present who also adapts well to change; and
3. When an effective business strategy is in place to supplement the organization's vision and values.

Of course, left unchecked, strong or cult-like cultures can become dangerous and dysfunctional. Indeed, the indoctrination practices of terrorist and other ethically questionable groups look very similar to those outlined by Collins and Porrass (Arena & Arrigo, 2005). A worst-case scenario is a company culture that supports unethical behavior. The following kinds of cultures are most likely to encourage questionable ethical practices:

1. A culture of broken promises
2. A culture where no one takes responsibility
3. A culture that denies participation and dissent

In 2002 the dramatic implications of questionable ethical practices within one well-known corporate culture—Enron—provided many people with new doubts about the benefits of working in a strong culture. In what was widely reported as a business culture of "cockiness and arrogance" that thrived on acute competitiveness among employees and intense aggressiveness in the marketplace, meteoric success quickly turned into dramatic failure (Sloan, 2002). Enron, a Houston-based natural gas and electricity company, boasted stocks valued at $84.87/share in December of 2000. The sign greeting visitors at the corporate headquarters welcomed newcomers to the "world's leading company," leaving no one in doubt of Enron's corporate culture. Less than one year later, the company found itself with shares trading for less than $1/share. The question quickly became: How did this happen? Soon, news reports of questionable or illegal accounting practices, dishonest communication with stockholders and customers, and insider loans to employees holding the highest positions in the company provided striking evidence of what can go wrong when the shared cultural values that help make a company strong cross moral, ethical, and legal boundaries.

Enron's collapse was not suffered in isolation, however, as corporate cultures around the globe came under scrutiny. New ethical questions regarding the need for corporations to keep their promises to employees, customers, and stockholders—as well as the moral climate informing accounting practices, and the role of employee voice and dissent—began to arise. Careful consideration of these questions has contributed to criminal indictments for executive officers of other large, publicly traded companies as well as major revisions to the codes of conduct guiding corporations and their boards. A new federal law now requires the signature of the CEO on all annual financial reports, which, for those who study organizational cultures, is a potent legal symbol that must be read as an important cultural sign.

Despite sustained criticism of the practical view as too controlling and reminiscent of Theory X, it continues to have currency in contemporary organizations and has brought certain benefits such as introducing a useful vocabulary for directing managers' attention toward communication practices and the human side of business (Alvesson, 1993; Smircich & Calas, 1987).

☐ An Interpretive View

While the practical assumption that culture can simply be imposed from above or engineered by well-meaning managers may be appealing to organizational leaders, interpretive organizational scholars believe that culture is too complex, holistic, and pervasive to be managed or controlled by any single individual or management team. Those who subscribe to an **interpretive view** treat culture as a process that is socially constructed in everyday communicative behaviors among all members of the organization and "find it ridiculous to talk of managing culture. Culture cannot be managed; it emerges. Leaders don't create cultures; members of the culture do" (Martin, 1985, p. 95).

From this perspective, culture is believed to emerge in the symbolism or discourse of everyday organizational life (Fairhurst & Putnam, 2004). Where the practical view was primarily interested in the meanings of such things as corporate logos and value statements, interpretive scholars focus on a broader view of symbolism in organizations. This interpretive view focuses on the subtle ways in which communication works to build, reproduce, and transform the taken-for-granted reality of organizational culture. How people dress, the stories that they tell repeatedly, the layout of offices and parking areas, the design of security badges and the length and tenor of staff meetings each communicate richly about an organization's unique culture. Research taking this perspective can be traced to a group of management and communication scholars who first met in Alta, Utah, in 1983. Organized by Linda Putnam and Michael Pacanowsky, this conference and a resulting edited book (*Communication and Organizations: An Interpretive Approach*, Putnam & Pacanowsky, 1983) helped legitimize interpretive and cultural studies of organizational communication. Around the same time, an influential article by Pacanowsky and Nick O'Donnell-Trujillo (1983) helped establish organizational communication as a form of cultural performance.

Some writers have argued that organizations are mainly storytelling systems (Boje, 1991, 1995). The stories or narratives about the organization's culture convey information about its current state of affairs, and as such the stories serve as resources for everyday sense making (Wilkins, 1984). As noted in Chapter 4, when an organization is viewed as a system — in this case, a storytelling system — modifications represent feedback. Paying attention to stories and how they change can be important for employees and managers alike (Mitroff & Kilmann, 1975).

Organizational stories may be found in speeches and casual conversations, as well as in employee newsletters, company brochures, strategic planning statements, corporate advertisements, fund-raising campaigns, and training videos (Goodall, 1989; Pacanowsky, 1988; Smith & Keyton, 2001). These forums provide opportunities for the organization to talk about its values and aspirations. However, different stories about the organization are told by different narrators. The corporate or official story about the organization may be told by advertising agents working in conjunction with high-level managers and stockholders. The inside stories are told by employees of the organization, who may offer different accounts. In two recent investigations into the working conditions of fruit pickers and employees of manufacturing plants in the Carolinas, the accounts given by the business owners and managers differed greatly from the accounts given by the employees. The story told by the owners and managers focused on the number of people employed by the companies, product quality, and reasonable cost to consumers. In contrast, the story told by employees focused on low wages (sometimes paid in the form of crack cocaine or alcohol) and unsafe workplaces.

Clearly, organizational stories represent the interests and values of the storytellers. In the preceding example, neither side's narrative captured the whole story. Usually, multiple stories or interpretations are needed to describe an organization's culture. These stories represent different voices as well as potential dialogues among individuals and groups within the organization. Therefore, we can think of an organization's culture as a potential dialogue of subcultures or as a many-sided story (Boje, 1995).

The interpretive approach to understanding culture has shifted our focus toward how people communicate and create meaning in dialogue. However, symbolic displays must be considered in practical contexts, not as isolated events. Just as a joke, a story, choice of words, or a ritual can be misleading out of context, symbols should be studied in ways that link them to the realities of work (Alvesson, 1993). In so doing, this view of culture gives us access to the social construction of meaning as well as its consequences.

As a case in point, in 1993, Gideon Kunda published an interpretive ethnographic study on the power relationships affecting workers' lives in a high-tech engineering firm that challenges many of the practical assumptions about corporate culture earlier identified by Peters and Waterman (1982). From interviews, observations, and a close reading of the culture's everyday activities, Kunda concludes that the control and commitment features of strong cultures are the most problematic. Specifically, leadership's attempt to "engineer culture" to look a certain way are flawed. Over time, workers may come to question the authenticity of any emotions and beliefs associated with company slogans and proclamations. Moreover, workers may learn the lessons of strong cultural performances so well that they seem driven to make irony "the dominant mode of their everyday existence" (Kunda, 1993, p. 216). In such an organization, employee talk is uniformly cynical and sarcastic, reflecting a deep discomfort with commitment to the "party line" that is continually pushed and endorsed by the organization. This has happened to a degree in the way some Disney employees talk about their "loyalty" to "the mouse." Kunda's interpretive study is valuable because it offers balance to what can at times seem to be a one-sided conversation about the benefits of a strong culture.

In his study, Kunda also describes the time-consuming, iterative process he used to both study and "write up" the culture. He makes clear that as symbols or texts, cultures can be interpreted in many different ways and, thus, there are often many potential tales to be told about the same culture (Van Maanen, 1988). Interpretive scholars are particularly interested in the form their studies take because they believe that the "tale" or the telling is as important as the culture it represents (Goodall, 2000). A recent volume, edited by Robin Patric Clair (2003), highlights the "novel" approaches to ethnography that interpretive scholars employ to bring organizational cultures to life on the page. Authors describe, in artful detail, how social and organizational cultures impact the birthing process and the stories mothers are able to narrate about their experience of childbirth, how corrections officers manage the dilemmas that characterize their everyday work worlds, and even how an organizational site, Comiskey Park, provided a context for and shaped a family's relationships (Krizek, 2003; Tracy, 2003; Turner, 2003). These cultural tales offer their readers new, engaging, and meaningful ways of "studying and speaking about culture" and, in turn, our lives (Goodall, 2003, p. 63).

Though interpretive studies provide insightful accounts, some have been critiqued for failing to adequately explore the power dimensions of organizational cultures, to address the relationship between the larger social context and the particular culture in question, and to offer prescriptive guidelines for improving cultural performance or facilitating change. Critical and postmodern scholars take up these criticisms directly.

☐ Critical and Postmodern Views

Research on organizational culture has moved significantly in the direction of the **critical and postmodern views**, each of which focus on challenges to power relationships and the status quo (which is why Chapters 6 and 7 are devoted to more detailed discussions of these topics). Two researchers who have made significant contributions to this line of work are Stanley Deetz and Joanne Martin.

Deetz and others (Atkouf, 1992; Smircich & Calas, 1987) argue that the managerial bias in culture research reinforces the "corporate colonization of the lifeworld" through which the interests of corporations frame all aspects of daily living for their employees (Deetz, 1991, 1995). These critics call for organizational ethnographers to examine issues of power and domination associated with the development, maintenance, or transformation of a particular culture. To do so, critics must expose how cultural elements, including stories, rituals, jokes, and mission statements, function to support and reproduce the power structure that privileges the interests of dominant organizational groups over others. Specifically, critics must reveal the cultural processes through which one particular and privileged social construction of reality comes to hold sway over other equally plausible constructions—that is, how the party line gets established and why it is accepted by employees (Mumby, 1987). Further, they believe the transcripts chronicling the lives of those with less power in organizations should be exposed and read, so that alternatives to the dominant culture can be considered.

Communication scholar Joanne Martin has developed a taxonomy of perspectives on organizational culture that takes into account the movement toward a postmodern view. According to Martin (1992), perspectives on culture can be characterized as highlighting integration, differentiation, or fragmentation. Although studies of organizations typically take one perspective, most organizations contain all three. Each perspective reveals a different orientation to three key features of cultural study: orientation to consensus, relations among divergent manifestations, and orientation to ambiguity. Let us consider each perspective in detail.

Integration

The **integration** perspective portrays culture in terms of consistency and clarity. From this perspective, it appears that cultural members agree about what they are to do and why they do it. There appears to be no room for ambiguity. In addition, an organization's culture is portrayed as a monologue, not a dialogue (May, 1988). This tradition in the cultural study of organizations is evident in Tom Peters and Robert Waterman's (1982) descriptions of excellent companies with strong cultures that adhere to a narrow set of shared values, meanings, and interpretations. Similarly, studies that analyze the influence of the organization's founder tend to trace those influences throughout the organization (Barley, 1983; Pacanowsky, 1988; Schein, 1991), sometimes to the neglect of competing values within the company (McDonald, 1988). Indeed, the integration perspective typically favors the story of those in power over other competing stories.

Differentiation

Whereas an integration perspective focuses on agreement, a differentiation perspective highlights differences. The **differentiation** perspective portrays cultural manifestations as predominantly inconsistent with one another (such as when the responsible party on an organizational chart is different from the person whom "everyone knows" is in charge). Furthermore, when consensus does emerge, the differentiation view is quick to point out its limitations (e.g., that agreement may only exist among a group or subculture of members). From the standpoint of the total organization, differentiated subcultures can coexist in harmony, conflict, or indifference to one another. These subcultures are viewed as islands of clarity, and ambiguity is channeled outside of their boundaries (Frost, Moore, Louis, Lundberg, & Martin, 1991).

In addition, the differentiation perspective sees organizational cultures as contested political domains in which the potential for genuine dialogue is often impaired. The various subcultures may seldom speak to one another, instead reinforcing their own accounts of organizational meanings without seeking external validation. As a result, they do not actively participate in the broader interests of the organization.

For example, one study revealed that a computer software firm had created barriers to its subcultures' communication when it moved to a new location (Goodall, 1990). Work groups were physically separated from one another, promoting competition for resources among them. In another study, a conflict between managers and employees over a pay freeze was masked at an annual breakfast by a group of speakers hired to create a story that favored management's position (Rosen, 1985). The ploy was unsuccessful and deepened the division between the two groups. Divisions among classes of employees often occupy the interests of subcultures, and the differentiation perspective can show how conflict among subcultures may be avoided, masked, or neglected.

Fragmentation

From a **fragmentation** perspective, ambiguity is an inevitable and pervasive aspect of contemporary life. Studies in this area focus on the experience and expression of ambiguity within organizational cultures, wherein consensus and dissensus coexist in a constantly fluctuating pattern of change. Any cultural manifestation can be interpreted in a myriad of ways because clear consensus among organizational subcultures cannot be attained.

Consistent with newer theories of organizations and society (see Chapter 7), the fragmentation perspective replaces certainty with ambiguity, contradiction, tension, and irony as models for interpretation. Furthermore, ambiguity can be manipulated by management to support management's interests and by disempowered employees to cope with their interests (Ashcraft & Trethewey, 2004; Eisenberg, 1984; Harter, 2004; Myerson, 1991; Stohl & Cheney, 2001; Trethewey, 1999). Researchers have applied ambiguity to organizational communication in a variety of ways. For example, it has been used to explain the divergent accounts of an airline disaster given by eyewitnesses (Weick, 1990) and the ways in which farmers in Nebraska negotiate their simultaneous but competing needs for rugged independence and collective interdependence and survival (Harter, 2004).

The meaning of ambiguity for our concept of organizational cultures as dialogue depends on how we define dialogue. If dialogue is viewed as a means of generating consensus, then ambiguity makes dialogue unlikely. Conversely, if dialogue is thought of as embodying a respect for diversity—and perhaps a form of consensus based on acknowledgment of differences—then ambiguity is a necessary component of dialogue. Furthermore, unlike ambiguity about shared meanings or interpretations of culture, multiple meanings are inevitably found in ambiguities about shared practices. Recall that in the interpretive perspective, shared practices and multiple interpretations of meaning for those practices are highly valued. For us, then, ambiguity is a necessary component of dialogue. Indeed, genuine dialogue probably would not exist without ambiguity, for if everything were clearly understood, there would not be much left to talk about (Boje, 1995).

An ethnography focusing on how one university selected its chief academic officer shows the usefulness of Joanne Martin's taxonomy (Eisenberg, Murphy, & Andrews, 1998). In this year-long study, various interpretations of the university's search process were offered by both participants and the researchers, and these accounts are shown to reflect all three of Martin's perspectives. Some saw the search process as highly rational, with the choice of the leading candidate an inevitable result. Others described the process as highly political; still others saw it as rife with ambiguity and confusion from the outset. A traditional researcher might ask, "Who is right?" The authors chose instead to describe the ways in which participants selected their interpretation with their audience in mind and felt free to offer differing interpretations at different occasions. They concluded that using all three perspectives provided a richer view of the search process than any one taken alone.

◪ RECENT TRENDS IN ORGANIZATIONAL CULTURE RESEARCH

The culture approach to organization has been applied in two interesting lines of research in communication. The first centers on organizational socialization, or the process of assimilating members into an organization's culture. The second focuses on the material impact of organizational cultures on members' bodies.

☐ Socialization: Integrating New Members into Organizational Cultures

A cultural approach acknowledges that transitioning new members into the organization requires much more than simply providing necessary task information. Successful socialization demands that organizations help new members feel integrated into the culture. "Workers who remain apart from the prevailing culture rather than becoming a part of it are unlikely to be as effective or as satisfied with the job as they could be" (Hess, 1993). **Socialization** is a process by which people learn the rules, norms, and expectations of a culture over time and thereby become members of that culture. We are all, to some extent, assimilated into a national and local culture. As children, we were taught by parents and others how to become members of a family, community, religion, or country. Thus, socialization involves learning the rules that guide what members of a culture think, do, and say. Socialization of members is essential in any culture and begins at an early age. For example, in the United States, children learn much about American culture during dinnertime conversations with family members (Ochs, Smith, & Taylor, 1989).

In organizations, describing the socialization process helps us understand how the new employee learns about and makes sense of the organization's culture (Jablin, 1987; Kramer & Miller, 1999). Although the employee's first week on the job is filled with surprises, over time the employee learns the formal and informal rules that govern behavior in the organization. This learning process has three broad stages: (1) anticipatory socialization, (2) organizational assimilation, and (3) organizational turning points or exits.

Anticipatory Socialization

Some of the lessons about the nature of work are learned long before the job begins. In the **anticipatory socialization** stage, people learn about work through communication. There are two forms of anticipatory socialization: vocational and organizational. The vocational type, which begins in childhood, involves learning about work and careers in general from family members, teachers, part-time employers, friends, and the media. Children and adolescents acquire a general knowledge of accepted attitudes toward work, of the importance of power and status in organizations, and of work as a source of meaningful personal relationships (Atwood, 1990; Gibson & Papa, 2000; Jablin, 1985).

Later in life, the organizational type of anticipatory socialization involves learning about a specific job and organization. It takes place before the first day of work and is typically accomplished through company literature, such as brochures, personnel manuals, and Web sites, as well as through interactions between job applicants and interviewers. Through such communication, individuals develop expectations about the prospective job and organization. However, their expectations are often inflated and unrealistic due to interviewers' tendency to focus on positive aspects of the job and the company. In fact, because job interviews typically result in more information for the prospective employer than for the prospective employee, some researchers (Wilson & Goodall, 1991) advocate changing the nature of the interview to more closely reflect the model of dialogue discussed in Chapter 2 (Defining Organizational Communication).

Organizational Assimilation

The experience of **organizational assimilation** involves both surprise and sense making (Louis, 1980). As new employees' initial expectations are violated, they attempt to make sense of their job and the organization. "The newcomer learns the requirements of his or her role and what the organization and its members consider to be 'normal' patterns of behavior and thought" (Jablin, 1987, p. 695).

For example, it is common for presidents and CEOs of companies to attend orientations for new employees and to deliver the message that their "door is always open" to employees who want to talk. In most cases, the employees who take this seriously are surprised by the likely reality that the president or CEO is either unavailable or unhelpful or that such conversations are not much appreciated by line and middle managers. After a few weeks, these employees come to make sense of "how things really work around here."

Newcomers' search for information carries a sense of urgency. Typically, new employees have some difficulty performing their jobs and getting along with others until they reach a level of familiarity. Potential sources of useful information for newcomers include (1) official company messages (e.g., from management, orientation programs, and manuals), (2) co-workers and peers, (3) supervisors, (4) other organizational members, including administrative assistants, security guards, and employees in other departments, (5) customers and others outside of the organization, and (6) the employee's assigned tasks. Newcomers thus attempt to "situate" themselves in an unfamiliar organizational context, but to do so they must first learn a great deal about how existing members define the organization's culture. To solicit the information they need, new employees tend not to rely on direct questioning because substantial risks may be associated with asking irrelevant questions. Instead, they use other tactics to solicit information about the organizational culture (Miller & Jablin, 1991; see Table 5.2). One of the more interesting tactics, "disguising conversations," involves making jokes about people, procedures, or activities and watching to see whether others think they're funny.

Over time, employees may evolve from newcomer status into full-fledged members of the organization (Jablin, 1987). This period of transition may or may not be lengthy, depending on the organization and the industry involved. In hotels and restaurants, for example, employees may feel like old-timers after only six months on the job, whereas in universities and professional associations, the transitional period may last nearly a decade. Of course, not everyone makes the transition to member. If there is a poor fit, either the organization or the individual may opt out of the relationship. Moreover, the assimilation process is rarely as neat as these "stages" make it sound; large organizations in particular often make room for numerous diverse voices and definitions of membership (Bullis, 1999).

During the transitional period of organizational assimilation, employees begin to differentiate between rules and norms that must be followed and those that can be ignored. Feeling more comfortable with the rules of the organization, employees begin to individualize their job, develop their own voice, and behave in ways

TABLE 5.2

Newcomer's Information-Seeking Tactics

TACTIC EXAMPLE

- Overt question: "Who has the authority to cancel purchase orders?"
- Indirect question: "I guess I won't plan to take a vacation this year." (Implied: "Do we work through the holidays if we don't finish the project?")
- Third parties: (To a co-worker) "I'm making a presentation to the president. Does she like it if you open with a joke?"
- Testing limits: Arriving at work wearing casual clothes and observing others' reactions.
- Disguising conversations: "That safety memo was sure a riot. Can you believe the gall of those guys?" (Waiting for reaction to see whether others also think it was funny.)
- Observing: Watching which employees get praised in meetings and emulating those who do, paying attention to specific individuals.
- Surveillance: Eavesdropping on peer conversations; paying careful attention at office parties; monitoring the environment for clues.

that both conform to and transform the existing rules. For example, a new supervisor who makes minor changes in how work is delegated distinguishes his or her department from others in the organization. Whereas newcomer behavior focuses on discovering constraints, the transition toward assimilation is marked by a greater degree of creativity. The degree of balance between the two—and of the employee's satisfaction with his or her role in the organization—largely determines patterns of cooperation, resistance, and exit.

Organizational Turning Points

In the course of one's engagement with an organization, much can happen that significantly changes the relationship. Research on organizational assimilation sometimes focuses on these critical moments, which have been called **turning points** (Bullis & Bach, 1989). Consider your experience as a student. The turning points in your experience probably include identifying with your college or university and its organizations or teams as well as choosing your major area of study. Together with other moments (some more positive than others), these turning points in your experience as a student have permanently altered your understanding and interpretation of the school and your membership in it. For example, you probably know students who are wholehearted supporters of your school's programs and teams and others who openly express more negative attitudes toward your college or university. In the same sense, employees come to understand their role in their place of work through organizational turning points. Examples might include receiving a favorable performance review, getting a long-awaited promotion, participating in genuine dialogue, or being unfairly criticized by a supervisor.

In addition to altering employees' perceptions of identification with the company, turning points can structure perceptions of career choices, job transfers, and even one's purpose in life. Turning points can change a person's life, influencing how the person sets goals, determines career paths, and makes the connection between work life and one's life course more generally (Fox, 1994). In the next section, we'll see how organizational turning points in high-reliability organizations, such as graduating from the training academy or receiving symbols of acceptance, are significant milestones in members' socialization.

Socialization and High-Reliability Organizations

Successful socialization efforts can serve as a means of reproducing and reinforcing an organization's culture. In **high-reliability organizations (HROs),** such as nuclear reactors or air traffic control towers, members continually operate in dangerous conditions where even a small misstep can lead to disaster. HROs avoid catastrophe by adhering to meticulously planned and coordinated safety rules and cultures, hence successful socialization can literally mean the difference between life and death. In practice, this means a combination of technical training and interpersonal tests to ensure a newcomer's trustworthiness (Myers, 2005).

Myers' (2005) study revealed how one HRO, a large metropolitan fire department, emphasized its cultural values of trust and member reliability through its extensive socialization programs in two ways. First, the fire department made membership contingent on a rigorous anticipatory socialization process. Second, the culture required new members to adopt a specific role, "the humble boot," before they were finally accepted and integrated into the culture. Long before new firefighters enter their fire stations as probationary firefighters, they are required to demonstrate their commitment to firefighting. There are formal hurdles the potential recruit must overcome before he or she can enter the twelve-week training academy. Candidates must pass a comprehensive exam on firefighting and rescue knowledge as well as physical endurance tests. Then they must successfully navigate two rounds of interviews where they are asked pointed questions about how they will "fit" in the organization's culture. Of course, successful responses require candidates to familiarize themselves with the culture by spending time in fire stations and performing ride-alongs on fire trucks. Many candidates supplement their direct knowledge of the culture through indirect knowledge obtained from family members—up to 70 percent of new recruits have relatives or close friends who are firefighters. Of the forty-five hundred candidates who apply each year, only the forty to fifty who demonstrate their commitment to and compatibility with the culture are invited to participate in the training academy.

Once the recruits graduate from the rigorous training academy, they become, in the language of the culture, "blue shirts." Even though they are able to wear the coveted "blue shirts" that symbolize their movement from recruit to firefighter, they must still spend their first year proving themselves as "booters" at the station. The "humble boots" are expected to continually demonstrate a good work ethic, be the last ones to sit down to eat and the first to get up to clean, speak only when spoken to, earn a good reputation, have a good attitude, haul equipment, all showing deference to senior members. These behaviors, enacted at the fire station and explicitly included in socialization efforts, lead more seasoned members to trust the booters in the context of a life-threatening fire. In this way, HRO culture, one based on trust, is reinforced and upheld. Some scholars argue that organizations can exert significant control over their members through socialization. Although the control and high degree of member conformity may be productive for some organizations and occupations, it may be counterproductive in others (Gibson & Papas, 2000).

Socialization and Technology

The intensive efforts to socialize firefighters into HROs result in a family-like culture of trust and a clear and shared understanding of the nature of the organizational rules and ropes. The socialization process that works for the fire department is not likely to work for virtual organizations (whose employees are dispersed geographically and rely on communication technology to stay connected) or those that hire contract or temporary workers. The nature of the workplace is changing, and socialization efforts have to keep pace. According to Flanagin and Waldeck (2004), **advanced communication and information technologies (ACITs)** such as Web pages, intranets, chat groups, instant messaging, PDAs, videoconferencing, on-line databases, and electronic bulletin boards impact socialization processes in two important ways. First, they offer potential and new employees a greater variety of channels to seek information about and communicate with organizations and their members. Second, the move toward virtual organizing means that new members may have fewer opportunities to engage in more traditional forms of socialization, including face-to-face meetings and orientation programs and casual conversations with peers.

Understanding the role that new communication technologies play in socializing new members is particularly important in traditional contexts, but is also useful in organizations that use ACITs. One consistent finding across studies of organizational socialization is that newcomers are rarely satisfied with the amount of information they receive during socialization. According to Flanagin and Waldeck (2004), "the increased use of communication and information technologies may expand opportunities for individuals to obtain information that may contribute to successful socialization" (p. 141). Indeed, a thorough review of an organization's Web site may help potential recruits to self-select such that the organization will save time and money in recruitment and retention costs.

Of course, not all cultural information is amenable to transmission via electronic media. Information about "acceptable" but informal standards, practices, and values of a particular culture may be impossible to convey over mediated channels. In fact, a recent study by Waldeck, Seibold, and Flanigan (2004) found that the most important predictor of effective socialization is still face-to-face communication, and the least important predictor is traditional technologies, including handbooks, other written materials, or telephone conversations. Advanced communication technologies still fall between face-to-face communication and traditional channels in terms of their effectiveness in helping new members to assimilate into their new organizational cultures. This finding highlights the "growing acceptance and reliance on more advanced technologies in the workplace" (p. 177).

The 2004 study by Waldeck and her colleagues revealed that members are likely to use technology when they perceive their communication tasks to be relatively complex and ambiguous or when interpersonal interaction cues are required. This study has several practical implications for organizations hoping to use technology effectively as a socialization tool. First, many employees are more comfortable learning about their new culture in the context of ACITs rather than from more traditional media like handbooks or memos. Second, organizations should match the complexity of the new members' communication tasks with an appropriate technology. Relatively simple tasks such as asking questions, staying in touch with

Socialization, Technology, and University Students

When we were applying to colleges, universities would stuff our mailboxes with letters, postcards, and glossy view books in the hopes that we would take the time to visit their campuses and even apply for admission. All of these advertising pieces contained the essentially the same information: accolades about the university's academics, details on the assorted types of student organizations that awaited us, and beautiful photographs of students laughing on their way to class or some fabulous activity. We would look at these photographs and wonder: Would we fit in at University X?

The days of such mailers as the university's primary way of communicating with students are long gone. The vast majority of schools have invested an incredible amount of time and money to develop elaborate Web sites that offer every possible detail about the school—from class offerings and dorm policies to professor profiles and drop-in tutoring hours. But how do universities go about crafting messages that are compelling to students and that present "the best" of the school now that they are not restricted to the page count of the view book? How does a college's Web site send a message about the school's culture and the potential student's likelihood to fit in? Let's take a look at two very successful, but very different, American universities, Yale and NYU, to see what the content and appearance of their Web sites reveal to students, as well as what messages the sites attempt to send about the culture of the university.

At the time of this writing (March 2006) the Yale University home page <www.yale.edu> presents us with an uncluttered, elegant background that highlights a single image: The Yale University shield. The surrounding text reminds us that the shield "recalls the University's origins in 1701 as a school 'wherein Youth may be instructed in the Arts & Sciences . . . [and] fitted for Publick employment both in Church & Civil State'" (Yale, 2006). A brief look through the links available on the site highlight not only student life and academics, but also Yale's history as one of our country's oldest institutions of higher learning. The home page for NYU also highlights the university's research, academics, and history, but none of these topics stand out as much as the vibrant images of the university's New York City setting. The surrounding text reminds us that New York is the city that never sleeps—a dizzying array of activities awaits NYU students, from lectures, art exhibits, and dance recitals to poetry readings and book signings. And that's just on a Tuesday!

Consider what you have read about the ways that organizations utilize advanced communication and information technologies to create messages and disseminate information and respond to the following questions.

DISCUSSION QUESTIONS

1. What does each of these home pages suggest about the image each institution is trying to promote? What clues do they give you about the likely culture at the university? How would you describe the mission of each school judging solely by its Web presence?

2. Think back to your experiences browsing through university Web sites as you were deciding where to apply to college. How did your university's efforts to recruit you as a new student through Web pages, e-mail correspondence, and other communication technologies influence your decision to enroll? What was it about your university's culture, as expressed through their Web presence, that led you to believe that you would be a good "fit" for the school and vice versa?

3. After you enrolled at your university, did you find that the culture and values of the school matched what was presented on the institution's Web site? Do you believe that your university makes adequate and accurate use of advanced technology for socializing new students into the culture?

other members, or exchanging information can be handled effectively with traditional media (e.g., phone calls or e-mail exchanges). Complex and ambiguous tasks including exchanging confidential information, negotiating or bargaining, getting to know someone, generating ideas, resolving disagreements, or making decisions more likely require face-to-face conversations or the use of advanced communication and information technologies. Over the next several years, we are likely to witness the increasingly central role technology will play in new members' socialization experiences because technology is an important component of an organization's culture.

☐ The Material Consequences of Organizational Cultures

Organizational culture is often assumed to influence the "hearts and minds" of employees by influencing their values, attitudes, and behaviors. In addition to these ideational effects, cultures also have material or "flesh and blood" consequences for their members. Some organizational scholars are beginning to examine how organizational cultures impact members' bodies (Murphy, 1998; Scott, 2005; Trethewey, 2000).

Organizational cultures influence how members understand themselves, their organizations, and their place within those organizations, but they also literally shape members' bodies in a variety of ways. Consider the lengths that exotic dancers go to ensure that their bodies conform to cultural norms of beauty. In one club, strippers found that the "Barbie Doll" look received the most attention and financial rewards from the (mostly) male customers. That look, characterized by a thin, lithe body, large breasts, blonde hair and light skin, is one that strippers go to great lengths to achieve. In an effort to succeed in and fit into the organizational culture, they often "manage" their weight through the use of addictive or illegal drugs, liposuction, and/or obsessive exercising. Dancers also used plastic surgery to "enhance" their bodies (Wesely, 2003). While exotic dancers may appear to embody an extreme form of femininity, as demanded by their organizational lives, women employed in professional occupations in corporate cultures routinely practice similar strategies. As Murphy (2003) argues, the jobs of professional women do not "have to require them to take their clothes off for them to feel that to be successful they must shape and discipline their bodies toward a prescribed feminine image" (p. 309).

In fact, Trethewey's (1999) research on professional women reveals that cultural expectations influence how women experience, manage, and control their own bodies. For women, demonstrating their fit within a professional culture often means inhabiting a "fit" body. As one health-care professional explains, in order to be successful, "You have to be fit—physically and emotionally—and that gives you the ability to be more productive, more efficient and more in control" (p. 436). In addition, professional women take great care to reveal only culturally appropriate nonverbal signs through their bodies. In the context of corporate culture, women often fear that their bodies may give signs they did not intend, thus compromising their image. Female bodies are often experienced as a professional liability because they may, at any moment, inadvertently reveal a woman's:

- Sexuality—through revealing or tight-fitting clothing
- Fertility—through pregnancy, menstruation, or lactation
- Emotionality—through tears

As they are currently constructed, many organizational cultures do not value these feminine markers. As a result, women often try to "keep the body in check, to prevent leaks," and to control their bodies in line with cultural dictates. And as one participant noted, "'It's a hard line to find,' and it is up to the individual woman to find it" (Trethewey, 1999, p. 433). Critical theorists would remind us that it is not women's bodies that are the problem in professional contexts; rather, it is constructed meanings for those bodies that are problematic.

Members of historically underrepresented groups in professional cultures may find "fitting" in to be particularly difficult and complex in dominant culture organizations. Seemingly simple decisions take on heightened importance — for example, how to style one's hair. As a young African American woman looking to succeed in a dominant culture organization, communication professor Regina Spellers (1998) felt her hair was "read" as symbol by others. A permed, short bob was a style in keeping with the dominant views of professionalism, but required a significant investment of time. Braids offered her an easy to maintain hairdo, but other African American women discouraged her from that style as it had the potential to be read as "unprofessional/too ethnic/too Black" (p. 56). Her experience reminds us that organizational members must consciously balance their own desires to be true to themselves with the constraints of their local organizational cultures.

▨ A COMMUNICATION PERSPECTIVE ON ORGANIZATIONAL CULTURE

Reviewing the body of research on organizational culture is a tantalizing and confusing task. Just about anything is regarded as culture, and studies purporting to study culture do so in dramatically different ways. As a result, no consistent treatment of communication has emerged in the culture literature.

For this reason, we propose a perspective in which theories of organizational culture have the following characteristics:

1. They view communication as the core process by which culture is formed and transformed and see culture as patterns of behavior and their interpretation.
2. They acknowledge the importance of everyday communication as well as more notable symbolic expressions.
3. They encompass not only words and actions, but also all types of nonverbal communication (such as machinery, artifacts, and work processes).
4. They include broad patterns of interaction in society at large and examine how they are played out in the workplace. Therefore, they view each organization's culture as a cultural nexus of national, local, familial, and other forces outside of the organization (Martin, 1992).
5. They acknowledge the legitimacy of multiple motives for researching culture, from improving corporate performance to overthrowing existing power structures.

SUMMARY

Cultural approaches bring the symbolic life of organizations to the forefront. Organizational cultures are constructed through language, everyday practices, and members' meaning making. Several cultural elements combine to create an organization's unique sense of place, including metaphors, stories, rituals, artifacts, heroes and heroines, performances, and values.

The focus on culture, and its constitutive elements, developed in response to three trends. First, competitive pressures from Japanese companies who were thought to have mastered building strong and responsive organizations through developing strong and unified cultures provided a model for many American corporations. Second, the increased use and acceptance of ethnographic and interpretive methods among communication scholars created a critical mass of research that sought to better understand members' cultural experiences. Third, the social climate that was beginning to value participation and diversity and recasting work as a more meaningful experience looked to culture as a vehicle for such change.

Three broad approaches characterize the study and practice of organizational culture. The practical view treats cultural elements as tools managers leverage to build more effective organizations or "cult-like" cultures. Using ethnographic methods, the goal of the interpretive view is to develop richer understandings of how cultures emerge through the everyday interactions of all organizational members, not just managers or leaders. Finally, critical and postmodern approaches unpack the power and politics that underlie organizational cultures and recognize that cultures are not always integrated, but can be differentiated and fragmented.

Recent scholarship in organizational culture highlights the importance of socializing new members into ongoing cultures through face-to-face and, increasingly, computer-mediated communication. Effective socialization, as a cultural practice, has been found to be particularly important for high-reliability organizations that operate in dangerous environments. Finally, while it would appear that organizational cultures are designed to win over the "hearts and minds" of employees, cultures also exert influence on members' bodies.

While several different and sometimes competing approaches to organizational culture exist, we suggest that a communication perspective on organizational culture provides a useful, but complicated and dynamic, framework for understanding, participating in, and transforming organizational culture. In conclusion, then, we offer the following thoughts on organizational culture and research:

> A culture—any culture—is like an ocean. There are many wonderful things and creatures in it that we may never understand; they change and so do we, regardless of the depth or perspective of our study. But the ocean is also made up of waves that are as regular as the cycles of the moon, and just as mysteriously musical, powerful, and enchanting. The top millimeter of the ocean is a world unto itself, and a vital one, in which the broader secrets of biological and evolutionary life . . . are contained. But even their meanings must be read in a vocabulary that is separate and distant. . . . So it is that within that millimeter, among those waves, we find clear and recurring themes. Like the great questions about culture that we pursue, those themes are always with us and not yet fully understood. (Goodall, 1990, p. 97)

QUESTIONS FOR REVIEW AND DISCUSSION

1. What is culture? What makes studying an organization's culture different from studying French or British culture?

2. Why are symbolic action and metaphor central to the study of organizational cultures?

3. What were the historical, political, and social trends that contributed to the development of cultural studies of organizations?

4. What major questions are posed by viewing organizations as cultures?

5. Compare and contrast the major characteristics of the three approaches to organizational culture (practical, interpretive, critical and postmodern).

6. Describe the various tactics that a new employee might use to learn more about an organization's culture. What is the role of advanced communication and Internet tecnologies in this socialization process?

7. What are the advantages and limitations of studying organizations as cultures?

8. What are the characteristics of a communication perspective on organizational culture?

KEY TERMS

Advanced communication and
  information technologies
  (ACITs), p. 151
Anticipatory socialization, p. 147
Artifacts, p. 129
Critical and postmodern views
  (of organizational culture), p. 143
Differentiation, p. 144
Ethnography, p. 131
Fragmentation, p. 145
Heroes and heroines, p. 129
High-reliability organizations
  (HRO), p. 149
Integration, p. 144

Interpretive view (of organizational
  culture), p. 141
Metaphors, p. 128
Organizational assimilation, p. 147
Organizational culture, p. 127
Performances, p. 129
Practical view (of organizational
  culture), p. 137
Rituals, p. 128
Socialization, p. 146
Stories, p. 129
Turning points, p. 149
Values, p. 129

CASE STUDY 1

The New Dojo

The sport of Judo has been good to Hank Tagawa. A sixth-degree (dan) black belt in the sport, Hank was born in Osaka, Japan, in 1965. He competed for years at the highest international level and won both a world championship and a silver medal in the 1992 Olympics. Eventually he settled in Pensacola, Florida, where he met and married an Anglo woman and began to put down roots in the community.

A shy, focused, but highly likeable man, Hank had been encouraged for years to consider opening his own judo school (dojo). About a year ago, Hank got the money together and did so. At first, the new dojo, at which Hank was the head teacher (sensei), had few students, but he was not interested in advertising, which he felt would appear too pushy. After a few months, however, there was an explosion of interest, both from parents bringing their small children for lessons and from men and women from a nearby military base who had heard of Hank's history and sought out the new dojo as a solid place to train. He set up classes for both children and adults and enjoyed both the cash flow and the camaraderie. He recruited a number of his former Olympic teammates from Osaka to visit for extended periods and to help out as instructors in the new dojo.

Hank's foremost concern is his desire to teach judo the "right" way, the way he was taught at the Kodokan Judo Dojo in Japan. This includes enforcing strict rules for the cleanliness and appearance of mats and uniforms, as well as rules for the respectful address of people of more senior ranks. Students are taught to bow to their teachers and superiors, speak some Japanese, and carry themselves with a quiet dignity both in and outside of the dojo.

After a year in operation, however, the dojo's attendance is starting to drop off. Sensei Tagawa has not deviated in his commitment to "doing things the right way," but many students have been unwilling or unable to tolerate his discipline. Furthermore, students from the military base resent his characterization of them as too aggressive, and parents are concerned about the visiting instructors, who force their children to do push-ups for bad behavior or, worse yet, to exercise to the point of exhaustion as a way of building endurance.

Sensei Tagawa has come to you for advice about saving his dojo. He's ready to conclude that he is just not cut out for teaching, but you suspect that there is more to the story.

ASSIGNMENT

Given what you know about organizational communication and culture, answer the following questions:

1. Describe the organizational culture of the dojo. What is the origin of these beliefs, assumptions, attitudes, and practices?

2. Would you characterize the dojo culture as strong or homogeneous? Why or why not? Are there subcultures? Kinds of resistance?

3. How would you describe the interaction among different cultural perspectives at the dojo?

4. How do you feel about the Sensei's desire to ensure that his school teaches the "right" way? What are the pros and cons of his taking this approach?

5. At this point in the story, what advice would you give Sensei Tagawa about future actions? Can the dojo be saved, and if so, how?

6. How is this case similar to challenges faced by other organizations? How might we apply lessons from the dojo to a start-up plan for another, similar organization?

CASE STUDY II

Studying the Culture of Meetings

Helen Schwartzman asserts in *Ethnography in Organizations* (1993) that "nothing could be more commonplace than meetings in organizations," yet most studies of organizational cultures fail to look closely at the exchanges of talk at those meetings (p. 38). She argues that close readings of those exchanges can tell us much about various aspects of a company's culture: power; domination; resistance to domination; gender, race, and class divisions; concepts of time and money; and regional differences, among others. Her argument is compelling.

ASSIGNMENT

As a student of organizational communication and a member of an organization (your class, college, sorority/fraternity, or place of employment), you are likely intrigued by the idea that meetings hold important clues to organizational cultures. For this case study, you will immerse yourself in a culture in order to understand, analyze, and write about it in the form of an ethnography. You will collect the data to be analyzed and then write about it using what you have learned in this and other chapters. Here are some guidelines for conducting your cultural study:

1. Record and transcribe the exchanges between members of the group, team, or organization at one or more of its meetings. Use the following questions and illustrations to guide your work:
   a. Who opens the meeting? Who takes notes? Answering these questions should tell you something about the leadership of the meeting, as well as the role of one or more of the group members.
   b. In general, who says what to whom and with what effect? Answering this question may help you isolate particular relationships and power structures.
   c. Pay close attention to exchanges of conversation—both on-topic and off-topic—that occur during the meeting. What are the exchanges about? What do they say about the role and relative power of the group members? What is the role of silence in the group? Is anyone excluded from the talk?
   d. What is the function of humor in the group, if any?
   e. What clothing do the group members wear to the meeting? Is there a relationship between their clothing and the conduct of the meeting (e.g., formal, informal)?

    f. Does the group use a particular style of language? For example, is it highly technical? Does it contain a lot of jargon or slang? Can you tell "who is in the know" just by listening? Can you tell who isn't? Is there any attempt to mentor newer group members? Are there any metaphors that recur in the group and seem to suggest a common understanding?

    g. What other affiliations or associations can you assume characterize these group members' lives outside of this meeting? How much of those extra-meeting cultures are brought into the culture of the meeting?

    h. How do the meetings end? Are assignments made? Are they equitably apportioned? How much does expertise play a role in the assignments? How about friendship?

2. Decide how you will analyze the data based on your reading in this and other chapters. For example,

    a. What management or communication approach (e.g., scientific management, human relations, human resources, systems, cultures, etc.) best characterizes the meeting?

    b. Does the group operate like a system? If so, how? If not, why not?

    c. What is the role of leadership in the group?

    d. How are power relations established and maintained? How are they challenged?

    e. What is the role of gender, race, class, or sexual orientation in the group? How do you know?

3. Perform your analysis.

    a. Write a narrative account (i.e., a story) about the group meeting. Be sure to include as much detail about the conversations and your impressions as you can. Make sure your story has an identifiable beginning, middle, and ending.

    b. Where possible, apply material from the chapters you have read to the story. When you are finished with a draft, add an introduction that theoretically frames the story and a conclusion that attempts to "sum up" what you have learned about this culture from the study.

4. Share your ethnography with your class.

CASE STUDY III

Cultural Constructions of Gender and Sexuality in College Fraternities and Sororities

Alan DeSantis and Audrey Hane (2004) provided a detailed and shocking ethnographic analysis of the cultural constructions of gender and sexuality in college fraternities and sororities. In their study, they highlighted the terminology used by both sexes to differentiate the sexual proclivities of undergraduate students. They showed how labels developed based on perceptions of bodies and the frequency of supposed (or real) sexual activities. They further described the influences these labels have on the meanings of gender and sexuality among women and men in fraternities and sororities.

ASSIGNMENT

If you are a member of a sorority or fraternity on your campus, write a brief account of the language used to describe gender and sexuality. If you are not a member of one of those social organizations, select a group that is interesting to you, or perhaps in which you are a member, and write a brief account of the language used to describe gender and sexuality. In either case, allow your writing to be guided by the following questions:

1. What specific terms (and definitions for those terms) derived from gender and sexuality are used to differentiate among members of the organization? How are those terms used to socialize new members? How are they used to control perceptions? How do they organize hierarchies within the organization?

2. What is the relationship between body size, shape, and habits of dress to perceived value and meaning within the organization? How do those values transfer into other aspects of academic life?

3. What activities are used in stories about group members to construct their gendered identities? Do the activities need to be true to be used?

4. How do rumors and gossip about sexual activities figure into the social and cultural construction of identities within the organization?

5. Who benefits from these constructions? Who suffers? What are the communication mechanisms for countering a negative construction?

6. How much of the everyday "work" of identity management in the organization is associated with management of gender, sexuality, and reputation?

CHAPTER 6

Critical Approaches to Organizations and Communication

The approaches to organizations discussed in prior chapters pose questions from within the dominant frameworks of Western capitalism, behavioral science, and modern organizational studies, but do not for the most part challenge these frameworks. While more recent cultural approaches have been more critical, blurring the distinction between cultural and critical approaches, even more subversive approaches exist.

The perspectives considered in this chapter examine and oppose the assumptions of the dominant frameworks. **Critical organizational theory** reveals the hidden but pervasive power that organizations have over individuals, and questions the assumed superiority of market capitalism and its attendant organizational structures, norms, and practices. Critical approaches, as we will see, pose difficult and important questions about power and control.

CRITICAL THEORY

☐ Historical and Cultural Background

When we think of someone as "critical," we imagine them as challenging some action or decision that they consider inappropriate or unfair. This is what critical theory and critical approaches to organizations do: They challenge the unfair exercise of power. Critical theory first emerged in response to the growing power that a small but elite segment of society held over the rest of the public during the Victorian period (1837–1901). This era was marked by a brutally abusive system of low wages, squalid working conditions, and wealthy, isolated business owners (Mead, 1991). Child labor was common, particularism was the rule, and employees had little protection from the cruel whims of their employers. Women, children, and minorities were paid far less than adult white men for performing the same work, and their opinions about how work should be done or how workplaces could be improved were ignored (Banta, 1993).

The roots of critical theory can be traced to Karl Marx (1818–1883). Marx viewed the division between business owners and paid laborers as inherently unfair, and predicted that it would lead inevitably to a violent overthrow of the owners as workers seized the means of production. The world has since witnessed many practical adaptations of Marx's ideas (e.g., China, Cuba, and the former Soviet Union), none of which have proven successful, as well-intentioned egalitarian ideals have been quickly usurped by autocratic dictators. Nonetheless, the impulse to challenge the abuses of power remains important. One particular theoretical adaptation of Marxist thinking merits special attention: that of a group of professors from the University of Frankfurt, referred to collectively as the Frankfurt School, who in the first half of the twentieth century developed what is now known as critical theory (Adorno & Horkheimer, 1972).

Recognizing the triumph of reason in modern society, these authors set out to demonstrate the seeming relationship between an overemphasis on reason and brutality. In their later years, they were deeply affected by the Holocaust, and more specifically the mass killings at the Auschwitz concentration camp, which they saw as a prime negation of the superiority of instrumental reason. Interestingly, they reserved their harshest criticisms not for the killers but for those adopting a "bourgeois sensibility"—that is, living an unreflective, materialistic life governed by instrumental rationality and the dispassionate routinization of brutality and abuse.

☐ The Rise of Critical Theorizing in the United States

Critical theory gained considerable popularity in the United States during the 1980s (Strine, 1991). Today, given the rapid and sustained development of critically oriented scholarship, it no longer makes sense to refer to "critical theory" as a unified and singular approach. Scholars and activists use a variety of theoretical and conceptual tools to help transform the way we think about and enact organizational life. Both practical and intellectual reasons account for the current interest in critical theory in the United States, and we discuss these next.

At the turn of the twentieth century, U.S. industrialists broke from traditional capitalism, which funneled the lion's share of wealth and responsibility to the ownership elite. For the first time, a connection was made between the wages paid to employees and their ability to be active consumers. At Ford Motor Company in the 1920s, for example, workers were paid the then high wage of $5 a day. Ford reasoned that to sell his cars to the masses, workers had to earn enough to buy them.

This strategy, known as **progressive capitalism**, dominated U.S. industry from the Industrial Revolution until the early 1970s, when the average, inflation-corrected weekly wage of Americans reached its peak. Throughout this period, both individuals and corporations experienced significant increases in economic well-being (Mead, 1991). In addition, for the first time in human history, a majority of individuals worked for someone other than themselves.

Decades of progressive capitalism eventually gave way to revolutionary changes in the world of work. With the globalization of labor and markets, "a phenomena that has remade the economy of virtually every nation, reshaped almost every industry, and touched billions of lives," employers had the option of hiring lower-wage workers overseas (Rosenberg, 2002, p. 28). Although this practice led to human rights abuses reminiscent of early capitalism, they occurred far enough away from home to be ignored by most people until recently.

Tina Rosenberg (2002) investigated the impact of globalization in Latin America and found that although it had indeed produced additional jobs, it has also led to dramatic increases in crime, the rise of new dictatorships, the economic collapse of Argentina, the financial panic that continually haunts Brazil, and the new economic woes of Uruguay and Venezuela. In India, Rosenberg discovered that the recent influx of new money to support high-technology investments by American firms has led to further economic and social division between the literate (30 percent) and illiterate (70 percent) populations, rekindling cultural and religious tensions over the importation of Western capitalist values. The same story has generally been true throughout Southeast Asia, where the widespread use of child labor in sweatshops over the past two decades by large American firms (e.g., Nike) has created a public outcry and has led to some reforms.

Beginning in the 1980s, elected leaders of both the United States and Britain adopted an economic philosophy opposed to decades of progressive capitalism. With this approach, more resources and support were given to big business (e.g., tax exemptions and reduced regulatory fines and controls) than to struggling individuals, with the expectation that increased profits would "trickle down" to the needy population (this approach has also been labeled "supply side economics"). Instead of promoting a more equitable sharing of wealth, however, the result has been a steady decline in the average employee's real wages, benefits, and standard of living. Today, many people work at one or more low-paying service job and struggle to make ends meet. In one notable investigative study, Barbara Ehrenreich (2001) decided to live as a minimum wage earner in Florida, Minnesota, and Maine by working as a waitress, hotel maid, nursing home aide, house cleaner, and Wal-Mart salesperson. She discovered, along with the estimated 12 million women who were moved off welfare roles into minimum wage jobs as a result of welfare reform legislation during the 1990s, that the work was physically, mentally, and emotionally exhausting and that one needs at least two of these jobs in order to live indoors.

The gap between people who *own* things (homes, cars, stocks, and stock options) and those who do not is big and getting even bigger. In addition, those who do have access to the trappings of a middle-class life are finding it more and more difficult to maintain it. Never in our history has it been this hard for families, even those with two working adults, to secure health insurance, job stability, and afford-able housing, the three basic elements of progressive capitalism and the American Dream (Shipler, 2004; Warren & Tyagi, 2003). As the divide between rich and poor has widened, new information technologies exacerbate the problem by offering companies unprecedented opportunities to send jobs overseas. By outsourcing to poorer nations and increasing their reliance on temporary workers, these firms max-imize profits for shareholders while at the same time contributing to the widening income gap worldwide (Townsley & Stohl, 2003). Some economists predict that as many as 14 million American jobs are now vulnerable to being sent overseas (Witte, 2004). These trends have squeezed the middle class by creating fewer jobs that support a living wage, while the ranks of the working class have swelled.

Together, these changes have had a revolutionary impact on all of our lives. The critical approach to organizational communication seeks to advocate for the interests of working people rather than the interests of corporate leaders and share-holders typically favored by management theory and practice. For many readers, critical approaches seem at first glance to pit people against profits. Particularly in a growing economy, critical approaches are often criticized for not taking a pro-profits stance and for underestimating the need for companies to remain profitable in an increasingly competitive global market (see the ethical questions emerging from this problem in *What Would You Do?* on p. 167).

One way the tension between people and profits plays out in real life is be-tween similar companies that take differing positions on the matter. Many describe Wal-Mart, the nations' largest retailer, as the epitome of the pro-profit position, while describing Costco Wholesale as occupying the pro-people position (Fried-man, 2005). Wal-Mart's revenue in 2003 was $256 billion. Of that, the company spent $1.3 billion (or .5 percent) on health-care coverage for its employees. Wal-Mart offers health care to 45 percent of its workforce. By contrast, Costco insures 96 percent of its full-time and part-time employees. Wal-Mart's pretax profit mar-gin is 5.5 percent of revenue. Costco's is only 2.7 percent of revenue. Stockholders and consumers value Wal-Mart's "flattening" process that takes all the "fat" (in-cluding labor costs, of course) out of its business practices. Yet, as employees we may prefer to have some of the "fat left on the bone," particularly when it means health-care coverage (Friedman, 2005, p. 220). Perhaps due to recent criticism, Wal-Mart recently announced a plan to make health care affordable to more of its workers (Barbaro, 2005).

Rather than framing the debate as an either-or choice between profits and peo-ple, we find it more productive to ask how the varied needs of all organizational stakeholders, including managers, workers, workers' families, host communities, and shareholders can be adequately addressed. Profitability is essential to the suc-cess of nearly all organizations, but should not be maximized at the expense of

From "The Ethicist" by Randy Cohen

In a letter to Mr. Cohen (*New York Times Magazine*, September 22, 2002), a reader from Fayetteville, Arkansas, wrote:

> When I hire local teenagers to do odd jobs, I pay about what they'd earn at a fast food restaurant. I pay adults doing similar work at least twice as much and add a hefty tip, since they have families and basic living expenses. It's not the money but the message: I don't want the teenagers to think this might provide a lucrative career. Is this pay inequality ethical?

On a separate piece of paper or working at a computer, write out your response to this question before reading Mr. Cohen's response. Given what you've learned thus far about critical theory and work, what constitutes an ethical stance on this issue?

Here is Mr. Cohen's printed response:

> Two people doing the same job are entitled to the same pay. How they spend it — on rent or renting video games — is not your concern. It might not be about the money for you, but I assure you it is for your hires. They're not hauling around your boxes for the career counseling you provide. Looked at benignly, you're giving a bonus to an older worker to help him meet his financial obligations. Looked at less generously, you're penalizing a teenager for not having a couple of kids. Is that what you mean by "the message"? Are you prepared to fully embrace your pay plan? If an employee wants to buy a second TV or have a third child, will you give him a raise? When one of his kids grows up and leaves home, will you cut his pay? The history of this sort of paternalism is not heartening. Such thinking was once used to justify paying single women less than married men because while men had families to support, the women didn't "need" the money. The ethical solution is to pay what in your area is considered a fair wage for the job — not just what the market will bear, but a decent living wage — and offer it to whoever can do the job. That is, determine pay by the act, not the actor.

Given Mr. Cohen's response, think about how this answer might be used to critique some existing corporate policies about hiring workers in developing countries to do jobs for a lot less money than is paid to workers in the United States. How does Mr. Cohen's phrase "pay what in your area is considered a fair wage for the job" complicate your answer? Or does it? Where does the global become local?

other equally important social needs, including living wages, sustainable development, quality of work-life and self-determination. In this chapter, we examine ideology, manufactured consent, concertive control, and the power of discourse as conceptual tools to better understand how our taken-for-granted beliefs about organizational life may inhibit our individual and collective abilities to balance the needs of people with the needs of profit. Central to this tension are notions of power.

□ The Centrality of Power

Early attempts to define **power** were based on the assumption that it is something a person or group possesses and can exercise through actions. In a classic paper on the subject, Robert French and Bertram Raven (1968) described five types of social power, following the assumption that person A has power over person B when A has control over some outcome B wants:

1. *Reward power.* Person A has reward power over person B when A can give some formal or informal reward, such as a bonus or an award, in exchange for B's compliance.
2. *Coercive power.* Person A has coercive power over person B when B perceives that certain behaviors on his or her part will lead to punishments from A, such as poor work assignments, relocation, or demotion.
3. *Referent power.* Person A has referent power over person B when B is willing to do what A asks in order to be like A. Mentors and charismatic leaders, for example, often have referent power.
4. *Expert power.* Person A has expert power over person B when B is willing to do what A says because B respects A's expert knowledge.
5. *Legitimate power.* Person A has legitimate power over person B when B complies with A's wishes because A holds a high-level position, such as division head, in the hierarchy.

French and Raven's approach to power is further reflected in some research on compliance-gaining (Kipnis, Schmidt, & Wilkinson, 1980) and behavior-altering techniques (Richmond, Davis, Saylor, & McCroskey, 1984). Examples include research on how supervisors can persuade subordinates to do undesirable tasks, how employees can persuade supervisors and co-workers to give them desired resources, and even how teachers can encourage students to complete assignments.

This traditional approach to understanding power, however, is incomplete. By focusing on the overt or superficial exercise of power by individuals, we learn little about the more covert or deep structures of power (Conrad, 1983). Unlike overt power, which is easy to spot and can in principle be resisted (though often at great costs), covert or hidden power is more insidious. Critical approaches focus on the control of employers over employees (Clegg, 1989) wherein power "resembles a loose coalition of interests more than a unified front. Critical theory is committed to unveiling the political stakes that anchor cultural practices" (Conquergood, 1991, p. 179). In short, critical theorizing seeks to expose the underbelly or dark side of organizational life by actively questioning the status quo—how it came to exist, whose interests it serves, and how it marginalizes and devalues some people while privileging others.

Consider, for example, just how much invisible power is exerted over your choice of major or, for that matter, of your even being in school. Since the Industrial Revolution, nations have funded "public schools" mainly to prepare society's youth for a lifetime of work in organizations. In 1862, the U.S. Congress passed the Morrill Land-Grant Act. The act enabled states to sell federal land, invest the proceeds, and use the income to support colleges "where the leading object shall be, without excluding scientific and classical studies . . . to teach agriculture and the mechanic arts [engineering] . . . in order to promote the liberal and practical education of the industrial classes in all the pursuits and professions of life" ("A Short Penn State History," 2002, para. 2). One such land grant institution, Pennsylvania State University, further defined their goal as to "apply scientific principles to farming, a radical departure from the traditional curriculum grounded in mathematics, rhetoric, and classical languages" (para. 1). Today's educational reforms are largely evolutionary and build upon this notion: The question everyone shares today is how to best prepare students for the new world of work. Critical approaches maintain that our system of education—and our outmoded assumption of lifetime employment with a company—are long overdue for reform.

POWER AND IDEOLOGY

An **ideology** is a system of ideas that serve as the basis of a political or economic theory (as in Marxist or capitalist or feminist ideology). In conversation, the term *ideology* refers to our basic, often unexamined, assumptions about how things are or ought to be. During the era of classical management, for example, the dominant ideology about work was based on various assumptions: that men (especially white men) were better suited to assembly lines than were women; that white men could learn faster than women and minorities and, therefore, should hold supervisory positions; that the U.S. system of work was second to none in the world; that Americans had a right to use the world's natural resources to build their cities, roads, and systems of commerce and industry; and that the American form of government was superior to all other forms (Banta, 1993).

Ideology touches every aspect of life and shows up in our words, actions, and practices. The existence of ideology helps us to understand that power is not confined to government or politics, nor is it overt or easy to spot. Because ideology structures our thoughts and interpretations of reality, it typically operates beneath our conscious awareness. Ideology is the medium through which social reality is constructed—it shapes what seems "natural," and it makes what we think and do seem "right" (Deetz & Kersten, 1983). Ideology tells us what exists, what is good, and what is possible in organizational life (Therborn, 1980). In so doing, it limits our socially constructed realities by preventing other equally plausible meanings for organizational life from coming to fruition. By constraining and limiting the possibility of alternative meanings and experiences, ideology can also contribute to oppression and domination.

One of the first efforts to investigate the relationship between ideology and everyday organizational culture is Dennis Mumby's (1987) critique of an oft-told cultural narrative from IBM. The story, about a new employee's encounter with IBM's CEO (Thomas Watson, Jr.), reads as follows:

> The supervisor was a twenty-two-year-old bride weighing ninety pounds whose husband had been sent overseas and who, in consequence, had been given a job until his return. . . . The young woman, Lucille Berger, was obliged to make certain that people entering security areas wore the correct identification. Surrounded by his usual entourage of white-shirted men, Watson approached the doorway to an area where she was on guard, wearing an orange badge acceptable elsewhere in the plant, but not a green badge, which alone permitted entrance at her door. "I was trembling in my uniform, which was far too big," she recalled. "It hid my shakes, but not my voice. 'I'm sorry,' I said to him. I knew who he was alright. 'You cannot enter. Your admittance is not recognized.' That's what we were supposed to say." The men accompanying Watson were stricken; the moment held unpredictable possibilities. "Don't you know who he is?" someone hissed. Watson raised his hand for silence, while one of the party strode off and returned with the appropriate badge. (pp. 117–18)

Organizational culture scholars interpret this story as providing two important messages to IBM members. For higher-status members, the story says, "Even Watson obeys the rules, so you certainly should." To lower status members, the story's message is "Uphold the rules, no matter who is disobeying" (Martin, Feldman, Hatch & Sitkin, 1983, p. 440). In his analysis, however, Mumby moves beyond illustrating how shared meanings are produced to expose how ideology functions through seemingly benign organizational narratives to suture or "fix" the meaning of the culture in ways that reinforce the power of dominant organizational members and oppress or marginalize organizational others. Specifically, he argues that ideology functions in four different ways to support the power of organizational elites:

1. *Ideology represents sectional interests to be universal.* In other words, ideology works to make the interests or concerns of the managerial elite appear to be the interests of all organizational members. The story seems to suggest that all "IBMers" should be concerned with upholding the rules. What is obscured, however, is that the rule system was created by the corporate

elite to protect both core technologies and their own interests. After all, managerial elites are much better served by security rules than are line workers.

2. *Ideology denies system contradictions.* Mumby claims that system contradictions are inherent in capitalistic organizational life. Foremost among those contradictions is the fact that we live in a democracy where one of our highest decision-making values is "one person, one vote," but at work we often willingly leave our democratic ideals at the door and operate under the assumption that "a few vote for everyone else." Mumby explains that the IBM story itself is contradictory because it suggests that at IBM "no one is above the law," but if Watson really was subject to the same rules as other employees, this story would have little significance. The story is only interesting and worth retelling because Watson chooses to obey the rules he could have clearly decided to break.

3. *Ideology naturalizes the present through reification.* **Reification** refers to the process whereby socially constructed meanings come to be perceived and experienced as real, objective, and fixed, such that members "forget" their participation in the construction of those meanings. In the IBM story, the rules, the organizational hierarchy, and traditional gender roles are reified such that they appear "just the way things are."

4. *Ideology functions as a form of control.* By creating an unquestioned agreement regarding the way the world "really" is, ideology furthers the control of dominant groups. Power and control are not explicitly exercised as much as embedded in routine thoughts, actions, and organizational processes. Ideological control is subtle and indirect, but highly effective. Known also as **hegemony**, ideological control "works most effectively when the world view articulated by the ruling elite is actively taken up and pursued by subordinate groups" (Mumby, 1988, p. 216). By enforcing a rule, Lucille Berger actively perpetuates the rule system that is created by and for the organizational elites. We see hegemony operating when the organization's interests and rules are maintained from the bottom up rather than having to be imposed from the top down.

The four functions of ideology—representing sectional interests as universal, denying contradictions, reification, and control—are often most evident in organizational narratives. Critical scholars recognize that organizational stories are quite literally "power-full" because they provide members with a "vision of the organization which is relatively complete, stable and removed from scrutiny" (Mumby, 1988, p. 125). Mumby's analysis provides a model for understanding how other cultural elements, such as jokes, rituals, or mission statements, can be critiqued to reveal the underlying ideology that privileges the interests of dominant organizational groups over those of others.

EVERYDAY ORGANIZATIONAL COMMUNICATION

Gender, Ideology, and Power in Career Paths

Ideologies are pervasive in nearly every aspect of daily life though they often remain implicit and unquestioned. Consider, for example, how ideologies about gender may affect the very activity in which you are currently engaged: studying and preparing for a career! Ideological constructions encourage us to consider particular kinds of work (whether in a professional organization or in a major course of study in college) as appropriate for men or women. For example, we might think that it is "natural" for women to choose to study elementary education, nursing, or social work and to enter the "caring" fields such as teaching young children. Men, according to such constructions, might find a better fit in the engineering, science, or business departments at the university and become tomorrow's scientific researchers, industrial engineers, and CFOs. Have you ever considered the ways in which your own choice of major or professional aspirations might have been influenced by gendered ideology?

Critical scholars would remind us that such seemingly "natural" and "normal" assumptions about gender, college majors, and career paths are often grounded in ideologies that support the interests of those in power. If our ideologies prompt us to associate men and masculinity with power, then we also come to associate "masculine" majors and professions with power, influence, and prestige. Is it more prestigious to be a third-grade teacher or a cardiologist? Whose starting salary will be higher — the social worker's or the engineer's?

The power associated with masculine professions is further evidenced in examples of men and women making career choices that run counter to ideological assumptions about gender. Even if women are not thought to be a "natural" fit for careers in science and engineering, they are often considered "trendsetters" and "role models" for pursuing careers in these prestigious fields. Dozens of organizations from the Women's International Science Collaboration Program to the Committee on Women in Science and Engineering aim to support women in overcoming ideological boundaries that keep them from entering such fields in larger numbers.

But is the same true for men who wish to enter less-powerful, less-prestigious feminine professions? Consider the example of Steve France, a recent college graduate, who chose to leave behind a powerful masculine career (in this case, the "corporate ladder") to have more regular working hours as a personal secretary. The ideological assumptions of his colleagues and supervisors often posed substantial challenges for Steve. He had to beg for his first job and prove himself *capable* by working for free while learning PowerPoint and Excel. The other secretaries—all women—frequently questioned him about his career choice: Why would he want to be a secretary (Pendele, 1999, para. 12)? Male nurses often face similar obstacles. Family members often question: "Why would you become a nurse when you could be a doctor?" Gene Tranbarger, associate professor of nursing at East Carolina University, notes that "male nurses who wish to work in obstetrics/gynecology still face obstacles and often have to resort to legal remedies" (Chung, para. 4).

DISCUSSION QUESTIONS

1. Consider the four functions of ideology described in this chapter. How does ideology operate in the examples of male secretaries and male nurses?
2. Ideologies are often difficult to recognize and articulate because they often come to be seen as natural, normal, and just "the way things are." It is often when we encounter an exception to the ideological "rule" that we are forced to think critically about power. How are male secretaries and male nurses the "exception" and more importantly, from a critical perspective, why are their stories exceptional?
3. Now consider your daily life. What experiences have you had or heard that have caused you to think critically about power and how it operates, especially in organizational contexts? Have you confronted exceptions to the rule (e.g., female airline pilots, male preschool teachers) that have given you pause? What do your responses to those exceptions tell you about our "taken-for-granted" assumptions of organizational life? Why do those ideologies persist?
4. Finally, consider your choices. Is it possible that your own choices about your major and your career goals are influenced by gendered ideologies? How? Do your choices extend the reach of hegemony? In other words, have your choices supported and reinforced gendered assumptions that maintain the power of dominant groups in organizational life? Alternatively, in what ways might your choices resist or transform those ideologies?

☐ The Hidden Power of Culture: Myths, Stories, and Metaphors

As Mumby's analysis of organizational ideology indicates, organizational culture, including the myths, stories, and metaphors that reproduce it, can be viewed as ideological outcroppings. **Myths, stories, and metaphors** are the surface structure forms of communication that contain implicit, hidden, and taken-for-granted ideological assumptions that reside at a deep structure level of power. Because ideology rarely announces itself, we must unpack ideological assumptions and functions as they are manifest in everyday elements of organizational culture.

Myths contribute to the strength of a culture's ideology and its sources of power. These specialized narratives often reveal the beliefs and values of a culture as they tell the stories of legendary heroes, of good and evil, and of origins and exits. In myths, we find evidence of basic metaphors that structure "our" view of things. For example, both H. L. Goodall (1995) and Janice Rushing (1993) suggest that in the American West there is a dominant mythic narrative that describes the origins of order and power and that features three main characters: (1) power, the expression of a sovereign, rational, unified, or modern self; (2) the other, the force that resists the domination of the self by glorifying its opposites; and (3) spirit, a mysterious force that is capable of resolving the differences between, and therefore uniting, power and other. The *Star Wars* story line is utterly familiar and resonates with us precisely because it reflects the dominant cultural narrative. On the one hand, there is Luke Skywalker who represents the forces of good; on the other there is the "Dark Side" led by Darth Vader (and others). At the same time, we learn from Yoda of a transcendent "force" that can somehow end the conflict for-ever. Nearly every popular American story—from movie to novel to television drama—reflects some version of this narrative.

More specific stories exist at the organizational level as well. Indeed, critical theory seeks to understand why organizational practices that maintain strong con-trols over employees are considered legitimate and, hence, are not resisted (McPhee, 1985). This kind of legitimation is maintained through such symbolic forms as metaphors, myths, and stories. Southwest Airlines, for instance, has been able to offer lower fares to its customers while consistently maintaining profitability in an industry that has been plagued by bankruptcy, labor strife, and other problems. A cornerstone of Southwest's success is its employees who accept the company "LUV" story. Part of that story can be read in its mission statement:

> We are committed to providing our Employees a stable work environment with equal opportunity for learning and personal growth. Creativity and innovation are encour-aged for improving the effectiveness of Southwest Airlines. Above all, Employees will be provided the same concern, respect, and caring attitude within the organization that they are expected to share externally with every Southwest Customer. (Southwest Air-lines, 1988)

The power of this story is evidenced in Southwest's recent history. Southwest Air-lines employees have twice taken voluntary pay reductions, once after the first Gulf War to offset rising fuel costs, and once again after 9/11 so the company did not have to cut back on its flight schedule as other airlines did. In return, their loyalty has been rewarded. In the past three years, the five union contracts have been ne-gotiated and "fresh pay raises" were awarded to all employees, according to a South-west vice president, Donna Conover ("100 Best," 2005, para. 20). Organizational

Metaphors Can Suspend Critical Thinking

Family is a common metaphor used by companies in the United States. For some companies, like entertainment giant Disney, the metaphor has been very useful. The ideal family includes a warm, wholesome, caring, mutually supportive set of interdependent relationships characterized by open and honest communication. Viewed in this way, family is a positive metaphor for any firm.

Not all families conform to this ideal, however. Do the terms for describing the ideal family sometimes obscure dysfunctional power relationships between parents and children, among siblings, and with relatives? Should all families strive to achieve the same ideals? Are all successful organizations alike in this regard? Consider these questions as you respond to the following situations:

1. You dislike your supervisor's frequent use of the family metaphor to explain his behavior (e.g., "Yes, I yelled at you about that report, but even in the best families that sometimes happens" and "We're all family here, so if you have personal problems, you can tell me about them"). You believe your supervisor uses the family metaphor as an excuse for his irrational behavior as well as to gain unwarranted access to employees' private lives. What is wrong with the supervisor's behavior? What should you do?

2. Your company has just announced that at its annual holiday party, skits will be performed by employee work teams. Your team has been asked to write, produce, and perform a skit that portrays the company as a family. You view this as an opportunity to reveal both the positive and negative aspects of the organization's use of power and informal relationships. However, two members of your team argue against your proposal; they agree with your ideas, but they fear management's response to the negative portrayals. How will you argue your case at the next team meeting?

3. What other metaphors can be used to describe and to organize work relationships? Describe at least one such metaphor and its ethical dimensions.

stories like these are regularly employed to justify managerial decisions regarding hiring, firing, promotions, and raises. Employees generally accept these controls as part of the "story" that distinguishes the organization and its culture. Over time, such myths, metaphors, and stories can come to define appropriate behavior and may suspend employees' critical thinking. (See *What Would You Do?* above.)

One of the most pervasive myths in American culture is the idea of what constitutes (and fails to constitute) a "real job" (Clair, 1996). Although the phrase has the effect of naturalizing the idea that some jobs are more "real" than others, it can also be seen as a way of privileging certain kinds of work. Specifically, most people think of a real job as one that involves collecting good wages from an organization. This relegates all kinds of important work—non-organizational, unpaid, home-based, odd-hours, service-oriented—to the margins. Another pervasive myth in our culture is the idea of a "career" being tied to societal norms or a "social contract" (Buzzanell, 2000). As Purdue University professor and communication scholar Patrice Buzzanell points out, when the old social contract (that idealized individual commitment, hard work, and loyalty to a company in exchange for lifetime employment and a good retirement program) was replaced with the new social contract (that promises only a series of work contracts over a lifetime to those able to keep abreast of technological change), the career aspirations of many "marginalized workforce members (people of color, white women, poor and lower class persons, and the less educated)" were sacrificed (p. 211). Once again, a critical perspective helps us see how our taken-for-granted ways of thinking and speaking can mask important power relationships (Clair, 1996; Mumby, 2000).

☐ The Hidden Power of Legitimation: Manufactured Consent and Concertive Control

The hidden power of organizational systems and structures has been a central focus of critical theory. Habermas (1972) argues that social legitimation plays a major role in holding contemporary organizations together. According to Habermas, capitalist societies are characterized by **manufactured consent**, in which employees at all levels willingly adopt and enforce the legitimate power of the organization, society, or system of capitalism. Furthermore, only when this perceived legitimate power is challenged might the basic order face a crisis.

The fact that this kind of power is hard to see only increases its strength. Practically from birth, westerners are immersed in capitalism and are trained to be consumers first, and citizens second, if at all. Most of our activities are structured around either consuming or finding ways to "add value" to ourselves and our families (Carlone & Taylor, 1998; Nadesan & Trethewey, 2000). Moreover, employees have, for some time now, accepted the odd label of "human resources," which suggests an objectification of people that in turn makes it easier to either mold or get rid of them. The magic of consent is that the people themselves buy into the vocabulary and, despite how it casts them as disposable objects, have difficulty imagining an alternative reality.

Manufactured consent has recently become unmoored from its bureaucratic heritage. Even in flatter organizations with ostensibly "democratic" aims, power and control feature prominently. Jim Barker's research on self-managing teams (1993, 1999) reveals the power of "concertive control" in seemingly more humane and democratic organizational forms. **Concertive control** occurs when employees police themselves, developing the means for their own control. "Workers achieve concertive control by reaching a negotiated consensus on how to shape their behavior according to a core set of values, such as the values found in a corporate vision statement" (Barker, 1993, p. 411). Workers in these systems do not need supervisors to create and maintain rules; rather, rules are created collaboratively among members themselves. Barker's ethnographic study of one communications company indicates that concertive control systems can become even more stringent and less forgiving than their traditional, bureaucratic predecessors. Their [self-generated] system of rational rules constrains them even further as the power of their value consensus compels their staunch obedience.

Manufactured consent is evident when an employee or manager says, "I was just doing my job," to justify a decision or action. As Dennis Mumby (1987) points out, domination involves leading people to organize their behavior around a rule system. The system, not individual managers or actors, can then be blamed—but not held accountable—for actions taken in its name. A recent law aimed at correcting this situation makes the senior management of large corporations personally responsible for any criminal actions taken on behalf of the company. Similarly, both Exxon and Union Carbide were held (somewhat) financially accountable for, respectively, a major oil spill in Prince William Sound, Alaska, and the release of deadly gas in Bhopal, India. Even more recently in the wake of the accounting scandals of 2002, the Securities and Exchange Commission (SEC) proposed holding corporate officers—CEOs and CFOs—personally responsible for the truthfulness, timeliness, and fairness of all public disclosures, including their financial statements. As a result, in 2005 Bernard Ebbers, the former chief executive of WorldCom, was sentenced to twenty-five years in prison for his role in the $11 billion accounting fraud case, the largest in our country's history. Likewise, John Rigas, founder of the cable company Adelphia, was sentenced to fifteen years in prison and his son Timothy, the former chief financial officer, was sentenced to twenty years in prison after being convicted on fraud and conspiracy charges in that same year.

Concertive control makes it difficult to hold on to the idea that organizational elites, namely managers, shape organizational meanings, rules, and structures to support their own interests at the expense of labor. A study by Larson and Tompkins (2005) revealed that "managers who implement a concertive-control system for employees may themselves come to be controlled by that same system" (p. 15). Larson and Tompkins thus render problematic the "neat dichotomy" between managers and employees that is often the basis for explaining relationships of power and control in organizational life.

Not all consent, however, has negative consequences for organizational members. The Grameen Bank in Bangladesh is an interesting example of how the self-policing quality of ideology can have its benefits. The Grameen Bank "enables the poor, landless, and mostly illiterate people of rural Bangladesh to assist themselves, by extending them small loans, loan utilization training, and various social services" (Papa, Auwal, & Singhal, 1997, p. 219). ɔple use the loans tɔ tart small enterprises that pull them out of poverty. Incredibly, the payback rate on these loans is 99 percent. This is because the members themselves maintain a structure of guilt and peer pressure that stigmatizes those who would fail to repay their debts. At the same time, this normative structure can be seen as a kind of support system, as the bank provides "required" motivational programs and strict daily monitoring of performance as well as weekly review meetings. In this way, members come to identify strongly with the bank and to feel a shared responsibility for the repayment of all loans. Defying simple analysis, it appears that Grameen is both incredibly empowering and controlling at the same time (Papa, Auwal, & Singhal, 1997).

▨ DISCOURSE AND DISCIPLINE

Critical approaches that focus on ideology are mainly interested in how dominant groups influence subordinate groups, treating power as a repressive force that is somehow "held" by these powerful groups or individuals. This view of power has recently been revised through a widespread turn toward postmodern understandings of power (Ashcraft & Mumby, 2005). Borrowing heavily from French philosopher Michel Foucault (1978, 1979), many critical scholars now view power as a widespread, intangible network of invisible forces that weaves itself into subtle gestures and intimate utterances. As such, power does not reside in things or in people but "in a network of relationships which are systematically connected" (Burrell, 1988, p. 227). In this view, power operates primarily in and through discourse. For Foucault, **discourse** is more than simply a shared system of meanings; rather, discourse is a site of power, a site of struggle over competing versions of knowledge, truth, and the self. What we understand to be true, what counts as a legitimate knowledge claim, and even our very identities are constituted or produced through discourse: "Discourses are more than ways of thinking and producing meaning. They constitute the 'nature' of the body, unconscious and conscious mind and emotional life of subjects which they seek to govern. Neither the body nor thoughts and feelings have meaning outside their discursive articulation" (Weedon, 1997, p. 105). As a discursive force, power works not to actively "repress" individuals or deny their "real" interests, but to literally "produce" them in a way that aligns with a preferred ideology. In organizational contexts, a focus on discourse encourages questions such as "How is 'truth' or knowledge produced through organizational discourse?" "Whose 'truth' counts?" and "With what effect?"

☐ The Hidden Power of Knowledge: Surveillance, the Panopticon, and Disciplinary Power

Foucault's (1979) work on the history of the prison systems reveals how contemporary penal discourses articulate and literally create the "subject" of punishment—namely the prisoner. The prisoner becomes defined and controlled through communication about and practices related to punishment. At the same time, discourse establishes the prisoner's relationship to society. Foucault's analysis suggests that a central feature of current modes of power is **surveillance** or constant supervision. Such supervision is a structural feature of modern power systems, epitomized in Jeremy Bentham's panopticon. The **panopticon**, which literally built surveillance into the design of an ideal prison, consisted of a central core that housed the guards and was surrounded by individual backlit cells such that the inmates were constantly visible. But because the inmates could not see the guards in the central core, they never knew if they were in fact being watched, only that the possibility existed.

Bentham's design assumed that power should be visible and unverifiable. "Visible: the inmate will constantly have before his eyes the tall outline of the central tower from which he is spied upon. Unverifiable: the inmate must never know whether he is being looked at any one moment; but he must be sure that he may always be so" (Foucault, 1979, p. 201). This created a system of disciplinary power in which inmates internalized the "gaze" of the guard by keeping a watchful eye on their own behavior.

While Bentham's prison never came to fruition during his lifetime, Foucault offers the panopticon as a useful metaphor to explain modern-day systems of power, including those found in most workplaces. Organizational members are increasingly subject to systems in which a real and present possibility of surveillance exists, whether it is in the form of "secret shoppers" who monitor customer service or recording devices that monitor telephone calls for quality assurance purposes. As a result, employees often behave as if they are being monitored, even when they are not. They correct, modify, and discipline themselves in the name of the organization. Thus, the primary effect of the panopticon is that the members are "caught up in a power situation of which they are themselves the bearers" (Foucault, 1979, p. 201). Critical scholars have examined the communicative dimensions of disciplinary power, the impact of discipline in the creation of scientific knowledge in a research laboratory, and the mutually reinforcing effects of technology and disciplinary power among workers in a call center, among other topics (Barker & Cheney, 1994; Brannan, 2005; Kinsella, 1999). Yet it is the expanding potential of technology to survey and discipline organizational members that has received the most attention from critical scholars and activists alike.

☐ The Technological Panopticon

Certainly, critical scholars recognize the benefits that technology affords individuals and organizations in their everyday lives. Who among us has not conducted our banking on-line, ordered music from the Web, or "Googled" someone or something? However, critics warn that that the taken-for-granted ideology that glorifies technology in general, and knowledge management systems in particular, is one that frames technology as "universally desirable" (Chan & Garrick, 2003).

Critical scholars encourage a more complex understanding of technology that reveals both its benefits and its burdens. Several features or by-products of technology have garnered attention from critical scholars. For example, for all their advantages, new communication technologies keep employees more tightly tethered than ever before. The proliferation of BlackBerry PDAs, laptops, and cell phones means that many workers have difficulty creating boundaries between work and the other spheres of their lives (Edley, 2001). **Knowledge management systems (KM systems)** such as searchable databases and interactive expert systems have been similarly critiqued. These systems (designed to "enhance and increase the value of the generation, sharing, and application of knowledge") effectively ensure that in order to "count," an employee's contribution to organizational knowledge must be in a form that the system recognizes, be compliant with the system, and be able to be coded and digitized in a way that the technological system can use (Chan & Garrick, 2003, p. 292). Thus, alternative ways of knowing (e.g., intuition, insights from other industries) are often rendered invisible and useless, and only the official "scorecard measures" adopted by the firm are found to be acceptable. Thus, the important, but not easily codified, knowledge that is necessary to perform vital "care" work (e.g., that which is regularly performed by nurses, day-care workers, and others) becomes easily overlooked and devalued in KM systems.

Finally, although the control of employees has always hinged on oversight and observation, technology, including KM systems, has created conditions for heightened, continuous, and more insidious forms of control. Technology is now in place that can monitor employees' speech, their every keystroke, and even their hygiene habits in the company washroom. The challenge organizations face is to build surveillance systems that are both productive and ethical. Critical organizational communication scholars are advancing precisely those sorts of models. For example, Trethewey and Corman (2001) have proposed a model that articulates two ethical dimensions that can be used to assess any particular KM system, the inclusivity-exclusivity dimension and the transparency-opacity dimension (see Table 6.1).

The first dimension centers on the degree of participation that KM systems enable and encourage. Those systems that are inclusive or designed with input from a variety of stakeholders toward a collective good are more ethical than those that are exclusive. Exclusive systems are designed for and by a certain segment of the organization. The second dimension refers to the degree to which KM systems and their uses are transparent or visible versus opaque or hidden from members who are impacted by them. In transparent systems, employees know when and how information is being collected and/or generated about them and their work, how those data are being used, and the consequences of such monitoring. The least ethical systems are those that most closely mirror the panopticon and are both opaque and exclusive. The most ethical are those systems that are inclusive and transparent.

Trethewey and Corman warn that the trend toward the commodification of knowledge, efficiency, and managerial control will lead to KM systems that are located at the opaque/exclusive ends of the continua unless participatory decision

TABLE 6.1

Ethical Dimensions of Knowledge Management Applications

A MODEL FOR KNOWLEDGE MANAGEMENT	TRANSPARENCY	OPACITY
Inclusivity	Active Consent Example: Technical support forums that use threaded discussion to share/collect problems, reports, and solutions	Passive Consent Example: Data mining forums that scour sources for discussion to share/collect information on relevant problems, reports, and solutions
Exclusivity	Technical/behavioral Control Example: Employees are notified of possible monitoring of their systems and phone calls they will get for training and quality assurance purposes.	Panoptic Control Example: E-mail monitoring systems that are installed and used without employees' knowledge

Source: Trethewey, A., & Corman, S. (2001). Anticipating K-Commerce: E-Commerce, knowledge management and organizational communication. *Management Communication Quarterly*, 14, 619–628.

making is enacted at all levels of the organization. Such decision making ensures that those who are most immediately impacted by both the opportunities and challenges of technological systems are represented in dialogue about what "counts" as organizational knowledge and how such knowledge can and should be used.

 # RECENT TRENDS IN CRITICAL ORGANIZATIONAL COMMUNICATION SCHOLARSHIP: ORGANIZING HEALTHY ORGANIZATIONS

One area of organizational life that is commanding increasing attention from critical scholars is employee health and well-being. Scholars have long been concerned with the devastating health consequences that work can have on employees. Hazardous working conditions, industrial accidents, and occupational disease take an alarming toll on human life in the United States each year. According to the Occupational Safety and Health Administration's "Healthy People 2010" report, each day in the United States 15 occupational fatalities occur, 130 employees die from work-related illnesses, and 11,000 workers become disabled from work-related injuries (Beato, 2004).

Critical scholars suggest that workplace accidents, occupational disease, and other work hazards are often a direct consequence of organizing practices that value efficiency and productivity over employee safety and health. For example, organizations often simply pay higher insurance premiums rather than redesign the workplace and work processes with an eye toward employee safety (Zoller, 2003). Those who escape physical harm at work may still find their health negatively impacted by the growing strain of occupational stress. Nearly 80 percent of U.S. employees report that work is their biggest source of stress. The consequences of stress include decreased physical and mental health (Farrell & Geist-Martin, 2005).

Because critical scholars are fundamentally interested in the well-being of employees, health has emerged as an important focus for scholarship. Assuming that our health is organized by a variety of everyday communicative practices, organizational communication researchers have explored the ideology that undergirds doctor-patient relationships, employees' consent to unhealthy work practices, and the social construction of risk at work, among other topics.

An example of critically oriented scholarship is Patricia Geist and Jennifer Dreyer's (1993) critique of the dominant ideology of health care in the United States. They explore this model's ability to define and control what is considered appropriate, professional, or ordinary health-care communication through the routine doctor-patient interview. The result often gives less weight to the patient's perspective because the doctor is assumed to be the knower and the patient is reduced to an object or case (e.g., disease, symptom) to be known. Using dialogic theory (Bakhtin, 1986), Geist and Dreyer propose an alternative model for communication encounters between health-care providers and their patients. By refocusing the dialogic encounter on what is created in communication (as opposed to what is given through scientific authority), Geist and Dreyer aim to empower those who seek medical treatment through the deliberate inclusion of the patient's voice in the doctor-patient interaction. Hence, two major challenges to the power of received ideology are present in their research agenda: (1) the power of the traditional medical model of scientific information gathering and (2) the power of traditional models that distance researchers—and research practices—from the people they study.

In a similar vein, Scheibel (1996) critiques the dominant medical ideology that informs how residents are trained to conduct pelvic exams. An ideology of excellence encourages medical students to treat women's bodies as "machines" and simultaneously disregards and minimizes the patient as a knowledgeable, communicative, and even conscious being (p. 318). Through the combined efforts of critical scholars, patient advocates, and more progressive elements of medical institutions, the dominant medical ideology is currently undergoing a transformation that moves away from treating patients as passive receptors of medical directives to more active and knowledgeable agents who collaborate, communicate, and share in decision making with their health-care providers (Yedidia et al., 2003).

Medical ideology can also serve to reify class- and race-based inequities in health-care provision. The many ways that a patient's socioeconomic status may impact his or her ability to comply with medical recommendations are often erased by existing medical ideology that treats the patient as a diseased body rather than a contextually bound individual. Gillespie's (2001) study of Medicaid patients' experiences navigating managed care for asthma treatments is telling in this regard. She notes:

> Left in the inner city by those who fled to the new, affluent suburbs decades ago, low-income families live in older homes filled with lifetimes of dust and molding timber. They breathe air polluted by factories that never cease production and by the cars of daily downtown professionals who sleep in clean, suburban air each night. Often depressed, they are more likely to smoke and less likely to eat well. Many sleep on the floor, knowing that the asthma this triggers could kill them, but afraid that a stray bullet shot through the window will do so sooner. . . . Without this knowledge, frustrated doctors and bureaucrats, certain their instructions are clear and motivating, may make sense of patient "non-compliance" as selfish resistance to efforts to help them. (p. 114)

Other researchers have addressed the difficulty many women have getting their health-care needs taken care of, and the even greater difficulty women of color have getting quality health care (Ellingson & Buzzanell, 1999). The problems that women of color encounter in the context of doctor-patient interactions are highlighted in Dixon's (2004) research. In her study, she follows the conversational twists and turns experienced by an aging, African American woman and her white, male physician. She reveals how inadequate intercultural communication results in a substandard health-care practice, as each party maintains a very different view of what constitutes health and illness. For many doctors, compliance, or the patients' willingness to follow doctors' orders, is often framed as a simple personal choice on the part of the patient. For many patients, however, compliance has much more to do with structural or environmental obstacles that can not be removed by simple "choices." Gillespie's (2001) research on Medicaid patients reveals that the doctor's wishes that patients better manage "environmental" factors that impact asthma, such as replacing old carpeting or draperies, are not feasible. On a more hopeful note, some researchers are exploring how patients are resisting dominant medical discourses in ways that afford them opportunities to receive better treatment and to create medical encounters that are more satisfying (Armstrong, 2005; Ellingson & Buzzanell, 1999; Wheatley, 2004). And other scholars are working with physicians to develop communication strategies that respond more effectively to the patient and his or her particular context (Eisenberg et al., 2005).

Although some patients are becoming more vocal advocates for their own well-being in the context of health-care organizations and relationships, many employees still remain relatively silent when it comes to advocating for healthier workplaces and work processes. As sobering as the statistics on workplace fatalities, injuries, and illnesses are, those numbers only reflect the incidents that were "officially" reported. Power relations and concertive control processes begin to explain why many workplace injuries and illnesses go unreported (Collinson, 1999; Zoller, 2003). Zoller's (2003) ethnographic study of an automobile manufacturing plant revealed that nearly every worker either experienced a physical ailment resulting from work or knew someone who did. Yet those same workers rarely reported injuries or work-induced health problems to management. As a result, the plant's injury rates decreased, and workers then used those rates to "prove" that the workplace was safe. Understanding communication processes, particularly those related to concertive control, can help to explain the contradictions between workers' actual experiences of health and safety and their reported or official injuries. Although Zoller revealed the subtle pressures that organizational leaders exerted to reduce the number of injuries reported to OSHA, employees themselves communicatively created norms that discouraged workers, or management, from addressing the systemic health implications of their work and workplace. Instead, the workers consented to risky work because they valued the active, "physical" nature of their work (particularly in relation to management work), and defined "good workers" as those who could "take" the demands of the job and not let the job get them down. The workers also respected colleagues who didn't complain, and felt that because they were paid relatively well the organization deserved their gratitude, despite the risks of their employment.

Zoller's study brings into focus the problematic and dangerous ways that employees consent to health risks. In a similar way, Clifton Scott's (2005) ethnographic study reveals how individual firefighters, despite their leader's adamant and repeated admonishments, often engage in high-risk behavior. Firefighters, who pride themselves on acting manly and heroically, often put themselves in harm's way, even when there is no immediate need to do so. The case presented at the end of this chapter is drawn directly from Scott's work and speaks to the very real and pressing ways that employee consent can negatively impact health and well-being. Future work in this area will undoubtedly continue to explore how organizing processes impact the health and well-being of individuals, organizations, and communities.

☐ Resistance: Challenging Organizational Power and Control

The emphasis in critical organizational communication studies on organizational power, control, and domination foregrounds the many ways that individuals are controlled by modern-day organizational forms and practices. Critical scholars call attention to the ways in which corporate ideology and managerial discourse have seeped into and shaped our daily lives, not just at work, but at school, at home, and through the media. Stanley Deetz (1992) calls this form of control the "corporate colonization of the life world" and believes it leads to the eventual breakdown of families, schools, and other social institutions. Issues such as childbirth, education, and even morality have been removed from the domain of the family and turned into externally purchased goods and services (Lukes, 1986). People's decisions about where to live, when to have children, and how to spend their leisure time are increasingly based on career-related concerns. Alienation and loss of identity result when people can no longer turn to the social institutions (e.g., school, church, neighborhood) that once fostered a sense of belonging to a family or community and turn instead to their work.

As noted, schools and the media also play a role in normalizing corporate colonization. For example, education reinforces the notion that corporate domination is both practical and acceptable as schools are increasingly concerned with training students for occupations. Indeed, corporate spending on training now outpaces government investment in public education! The media, too, sponsors a corporate vision of success through its literal (e.g., product placements in films and television programs) and figurative representation of the "good life," grounded in material wealth and consumption (Deetz, 1995). In sum, we consider again Deetz's words:

> With such institutional domination in place, every other institution subsidizes or pays its dues for the integration given by the corporate structure, and by so doing reduces its own institutional role. The state developed for public good interprets that as the need for order and economic growth. The family that provided values and identity transforms that to emotional support and standard of living. The educational institution fostering autonomy and critical thought trains for occupational success. (1992, p. 17)

Under the enormous and ubiquitous weight of market-driven, corporate colonization of our everyday lives it is hard to imagine a way to push back.

Yet, what often remains "hidden" but is always present is resistance to organizational and increasingly corporatized power and control (Scott, 1990). Despite the best efforts of organizations to fully control their members, those members often engage in **resistance** — distancing and defending themselves from organizational power (Fleming, 2005). Resistance to organizational domination can take a variety of forms, ranging from large-scale social movements including boycotts and strikes to individual tactics designed to carve out a small, but satisfying space of agency, action, and autonomy (Holmer-Nadesan, 1996).

Shiv Ganesh, Heather Zoller, and George Cheney (2005) are critics who urge organizational scholars to devote increased attention to **global transformation**. *Transformation* is a term that highlights how local social movements attempt to "effect large-scale, collective changes in the domains of state policy, corporate practice, social structure, cultural norms, and daily lived experience" (p. 177). These social movements often begin as locally based and loosely organized groups of people who are working toward change. The Internet has become a valuable tool in mobilizing grassroots campaigns against corporate domination. The effects of these resistance movements have real and material effects. Ganesh, Zoller, and Cheney point to several successful examples:

- The protesters involved in the "Battle of Seattle" claimed a significant role in halting the Multilateral Agreement on Investment during the World Trade Organization meeting in 1999 (Ganesh, Zoller, & Cheney, 2005).
- In 2000, poor Bolivians took to the streets in Cochabamba to resist Bechtel corporation's purchase of their national water system (Ganesh, Zoller, & Cheney, 2005).

- In November 2005, thousands of individuals in Argentina gathered in Mar del Plata, site of the Summit of the Americas, to protest free trade agreements that are thought by many to "enslave" Latin American workers (Bash, Mirian, & Newman, 2005).

Organized activist movements like these that center on issues such as fair trade, social justice, and corporate responsibility are one means through which individuals can effect change. Many organizational members, however, find themselves hard pressed for the time and energy it takes to participate in organized activism. Moreover, as forms of workplace control and surveillance have increased in both "strength and ubiquity," the possibility for collective, confrontational forms of worker resistance has waned (Mumby, 2005, p. 38). Instead, many members now turn to more subtle, covert, and hidden tactics to create momentary, but potentially transformative, "resistant spaces" (Gabriel, 1999). Critical scholars have documented how members have used humor, irony, "bitching," "hidden transcripts," and cynicism in pursuit of some measure of autonomy (Bell & Forbes, 1994; Collinson, 2002; Fleming & Spicer, 2002; Martin, 2004; Murphy, 1998; Sotirin, 2000; Trethewey, 1997, 1999). Consider the following examples:

- The McDonald's employee who wears a shirt with the phrase "Mc[expletive]" emblazoned across his chest under his official uniform (Fleming & Spicer, 2002).
- The flight attendant who wears her high heels only in the concourse where she knows supervisors are looking, then quickly changes into comfortable loafers once she's in an unsupervised zone (Murphy, 1998).
- The client who "performs" an appropriately subservient role in order to receive material assistance from a social service agency (Trethewey, 1997).
- The worker who privately relates a representative story about an alienated, displaced, anxious, or angry worker. This story can function as a therapeutic tool for relieving job pressure, assessing work-related situations, and regaining control over emotions (Goodall, 1995).
- The working-class secretary who decorates her cubicle with cartoons that decry, albeit in a humorous way, her overworked state (Bell & Forbes, 1994; see Figure 6.1)

What these organizational members share is the desire to assert control in an oppressive context. Of course, what is notable about all these forms of resistance is that they operate under the managerial radar screen. These tactics make clear that resistance is never enacted outside of dominant forms of power; rather, resistance is always performed in direct response to power. Resistance emerges in the ever-changing and contestable space between acceptance and revolting. A Malaysian proverb illustrates this dialectical relationship between resistance and control: "When the great lord passes, the wise peasant bows deeply and silently farts" (qtd. in Mumby, 2005, p. 21). Critical organizational scholars, then, should focus not only on the "bow (an ostensible act of obeisance to power)," nor should they focus exclusively

FIGURE 6.1

Cartoons as Micropractices of Resistance

Source: Bell, E., & Forbes, L. C. (1994). Office folklore in the academic paperwork empire: The interstitial space of gendered (con)texts. *Text and Performance Quarterly*, 38, 187.

on "the fart (a covert act of resistance to power)," but rather on the "complex ways in which these intersect in the moment to moment to produce complex and often contradictory dynamics of control and resistance" (Mumby, 2005, p. 21). Importantly, these small-scale forms have the capacity to bubble up into larger organizational changes and transformations. Murphy's (1998) research, for example, demonstrates how flight attendants resistance to body regulations eventually led the airlines to drop some of their more stringent weight requirements for attendants.

Critical scholars, despite their rather dire descriptions about the oppressive state of organizational life, hold out hope of change at the individual, organizational, and cultural level. Resistance to organizational oppression is necessary if we hope to reclaim and retain the democratic potential of our contemporary lives. According to Deetz, the basic problem is not a lack of awareness about what to do; much help is available there. After all, communication scholars and students, in particular, are armed with communication tools (e.g., listening, decision making, persuasion, leadership) that can enable them to be active change agents through resistance. Rather, the problem is *wanting* to do it, seeing the necessity of change, and taking the risks that accompany change (Deetz, 1995). This chapter may challenge you to consider the ways you might resist organizational power and control to create more empowering and enabling opportunities for yourself and others. In so doing, you may decide that you are interested in taking on the role of the critical theorist/activist.

□ The Role of the Critical Researcher

In many respects, research from a critical perspective is similar to that of the cultural approach (see Chapter 5). To discover the deep structures of power, the investigator must look for details about not only what happens in the organization and why it happens, but also how it is shaped by economic, political, and social forces worldwide. From a critical perspective, the cultural approach moves in a useful direction by focusing on meaning and sense making, but it neglects to ask in whose interest certain meanings and interpretations lie. A critical theorist, then, gathers interpretive cultural data about race, class, gender, age, language, motives, and actions and makes judgments about the power relationships that exist in all aspects of organizing. This is a very subjective enterprise; not only can critical theorists be criticized for all of the same faults as cultural researchers (e.g., narrow samples and bias in selecting participants and events), but they can also be called "elitists."

Critical theorists have been classified as elitists because, in practice, they must be willing to argue that certain individuals or groups are oppressed but are unaware of their oppression. This is the most serious problem with asserting the existence of hegemony. In a marked departure from the cultural approach, critical theorists may maintain that people do not know their own minds (Clegg, 1989). Perhaps this is one reason why more recent critical studies of organizations openly embrace an advocacy role and political agenda, and why critical and cultural studies theorists often rely on passionate, highly personal experiences and arguments to make their cases.

As champions of organizational "underdogs," critical scholars have often conceived of their task as one closer aligned with social activism than with traditional objective science. The role of the critical scholar has been described in terms of critiquing dominant discourses; educating organizational members, leaders, and the larger culture on the inequities of contemporary organizations; and emancipating organizational members from oppression through the articulation of positive and transformative alternatives to present structures and processes. Deetz (2005) claims that critical theory means more than adopting a particular role; rather, it is a way of life characterized by the three following tension-filled, **critical modes of being**.

- *Being filled with care*: Caring for and directing attention to others characterizes this way of being. At root, it involves efforts to understand others on "their own terms," and in so doing, the self's "values become exposed as partial and incomplete" (pp. 101–102). Of course, when we begin to take seriously the "other," our understanding of our own self and our world becomes much more complicated, complex, and, sometimes, problematic. Barbara Ehrenreich and David Shipler are two writers who embody this ethic of care in their respective texts, *Nickel and Dimed: On (Not) Getting By in America* and *The Working Poor: Invisible in America*. Both authors were invested in telling the story of the working poor from the perspective of the diverse individuals who make up the largest cadre of employees in our country. Both texts are grounded in the lives, meanings, and everyday experiences of the working poor in our country. Shipler's text, for example, follows several working-class workers over several years as they attempt to pull themselves out of poverty, often repeatedly, and only occasionally with any success. Hearing the stories of these individuals' lives, told from the perspective of their complex and difficult lived experience, makes it difficult for the reader to do anything but care about their plight. Being empathic is only one aspect of living life as a critical scholar.
- *Being filled with thought*: Moving from caring about or empathizing with individuals to considering and acting on the larger social and political ramifications of seemingly "individual" stories is a hallmark of being filled with thought. For example, both Ehrenreich and Shipler's texts move beyond revealing personal stories to address the systematic and structural causes and consequences of class divisions in our country. Additionally, both texts invite (middle class) readers to recognize their often-unwitting complicity in systems that perpetuate the deep class divisions in our country and to work toward changing those systems.
- *Being filled with good humor*: While care and thought require seriousness, a critical way of being also requires a willingness to recognize the ironic and contradictory aspects of life. Good humor means accepting uncertainty and embracing a willingness to "make it up as we go" (Deetz, 2005, p. 103). It means realizing that we can never "fix" social problems with a singular or final response, but we must act anyway to provide solutions (that are inherently

partial, partisan, and problematic). Although some may feel that despair is the most appropriate response to this ontological insecurity or fundamental openness, we believe that good humor, even laughter, is a more appropriate response. The critique of organizational inequities and laughter can go hand-in-hand (Trethewey, 2004). Critical scholars have explored the ways marginalized organizational members, including women, middle managers, secretaries, female clients in social service agencies, and male shop floor workers, have used humor to resist oppression and to create spaces of empowerment at work (Bell & Forbes, 1994; Collinson, 1992; Martin, 2004; Trethewey, 1997).

These three modes of being can be harnessed in service of organizational empowerment and justice.

SUMMARY

Critical theories emerged when scholars recognized a lack of attention in previous scholarship to the pervasiveness of power and control in shaping members' experiences of organizational life. The principle observation is that power in organizations is important because it is often exercised inequitably, resulting in the reproduction of organizational "haves" and "have nots." The roots of critical theorizing can be traced back to the work of Karl Marx and, later, the Frankfurt School. Since that time, critical approaches have moved away from economic explanations of power inequities to address the myriad ways power operates through everyday communication practices such as storytelling, language use, and the establishment of routine. With the collapse of progressive capitalism, critical approaches have become an ever more necessary counterbalance to organizational theorizing that privileges those who already possess power (e.g., reward, coercive, referent, expert, or legitimate), including managers, leaders, white-collar employees, and professionals.

Critical approaches remind us, however, that power is more than simply the ability to get someone else to do one's bidding. Power and its attendant inequities are also reproduced through ideology. Ideology both shapes and limits our social constructions of reality by providing a sense of what is good, right, and possible. Critical theorists point out that ideologies are never neutral; rather, ideologies serve some organizational groups and interests better than others. The functions of ideology include (1) representing sectional interests to be universal, (2) denying system contradictions, (3) naturalizing the present through reification, and (4) serving as a form of control. Ideologies rarely announce themselves so critical scholars often tease out ideologies as they are manifest in organizational myths, metaphors, stories, and other cultural practices. Moreover, critical theorizing suggests that ideology is not only imposed on members from those in power; rather, through processes of manufactured consent and concertive control, employees often willingly participate in power systems that are not necessarily in their best interests.

Recent trends in organizational communication research have focused attention on the power of organizational discourses and the knowledge they enable and create. Borrowing from French social philosopher Michel Foucault, scholars have revealed how knowledge gathering and knowledge management practices have increased the opportunity for organizational surveillance and discipline. Such heightened surveillance strategies find their most problematic expression in the technological panopticon. Critical scholars warn that we must find ways to use technology ethically if we are to avoid the most dangerous features of the technological panopticon. In addition to technology, critical scholarship has also emerged in the area of health communication to better understand, challenge, and transform how ideology and consent shape health-care encounters and employee wellness programs.

While critical theorists are quick to point to the (many) problems and power imbalances in organizational life, they are also interested in how members of society and members of organizations can bring about positive change. The study of organizational resistance centers on challenges to power and control in contexts ranging from global social movement to individualized "micropractices." And it reminds us that the role of the critical researcher is one that embraces care, thought, and good humor in service of organizational empowerment and justice.

QUESTIONS FOR REVIEW AND DISCUSSION

1. What are the advantages and disadvantages of viewing organizational communication in terms of power?

2. Trace the historical roots of critical approaches. Do you think critical theorizing is still relevant today? Why or why not?

3. What are some different views of the nature of power in organizations?

4. What is ideology, and how does it both enable and constrain communication in organizations?

5. What roles do metaphors, myths, and stories play in maintaining and transforming existing power relations?

6. What is concertive control? What are some examples of concertive control that you have experienced as an employee or a consumer?

7. What is discourse? How are discourse and organizational knowledge related to one another?

8. What elements, if any, of the panopticon still exist in contemporary institutions?

9. What role does electronic surveillance play in the exercise of power at work?

10. Why is health care an important context for critical inquiry? What concepts from the chapter might provide the most leverage in terms of creating change in health-care contexts?

11. Of the forms of resistance discussed in the chapter, which ones have the greatest potential to effect change? Given what you have read in this chapter, why do you think resistance movements are not widespread?

12. What modes of being are encouraged by critical approaches to organizations? As a critical student of organizational life, what is the one issue or problem you are most concerned about? How is that issue or problem an outgrowth of ideology, hegemony, or concertive control? What can *you* do to transform that issue or problem?

KEY TERMS

Concertive control, p. 177
Critical modes of being, p. 189
Critical organizational theory, p. 163
Discourse, p. 178
Global transformation, p. 186
Hegemony, p. 171
Ideology, p. 169
Knowledge management systems
  (KM systems), p. 180

Manufactured consent, p. 176
Organizational myths, stories, and
  metaphors, p. 173
Panopticon, p. 179
Power, p. 168
Progressive capitalism, p. 165
Reification, p. 171
Resistance, p. 186
Surveillance, p. 179

CASE STUDY I

Risky Business:
Consent, Safety, and Firefighter Culture

The Bay City Fire Department (BCFD) provides fire and emergency medical service to a major U.S. city and is widely regarded in the fire service community as one of the most advanced in the country. However, department leaders have become increasingly concerned about safety issues. For example, a firefighter was recently killed in a fire at a hardware store, two clients were killed in ambulance accidents, and several firefighters were injured when two fire engines collided while driving to the same fire. What most disturbs administrators is that all of these injuries and deaths could easily have been prevented if members had followed the standard operating procedures in which they were trained. For example, the firefighter who died did so when he and his peers were still trying to put out the fire from the inside even though they knew that potential victims had been rescued and that the building was already a total loss. The fire engines that collided were racing each other to a fire scene, competing to be the first truck on the scene, a common scenario.

It's not as if BCFD has failed to be "safety minded." Many of the safety reforms implemented in fire departments nationally and internationally were first developed at BCFD, and members regularly participate in a variety of safety training exercises. However, there has been some resistance to the increased dialogue about safety. Some members actually believe the department is too conservative in the way it manages fire incidents. They want to stay in fires longer, fighting "the beast" and "getting it on" from the inside rather than using the "surround and drown" from outside approach. The union chief complained, "Don't they call 911 because they want us to put out the fire?"

Newer firefighters who have received the most safety training and claim to be more safety-conscious than senior members seem to be the biggest violators. Both of the ambulance deaths occurred while a second-year firefighter was driving, and two novice firefighters were nearly killed recently after disobeying orders to leave a burning building for safety reasons. Internal investigations revealed that the two stayed in the fire because they had been trying to melt their helmets. In the culture of the fire service, a disfigured helmet is a sign that one is a "real" firefighter because he or she can "take it." Investigations have also revealed that novice firefighters have broken driving regulations in an effort to prove themselves as "real" firefighters, attempting to shield themselves from the "care bear" label often applied to those who staff the department's ambulances.

(continued, Risky Business)

Similarly, the investigation concluded that the two fire engines collided because they were racing one another for the chance to arrive first on the scene and enter the blaze at its peak.

The fire chief and his assistants aren't sure how to handle these problems. The fire chief recently said in a staff meeting, "We are killing our customers as we try to help them, and we are killing firefighters for empty buildings that are going to be torn down anyway. I shouldn't have to tell our guys that it's not okay to die in a fire." After years of trying to fix the problem with better training, they are beginning to think that training deficiencies are just a small part of the problem.

Source: Scott, C. (2005). *The discursive organization of risk and safety: How firefighters manage occupational hazards*. Unpublished dissertation, Arizona State University.

ASSIGNMENT

1. Why do you think firefighters are violating standard operating procedures? How might your response be informed by an understanding of ideology, manufactured consent, or discipline?
2. How does organizational discourse enable and constrain the occupational behaviors of these employees?
3. You are an organizational communication consultant hired to increase firefighters' compliance with safety procedures. What would you do?

The Brilliant Engineer

Carl McKnight is an electrical engineer with twenty-seven years of experience at a major aerospace firm in California. During his long career, Carl has played many pivotal roles in the company, particularly in its development of the space program. He is well respected by his peers and has received a number of awards from both the company and government agencies for his work. Other than reading scientific journals and attending an occasional conference, Carl does not need to do much else to stay current in his field. He came to it as an electrical genius. Even in college he did not have to work as hard as other students to succeed.

Recently, however, Carl has sensed that his technical expertise seems to carry less weight. In the past, his colleagues regarded his role in designing a new satellite or spacecraft component as crucial. Now, however, his comments are often met with groans. Carl is not sure what to make of this change, but he suspects that it may be related to changes in what customers are looking for in electrical and aerospace design. Carl feels that the customers are too willing to forgo cutting-edge design in exchange for lower cost. He is offended because his expertise, in a sense, has become irrelevant.

ASSIGNMENT

Apply what you have learned in this chapter about critical theory and related concepts to envision a future for Carl McKnight. When responding to the following questions, be sure to address the connections among sources of expertise, sources of overt and hidden power, and processes of overt and covert communication.

1. From his manager's point of view, what plans should be made for Carl's future? How can he best be made a part of the changing situation?
2. From his peers' perspective, what is the best possible future for Carl?
3. From Carl's point of view, what has happened, and what should happen next?

PART III

CONTEXTS FOR ORGANIZATIONAL COMMUNICATION

CHAPTER 7

Identity and Difference in Organizational Life

Organizations are primary sources of meaning in contemporary life. Through our attempts to coordinate our activities with others, we come to understand both who we are and who we might become. As we argued in Chapter 6, organizational communication often serves to create partisan meanings that privilege the interests of elites over the interests and concerns of the relatively powerless. Thus, organizational meaning-making processes tend to create, emphasize, and value "differences that make a difference" as they are constructed around issues of race, sexuality, class, age, and gender.

In this chapter, we take up meaning-making processes that center on difference in more detail. Specifically, we explore how some socially constructed differences (including gender, race, and class) are produced through everyday organizing. We will also examine the symbolic and material consequences of those socially constructed differences for organizational members. Our understandings of how we are both similar to and different from others shape our very sense of self, and this is particularly true in the context of organizational life. In short, this chapter centers on the concept of organizational identity. **Identity** is defined as how individuals position themselves in the world through language and action. First, however, we provide a historical context for current understandings of identity.

▧ THE HISTORY OF IDENTITY IN ORGANIZATIONAL COMMUNICATION

In Chapter 2, we introduced the concept of the *situated individual* in describing how we all live our lives in the shadow of powerful organizations. Our take on identity has a similar flavor. As we discussed earlier, however, the degree to which organizations have permeated personal life has varied throughout history. Prior to industrialization, notions of the self were largely fixed and mainly unitary; an individual's self-definition came largely from his or her craft, locale, and family, and did not vary much throughout the course of life. In contrast, classical management theories regarded the individual as an inhuman cog in a complex machine, a state accomplished through the bureaucratic separation of the personal and public self. Bureaucracies sought to establish control over the public side of each employee, or the side related to work. This realm was called the individual's *zone of indifference*. Consequently, throughout the industrial era (most of the twentieth century), employees identified their so-called real selves as existing mainly outside of the work setting and appearing only when the artificial rules and roles of work life were loosened.

In recent years, powerful organizations have lost a great deal of their ability to control what individuals can become, thus allowing for a broader range of employee identities. Interestingly, many young people are seeking to reintegrate their work selves with their personal selves, producing a greater continuity of identity across public and private contexts. This trend is propelled by a growing desire for **authenticity**, or for being real and honest in how we live and work with others. Whereas earlier notions of identity referred to an individual's ability to look inside oneself (or outside of one's professional work) to find one's real self, contemporary ideas of authenticity focus much more on the ethics and consistency of one's behaviors. In other words, we must reveal our true selves not only in personal relationships and during our personal time, but also through our choices of professional and organizational affiliation. The motto for those who hold such beliefs might be something along the lines of the popular career guidance advice to "Do what you love!"

Despite our attempts to achieve consistency across contexts, we are continually bombarded by media images from popular culture that offer infinite examples of competing identities. Think of the plethora of ways that the identity of "working mother" is represented in the media; clearly there is no single or preferred identity represented across magazines (parenting magazines, fashion magazines, *O, The Oprah Magazine*), television programs (from soap operas to *Desperate Housewives*), and books, such as Allison Pearson's *I Don't Know How She Does It* (2003). While there may be some common themes in all these representations — namely that women bear the burden of balancing work and life — there is not a clear, consistent, or consensual model available. The same could be said for working fathers, organizational leaders, and successful employees. Thus, most Westerners' identities tend to be both fluid and multiple, or what Kenneth Gergen (1991) describes as a state of "multiphrenia." For most of us, this situation is complex, stressful, and at times tenuous, as we seek to establish core values that will serve us as we perform multiple, varied roles (e.g., student, parent, citizen, employee, fan, congregant, girlfriend, etc.). The proliferation of multiple possible identities makes it even more critical that we select some "horizons of significance" toward which to orient ourselves (Taylor, 1991). These horizons are the most critical values or beliefs about which we may be authentic or, to paraphrase Dr. Martin Luther King, they are the content of our character.

Not all identities, however, are equally welcome in the world of work. For many reasons, organizational members use identity markers to create and highlight differences between people, and then use these marked differences as reasons for treating them differently. The next section begins the discussion of how difference is created in organizations and its implications for individual and organizational well-being.

ORGANIZING DIFFERENCE IN ORGANIZATIONS

In Chapters 5 and 6, we introduced the idea that a significant goal of many organizations is to regulate and control their members' identities. Alvesson and Wilmott (2002), two European critical management scholars, describe several specific practices that organizations use to "make" members' identities, including:

1. *Defining the person directly*: Those who are described as midlevel managers, as opposed to senior-level managers, have their leadership capacities curtailed, by definition.
2. *Defining a person by defining others*: Many organizational members create positive identities by contrasting their positions with the positions of others. For example, low-level hospice care providers who have little organizational status or authority often describe themselves as providing real, hands-on care, while describing registered nurses as paper-pushers.
3. *Providing a specific vocabulary of motives*: Organizations often explicitly describe the motivations that drive their ideal employees. An elementary school that recruits and retains only those employees who passionately care about children and education provides employees with a road map for successful identities. For example, a "successful" teacher is one who does not request a higher salary or a stipend to buy items for his or her classroom. A successful teacher is "in it for the kids."
4. *Explicating morals and values*: Organizational cultures, as discussed in Chapter 5, routinely offer employees an explicit set of guiding values such as innovation, customer service, or efficiency that they may use to craft and/or regulate their identities at work.
5. *Knowledge and skills*: Having access to specific knowledge (of the law or of medicine, for example) or the skills necessary to execute a specific process or practice enables organizational members to define themselves in particular ways.

6. *Group categorization and affiliation*: When organizations foster feelings of "us" and, often less explicitly, "them," they generate feelings of community, belonging, and loyalty. Students, for example, who are integrated into the fabric of the university are more likely to retain spirited connections to their alma maters.

7. *Hierarchical location*: One of the central ways that we answer the question "Who am I?" is by figuring out the superiority/subordination dynamics between ourselves and others. Those relations are often both symbolically and materially reinforced in organizations.

8. *Establishing and clarifying a distinct set of rules of the game*: Organizational communication creates and naturalizes rules and taken-for-granted ways of doing and being. For example, specific ways of being a "team player" (e.g., working without complaint, not outdoing a superior, protecting teammates from mistakes) often serve to regulate employees' behavior.

9. *Defining the context*: Organizational leaders often define the environment in which employees operate. When globalization, excessive competition, and rapid and unpredictable change are said to mark the environment, then organizations tend to value those who are adaptable, aggressive, and entrepreneurial.

While organizations do, in fact, make explicit attempts to manage diverse identities, those efforts are not always entirely successful or seamless. A focus on gender as a difference that makes a difference in organizational life points to the complexities of identity construction. One group that has provided considerable insight into those complexities are the feminist organizational scholars who study the impact of communication on public and private gendered identities.

One of the key reasons that feminist organizational communication scholars have been interested in the question of identity at work is because of the marginalization women have experienced historically in public and organizational life, particularly through wage, access, and mobility inequities. In response, feminist research has attempted both to explain women's marginal position and to develop alternative organizational structures, policies, and identities that enable women to participate more fully in organizations.

Feminist research takes on a variety of forms and is influenced by several different traditions. For example, whereas **liberal feminists** are most interested in changing government and company policies to level the playing field for women in organizations, **radical feminists** might be more interested in dismantling those very organizations and replacing them with feminist-inspired, nonhierarchical structures. Recent feminist scholarship has moved beyond studying gendered organizational dynamics to exploring the intersections among gender, race, class, sexuality, and other aspects of individual and social identities.

Despite these many variations, feminist scholarship on identity, particularly in the context of organizations, is united by the assumption that the socially constructed (and ideological) split between the public sphere of work and the private sphere of home has led to significant symbolic and material consequences for both men and women. Historically, men and men's work have been linked to the public sphere and public organizational life, while women and women's work have been associated with the private or domestic realm. The public/private split has resulted in several implications for men and women in contemporary organizational life, including the

- exclusion and control of women in the public sphere;
- denial of women's domestic work as legitimate and valued labor;
- devaluation of feminized labor in the public sphere (e.g., nursing, teaching, and other caring professions);
- reduction of men's participation in domestic work and family life;
- construction of work/family conflicts as a private problem rather than a public or social issue (Ashcraft, 2005, pp. 153–54).

Recently, feminists have adopted a number of different approaches to explore the implications of the public/private split of gendered identity. One direct outgrowth of their interest in this divide is focused attention on work/family conflict or, more recently, work/life conflict (Kirby, Golden, Medven, Jorgenson, & Buzzanell, 2003). The term **work/life conflict** refers to the simultaneous influence of work on members' lives away from work—at home, at leisure, and in families and communities—and the influence of personal life responsibilities and aspirations on members' experiences at work. Work/life conflict has been of interest to feminist scholars because women's ability to successfully negotiate work/life balance and to craft satisfying identities is hampered by social constructions of gender that encourage women to take on significant duties in the private sphere, such as child care and domestic labor, once they get home from work (Hochschild, 1989). As feminist scholars are a diverse group, they approach this important topic in a variety of ways that offer a number of potential solutions for working women and men.

Karen Ashcraft (2004), a leading feminist organizational communication scholar, outlines four approaches or "frames" that are particularly relevant to questions regarding the public/private spheres, work/life balance, and gender concerns. Work/ life identities are ongoing accomplishments that are continually informed and constructed by discourses of gender, power, and organization. Yet, each frame adopts a different way of considering the relationships among communication, gendered identity, and the organization. Each frame also constructs the "problem" of gender in a particular way, and in so doing, also suggests a potential solution to the "woman question" at work.

In the following sections, we take a close look at Ashcraft's four frames of identity (Gender Difference at Work, Gender Identity as Organizational Performance, Gendered Organizations, and Gender Narratives in Popular Culture), using examples of work/life conflict research to highlight the ways that gendered identities—both at home and at work—are impacted, created, and transformed by organizational communication.

□ Frame 1: Gender Differences at Work

The popularity of John Gray's book *Men Are from Mars, Women Are from Venus* attests to the cultural belief that men and women communicate in fundamentally different ways. The first frame assumes that gender is "a socialized but relatively fixed identity . . . organized around biological sex and which fosters fairly predictable communication habits" (Ashcraft, 2004, p. 276). Men and women's communication styles, therefore, are outgrowths of gendered socialization and are made manifest in organizational contexts. The scholarship on gender communication differences supports this frame.

Sociologist Deborah Tannen's (1994) book *You Just Don't Understand: Women and Men in Conversation* provides a comprehensive view of how gendered identities, learned in childhood, drive men's and women's conversational styles. Men treat conversations as a hierarchically ordered space in which they can demonstrate and vie for *status*; women treat conversations as a web-like space in which they can demonstrate and vie for *connections*. Men seek status by engaging in **report talk**, a style of speaking that emphasizes:

- demonstrations of knowledge, skill, and ability
- instrumentality
- conversational command
- direct and assertive expressions
- abstract terms over personal experience (Tannen, 1994)

Women use conversations to build relationships using rapport talk. **Rapport talk** emphasizes:

- demonstrating equality through matching experiences
- providing support and responsiveness
- conversational maintenance
- tentativeness
- personal, concrete details (Tannen, 1994)

According to this literature, these different conversational orientations can often lead to misunderstandings between men and women who often experience the same conversation in very different ways. "Troubles talk," or discussions of personal or professional problems, is one arena where men and women tend to adopt distinct approaches. Tannen claims that when women share their troubles with a conversational partner, they often hope to hear messages of support ("That must be difficult for you"), reciprocity ("I know how you feel; I remember when something similar happened to me"), and connection. When sharing their stories with other women, they often receive precisely those messages. However, when sharing problems with male conversational partners, women often receive solutions and directives ("You should just confront your colleague"). A woman might interpret a man's instrumental approach to troubles talk as a move to cut her off or diminish her experience. Similarly, when men engage in troubles talk with women, they are often disappointed with women's tendencies to immediately match troubles. Such a conversational move is interpreted by men as simply wallowing in self-pity or complaining without taking action. Tannen (1994) suggests that the trick to conversational success is for men and women to learn to interpret one another's speech styles in new ways and to develop a larger conversational repertoire so that it becomes easier to be heard by those who occupy different gendered speech communities.

Early research on gender in organizational contexts sought to document men's and women's different communication styles and their effects on organizational processes and outcomes. In such studies, women's seemingly tentative, self-deprecating, and inclusive speech was initially assumed to be ill-suited to the hard-driving demands of organizational life, and management in particular. Women's communication style was perceived as preventing them from forming networks and moving up the career ladder (see, for example, a study by Reardon, 1997). More recent research suggests that women do not ask for things (e.g., raises, promotions, etc.) or negotiate on their own behalf as often or as forcefully as their male counterparts. The lack of this specific communication behavior can lead to fairly dramatic and troublesome outcomes. Consider the following example:

> Suppose that at age 22 an equally qualified man and woman receive job offers of $25,000 a year. The man negotiates and gets his offer raised to $30,000. The woman does not negotiate and accepts the job for $25,000. Even if each of them receives identical 3 percent raises every year throughout their careers (which is unlikely, given their different propensity to negotiate and other research showing that women's achievements tend to be undervalued), by the time they reach age 60 the gap between their salaries will have widened to more than $15,000 a year, with the man earning $92,243 and the woman only $76,870. While that might not seem like an enormous spread, remember that the man will have been making more all along, with his extra earnings over the 38 years totaling $361,171. If the man had simply banked the difference every year in a savings account earning 3 percent interest, by the age of 60 he would have $568,834 more than the woman—enough to underwrite a comfortable retirement nest egg, purchase a second home, or pay for the college education of a few children. This is an enormous return on investment for a *one-time* negotiation. (Babcock & Laschever, 2003, p. 5)

Linda Babcock, an economics professor at Carnegie Mellon University, and Sara Laschever, a journalist, argue that women need to follow the assertive man's lead and ask for what they deserve. Failure to do so results in "molehills" (a one-time missed negotiation) becoming "mountains" (lack of a comfortable retirement).

While much of the early research treated women's communication style as a deficit or a liability at work, some scholars attempted to demonstrate the utility, perhaps even the superiority, of "women's ways" of knowing, being, and leading. For example, women tend to think of organizations in terms of networks or webs of relationships, with leadership at the center of the web rather than on top of a pyramid (Helgeson, 1990). Further, in contrast to traditional models, narratives by and about women tend to value:

- fluid boundaries between personal life and work life
- relational aspects of work

- a balanced lifestyle
- a nurturant approach to co-workers
- a network of relationships within and outside the organization
- a service orientation to clients
- work as a means of developing personal identity (Buzzanell, 2000; Grossman & Chester, 1990; Helgeson, 1990; Lunneborg, 1990; Rosener, 1990)

Valuing "women's ways" in organizations means opening organizational dialogue to a different set of assumptions: Can we define competition as "doing excellently" instead of "excelling over" (Calas & Smirich, 1996)? Can we define power in a way that enhances, rather than diminishes, the power of everyone (Reuther & Fairhurst, 2000)? Can we value and seek diversity in organizations (Allen, 2004)? Can we view organizations as being responsible for social change (Marshall, 1984)? Can hierarchies be abandoned or reenvisioned as networks (Ferguson, 1984)? Can we learn to ask "whom does my work benefit" (Buzzanell, 2000)?

Women's ways of operating in organizations bear a striking resemblance to more general prescriptions for effective and progressive leaders and managers, which we discuss in detail in Chapter 9. Specifically, there is a growing consensus that the traditionally male form of leadership that highlights command and control does not work in today's complex and dynamic organizations. Moreover, it is increasingly clear that leaders must share responsibility, develop and invest in others, and build and maintain a network of relationships to effectively manage diverse and often competing stakeholders. What is fascinating is that few male writers have been willing to characterize these new leadership models as in any way feminine! One advantage of doing so is that it would allow us to see the masculine hegemony evident in traditional, purportedly gender-neutral organizations (May, 2000; Mumby, 2000).

With some notable exceptions (e.g., women's asking behaviors), it is important to note here that the research on gender differences over the last three decades has yielded little empirically supported behavioral differences between men's and women's communication in organizational contexts (Canary & Hause, 1993). Yet, even when men and women engage in similar behaviors, it is often made meaningful or interpreted in very different ways. What persists is a well-entrenched ideology of "gender differences" that continues to hold sway in the popular imagination. As a result, even when men and women engage in the same behaviors, those behaviors are interpreted differently in organizations that often privilege masculinity over femininity.

☐ Gender Differences in Work/Life

The assumption that men's and women's communication styles are fundamentally different has implications for the ways that men and women negotiate their work and their personal lives. Because women are assumed to be more nurturing and relationally focused, women's caregiving at home has been viewed as a "natural" outgrowth of women's love for their partners and children. As a result, women have often assumed greater responsibility for domestic labor, even when they work as many hours outside the home as their partners (Coltrane, 2000; Erickson, 2005). Sociologist Arlie Hochschild (1989) labeled this phenomenon the **second shift**. The term captures the significant labor that women perform in the private sphere for which they receive little compensation or gratitude (Hochschild, 2003). Current research suggests that women who work outside of the home typically still do twice as much routine housework as their male partners, despite the fact that men's participation in household labor has increased slightly over the past several years (Coltrane, 2000). Not surprisingly, working women participate in fewer hours of leisure activity, including exercise, than their male partners, particularly in families with young children (Nomaguchi & Bianchi, 2004).

Even in occupations with more flexible hours, gender inequities persist in the division of domestic labor. The new knowledge- and service-based economy and the development of the Internet have enabled many changes in the way employees accomplish their work/lives. Communication technologies can free employees from working on-site, thus "extending the range of locations [and times] from which paid work can be carried out," but technology can also be a "means of work invading the home" (Perrons, 2003, p. 69). Thus, negotiating work/life balance becomes even more complicated as the boundaries between public life and private life become blurred. In one study, some women who used communication technology to perform their work found it to provide greater flexibility and "time sovereignty" that enabled them to combine "interesting, enjoyable, intellectually challenging and highly satisfying work with family life" (Perrons, 2003, p. 88). Yet, the majority of women still experienced significant tensions between work and life, particularly among women with children or other caring responsibilities. So, while communication technologies have created new ways of working, our ways of living have not caught up. Most families still rely on the female parent to negotiate child care and domestic labor, men are still wary of taking parental leave and using other family-friendly policies, and children are still treated as an individual choice rather than a public good. These assumptions prevent many working women (and men) from creating the flexibility that is so sorely needed and desired by much of the current and future workforce (Stork, Wilson, Wicks, Sproull, & Vena, 2005).

While this frame has the deepest roots in organizational communication research, it is problematic because it assumes that perceived differences between men and women are innate, highlights those differences rather than similarities, and often reinforces the idea that women's ways of speaking and being are less valuable than men's, particularly in organizational contexts.

☐ Frame 2: Gender Identity as Organizational Performance

While early research assumed that identity was a relatively fixed and stable effect of biology or socialization, later approaches treated gender as a communicative accomplishment or performance. Treating gender as a fixed biological or learned source of communication behavior overlooks the ways individuals create their gendered identities through communication in everyday interactions. Karen Ashcraft's second frame foregrounds gender as an ongoing accomplishment, as an identity that is accomplished through "doing" rather than "being" (West & Zimmerman, 1987). Feminist scholar Judith Butler suggests that we do gender in and through everyday performances or micropractices that are carried out on the organizational stage. **Micropractices** refer to the moment-to-moment behaviors, actions, and communication messages that we use to bring ourselves into being in everyday life.

Like actors who create their characters for the audience, organizational members enact a gendered self on the organizational stage, using gendered norms and expectations as their scripts that they then improvise in everyday contexts (Goffman, 1959). From this angle, gender is not an essential or "natural" or fixed aspect of our identities, "but practices learnt and enacted in appropriate occasions" (Bruni, Gherardi, & Poggio, 2004, p. 407). In fact, Frame 2 suggests that gender is an aspect of our identity that is negotiated and renegotiated anew each and every day, across a variety of contexts. Thus, how a person performs masculinity or femininity will change depending on the context.

A study by Alexandra Murphy (2003) reveals how exotic dancers perform multiple forms of femininity in multiple contexts. On the stage, dancers (literally) embody a highly stylized and overtly feminine identity that is based on a caricature of male desire. As one dancer commented, to be successful, "you become whatever they [the customers] want you to be" (p. 314). Murphy reminds us that "she is not saying that the strippers *are* what the customers want them to be. They become or they *perform* what the customers want them to be" (p. 314). While clearly a job that requires a staged performance would demand that employees negotiate their gendered identity regularly, Murphy's work also points to how dancers have to negotiate their identities in "backstage" contexts as well. For many dancers, negotiating an acceptable identity as a "good girl" with friends and family becomes equally complex. Dancers find ways of describing their work in strategically ambiguous terms (e.g., telling children that mommy works in a "big people's place," avoiding conversations about their work, or simply lying about what they do).

Murphy's research raises the question, why do organizational members go to such lengths to perform "appropriate" gender identities? The answer is that successful gendered performance is richly rewarded. Dancers who enact a "proper" feminine gender identity are rewarded with higher tips, and male oil rig workers who demonstrate stoicism in the face of work hazards and even injuries are more likely to retain their often precarious jobs (Collinson, 1999; Murphy, 2003). Those who fail to perform their gender correctly are routinely punished (Butler, 1988). Indeed, there are severe penalties for failing to enact or perform an appropriate organizational gender, including lack of upward mobility and less access to employment. Employees who embody a preferred gender identity and are more attractive than their average counterparts are more likely to receive job offers and higher starting salaries (Watkins & Johnston, 2000).

While much of the research on gendered organizational performances has focused on white, middle-class women's identity performances (Ashcraft, 1999; Brewis, Hampton, & Linstead, 1997; Murphy, 1998), scholars are also beginning to explore how women's gendered identity performances are complicated at work by issues of race (Allen, 2005; Parker, 2003), class (Hughes, 2004), age (Trethewey, 2001), and sexuality (Spradlin, 1998). Patricia Parker (2003) documents the contradictions that African American women often experience between their own empowered self-definitions of African American womanhood and the social and organizational constructions that relegate them to a position of "difference" or "marginality" in organizational life. In order to craft successful identity performances, African American women must often

- seek and gain high visibility projects;
- exceed performance expectations;
- use an acceptable (read: white, middle-class, professional) communication style; and
- obtain an influential mentor or sponsor (Parker, 2003).

Because prejudice and discrimination are still unfortunate features of many organizations, these tasks are often challenging for African American women. Relying on other African American women in the community for support is another strategy for crafting successful identities at work (Parker, 2003). Many African American women develop networks outside their workplaces to help them navigate the difficulties of operating in dominant culture organizations. Those external social support groups become a place where African American women can find emotional and social support and engage in authentic, less guarded conversations about work life.

Another area of current inquiry that points to the performed character of identity is emotion labor. **Emotion labor**, a term made popular by Arlie Hochschild, refers to "a type of work wherein employees are paid to create a 'package' of emotions" (Tracy, 2000, p. 91). Hochschild's (1983) early study of flight attendants revealed that the organization proscribed "feeling rules" for the flight attendants that made explicit the particular emotional displays or performances that the attendants were required to enact. Flight attendants' main tool for ensuring that passengers enjoy the ride is their "happy face," and flight attendants are encouraged not to drop this "tool," even in the event of an emergency (Murphy, 2001, p. 34). From Hochschild's perspective, emotion labor can be damaging over time as employees become estranged from their "real" feelings after performing "fake," commodified, instrumental, and organizationally controlled feelings. Moreover, extensive emotion labor has been linked with increased stress and burnout (Tracy, 2000, 2005). Communication scholars have extended Hochschild's early research by demonstrating that performed emotions, and their resultant organizational identities, are no less "real" than their seemingly "authentic" counterparts. Sarah Tracy studied the emotion labor performances of cruise ship employees and corrections officers. Her research revealed that in a very real sense employees, over time, become the characters they perform. Employees who are ̄ed to "put on a har y face" at work, like cruise ship employees, come to understand themselves and their identity in those terms (Tracy, 2003). In one particularly troubling incident onboard, a female employee withstood rather blatant sexual harassment from a male customer because she wanted to maintain her "happy, smiling" and gendered emotional display. Similarly, corrections officers, who are primarily men, are explicitly asked to demonstrate a suspicious and detached demeanor at work. These individuals often continue to embody that persona at home (Tracy, 2005).

☐ Performing Gender in Work/Life

For many employees, emotion labor is a primary means through which they perform a gendered work(ing) identity. However, gendered performance continues after the work day comes to a close; it seeps into employees' home lives as well as the "third spaces" between work and home (e.g., the gym, communities of faith, the laundromat) (Oldenberg, 1999). David Collinson, a British critical scholar, found that shop floor workers embodied distinct performances of masculinity at work and at home. At work, the shop floor workers demonstrated a very public form of working class masculinity that is characterized by cursing, reinforcing the value of physical labor as a symbol of honesty and integrity, emphasizing their (hyper) sexuality (e.g., telling tales of prowess), and "piss taking," a form of macho joking with one another (Collinson, 1992, p. 115).

At home, those same men, however, enact a very different private role. They continue to perform what they believe to be the role of a real man, but they do so using different private strategies. They do not curse, many do not reveal their salaries or "wage packets" to their wives because to do so would undermine their breadwinner role, and they try to maintain strict boundaries between their lives at work and their lives at home. Unlike salaried managers, the shop floor men resisted and denigrated those (managers) who would "take work home" (p. 95); rather, as "masculine breadwinners" they describe themselves as "free," at least from the burden at work, once they clock out. Interestingly, however, those men described feeling much more comfortable and relaxed with their fellow workers in public interactions than with their own wives in private ones. Collinson concludes that such gendered identity performances tend to reproduce traditionally gendered scripts at home and class-based scripts at the office.

Gendered performances may even be part of the work contract, as we saw with the flight attendants in Hochschild's study who performed emotion labor. While Hochschild treated emotion labor exclusively as part of paid employment, others now suggest that emotion labor, though often overlooked, is a regular part of domestic labor at home (Erickson, 2005). Given cultural understandings of gender that position women as "naturally" caring, it is not surprising that women tend to bolster the emotional well-being of their partners and families as well as manage the "emotional climate" in relationships (p. 338). One study found that those who constructed their gender in feminine terms tend to do significantly more emotion work in their personal lives. Moreover, in that same study, the tendency "to conceptualize emotion work as *work* suggests that women recognized that they are held accountable for the performance of this work in ways that men are not" (p. 348). Like emotion labor at work, emotion work at home is a gendered performance that "does not just emanate from within, but must be managed, focused, and directed so as to have the intended effect on the care recipient" (p. 349). This important aspect of family work has often been excluded from studies of the division of household labor, and yet it is an ongoing and demanding gendered performance. This frame shines a spotlight on the everyday performances that make up gendered identities. The organization, however, remains a neutral stage on which those performances are enacted.

☐ Frame 3: Gendered Organizations

Frame 3 brings the gendered character of organizations themselves into sharp relief. Here, the assumption is that organizational forms or structures, "like gender identity—[are] constantly in process, brought to life, sustained and transformed by interaction among members. Simultaneously, organization guides interaction, predisposing and rewarding members to practice in particular ways" (Ashcraft, 2004, p. 281). The organization acts like an agent or a character that both produces and is a product of gendered scripts or discourse. Here, gender is a fundamental feature of organizations that impacts identities in a variety of taken-for-granted ways.

In a foundational essay, sociologist Joan Acker argued that far from being "neutral" backdrops, organizations are themselves gendered structures that reflect and reproduce patriarchy or the systemic privileging of masculinity. To say that an organization is gendered means that "advantage and disadvantage, exploitation and control, action and emotion, meaning and identity, are patterned through and in terms of a distinction between male and female, masculine and feminine" (Acker, 1990, p. 146). The gendered organization emerges out of at least five processes, including:

- The social construction of divisions of labor, positions, and types of work along gendered lines. The types of work that women and men do are often differentiated in organizations such that women assume support roles and men assume leadership roles.
- The social construction of symbols and images that reinforce gender divisions. Images of leadership often rest on a masculine model.
- The mundane communication interactions between men and women, men and men, and women and women often reproduce gender divisions in ways that reinforce men's (relatively) powerful position. Women's speech is often presumed to be ill-suited to organizational life.
- The ways in which individual actors often take up identities that reinforce the three processes described above. Career choices, style of dress, interaction patterns, and everyday performances result in gendered identities.
- Gender is, then, a fundamental element in "organizational logic" or a "gendered substructure that is reproduced daily in practical work activities" (Acker, 1990).

Through these processes, organizational structures, jobs, and even bodies are gendered in specific ways. For example, Acker argues that the dominant organizational logic creates a preference for a "male worker whose life centers on his full-time, life-long job, while his wife or another woman takes care of his personal needs and children" (p. 151). Even management theory has often assumed that career paths unfold in upward, linear, sequential, and cumulative ways, with few breaks, disruptions, or interruptions. Feminist scholars suggest that, as such, the very notion of career has been biased in ways that have favored men (Ashcraft, 1999; Marshall, 1989). For women, embodying the "ideal" worker is difficult, as that which is associated with the private sphere and domesticity is excluded from organizational logic. Thus, "women's bodies — female sexuality, their ability to procreate and their pregnancy, breast-feeding, and child care, menstruation, and mythic 'emotionality' — are suspect, stigmatized and used as grounds for control and exclusion" (p. 152).

When domesticity, the private sphere, and femininity are devalued and assumed to be abnormal or less than ideal, organizational hierarchies come to reflect and reproduce those values. It is not surprising, then, that many positions involving care and support (e.g., administrative assistants, nurses, and human resource professionals) are treated as "women's work" and often located near the bottom of organizational hierarchies. And even men who demonstrate a commitment to their family or other nonwork activities may be perceived as having less career potential.

Acker's model of the gendered organization has influenced many communication scholars who have studied its consequences. Patricia Parker's (1997, 2003) research extends Acker's model by suggesting that, in addition to being gendered, organizations are also "raced" and "classed" in ways that reflect and reproduce inequitable divisions in everyday organizational life (see also, Allen, 2004; Allen & Aschraft, 2003). Recruiting and promoting practices, for example, contribute, however unintentionally, to job segregation along gendered, raced, and classed lines. For example, young African American women may received negative or indifferent messages about academic and career achievement from their teachers, counselors, and school administrators and are thereby discouraged from pursuing careers where African American women are underrepresented. If African American girls do successfully negotiate raced and classed school environments, empirical evidence suggests that they are often confronted with race-based discrimination during initial employment interviews (Holzer, 1996).

One recent study suggests that while racial discrimination has decreased somewhat over the past two decades, African American men are still disadvantaged compared to similarly skilled white men, particularly when applying for jobs in organizations that assess social skills according to "ambiguous evaluative criteria" (Kim & Tamborini, 2006). The organizational logic that defines "whiteness" as the unspoken but pervasive norm also requires that African Americans prove to potential employers that they do not conform to racial stereotypes by adopting a "middle-class" persona, including appearance, style of dress, and manner of speech (2006). The gendered, raced, and classed character of organizations enables and constrains the identities that employees and employers perform in their daily organizational activities. The gendered organization also extends its reach into nonwork arenas.

☐ Gendered Organizations and Work/Life

The gendered organization exists at an abstract and theoretical level, but is manifest in very specific, material, and codified ways at the level of organizational policy. Policies centered explicitly on work/life issues, including family leave, flextime, and the "mommy track," dictate both the organization's and the employee's rights, responsibilities, and privileges. Far from being simply legalistic and neutral, policies, too, can be read as gendered narratives and outgrowths of the gendered organization.

Peterson and Albrecht (1999) point out that maternity leave is often framed as a "benefit." In so doing, policies treat maternity leave as a bonus rather than an automatic right, such as sick leave or vacation time. Whereas some employees can forego sick or vacation leave in favor of pay, "it would be a rare occurrence, indeed, that an employee would be paid for not taking a maternity leave" (p. 174). Moreover, pregnancy is often cast in policy texts as a sickness, disability, or limitation, rather than an important family/life event or process. This clinical, rational approach to pregnancy is further evidenced by the language of organizational documents. As noted by Peterson and Albrecht, "The neutral, rationale tone of the text symbolizes the language of the public domain. . . . The language of emotion and nurturance . . . is part of the private domain and thus inappropriate for an organizational document" (p. 177). Peterson and Albrecht also note that leave policies—while involving the mother, the father, and the child—tend to focus on the mother/employee. Fathers and children are largely written out of story. So rather than being "benign" documents, policies are a "discursive site where gendered identities are produced and reproduced" such that pregnancy is associated with organizational abnormalities, parenting is treated as a "women's issue," and domestic life is rendered less central than organizational life (p. 179).

Buzzanell and Liu (2005) examined the experience of several women during their maternity leaves and found that many had difficulty maintaining a gendered identity that was valued, recognized, and rewarded. In their study, the authors suggest that organizations could develop more gender equitable policies by:

- establishing an advocate in the human resource department who would assist women in their negotiations for leave, special accommodations, and career opportunities with their supervisors,
- making parental leave policies unambiguous, automatic, and streamlined, so that they serve as a "baseline" from which case-by-case negotiations can proceed,
- rewarding and promoting competent women while they are pregnant or on maternity leave, or during their return to work,
- providing flexible work schedules and [rewarding] employees for efficiency rather than extensive "face time" at work (Buzzanell & Liu, 2005).

Fortunately, there are some organizations that are making system-wide changes to better accommodate and serve the diverse needs of their working men and women. Deloitte & Touche, an international accounting and consulting firm, recognized that the gendered character of their organization was resulting in a high turnover rate among its most highly qualified women and dissatisfaction among many of its employees, who felt they could not effectively balance work and life concerns. In response, the organization made large scale changes in eight areas: child care, organizational culture, flexible schedules, generous parental leave policies, women's advancement programs, total compensation, work/life culture, and family-friendly programs. As a result, the company has won numerous awards, including recently being named to *Working Mother* magazine's "100 Best Companies for Working Mothers" for the twelfth consecutive year ("100 Best," 2005). These instrumental changes have nearly eliminated the gender gap in turnover and serve as a model for other organizations hoping to reduce gender inequality.

As this example suggests, an important implication of Frame 3 is that it demonstrates that identities can usually not be changed simply through individual choices or performances; rather, the organizational systems, structures, and policies that reflect and reproduce gendered inequities must change. Feminist scholars and activists continue their attempts to design and implement equitable organizational structures and policies (Ashcraft, 2001; Martin, 1990, 1994). While fully feminist organizations are difficult to maintain, many of the principles they advocate have found their way into more mainstream organizations.

☐ Frame 4: Gendered Narratives in Popular Culture

Frames 1 and 2 focus on gendered individuals within organizations, and Frame 3 is centered on the gendered organization. Frame 4 directs our attention outside the organizational context to the broad social discourses that shape both gendered identities and gendered organizational forms. This frame "shifts attention from communication *in* organizations to communication *about* organization, or how a larger society portrays and debates its institutions and the very notion of work" and workers (Ashcraft & Mumby, 2004, p. 19). The assumption is that social texts that exist outside the organization, such as those found in popular culture, reveal and reproduce cultural understandings about the nature of work, life, and identity. In other words, the meanings we assign to ourselves, our work, and our organizations are significantly influenced by the texts — films, books, television shows, news reports, magazines, fashions, and even scholarship — we consume in our everyday lives. Social texts like these provide us with discursive fragments or raw materials for constructing our own gendered identities in everyday life. Think, for example, about how television programs such as *The Apprentice* might influence the young viewers' ideas about superior-subordinate relationships, the seemingly competitive character of work life, and the gendered nature of leadership ("You're fired!").

Of the frames we have addressed thus far, Frame 4 is the most recent development in organizational communication theorizing and research. The few studies using this approach have traced representations of executive women and white-collar masculinity in film and representations of working women in magazines (Ashcraft & Flores, 2003; Schuler, 2000; Triece, 1999). The most comprehensive study to date that adopts this framework is Ashcraft and Mumby's (2004) project that explores the historical emergence of contemporary understandings of airline pilots as (largely) white, male, middle-class professionals. Through a critical reading of diverse texts, including historical texts and images, museum displays, poetry, films, government documents, and personal interviews, the authors track the shifting identity position of pilots from the end of World War I to the beginning of the twenty-first century.

After the war, popular images portrayed pilots as "hard-living, hard-drinking playboys" who "embodied distinctively masculine themes of physical and sexual prowess, individualism, debonair courage and rugged adventure, peppered with a dash of science" (Ashcraft & Mumby, 2004, p. 135). While romantic, appealing, and fascinating, the images did little to alleviate the public's fear of flying, which was shaping up to be a new mode of public transportation. Perhaps, not surprisingly, a new discourse emerged to ease the public's concern. This discourse featured "lady-fliers," "ladybirds," or "lipstick pilots" who took up flying as a "graceful sport" and managed to fly airplanes while maintaining their physical grace and beauty. During the late 1920s and early 1930s, this discourse (which was reproduced in advertisements for beauty products and cigarettes), reassured the public that flying was easy (since women could do it!) and planes were trustworthy. However, this discourse also proved risky and threatening to prevailing gendered assumptions. The lady-flier raised the possibility that, at least in the air, men and women could be equals! Rather than questioning the assumption that there really were few differences between men and women pilots, the public perception was that flying was simply easy, or that it was not real work.

The move, again, to establish flying as a masculine activity emerged in the late 1930s and early 1940s. At that time, the airline industry was struggling to become profitable and looking for ways to ensure long-term viability. The lipstick pilot heightened interest in flight, but not necessarily as a safe and reliable form of transportation. So, the airline industry created a public relations campaign designed to give pilots a "makeover" (Ashcraft & Mumby, 2004, p. 147). The body of the pilot was remade in the image of the authoritative sea captain, complete with uniforms. The new bureaucratized pilot was explicitly white, male, professional, and disciplined. Indeed, fearing that non-white pilots would damage the image of the "clean-cut Anglo-American type" pilot the airlines were trying to create, the Air Line Pilots Association adopted a "formal whites-only clause until 1942, retaining a tacit prohibition against pilots of color for sometime thereafter" (p. 147). This new image commanded professional privilege that is, in many ways, still unmatched. While the professionalized, racialized, and masculinized pilot garnered public and federal support, secured a professional monopoly, and institutionalized high salaries, the lady pilot did not disappear entirely from view. She simply was moved from the aptly named cockpit to the cabin, where she was transformed into a domesticated and feminized stewardess. It is that model that still frames current understandings of gendered relations, identities, and the division of labor in the aviation industry. Ashcraft and Mumby's analysis using the fourth frame productively moves between historical and contemporary texts and between micro- and macro-discourses as they impact, in material and symbolic ways, individual and collective identities.

☐ Gendered Narratives of Work/Life

In an increasingly media-saturated world, we are routinely bombarded with cultural texts that offer representations of work, workers, and work lives. A Frame 4 approach to work life explores how popular texts shape identities in the larger culture and how those culturally conditioned identities impact work life. For example, many scholars suggest that a growing force in popular culture is consumption (Schor, 1998). **Consumption** is a cultural practice through which individuals craft a self. Our consumptive choices regarding work (e.g., cell phones, PDAs, laptops, vehicles, dress) speak volumes about how we wish to show ourselves to family, friends, and colleagues.

In another example of culturally conditioned identity and its impact on work/life, Nadesan and Trethewey (2000) examined how the discourse of the burgeoning self-help industry — as revealed by the growing number of books on women's workplace success — articulates the internal (cognitive) and external (embodied) "barriers" that prevent women from achieving their full potential while offering advice on what women can do to overcome these obstacles. These popular success texts often presume that young women are wary of power, conflict, and success in professional environments. Thus, women are encouraged to develop strategies to overcome their internal barriers and also to mold their external images, through dress, makeup, and comportment, to match or approximate the organizational ideal.

In addition to revealing the prescriptions offered to working women in the popular success literature, Nadesan and Trethewey's (2000) study also described how individual professional women often reinforce and, sometimes, resist the identity positions outlined by such literature in their everyday practices. Several women in their study, for example, bemoaned the fact that women, unlike men, have never learned to separate business and friendship, confront conflict, or engage in competition. Thus, the participants claimed that women get bogged down in relationship maintenance at work in ways that their male counterparts do not. In so doing, these women reproduced the notion that is so common in popular success texts that men are more "naturally" suited to the demands of organizational life. And yet, even while expressing misgivings about "feminine" relational orientations, many of these same women also value themselves and others for building relationships, despite the fact that it takes time, energy, and effort and is not often explicitly valued in either the popular success literature or in their workplaces. This research indicates that popular texts are identity resources that real women employ in their attempts to perform appropriate, successful, and "entrepreneurial" workplace identities.

Through a variety of popular texts, employees are increasingly encouraged to treat the self as an enterprise, an ongoing project, and even a brand that can be managed (Lair, Sullivan, & Cheney, 2005). The entrepreneurial self, so pervasive in popular culture, "relies upon the image of an independent, resourceful, creative, and aggressive professional. This person is expected to be agile in a fluctuating job market, responsive to any opportunities, self-motivating and self-promoting" (p. 318). And the best way to do this is to literally turn one's self into a value-added commodity, or a **personal brand**. Even stay-at-home mothers are adopting this strategy by defining themselves as "family CEOs," developing family "mission statements" and treating the family as an enterprise (Medved & Kirby, 2005). While this model may, in fact, increase the likelihood of workplace success, it has rather problematic implications for success in other spheres. First, the entrepreneurial self, in a constant bid to enhance one's personal brand, often sacrifices family and relationships to work. Second, while the popular texts that espouse personal branding imply that everyone is equally able to create a successful "brand," personal branding:

> encourages women to get ahead at work, work as hard or harder than their male counterparts, and reach for the top but also to look womanly, take care of their external appearance, be there for their children and husbands (if a woman has them — but recognize that if she does, she may not be viewed as a 100% company woman), and routinely act in the caretaker role at work. (Lair, Sullivan, & Cheney, 2005, p. 328)

This is a tall order that few can achieve, and yet the popular narrative places the burden squarely on the woman's shoulders if she fails to achieve the entrepreneurial ideal. These social texts rarely address the ways that culture, organizations, and families make many unrealistic demands on working women. The personal branding texts similarly ignore the difficulties that aging, disabled, minority, or working-class individuals may face in creating a "winning" personal brand that is based on a white, middle-class, male model. Indeed, it is often the case that successful entrepreneurs often rely on working-class, third-world individuals to take on the burdens of the domestic sphere, including child care, housework, and yard maintenance, so that they can focus on success in the public sphere (Flanagan, 2004). Thus backstaged others often make significant, though undervalued and unrecognized, contributions to what appears to be an individual's success at work.

Finally, Frame 4 assumes that although popular culture impacts individual identities by offering resources through which individuals can craft identities, those narratives are rarely adopted wholesale. Moreover, this frame develops an historic and holistic understanding of gendered discourse as it encourages scholars to trace the emergence of particular identities in popular culture. Such analyses of popular culture may encourage individuals to be more critical consumers of cultural identity narratives. In short, individuals have the power to adopt, reject, and even transform the social narratives that guide them. Or, as Goodall (2004) asks, are you a character in someone else's story or are you the author of your own?

Table 7.1 summarizes the four frames. Clearly, these frames provide four very different models of identity. We believe that having a broad repertoire of models to apply to organizational life provides a wider set of possible points of intervening, transforming, and crafting empowering identities in organizational contexts.

TABLE 7.1

Four Frames for Communication, Organization, and Gendered Identity

FRAME	VIEW OF COMMUNICATION	VIEW OF GENDER	VIEW OF ORGANIZATION	ILLUSTRATIVE SCHOLARSHIP
1. Gender Difference at Work	Communication styles are an effect of gender	Individual identity is socialized and stable	Physical site of work where predictable communication patterns are manifest	Gender differences in organizational communication styles; women in management
2. Gender Identity as Organizational Performance	Everyday interaction is influenced by social scripts and narratives	Individual identity constantly negotiated; an effect of discourse	Physical site of work where gender identities are continually produced and reproduced	"Doing gender" at work; routine performance of masculinity and femininity in organizational life
3. Gendered Organizations	Gendered narratives embedded in organizational systems, structures, and policies and enacted in everyday interactions	Individual and collective identity is a process and product of organizing	Subject and object of gendered discourse; physical site of work	Organization as gendered; feminist forms of organizing
4. Gendered Narratives in Popular Culture	Gendered narratives embedded in cultural/societal representations of organization	Identity is a process process and object of gendered social discourses	Gendered labor relations are produced in sites external to the organization, particularly popular culture	Popular culture as gendered; cultural studies of gendered organizations

Adapted from Ashcraft, K. L. (2004). Gender, discourse and organization: Framing a shifting relationship. In D. Grant, C. Hardy, C. Oswick, & L. Putnam (Eds.), *The Sage handbook of organizational discourse* (pp. 275–91). London: Sage, p. 286.

EVERYDAY ORGANIZATIONAL COMMUNICATION

"Framing" Your Identity in College

The following quotation is an excerpt from a blog written by a recent college graduate who returned to her alma matter to find a large-scale campus reconstruction project in the works:

> When I think about how I changed in college, about the person I was when I started versus the person I was when I finished, it's fitting that I was there to witness and participate in such a reconstruction. Because, those four years brought on a rebuilding project of my own. At every turn, it seemed, ground was being broken on an old site of my ignorance or my immaturity. And while the reconstruction process was costly and painful, the end result is something that is more functional, more useful, a more practical structure for its intended purpose.
>
> It was messy but oh, so necessary, ("how now, wit?," 2006)

As this recent graduate indicates, college can be a time of great transition for many students as they learn new perspectives and develop new interests and friendships; some may even begin to experience adult responsibilities for the first time; still others learn a new juggling act in balancing work, family, and school.

Given these changes, it is not surprising that college is also a time when many students begin to develop new facets of their identities and shed others. A resource guide to the first year experience at Minnesota State University at Mankato puts it best:

> As students ask themselves, "Who am I and who do I want to become?" they may also try out new values and experiment with new roles. They may seek out new challenges or take risks, small and large, that they have not tackled before. For some students, this means adopting a new image—different clothes, different friends; for others it may mean testing out new behaviors. Still others will be confronted with new views on politics, morality or religion and may consider adopting a new view for a short time or for longer. ("The College Transition," 2006)

Think back to your first few days on campus. How are you a different person today? How are you similar to the person you were that first day on campus? In the discussion questions below, use the four frames we have discussed in this chapter to help you analyze how your own identity was influenced by your new environment and how you actively enacted and embodied a work/life identity in your new context.

(continued, "Framing" Your Identity in College)

DISCUSSION QUESTIONS

1. Frame 1 Questions: What were the key differences that made a difference to you in your interactions with others on campus? Did those differences center on gender? Age? Race? Ethnicity? Sexuality? What assumptions did you bring to your interactions that were based on presumed differences?
2. Frame 2 Questions: How did you perform your identity in a new environment? What aspects of your identity did you foreground in your interactions with your new peers? What aspects of your identity did you highlight in your interactions with your friends at home, your colleagues, your family, or your professors? Did those performances always mirror one another or were they quite varied across contexts? How were your identity performances scripted for you by the new context? How did you challenge those taken-for-granted scripts?
3. Frame 3 Questions: What about your university's policies and practices influenced your emerging identity? How did the dominant organizational narrative, as manifest in structures, policies, and practices, create conditions for you to develop new facets of your identity? How did the organizational narrative prevent you from developing new facets of your identity?
4. Frame 4 Questions: How did you develop preexisting ideas about what it meant to be a student? What cultural texts did you rely on to help you craft a narrative of the self when you arrived on campus? Did those cultural representations of student life enable or constrain your ability to create a successful identity? How does your own identity work reproduce and/or challenge the texts of student life that are found in popular culture?

◧ BEYOND GENDER: INTERSECTING IDENTITIES IN ORGANIZATIONS

While the four frames provide a useful set of lenses to better understand and dissect questions of identity in organizational life, their focus on gender tends to eclipse the importance of other social identity categories. While we may choose to focus attention on gender as an analytic category, in practice, as we have indicated throughout this chapter, organizational members live, experience, and negotiate gender identities in relation to a variety of other identities, including aged, raced, classed, and sexed identities. In our discussion of the four frames, we saw examples of ways that race and class complicate an easy analysis of gender in organizational contexts. In this section, we explore the concept of **intersecting identities** or the complex, fluid, and sometimes contradictory ways in which multiple social identity categories (including gender, race, class, age, ability, sexuality, and others) combine.

□ Negotiating Multiple Identities

Power and ideology impact how various aspects of one's social identity are valued. Within most organizational settings, "members tend to enact dominant norms and communication styles during everyday interactions. As a result, organization members may negatively judge persons who do not meet (or do not seem to meet) expectations related to white, middle-class values and attitudes" (Allen, 2003, p. 86). While organizations have traditionally favored masculinity, issues of class, race, age, and ability impact how individual men are able to enact a valued identity at work. An aging middle manager who has had a fairly successful career may find that he is increasingly compared to younger men who are described as being more "hungry" and having more energy, drive, and fire. Likewise, while a white, professional manager may find her femininity challenged in some organizational contexts, her privileged class status, ethnicity, and (hetero)sexuality may enable her to negotiate a successful and (relatively) powerful identity at work. In many ways, her ability to embody a satisfying and valued sense of self is enabled by an **ideology of white supremacy** or an institutionalized though often unintentional belief in white superiority (Allen, 2003). Similarly, a Latino middle manager may have access to structural power as a decision maker, but may also find that he has to guard his personal life as a gay man of color carefully so as not to lose status at work where white heterosexuality is the assumed norm (Spradlin, 1998; Ward & Winstanley, 2004).

These examples point to the complexity of identity negotiations in organizational contexts. Clearly, relying on simple binary categories (e.g., men/women) fails to capture the dynamic, fluid, communicative, and "crystallized" character of contemporary workplace identities (Tracy & Trethewey, 2005). Martin and Nakayama (1999) remind us that identity can be better understood as a dialectical and sometimes simultaneous process of privilege and disadvantage that is produced and reproduced in everyday conversations, organizational practices, and cultural texts.

Negotiating multiple identities simultaneously is an ongoing project for most individuals. That negotiation process often takes on heightened importance for some organizational members, particularly for those who are other than the assumed norm. First-generation college students are one such group. Mark Orbe, a professor of intercultural communication and women's studies at Western Michigan University, studied the complex ways that first-generation college (FGC) students negotiate their identities. Often, though not always, FGC students are more economically disadvantaged than their second-generation counterparts. They also tend to have lower SAT scores, make the decision to attend college later in their high school careers, choose less selective colleges, receive less support from their parents, tend not to participate in student groups, and tend to work more hours outside school than second-generation college students. Not surprisingly, college often feels like an "alien culture" to many FGC students (Orbe, 2004, p. 132). Moreover, those students must also negotiate the issue of **marginality**, or feeling like their identities are not like those in the "center" or the dominant group both at school and at home as they "work to bridge the worlds of their homes/families/neighborhoods and college life" (Orbe, 2004, p. 132).

In the context of home, many of the FGC students in Orbe's study enjoyed special attention from friends and family members when they visited for weekends or school breaks. At the same time, however, many (particularly African American FGC students) felt the burden of being "the one who made it out" of a disadvantaged neighborhood or family situation, having moved on from the community to "bigger and better things." While their privileged status as a college student can bring accolades, it can also generate jealousy and make others back home feel threatened. Thus, FGC students must walk a fine line between highlighting and downplaying their college status at home in their everyday micropractices or performances of identity. Despite being known as first-generation students at home, FGC students tended to keep this information private in the context of campus (or work). Being the first in the family to attain a higher education is not noted as a position of privilege — it is not an identity category that is immediately "marked" by others. In fact, many study participants felt that first-generation status is imbued with negative connotations and were, therefore, unlikely to foreground that aspect of their identities in interactions with peers and professors (Orbe, 2004)

While Orbe (2004) did not employ the four frames we have used to discuss identity in organizational/home contexts, those frames may prove useful in further explorations of college students' identity challenges and opportunities. This study attended most closely to identity performances among college students (Frame 2). Other research conducted from a Frame 3 perspective might explore how universities and colleges are structured in classed ways that assume students are familiar with, are equipped for, and have the material resources available to be successful in college life. Finally, a Frame 4 lens on college student identity might examine how student identities are represented in popular culture in film (e.g., *Animal House*, *Harold & Kumar Go to White Castle*, *Van Wilder*), television (*Tommy Lee Goes to College*, *The Real World*), and books (*I Am Charlotte Simmons*, *Prep: A Novel*), and how those representations influence first-generation college students' decisions about, and performances in, school.

☐ Communicating Multiple Identities

As symbol users (and abusers), human beings use communication to construct their own and others' identities. In this chapter, we have pointed to the ways that interpersonal interactions, organizational structures and policies, and larger social discourses of power shape, privilege, and disadvantage different social identities as they are enacted at work and in life. As Allen (2003) says, difference matters. How difference matters is up to us. Thoughtful and responsive communicators will make conscientious decisions about communicating in ways that value difference, resist stereotyped assumptions about particular social identities, acknowledge the power of communication, and foster agency (Allen, 2003). Brenda Allen (2003) offers three specific strategies that enable individuals and groups to better communicate multiple identities:

1. *Be Mindful*: When you communicate with others, be conscious about your own responses. It is helpful, though often difficult, to note your own privilege. What are the ways in which your social identity is privileged or valued in the communication context? How might your own privilege influence the responses you have to others? Are your attitudinal and behavioral responses based on stereotypes or other socially constructed assumptions? If so, consider the ways you might reframe your approach.

2. *Be Proactive*: When you communicate with others, take the initiative to create positive changes or be "response-able" (p. 193). For example, once you are mindful of the ways you are privileged, you can use your privilege to mentor, network with, or support those who are less so. Alternately, you might put the person as a unique and complex individual first rather than foregrounding and responding to a noticeable identity category (like gender, race, or ability). If you are in a position of power, you might try to be more flexible in your role. As a "child-free" manager, you might look for more ways to be responsive to your employees who are parents of young children. Being proactive means responding to behavior that is discriminatory or inappropriate (e.g., not laughing at racist jokes). There are many ways to be proactive; your challenge is to become more "response-able" each and every day.

3. *Fill Your Communication Toolbox*: The most "response-able" communicators are those with the widest array of tools or the broadest communicative repertoire. Utilizing effective listening and critical thinking, building persuasive arguments, using theories in applied contexts, creating the space for real dialogue, and balancing the constraints of any given situation with the needs (or the creativity) of the parties involved are all potentially useful skills for bridging differences at work and in life.

We encourage you to use your tools well in the service of creating richer and more fulfilling identities for your self and for others.

WHAT WOULD YOU DO?

The Secret Identity of an English Professor

It's Thursday morning and Michael Carter, an assistant professor of English at a large research university in the Midwest, sits at his desk and looks at the mounting pile of student papers that he needs to grade. But Michael is not resentful—he loves his work and was overjoyed at landing a tenure-track position in a competitive, overcrowded field. Even though he has two Ivy League degrees, numerous teaching awards, and several prestigious publications, Michael knows that he is lucky to have any job at all—let alone one at a solid school located only two hours from his wife's family. Michael vows that he will never again face the exhausting academic job search and interviewing process. He must work hard to earn tenure. It is the only way to secure a permanent academic position.

Fortunately, Michael is well on his way to making himself an invaluable member of the English department. He is well respected by his colleagues and his students and he has earned a reputation of being dedicated and hard working. Michael frequently volunteers for academic committees and departmental projects while still teaching three courses a semester (one of which he designed from scratch) and working on a book project that he hopes will end in a prestigious publication with a university press. He works long hours grading papers, advising students, and socializing with department faculty.

But Michael has a secret. Approximately three years ago, while he was finishing his dissertation, he began to experience episodes of trembling, dizziness, and blurred vision. He attributed these episodes to stress (and to staring at a computer screen all day!), but gradually the bizarre symptoms began to increase—and new ones formed. Fearing that his job was destroying his health, Michael sought professional help to learn to control the symptoms. He was, however, met with an extremely shocking and upsetting diagnosis: multiple sclerosis (MS), a disease of the central nervous system that can, in some cases, lead to paralysis, difficulty in communication, and cognitive challenges.

Michael's doctors informed him that he should, by all means, continue to work and lead a normal life. But they warned him that he may suffer from fatigue (particularly as MS treatments can sometimes cause flu-like symptoms) and that he may need to cut back on a few of his time-consuming commitments. Thinking about the possible progression of the disease, Michael knows that he may also need to request special accommodations from his employer, as guaranteed by the Americans with Disabilities Act.

In his mind, Michael knows that his university cannot discriminate against him for suffering from an illness. But he also knows that his job is not secure until he receives tenure, and he worries that his colleagues will view him as use-less if he doesn't volunteer for committees and develop new courses. He worries that his teaching evaluations will suffer if he takes too long to return papers—even if he has a valid, medical reason for taking time for his personal health. He considers keeping his news a secret from his colleagues and supervisor, hopefully until after he is tenured or until a time arises that they need to know his situa-tion. What should he do? What would you do if you were in his position?

DISCUSSION QUESTIONS

1. Consider the positions of power that Michael has enjoyed. He is a young, white, heterosexual man with a prestigious education and job. How might his sense of power change when his privileged position intersects with an ill-ness or disability?
2. Should Michael tell his supervisor and his colleagues about his condition? Should he tell his students? Why or why not? If you were Michael's friend, how would you advise him?
3. If Michael shares his condition at work, what types of struggles might he find in negotiating multiple identities? If he keeps his news a secret, will he en-counter similar struggles?

SUMMARY

Difference is created, reinforced, rewarded, and transformed in organizational life. While early theories of identity assumed that the self was fixed, unitary, and essen-tial, more recent identity theories explain identity as a dynamic product of ongoing communication processes. While identities or differences are now viewed as more fluid, it is still the case that some identities are more valued in organizational con-texts than others. And organizations engage in a variety of strategies to encourage members to align their identities with the organizational ideal.

Feminist theorists have long been interested in identity issues in organizational life because gender-based differences have been used as a justification for women's exclusion from various aspects of public, organizational life. As a result, women's ability to successfully navigate and create effective identities that transverse the boundaries between private (home) and public (work) life has been compromised.

Karen Ashcraft's four frames of identity highlight the various ways that schol-ars have conceived of the relationship between gender, communication, and orga-nizations. These frames also provide a useful lens for helping us think through work/life issues. Frame 1 suggests that gender identities are products of biological or socialized differences that are manifest in different communication styles and are evidenced in organizational behaviors. Frame 2 suggests that gender identities are ongoing accomplishments that are performed into being in and constrained by organizational contexts. Frame 3 moves beyond the individual to suggest that organizations themselves are gendered by structures, policies, and practices that produce and reproduce gendered scripts. Finally, Frame 4 points to the ways that larger social discourses, including popular discourses, represent organizations, organizational actors, and notions of work in ways that impact how individuals make sense of, experience, and perform gender in their everyday lives. These four frames help us to think about issues of identity, difference, and gender in a variety of ways. Having the ability to view identity through multiple lenses also suggests that there may be a variety of useful responses to dilemmas (based on gender or work/life).

Ashcraft's four frames can be usefully extended to better understand other "differences that make a difference" in organizations, including issues related to race and class. Specifically, we discuss how understanding identity is complicated and nuanced by addressing the many ways that multiple identities intersect in organizational contexts. Finally, we offer three strategies for communicating multiple identities, including being mindful, being proactive, and filling your communication toolbox.

QUESTIONS FOR REVIEW AND DISCUSSION

1. What are the ways in which organizations routinely seek to regulate and control members' identities? Is identity regulation a legitimate organizational concern? Why or why not?
2. Describe the public/private split. What do you think are the most problematic outcomes of this socially constructed split for men and women?
3. Frame 1 suggests that gender differences exist. Do you believe that to be true? If so, why? If not, why not?
4. Frame 2 argues that gender identities are performed. How do you perform your gender in your everyday life? What aspects of those performances are useful or beneficial? Which aspects are problematic? How might you transform your gender identity through engaging in different performances at home? At work?
5. Frame 3 suggests that the "ideal worker" is one who is masculine. Is that true across all organizational contexts? Where and how is that ideal challenged?
6. Frame 4 asks us to consider how popular culture impacts our understandings of work and life. What are the popular culture images that have had the most impact on your understanding of gender at work and in life?
7. What are some of the strategies you use to successfully enact and embody multiple and intersecting identities everyday in work and in life? How do the concepts presented in this chapter help you to do that more successfully?

KEY TERMS

Authenticity, p. 200
Consumption, p. 216
Emotion labor, p. 209
Identity, p. 199
Ideology of white supremacy, p. 221
Intersecting identities, p. 221
Liberal feminists, p. 202
Marginality, p. 222

Micropractices, p. 208
Personal brand, p. 217
Radical feminists, p. 202
Rapport talk, p. 204
Report talk, p. 204
Second shift, p. 207
Work/life conflict, p. 203

CASE STUDY

Rx for Sales: Recruit Cheerleaders!

Gendered identity performances are increasingly gaining the attention of savvy organizational recruiters as well as organizational theorists, as noted in "Gimme an Rx! Cheerleaders Pep Up Drug Sales," a *New York Times* article detailing the success of young, beautiful, fit, and personable former NCAA female cheerleaders in obtaining positions as pharmaceutical sales representatives (Saul, 2005).

In 2004, Gregory C. Webb founded the employment firm Spirited Sales Leaders (which maintains a database of thousands of cheerleaders interested in sales positions) because "so many cheerleaders were going into drug sales" (Saul, 2005, para. 13). With top performing salaries and bonuses averaging between $50K and $60K a year, as well as the use of a company car, there is no denying the appeal of such a job for recent college graduates. But why are pharmaceutical companies particularly interested in hiring female cheerleaders? Webb notes that cheerleaders are now "high-profile people" and "the top people in universities"; T. Lynn Williamson, a cheerleading advisor from the University of Kentucky, states that cheerleading teaches prospective sales representatives the skills they need to succeed on the job: "Exaggerated motions, exaggerated smiles, exaggerated enthusiasm—they learn these things, and they can get people to do what they want" (para. 10).

Critics, such as Dr. Thomas Carli from the University of Michigan, however, note that pharmaceutical companies are clearly utilizing beautiful women to seduce male doctors into buying their products. Jamie Reidy, a former sales representative, recounted a notable sales call with a very attractive female colleague: 'At first' he said, the doctor 'gave ten reasons not to use one of our drugs.' "But," Mr. Reidy added "She gave a little hair toss and a tug on his sleeve and said, 'Come on, doctor, I need the scripts.' He said, 'O.K., how do I dose that thing?'" (para. 26). Naturally, recruiters from the pharmaceutical industry often deny that attractiveness has a role in their decision making: "People hired for the work have to be extroverts, a good conversationalist, a pleasant person to talk to, but that has nothing to do with looks. It's the personality," said Lamberto Andreotti, the present of worldwide pharmaceuticals for Bristol-Myers Squibb (para 20).

Certainly in the short term, these new reps recognize the competitive advantage they enjoy due to their former cheerleader status. One downside to this otherwise potentially lucrative career is that male physicians' responses to perceived "cheer"fullness (e.g., attractiveness, enthusiasm, exaggerated smiles, and body motions, etc.) range from appropriate professional conduct to clearly inappropriate behavior. In fact, an "informal survey, conducted by a urologist in Pittsburgh . . . found that 12 or 13 medical saleswomen said they had been sexually harassed by physicians" (para. 28). Another disadvantage is that hiring decisions based on cheerleading skills may perpetuate a negative stereotype that further diminishes other women. If the most important qualifications for a good job are attractiveness and a perky demeanor, what does that say about the importance of developing critical thinking skills and a quality of intellect in young women?

Adapted from Saul, S. (2005, November 28). Gimme an Rx! Cheerleaders pep up drug sales [Electronic version]. *The New York Times*, Section A, Column 1, National Desk, Pg. 1. Retrieved March 3, 2006, from www.nytimes.com.

ASSIGNMENT

This case study raises a host of issues discussed within the chapter section on the four frames of gender, communication, and organization. Reflect on these frames and consider the following questions about this case:

1. Frame 1 assumes that gender differences are real and persistent. Are women naturally inclined to display "exaggerated enthusiasm," or is that a gendered/sexualized micropractice that is reinforced and rewarded in organizational contexts, as Frame 2 might suggest?
2. Interestingly, male cheerleaders, who have also demonstrated cheer skills, are not being recruited to the same degree as their female counterparts. What is it about our social constructions of gender and organization that might discourage pharmaceutical representatives from recruiting male cheerleaders?
3. Sales representatives and former cheerleaders are hired for their ability to perform and display particular emotions (e.g., enthusiasm). What sorts of emotion labor benefits and burdens come with the (sales) territory?
4. A Frame 3 lens suggests that when pharmaceutical companies recruit young women to be sales representatives, specific gendered organizational narratives are produced and reproduced. What sorts of organizational narratives or scripts are created when companies explicitly recruit female cheerleaders into support staff roles? In what ways are those gendered narratives helpful? In what ways are they problematic?
5. In the spirit of Frame 4, spend some time exploring mediated representations of working professional women. What types of images of working women do you see in film, television, and print? How do those images align with the image of cheerleaders? What are some alternative images of successful professional women?

CHAPTER 8

Teams and Networks: Collaboration in the Workplace

As a global economy fueled by advances in communication technology emerged in the late twentieth century, five key changes to the nature of organizing occurred. Thus far in this book we have discussed two of them: the emergence of flatter organizational structures and other alternatives to hierarchy, and the birth of the "customer-supplier" revolution, propelled by the demand for organizations of all kinds to work together to provide ever-improving quality in products and services to the global marketplace.

This chapter addresses the final three changes: the global emergence of a demand for increased participation in information sharing and decision making; new models of collaboration between and among managers and workers; and a gradual and not always welcome changeover from traditional bureaucratic "top-down" models of communication and management to newer team, group, and network-based models. Central to all of these new ways of working together is the need for new and improved forms of organizational communication.

◸ PARADOXES OF PARTICIPATION

Before turning our attention to specific forms of participation, collaboration, and democracy that characterize contemporary organizations, we must first discuss what Cynthia Stohl and George Cheney (2001) call the paradoxes of employee participation and **workplace democracy**. We do this to acknowledge from the outset that while most of us believe that increased employee participation in decision making will lead to improved outcomes, the reality is not so clear-cut. Simply put, a **paradox** is a particularly thorny contradiction. Stohl and Cheney elaborate on this definition by describing paradoxes as "pragmatic or interaction-based situations in which, in pursuit of one goal, the pursuit of another competing goal enters the situation (often without intention) so as to undermine the first pursuit" (p. 354). In organizational life a common example of paradox is the tension many employees with families feel when they wonder how they can put in the requisite amount of hours at work while remaining good spouses and parents at home.

As Stohl and Cheney point out, a pragmatic paradox exists within most organizational plans for increasing employee participation. Viewed positively by management as a means of giving voice to employees and empowering them to take responsibility for decisions they have fashioned, the downside is that these participation programs are often viewed by employees as "add-ons" to an already crowded workday. As a result, increased participation usually means doing more work for the same pay. Taking responsibility for decisions that a workers' council or quality improvement team makes means spending more time in meetings, taking more time to read and write reports, and, in the process, becoming even more accountable to management for results. This is the pragmatic paradox of participation. While it sounds like a good thing for improving bonds among workers and between workers and management, it may also mean accepting more of a workload, increasing personal anxiety over decisions, and being held to an even higher standard of performance. Consequently, in real life, increased participation is often both welcomed and resisted by employees. In Table 8.1, Stohl identifies seven paradoxes of participation based on critical frameworks.

The experience of paradox is not, of course, limited to workers. Managers often feel the same tensions as their authority for making important decisions is shared with team members who do not have their same level of training or expertise. Additionally, midlevel supervisors may feel threatened by shortcuts to decisions or violations of accepted procedures enacted by employees who find more efficient ways to complete their assigned tasks. By contrast, some managers interviewed by Stohl (1996) reported becoming "frustrated when their team 'wasted so much time' analyzing the issues and not solving them" (p. 367).

An interesting example of this dynamic can be found in our recent experience with the newly constituted leadership team of a multicampus university system. The newly designated system leader (the chancellor) has both a high need for information and a strong commitment to team problem solving. Consequently, he holds weekly, two-hour meetings with his campus presidents and CEOs to encourage dialogue about system-wide issues. Things are not going smoothly, however. While two-thirds of the meeting participants (mainly those from the smaller campuses) find great value in the team conversation, the remainder see the meetings as a colossal waste of time and an intrusion into their ability to manage their campuses. What looks like participation to the leader and most of the team feels like unnecessary micromanagement to some of its most powerful members.

TABLE 8.1

Paradoxes of Employee Participation and Workplace Democracy

A. *Paradoxes of Structure*: Concerning the architecture of participation and democracy (e.g., "Be spontaneous!").
   1. *Paradox of Design*: Imposing or mandating grassroots participation from the top; for example, as with Total Quality Management or Participative Management.
   2. *Paradox of Adaptation*: While trying to preserve the organization's essential qualities, adapting so much to outside forces or expectations that the organization's soul is lost.
   3. *Paradox of Punctuation*: Short-cutting the democratic process in practice (because the process takes so much time) in such a way that, over time, the vitality of the system is lost.
   4. *Paradox of Formalization*: Institutionalizing democracy such that spontaneity is gone through the routinization of what should be invigorating and inspired.

B. *Paradoxes of Agency*: Concerning the individual's (sense of) efficacy within the system (e.g., "Be yourself!").
   1. *Paradox of Responsibility*: Relinquishing individual decision rights to a group, particularly while insisting that the individual right to participation be maintained.
   2. *Paradox of Cooperation*: Following formal or informal procedures in a way that hinders rather than promotes cooperation, including the pattern of "nonparticipation" in the interest of furthering cooperation.
   3. *Paradox of Sociality*: Intense involvement at work as an ironic constraint on other forms of participation (e.g., in family and community) such that all types of participation become undermined.
   4. *Paradox of Autonomy*: Giving up more individual rights than one intended to through a contract with a highly democratic organization; surrendering individual agency for that of the collective. The gains to the individual through adhesion to the whole community are outweighed by the sacrifices.

C. *Paradoxes of Identity*: Concerning issues of membership, inclusion, and boundaries (e.g., "Be self-managing to meet organizational goals!").
   1. *Paradox of Commitment*: Making commitment to and enactment of the group's espoused values and beliefs about voice and participation a test that ironically leads to exclusion rather than inclusion.
   2. *Paradox of Representation*: Becoming co-opted by dominant interests; losing one's "voice" unexpectedly; for example, when labor thinks like management and forgets about workers' interests yet still insists its own role is distinct.
   3. *Paradox of Compatibility*: The potential problems with exporting a particular model of democracy or participation to another society or culture where it fits less well.

D. *Paradoxes of Power*: Concerning the locus, nature, and specific exercise of power in the organization (e.g., "I insist that you reach consensus!").
   1. *Paradox of Control*: Encountering less, not more, freedom within team-based structures, at the group or organizational level.
   2. *Paradox of Leadership*: Waiting for a charismatic leader to inspire, create, and maintain democracy.
   3. *Paradox of Homogeneity*: Failing to see the value of resistance or oppositional voices; excessive valuing of agreement, cooperation, and consensus, while preaching diversity of opinion.

Adapted from C. Stohl and G. Cheney. "Participatory Processes/Paradoxical Practices: Communication and the Dilemmas of Organizational Democracy," *Management Communication Quarterly* (2001) 14: 349–407.

This kind of conflict is typical. While participation is a key value in implementing or even encouraging democracy in the workplace, the practice of participation is often inhibited by paradoxes. That doesn't mean that increased worker participation and democratic ideals shouldn't be used to guide methods for improving the efficiency of organizations. But understanding the paradoxical nature of participation in advance sensitizes both managers and researchers to the likelihood that their implementation will always be contested and in some way problematic.

▧ DEMOCRACY IN THE WORKPLACE

Organizational scholar Stan Deetz's (1995) multiple stakeholder model provides a useful way of thinking about the importance of increased participation and workplace democracy. The **multiple stakeholder model** asserts that organizations ought to be concerned with the interests of many different individuals and groups and not just shareholders or stockholders (see Figure 8.1). Deetz's model seeks to balance the demands of global economic competition with a respect for the well-being of the planet and its citizens. As such, it raises critical questions about the potential (and generally negative) consequences of a powerful economic elite and of centralizing decision making in the hands of multinational corporate and govern-

FIGURE 8.1

Multiple Stakeholder Model of the Corporation in Society

STAKEHOLDER GROUPS	MANAGING PROCESS	OUTCOME INTERESTS
Consumers		Goods and services
Workers		Income distribution
Investors	Coordination ⟶	Use of resources
Suppliers		Environmental effects
Host communities		Economic stability
General society		Labor force development
World ecological community		Lifestyles
		Profits
		Personal identities
		Child-rearing practices

Source: Stanley Deetz, *Transforming Communication, Transforming Business* (Cresskill, NJ: Hampton Press, 1995), p. 50.

mental leaders. Instead, the model promotes greater voice and broader involvement in decision making by multiple stakeholders and stakeholder groups, in the service of a more democratic work environment. How can this model about the political ramifications of global organizational systems be applied to the idea of increased participation at a local organizational level? Deetz outlines four steps toward workplace democracy in which shared decision making among stakeholders is crucial.

1. *Create a workplace in which every member thinks and acts like an owner.* The point of business is to be of service; this is best accomplished when every stakeholder becomes responsible for decision making and is accountable for the outcomes of those decisions both to the business and to society.

2. *The management of work must be reintegrated with the doing of work.* The cost of people watching other people work for the purpose of controlling what gets done and how it is done can no longer be seen as economically efficient. Moreover, it leads to bad decisions (i.e., decisions about how to do work are best made by those who actually perform it and will be rewarded by its outcomes) and to less accountability (i.e., "watched" people tend to resist domination by finding ways to slow down work processes or to goof off on the job).

3. *Quality information must be widely distributed.* To fully empower workers and the societies they serve, the current system of filling up the day with mostly meaningless memos, letters, faxes, and newsletters that only encourage control and domination should be replaced by bringing to the attention of workers "real" information about the business and how it is affecting society and the planet.

4. *Social structure should grow from the bottom rather than be reinforced from the top.* If the basic idea of a participative democratic workplace values the consent of the governed in the governance of everyday affairs, everything from routine office policies to limiting the terms of managers should be accomplished by ongoing negotiations among the multiple stakeholders. (pp. 170–171)

Although practically difficult to implement, Deetz's suggestions move us toward a more democratic dialogue, or what he calls "constitutive codetermination" (1995, p. 174). Similar strategies have been implemented in newer manufacturing plants, such as BMW of North America. Indeed, Deetz's model may be easier to implement in new companies than in existing corporate and governmental structures.

The majority of strategies used to move workplaces toward more democratic and responsive structures and practices involve organizing the labor into groups, teams, and networks. The drive to organize in such a manner comes from the realization that no single individual, or for that matter no pair of individuals, is sufficient to achieve complex goals. Moreover, when people seek to make sense of their work lives, they tend to identify with larger groups (e.g., my department, my division, my building). In the following sections, we build on the previous discussion of participation and democracy by addressing communication that occurs in teams and networks. Today, most work that goes on inside organizations utilizes a team approach, whereas work that takes place outside of organizations (e.g., entrepreneurship, outsourcing, or consulting) relies even more heavily on networks and networking. If knowledge is power, such power is inevitably exercised in webs of relationships.

◪ COMMUNICATING IN TEAMS

☐ What Is a Team-Based Organization?

Most American employees now work in some form of **team-based organization**, where in addition to their individual responsibilities they also serve as members of one or more working groups. The importance of teamwork has long been appreciated. Filene's, a Boston-based department store recently bought by Macy's, introduced the concept of teamwork in the United States in 1898. However, today's emphasis on teams goes far beyond the original meaning of teamwork, of simply working together. A team-based organization is one that has restructured itself around interdependent decision-making groups, not individuals, as a means of improving work processes and providing better quality and service to customers.

Team-based organizing differs sharply from bureaucratic forms of organizing. First, consistent with the human resources approach, in team-based companies every employee is seen as possessing valuable knowledge that must be widely shared for the benefit of the whole. **Teams** are groups of employees with representation from a variety of functional areas within the organization (e.g., sales, manufacturing, engineering) to maximize the cross-functional exchange of information. In a bureaucracy, a hierarchical chain of command distinguishes managers (as "thinkers") and workers (as "nonthinkers"), emphasizing the need for division of labor and close supervision. Team-based organizations, in contrast, encourage informal communication and view all employees as capable of making decisions about how to manage work tasks. In the most progressive team-based organizations, supervisory work is conducted by self-managed work teams. In these settings, employees become "knowledge workers" dedicated to self-improvement, positive results, and productive collaboration:

> In the conversion to post-bureaucratic organizations, teams form the basic unit of empowerment, small enough for efficient high involvement and large enough for the collective strength and the synergy generated by diverse talents. Within teams, people can take wide responsibility for one another, for the organization, and for the quality of their products and services. (Pinchot & Pinchot, 1993, p. 194)

A recent job ad for positions at the search engine giant Google highlights this general trend: "We're looking for people with world-class skills who thrive in small, focused teams and high-energy environments, believe in the ability of technology to change the world, and are as passionate about their lives as they are about their work" (Google, 2006, para. 2).

The current interest in work teams is rooted in both the Hawthorne Studies (which attest to the importance of informal groups; see Chapter 3) and European experiments with autonomous work groups (Kelly, 1992). Research in Europe — Scandinavia, in particular — has been on the forefront of these new forms of organization, beginning with the development of the sociotechnical school in the 1950s (Trist, 1981). This school of thought maintained that organizational effectiveness depends on a proper blending of technical and social factors at work and stressed the importance of communication and collaboration. One study of British coal miners, for example, emphasized how communication processes optimize social and technical systems. In this study, there were clear indications of higher productivity and job satisfaction among those workers who were given more control of their jobs. Eric Trist's studies also indicated that organizations with workers who were more involved in the operation were better equipped to respond to changing markets and political conditions — something that large and rigid organizations found difficult (Wellins, Byham, & Wilson, 1991).

☐ Types of Teams

Despite widespread enthusiasm for team-based organizing, definitions of what constitutes a team remain ambiguous. However, all groups in an organization are not necessarily sufficiently interdependent to be classified as teams. A collection of working people may be a committee, a task force, or an ad hoc group. Teams, in contrast, generally fall into three categories or types: project teams, work teams, and quality-improvement teams. Depending on the location of its members, any of these types of teams may also be classified as a virtual team.

Project Teams

Project teams, which help coordinate the successful completion of a particular project, have long been used by organizations in the design and development of new products or services. For example, a project team might include software and hardware engineers, programmers, and other technical specialists who design, program, and test prototype computers. A project team might also be assigned to address a specific issue or problem. For example, a savings and loan recently charged a project team made up of representatives from all the major areas of the bank with the task of developing ways to bring in new business.

Project teams may struggle because people lack the communication skills needed to collaborate across significant functional divides. Collaborative behaviors are hard to learn; hence, while many project teams are formed with great optimism, few are managed for success (Jassawalla & Sashittal, 1999). Management must actively work to build real collaboration, by increasing commitment to team decisions, and to demonstrate a deep caring about team outcomes and accomplishments.

A special type of project team exists within **matrix organizations**, which are characterized by dual reporting relationships. Imagine a large matrix (like an expanded tic-tac-toe board) where the columns represent organizational functions like research and development, sales, production, and information services. Imagine also that the rows represent particular projects or product lines, like shampoo, conditioner, and hair mousse. In a matrix organization people's "home" departments are their functions (e.g., a chemical engineer would reside in research and development), but they are also assigned to a project team responsible for producing a particular product. This results in most employees reporting to two different supervisors. Although this form of organizing was very popular over the last few decades, it is less common today due to the tensions that can result from having multiple supervisors.

Work Teams

A **work team** is a group of employees responsible for the entire work process that delivers a product or service to a customer. One such work team at a California aerospace company is responsible for all metallizing of components in the company. The team resides together, outlines its own work flow (e.g., the steps for applying metal coatings to parts), and is engaged in making ongoing improvements in the work process (e.g., making the metal coating as thin as possible).

Such teams have been found to aid an organization's efficiency. Federal Express, General Electric, Corning, General Mills, and AT&T have all recorded significant productivity improvements after incorporating work teams (Wellins, Byham, & Wilson, 1991). Kodak reduced its turnover rate to one-half of the industry's average and improved its handling of incoming customer calls by 100 percent after reorganizing into work teams. Similarly, Texas Instruments Malaysia managed to boost employee output by 100 percent and cut production time by 50 percent after moving to a team-based approach. Recently, Detroit automakers passed on manufacturing hybrid vehicles, choosing instead to focus on fuel-cell technology, which has yet to come to fruition. In the meantime, Toyota built the Prius, a hybrid car now in its second generation. Toyota anticipates selling 300,000 Prius cars this year. The president of Toyota explained their success, saying, "Detroit people are far more talented than people at Toyota. . . . But we take averagely talented people and make them work in spectacular teams" (cited in Evans & Wolf, 2005, p. 104). Team work is the basis of Toyota's high-performance organization.

Successful work teams are supported by a commitment to empowerment. Because they are given the discretion and autonomy to make decisions and to solve problems, empowered teams are not frustrated by a lack of authority to implement their ideas and solutions. More generally, a group can do a better job of managing its resources when it understands the big picture, has the authority to adapt to changing work conditions, and feels that its work is meaningful and has an impact (Churchman & Rosen, 1999).

In practice, of course, work teams differ in degree of empowerment, as indicated in Figure 8.2. As empowerment increases, the team assumes responsibility for the continuous improvement of work processes, the selection of new members, the election of a team leader, and capital expenditures. At the highest level of empowerment, the self-directed work team is also responsible for performance appraisals, disciplinary measures, and compensation (Wellins, Byham, & Wilson, 1991). This type of self-directed work team is not yet common but is becoming more prevalent today.

FIGURE 8.2

The Empowerment Continuum of Work Teams

Source: Richard Wellins, William Byham, and Jeanne Wilson, *Empowered Teams* (San Francisco: Jossey-Bass, 1991), p. 26.

For teams to succeed, the company reward system has to recognize the contributions of both the team and its individual members. Organizations continue to struggle with the challenges posed by evaluating and rewarding teams whose members contribute unequally. Similarly, differences in the knowledge and skills of team members can cause some members to work harder than others and, therefore, to be more deserving of rewards for their efforts. The empowerment process may involve an employee stock ownership program (ESOP) to encourage team members' motivation and dedication to the team approach: "I will be motivated to do my best because the fruits of my labor are now visibly mine." ESOPs vary in structure—stock may be purchased by employees or given as a benefit—but they all share a common principle, which is getting shares of the company in the hands of its employees. Many line employees at Home Depot and Microsoft, to offer two examples, have become wealthy from employee stock. Companies create ESOPs with two very different purposes. The first approach is limited to seeing the stock as a financial benefit but is not tied to any increased opportunities for participation on the part of employees in company decision making. The second approach is ideologically motivated, with greater employee involvement accompanying equity (stock) participation. Not surprisingly, it is this latter form of ESOP—stock plus greater employee involvement—that has the most positive effects on employee motivation, identification, and commitment (Harrison, 1994).

One potential barrier to the effectiveness of work teams is union agreements, which may prohibit cross-training or may specify rules that conflict with self-management goals. For example, some union rules specifically limit the extent to which one classification of worker can cover for others in their absence. Where these conditions exist, there must be sustained collaboration between unions and management to establish rules beneficial to both parties.

As we discussed earlier, managers sometimes resist the move to empower self-directed work teams (Tjosvold & Tjosvold, 1991). For managers and supervisors, team-based organizing requires a fundamental change in their role, from operational expert or overseer to coach or facilitator. The ability to oversee an empowered work team has become an increasingly important management skill. It requires the supervisor overseeing a team to:

- act as a facilitator to keep the group on track while respecting a free exchange of ideas;
- be hard on rules, agenda, goals, and accountability but soft on the means by which the team chooses to organize itself and do its work; and
- communicate extensively with others to keep the team informed of the work of other teams and of the organization as a whole.

Effective managers of work teams create a climate for honest and supportive dialogue and possess the necessary communication skills to do so. The considerable challenges involved in such an undertaking are reflected in *What Would You Do?* on page 240.

The Dilemmas of Participative Management at a University

Joan Brittle is the new president of a large public midwestern university. Recently, she attended a workshop for new university presidents where she learned that most successful educational institutions today have adopted participative, team-based structures. While she has little formal education in management (she is a physicist by training), the team approach makes sense to her and fits with her personality and management style, which is all about cultivating strong relationships.

Following the workshop, she returns to her campus and enthusiastically charges a team of her top faculty to design a series of strategic initiatives for the school that both capitalize on existing strengths of the institution and are responsive to emerging social trends. To ensure that she does not impede their dialogue, she does not join the team but asks one of the more senior faculty members whom she trusts to lead the team and provide her with periodic updates. She is confident that "many heads are better than one" and anxiously awaits the team's report, which she believes will affirm and extend her ambitious vision for the future of the institution. She feels that both the opportunity and the optimal path to greatness for the university are fairly clear.

The strategic initiatives team attacks the new challenge with enormous energy and enthusiasm. In three short months, they have developed a comprehensive plan featuring five initiatives for the school to pursue over the next ten to twenty years. When President Brittle receives their report, she is both stunned and disoriented. Based on her beliefs and perspectives, she assumed that the team would come back with a plan that was responsive to changing environmental conditions and apparent opportunities in the state. Instead, their proposal was mostly an (admittedly ambitious) extension of current faculty interests and offerings, but did not suggest any kind of new direction or breakthrough. She wonders: How could this superb group be so far off base? From her perspective, the initiatives are too internally focused, reflecting faculty interest and expertise, and out of touch with the needs and desires of the Board of Trustees, the legislature, and the community. In addition, they do not represent any of her personal and professional interests in health and the life sciences.

DISCUSSION QUESTIONS

1. How did the group wind up with initiatives that differed so much from the expectations of President Brittle? What steps could President Brittle have taken to avoid the polarity of this outcome?

2. What does this situation tell you about risks and pitfalls in encouraging employee participation in decision making?
3. Based on your reading about teams what would you advise the President to do now? Why?

Quality-Improvement Teams

Popular in organizations in the 1980s, informal problem-solving groups called *quality circles* met voluntarily to address work-related issues on a weekly basis (Kreps, 1991). Quality circles have since been replaced by **quality-improvement teams** whose goals are to improve customer satisfaction, evaluate and improve team performance, and reduce costs. Such teams are typically cross-functional, drawing their members from a variety of areas to bring different perspectives to the problem or issue under study. In theory, a quality-improvement team uses its diverse talents to generate innovative ideas.

One example of a quality-improvement team is a program called *Work-Outs* at General Electric, which was initiated by CEO Jack Welch in 1989, management selects forty to one hundred employees to attend a three-day conference (Stewart, 1991). A facilitator divides the employees into five or six smaller groups, and each group works independently for two days to identify problems with the company and to prepare a presentation to senior management regarding recommended changes. On the third day, the panel of senior managers is confronted by each group and its proposals, and the managers must agree or disagree with each proposal or ask for more information (in which case, the group agrees to supply it by an agreed-on date). One vice president describes the experience in this way: "I was wringing wet within half an hour. . . . They had 108 proposals, and I had about a minute to say yes or no to each one" (Kiechel, 1994, p. 70). This is a dramatic example of how organizations are using teams to encourage creativity and to open the dialogue between managers and employees.

Virtual Teams

In response to a dynamic global economy, many organizations (and most large ones) have found it advantageous to maximize their geographical reach and become immersed in a wide range of local cultures. Companies ignore cultural differences at their own peril. Unfortunately, the geographical distribution of employees creates predictable communication difficulties associated with time and space, often resulting in serious misunderstandings. Fortunately, a range of technological tools has evolved to support these groups of people who work together across time and space in what are called **virtual teams**.

A superficial analysis of virtual teams can identify likely problems to watch out for, such as language barriers and differences in cultures, religions, work customs, and work habits. But deeper consideration reveals that all virtual teams engage in a developmental process that builds a negotiated order — a shared set of practices or "micro-cultures" that emerge among members (Gluesing, 1998). Some of the items that are typically up for negotiation include division of labor, sequencing of activity, and the nature and regularity of outcome assessment. In addition, virtual teams must work out more mundane but still vexing issues surrounding the use of list-servs, intranets, e-mail, and document transfers. This team development process is highly social (if largely through electronic media) and involves the development of mutual respect and trust (Baba, 1999).

Pamela Shockley-Zalabak (2002) conducted an important study of an international, self-managing, virtual team created by a technology company seeking to do a better job of meeting customer needs. She describes the functioning of this team over a two-year period as "protean," constantly changing in structure and form. Her research revealed some of the challenges associated with these kinds of structures. Two years into this experiment, while the members of this team did not want to return to hierarchy, they did express a strong desire for more structure, in the form of better processes and clearer work rules. While the idea of geographical boundaries was no longer relevant, a new kind of boundary was important to the team. Specifically, they wished for "boundary as guide, sense of place, commitment, relationship, and shared meaning [amidst continuous change]" (p. 249). Future studies of virtual teams will no doubt shed more light on the pragmatics of succeeding with this new organizational form. One important factor that team members must consider in a global world is how cultural influences may impact communication among virtual team members. Some of these cultural influences are described in Table 8.2.

☐ Communicative Dimensions of Teamwork

Simply calling a group a "team" does not make it one. A group becomes a team through the kinds of communication it displays over time and the resulting feelings of trust and interdependence. More specifically, there are five communicative elements of team interaction that are essential to consider: roles, norms, decision-making processes, management of conflict and consensus, and cultural diversity. The following sections address each of these elements.

Roles

Inherent in effective teamwork is the need to achieve a balance between the goals of individual members and those of the team. While individual behavior can vary significantly, team members tend to enact predictable **communication roles**, which are consistent patterns of interaction within the team (Goodall, 1990a). According to

TABLE 8.2

Cultural Influences on Global Virtual Teams

VARIABLE	IMPLICATION FOR MULTICULTURAL TEAMS
Individualism vs. Collectivism	• Individualistic team members will voice their opinions more readily, challenging the direction of the team. The opposite is true of collectivists. Collectivists will also want to consult colleagues more than individualists before making decisions. • Collectivists don't need specific job descriptions or roles but will do what is needed for the team, ideally together with other team members. Individualists will take responsibility for tasks and may need reminding that they're part of the team. • Individual-oriented team members will want direct, constructive feedback on their performance and rewards tied closely to their individual performance. Collectivists, however, might feel embarrassed if singled out for particular praise or an individual incentive award. • Collectivists prefer face-to-face meetings over virtual ones.
Power Distance	• Team members from cultures that value equality (i.e., low power distance) expect to use consultation to make key decisions. From the viewpoint of a team member from a higher power distance culture, however, a team leader exercising a more collaborative style might be seen as weak and indecisive. • Members from high power distance cultures will be very uncomfortable communicating directly with people higher in the organization.
Uncertainty Avoidance	• In a culture where risk taking is the norm or valued, team members tend to be comfortable taking action or holding meetings without much structure or formality. Members who are more risk averse need a clearer, prepared meeting structure, perhaps with formal presentations by all members of the team. They're unlikely to take an active part in brainstorming sessions. • Members from lower uncertainty avoidance cultures will not respond well to "micromanagement." They may also be more willing to use new technologies.
Task/Relationship Orientation	• Team members from relationship-oriented cultures want to spend extra social time together, building trust, and may have problems interacting smoothly with short-term members.

Source: J. Goodbody, "Critical Success Factors for Global Virtual Teams." *Strategic Communication Management* (February/March 2005) 9: 20.

the classic typology, the three broad types of communication roles are the task, maintenance, and self-centered roles (Benne & Sheats, 1948).

In performing the task role, the team member summarizes and evaluates the team's ideas and progress or initiates the idea-generating process by offering new ideas or suggestions. In the maintenance role, the team member's communication seeks to relieve group tension or pressure (e.g., by telling jokes or by changing the subject of a conversation) or to create harmony in the group (e.g., by helping to reconcile conflict or disagreements) (Shockley-Zalabak, 1991). Enacting the self-centered role, the team member seeks to dominate the group's discussions and work or to divert the group's attention from serious issues by making them seem unimportant. Unlike the positive effects of task and maintenance roles, the self-centered role is always considered inappropriate and unproductive.

Goodall (1990a) has identified two other roles, the "prince" and the "facilitator." The prince role is exhibited by group members who view themselves as brilliant political strategists and the world as a political entity. In the facilitator role, a team member focuses on group processes (e.g., following an agenda and maintaining consensus in decision making) for the benefit of the team, while refraining from substantive comments on issues.

Some people both serve on teams and facilitate team communication, playing different roles in various group situations. A training manager, for example, may act as a facilitator if during a team meeting the conversation drifts off topic. At the same time, the manager may suspend the facilitator role by offering information or opinions relevant to the discussion. Two other roles played by team facilitators — sponsor and coach — can help organizations ease the transition to a team-based approach. A sponsor who is not a member of the team and who has significant power in the organization is responsible for keeping the team informed of organizational developments, removing obstacles to effective teamwork, and advocating on behalf of the team for access to necessary resources. A coach, typically a former supervisor and a respected team member, is responsible for helping the other members acquire the cross-functional skills needed to accomplish team-based tasks. Coaching is especially important to team success because it addresses the specific problems associated with transitioning from a classical management approach to a team-based one. In addition, a coach teaches team members how to ask for coaching and thereby how to deal with errors, weaknesses, or deficiencies in productive ways that promote the team's performance.

Norms

Norms are the informal rules that "designate the boundaries of acceptable behavior in the group" (Kreps, 1991, p. 170). For example, team members may be expected to attend meetings on time, prepare for meetings in advance, and distribute the meeting's agenda by an agreed-on deadline. Norms about conflict may express varying degrees of tolerance for disagreement. Some observers attribute Motorola's success to its norm about conflict, which encourages team members to engage in loud debates at meetings (Browning, 1992b). Taking a different tack, one software company CEO insists that no one should ever kill a new idea. He instead encourages "idea angels" who are charged with saying something positive about any new idea that is introduced. 3M's success has often been attributed to a similar approach to innovation. 3M lives and dies by a norm that says, in effect, "when in doubt, try it."

Team norms, which are shaped by the national and organizational culture as well as by personal agendas, strongly affect member roles. For example, a large

U.S. insurance company emphasizes positive employee relations so much that the organizational culture is largely intolerant of conflict. As a consequence, work teams tend to avoid conflict and fail to deal with key issues involving poor performance and accountability.

Decision-Making Processes

Team decision making is as a rule more effective than decision making by individuals. Teams get more people involved in the decision-making process and generate more information and ideas. In addition, the simple act of participating in decision making makes team members more aware of important issues, more likely to reach a consensus, and better able to communicate about issues with co-workers.

In a departure from the classical management approach (which separates the tasks of making decisions from implementing them), the team-based approach gives employees more control over decisions that affect their work and has been shown to decrease job stress. Moreover, "the more complex and challenging the issues under evaluation, the more powerful the outcomes of decisions, and the greater the number of people affected, the better groups are for making the decisions" (Kreps, 1991, pp. 173–174).

Group decision making also poses a number of problems. In what is called the "risky shift phenomenon," a team may tend to make decisions that involve more risks than decisions made by individuals do because of perceived safety in numbers (Cartwright, 1977). In addition, strong-willed or verbose team members may dominate conversations, intimidate others, or manipulate team decisions to benefit themselves in an effort to gain power or to improve their image. **Groupthink**, a well-known problem associated with team decision making initially identified by psychologist Irving Janis (1971), occurs when team members go along with, rather than evaluate, the group's proposals or ideas. According to Janis (1971):

> In a cohesive group, the danger is not so much that each individual will fail to reveal his [or her] objections to what the others propose but that he will think the proposal is a good one, without attempting to carry out a careful . . . scrutiny of the pros and cons of the alternatives. When groupthink becomes dominant, there is also considerable suppression of deviant thoughts, but it takes the form of each person deciding that his misgivings are not relevant and should be set aside, that the benefit of the doubt regarding any lingering uncertainties should be given to the group consensus. (p. 44)

A number of strategies for dealing with groupthink are consistent with our ideal of promoting organizational dialogue:

1. Encourage team members to voice their objections and to evaluate others' ideas.
2. Encourage team members to remain impartial and, therefore, to maintain objectivity in decision making.
3. Use more than one group to work on a problem to generate a variety of proposed solutions.

4. Encourage team members to discuss the team's deliberations with people outside of the group to obtain feedback.
5. Invite outside experts into the group to obtain their input and feedback.
6. Make one team member responsible for ensuring that the team explores all sides of an issue.
7. Divide the team into subunits that work independently on a problem and then report back to the team.
8. Arrange a special meeting after a consensus has been reached to give team members the opportunity to discuss any doubts or concerns that remain. (Gibson & Hodgetts, 1986).

Decision making by teams also requires team members to face the challenge of sorting through multiple interpretations of a problem or issue to find the single best recommendation or course of action. Members who are intolerant of others' perspectives may find this task especially challenging. For this reason, extensive research has been conducted on identifying effective decision-making strategies.

Aubrey Fisher's (1980) model of group decision making sees decisions as the product of four stages:

1. Orientation
2. Conflict
3. Emergence
4. Reinforcement

In the orientation stage, the members of a newly formed team get to know and trust one another. Their communication tends to focus on clarifying the team's purpose and function and on reducing tension and uncertainty. After the orientation stage, communication about tasks inevitably initiates the conflict stage, as team members express and debate different ideas, perspectives, positions, styles, and worldviews, forming alliances and coalitions in the process. A team that manages the conflict stage well will emerge with a diverse assortment of perspectives and valuable information that it uses to move toward a single position. In the emergence stage, coalitions give way to a working consensus as a delicate balance of compromise and negotiation is worked out. Emergence involves moving toward action, and determining how to implement the decision. Finally, the reinforcement stage is marked by a strong spirit of cooperation and accomplishment among team members (Fisher, 1980).

Teams that skip the orientation phase for whatever reason may never truly feel comfortable as a group, inasmuch as members know one another only as roles, not as people. They may also lack direction. Teams that avoid the conflict stage—mainly through cowardice in the face of difficult conversations—run a decided risk of groupthink, of agreeing on a course of action before exploring all of the available information or alternatives. Teams lacking in communication skills often fall apart at the emergence stage, as group members find it impossible to work together and agree on a common direction. Many teams don't survive to experience the reinforcement stage.

Other studies of team decision making challenge the stage models proposed by Fisher and others by suggesting that most teams follow a less linear path toward decision making. These writers believe that group decision making is more varied and complicated than these models suggest (e.g., Poole, 1983; Poole & Roth, 1989). Seen this way, teams experience periods of disorganization that are unpredictable, tend to go through cycles and to repeat stages multiple times, and may engage in activities (e.g., managing tasks and establishing work relationships) in a haphazard rather than a coordinated fashion. In many cases, stages do not occur in an orderly or predictable pattern.

Similarly, the punctuated equilibrium model suggests an intriguing way of viewing the group decision-making process (Gersick, 1991). If trust is lacking in the group, or if members' differences are significant, the team will be unable to function. Some members may withdraw, while others may assert their power over the rest of the group. Drawing on similarities across various fields and subject areas (e.g., individuals, groups, organizations, academic disciplines, and species), this model offers three concepts related to group development: (1) deep structure, which is the set of assumptions and performance strategies that the team uses to approach the problem; (2) the equilibrium period, during which the team works within the established framework without questioning its fundamental approach to the task; and (3) the revolutionary period, when the team examines its operating framework and reframes its approach as a basis for moving forward. Note that the three concepts do not apply to all teams. At a point about halfway between a team's inception and a predetermined deadline, the opportunity to embark upon a revolutionary period arises. Whereas successful teams regard this potential crossroads as an opportunity to examine their basic assumptions, unsuccessful teams bypass the revolutionary period altogether, ignoring the opportunity for self-examination and proceeding on the basis of their initial assumptions.

Other important contributions to our understanding of effective group decision making include the argument that effective teams give more attention to the group process (i.e., the procedures used to solve problems) than do ineffective teams (Hirokawa & Rost, 1992). Referred to as "vigilant interaction theory," this theory holds that successful teams focus on four areas of self-assessment: (1) the nature of the task, (2) the standards for evaluating various decision options, (3) the positive aspects of the various options, and (4) the negative qualities of the various options. The theory claims that "group decision performance is directly related to a group's efforts to analyze its task, assess evaluation criteria, and identify the positive and negative qualities of alternative choices" (p. 284).

Finally, in a sustained effort to apply communication technology to group decision making, group-decision support systems (GDSSs) are used to give teams access to various decision-making tools (Poole & DeSanctis, 1990). For example, software that creates an electronic display for input and accepts input from all group members, and software for problem solving, decision analysis, and expert systems, can help teams make better decisions (Contractor & Seibold, 1992). This kind of technology is increasingly available to assist in the operation of all kinds of teams, both geographically co-located and virtual.

Management of Conflict and Consensus

Conflict occurs among members of organizations and teams largely because people in different positions of power pursue different interests. Here we are concerned with teams as sites of conflict and with team-based strategies for achieving consensus. Team conflict may occur among members who come from different fields or professions, such as in a cross-functional project team, or between line workers (who work directly with the product or service) and staff teams (who provide behind-the-scenes support). It may also occur as a result of perceived inequities in group member status or productivity, personality differences, or other work-related problems.

Conflict is defined by Putnam and Poole (1987) as "the interaction of interdependent people who perceive opposition of goals, aims, and values, and who see the other parties as potentially interfering with the realization of these goals" (p. 552). In organizations, conflict most often arises from the acquisition and use of resources. Like other types of communication, conflict changes or evolves over time and is unpredictable. It also takes place in the interdependent relationships among people who rely on one another to some extent for resources.

Attitudes toward conflict in U.S. organizations have changed significantly since the 1950s, when overt conflict was viewed as counterproductive and to be avoided. By the 1970s, however, some recognition of the benefits of conflict had emerged, such as its role in generating different ideas and perspectives (and thereby helping to avoid group think) as well as in facilitating the sharing of information. Studies have found that some degree of team conflict is essential to achieving high levels of productivity and effective communication (Franz & Jin, 1995). An absence of conflict over an extended period of time is more likely a sign of group stagnation than of its effectiveness. The constructive role of conflict is mostly understood today, although it remains difficult to realize in practice.

Research on conflict in organizations includes classical management studies that view conflict as a breakdown of communication (Hunger & Stern, 1976) and cultural studies that define it as a dispute over different perspectives of organizational realities (Smith & Eisenberg, 1987). Most research on the cycles and escalation of conflict has been approached from a systems perspective (Putnam & Poole, 1987), whereas critical theorists view conflict as reflecting deep imbalances of power in the organization and society (Mumby, 1993).

Because team conflict is inevitable, we are most concerned with how team members handle it. Broadly distinguished as emphasizing either a "concern for self" or a "concern for others," conflict style is also marked by degrees of assertiveness and cooperation (Kilmann & Thomas, 1975). Collaboration, which is generally seen as the most effective conflict style, emphasizes high assertiveness combined with high levels of cooperation. In contrast, compromise is considered less effective in resolving conflicts because neither party's preferred solution is adopted. Collaboration is more likely to lead to a novel solution that satisfies both parties. In addition, accommodation may at times be effective, but in most conflict situations, it is counterproductive because it causes stress for the team member who accommodates others and undermines the team's ability to generate creative ideas.

Unfortunately, there is often a significant gap between individuals' expressed or preferred conflict style and how they behave across a variety of conflict situations. For example, while supervisors' strategies for dealing with problem employees reflect their styles when the conflict first surfaces, over time they tend to use more coercive strategies regardless of their expressed conflict style (Fairhurst, Green, & Snavely, 1984). Therefore, because multiple situational factors and goals affect conflict strategy selection, conflict style is not always a good predictor of communication behavior (Conrad, 1991).

A team's commitment to collaboration and consensus, however, involves ongoing communication and results in good decisions with long-term impact. **Consensus** does not mean that all team members agree with a decision but feel instead that their views are adequately considered by the team. "If there is a clear alternative which most members subscribe to, and if those who oppose it feel they have had their chance to influence, then a consensus exists" (Schein, 1969, p. 56). Naturally, people agree to a group consensus with the understanding that their point of view will be accepted at least some of the time; otherwise they would most likely leave the group. Consensus reflects an overarching belief that in the long haul, "all of us are smarter than any one of us." Effective conflict management through consensus thus means accepting the inevitability of differences and remaining committed to an ongoing dialogue that is open to alternative perspectives and that encourages creative decision making.

Cultural Diversity in Teams

As corporations make greater use of intercultural teams in response to global competition, researchers are increasingly concerned with the effects of cultural differences on team member communication. In one such study, communication scholar Charles Bantz (1993) reports on his experiences as a member of a ten-person intercultural research team. Starting with four well-accepted dimensions of cultural diversity (power distance, uncertainty avoidance, individualism, and instrumentalism or expressivity) and four difference factors (language, norms, status, and politics), he offers the following conclusions:

> The range of difficulties generated by the diversity in a cross-cultural research team [leads] to a variety of tactics to manage those differences. The tactics include . . . alternating leadership styles across time and tasks; agreeing on long-term goals, while continuing to negotiate shorter-term goals; building social cohesion; [ensuring that] longer-term goals [meet] individual needs; alternating task and social emphases; maintaining

social support by engaging in confirming communication even when disagreeing; adapting to language difference[s] by slowing down, checking out, restating, and using more than one language; discussing work schedules; using varying conflict modes across different issues; discussing group procedures; initiating social discussion of work life to ascertain perspectives; and responding to political differences. While . . . tactics vary, [the] four [most] common [ones are] (1) gather information, (2) adapt to differing situations, issues, and needs, (3) build social as well as task cohesion, and (4) identify clear, mutual long-term goals. (p. 19)

He also points out that "awareness of cultural differences is necessary, but not sufficient for the accomplishment of cross-cultural team research" (p. 19).

Negotiation is another key to managing intercultural team differences. The following four phases in the negotiation process occur in all cultures (Varner & Beamer, 1995), but the amount of time devoted to each phase and its relative importance may differ:

1. *Developing relationships with others.* For the members of a newly formed intercultural team to develop productive work relationships, they need to be given sufficient time to explore long-term team goals, build trust, and adapt to cultural differences. In most cultures, candid answers to questions mark the beginning of a productive relationship, even when the required answers may be perceived as self-disclosing. However, face saving is just as important to members of Asian, African, and Middle-Eastern cultures as candidness is to other cultures. Therefore, it is wise to avoid insensitive remarks, to express tolerance of others' goals and values, and to respect the status that others enjoy in their native culture.

2. *Exchanging information about topics under negotiation.* Honest or frank disclosures are one way to generate trust among members of an intercultural team, but information exchange may also be enhanced by responding to questions with other questions that open up the team dialogue. Questions can be used not only to access information and to clarify ideas, but also to call bluffs, to show interest in another's ideas, to control the direction of a conversation, and to address controversial issues in nonthreatening ways. The types of exchanges generated by such questions help team members adapt to their cultural differences while also communicating with trust and openness. Team members also become more aware of how culture plays a role in the answers generated by questions; for example, "Why?" questions are answered with explanations of cause and effect in Western cultures, but they are answered more generally through stories, personal narratives, and cultural myths in non-Western cultures.

3. *Recognizing multicultural techniques of persuasion.* Rational arguments are considered persuasive by members of many cultures, but different perspectives on what is considered rational, and different ways of communicating rational arguments, can pose difficulties in intercultural teams. It is thus recommended that teams focus more on gaining information than on per-

suading and that team members respect their cultural differences when persuasion is necessary. For example, using "I" is less persuasive than the more inclusive "we," and using such words as *must, should,* and *ought* may be viewed as arrogant by members of non-Western cultures.

4. *Emphasizing the role of concession in achieving agreement.* Most cultures appreciate the value of fair exchange, including the value of concession in gaining agreement. In general, concessions are best expressed as "if" comments (e.g., "We can deliver those services if your suppliers can meet this schedule"), rather than as directives (e.g., "We can deliver those services but your suppliers must meet this schedule"). However, while Americans tend to emphasize the importance of concessions in the form of a well-executed plan, such as a business contract, Asians tend to emphasize the same principles in a different form — in their informal relationships with others. Thus, for example, an American businessperson may be surprised when an Asian businessperson does not observe the stipulations of a signed contract. A contract is considered binding in American culture, but in most Asian cultures, a contract may be superseded by informal relationships. Similarly, an American conducting business in Finland may be surprised to learn that formal written agreements are often considered unnecessary because verbal agreements are executed with trust.

□ Team Learning

Successful team-based organizations foster an environment that values and rewards team learning (Pinchot & Pinchot, 1993; Senge, Roberts, Ross, Smith, & Kleiner, 1994). MIT management and systems experts Peter Senge and colleagues (Senge et al., 1994) define **team learning** as "alignment" or the "functioning of the whole":

> Building alignment is about enhancing a team's capacity to think and act in new, synergistic ways, with full coordination and a sense of unity [among] team members. . . . As alignment develops, [members do not] have to overlook or hide their disagreements to make their collective understanding richer. (p. 352)

Senge and colleagues (1994) go on to suggest that team learning transforms the skills of "reflection and inquiry" into "vehicles for building shared understanding" (p. 352). More specifically, they identify the following guidelines for team communication:

1. *Balancing inquiry and advocacy.* Teams need to balance inquiry (i.e., asking questions that challenge the existing assumptions and beliefs about work) with advocacy (i.e., stating opinions and taking action). Neither inquiry nor advocacy should control the team's learning process. Figure 8.3 identifies various types of inquiry and advocacy commonly used by teams.
2. *Bringing tacit assumptions to the surface of team dialogue.* Senge and colleagues (1994) suggest that because "we live in a world of self-generating beliefs

FIGURE 8.3

Balancing Inquiry and Advocacy

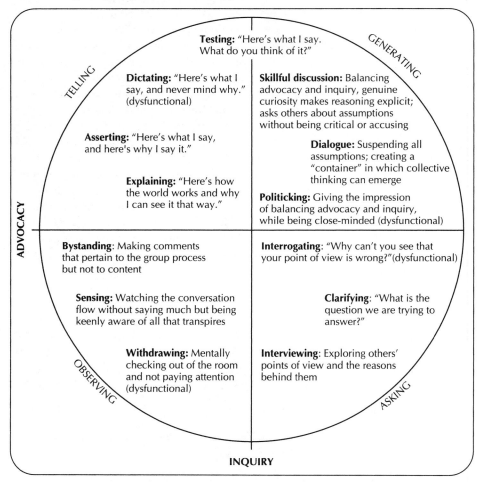

Source: Peter Senge et al., *The Fifth Discipline Fieldbook* (New York: Currency Doubleday, 1994), p. 254.

which remain largely untested" (p. 242), our beliefs appear to be the truth, the truth seems obvious to us, and the evidence for our beliefs is limited to the data we select from our experience. A team that learns to question these assumptions moves down the "ladder of inference" revealing the motivations behind our beliefs (Figure 8.4). As the team brings tacit assumptions to the surface of its dialogue, it discovers the role of those assumptions in the development of beliefs and conclusions.

FIGURE 8.4

The Ladder of Inference

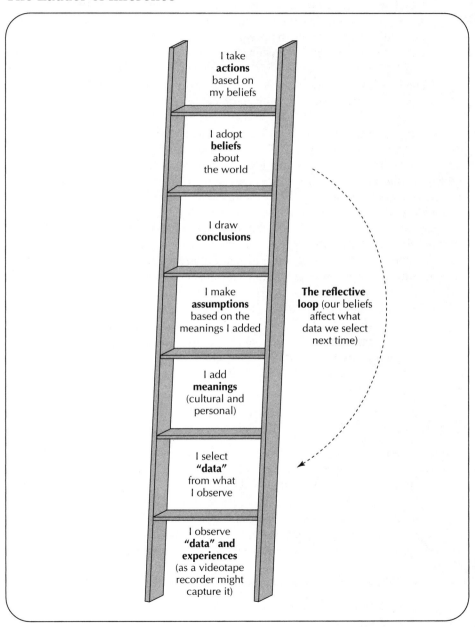

Source: Peter Senge et al., *The Fifth Discipline Fieldbook* (New York: Currency Doubleday, 1994), p. 243.

3. *Becoming aware of the assumptions that inform conclusions.* Once assumptions have surfaced, it is beneficial for teams to reflect on how these particular beliefs give rise to interpretations of events that support specific conclusions about work processes, employees, or customers. Making these connections explicit makes them easier to change. Conclusions, then, are filtered through members' assumptions and beliefs, which are unobservable and highly personalized. This is what makes the generation of new ideas challenging. However, by counteracting these abstract influences on the thought process, teams can promote creative thinking.

Dialogue is important to team learning. According to Senge and colleagues' (1994) model of the "evolution of dialogue" (Figure 8.5), team dialogue moves initially from invitation to conversation to deliberation. From deliberation, the dialogue may follow a path to discussion or to suspension and dialogue. Team learning thus encourages members to think about dialogue as allowing the "free flow of meaning," unencumbered by logical analysis (e.g., skillful discussion) or debate. People from Western cultures may find it difficult to learn the speaking and listening skills associated with this type of dialogue because of the value they are accustomed to placing on advocacy and rational argument. In addition, such dialogue challenges many of the assumptions of traditional communication in organizations. In dialogue, the objective is not to argue a point effectively but to balance inquiry with advocacy in ways that contribute to the knowledge of the team as a whole.

In the transition to a team-based approach, therefore, the organization not only must help employees cope with change, but also must help them learn new ways of communicating. This is a formidable challenge that requires a constant commitment to training and team learning.

☐ A Retreat from Teams?

Ideally, self-directed work teams help contemporary organizations deal with the pressures of global competition and help promote autonomy, responsibility, democracy, and empowerment in the workforce. In practice, however, the ideals of the team-based approach are often not realized by organizations.

In one recent case, a small airline tried to implement self-directed work teams but found that decision making was hindered by disagreements among team members. For example, the mechanics were frustrated by other groups' unwillingness to defer to them on all safety issues. This company's experience reveals the importance of the following factors in successful team formation:

1. Teams are only as good as their members; the careful selection of members is thus essential.
2. Teams must be trained in group decision making and communication.

FIGURE 8.5

The Evolution of Dialogue

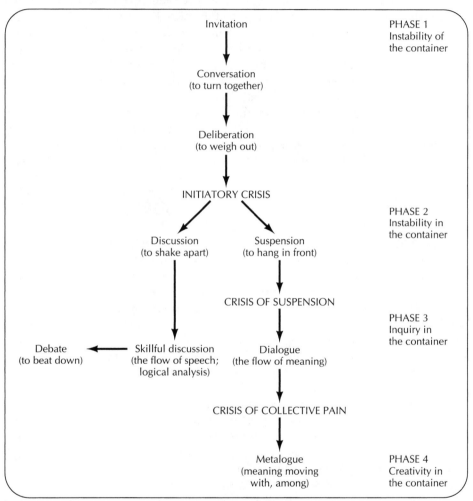

Source: Peter Senge et al., *The Fifth Discipline Fieldbook* (New York: Currency Doubleday, 1994), p. 361.

3. Only some decisions can be assigned to teams: those involving a significant challenge where the outcome affects many people. Simple tasks with limited impact are best assigned to individuals.

4. Some members of a team have more expertise and experience than do other members; therefore, all members do not contribute equally.

At various times in the past, a number of companies (e.g., Ford, Procter & Gamble, and Honda) have found that teams require too much time to make decisions and tend to shield their members from responsibility (Chandler & Ingrassia, 1991). Because teams require a radical reframing, traditional employees may also tend to view teams with skepticism, at least initially. If employees are empowered by the team approach, they become its strongest advocate. More often, however, management does not follow through on its promise of empowerment, and teams fail. Teams also fail when they believe they haven't reached their goals, or that their productivity hasn't been enhanced by teamwork (Coopman, 2001). Finally, teams fail when management neglects to define the types and functions of the teams it seeks to establish (Drucker, 1992b). As a result, teams do not have a clear understanding of their function in the organization. A highly empowered, cross-functional team that does not receive strong leadership support is likely to fail.

▨ COMMUNICATING IN NETWORKS

We have observed that contemporary organizational communication has expanded rapidly from face-to-face teams to real and virtual networks of people across multiple locales organized for a common purpose. Although networking has always been key to business success, defined **communication networks** — groups of individuals who may be identified as sharing regular lines of communication — have become a primary mode of organizing in the new economy. Networks are emergent, informal, and somewhat less interdependent than teams. Networks matter because regular contact between identifiable groups of people, whether they be scientists or political action groups, can play an important role in establishing access to information and in the quality and direction of decision making.

Within organizations, the concept of a network has emerged as a result of researchers' enduring interest in the structure of organizational groups. Human relations theorists recognized that small groups do much of the important work in organizations. The pattern of communication among group members, called the group's *communication structure*, is affected by many factors. For example, management may design a group in a way that hinders its communication, or employees with low status in a group (e.g., newcomers) may be less willing to communicate freely than those with high status. Formal lines of authority and rules about communication may also restrict the flow of information in a group. These investigations into communication structures have led to the idea of communication networks.

☐ Types of Communication Networks

Small-Group Communication Networks

Early research on communication structure focused on examining **small-group communication networks** (groups of five people) to determine the effects of centralized versus decentralized networks on decision making. In a well-known example,

> a small number of individuals are placed in cubicles and allowed to communicate only by means of written messages passed through slots in the cubicle walls. The slots connecting each cubicle can be opened or closed by the experimenter, so that different communication patterns can be imposed on the interacting subjects. . . . A typical task presented to groups of individuals placed in these networks is to provide each individual with a card containing several symbols, only one of which is present on the cards of all subjects. The task is . . . completed when all participants are able to . . . identify the common symbol. (Scott, 1981, pp. 148–149)

Four types of small-group communication networks were typically studied: circle, wheel, chain, and all-channel (Figure 8.6). The circle and all-channel networks are highly decentralized, whereas the chain and wheel are centralized. It was found that centralized networks are more efficient than decentralized networks, as reflected in the speed with which they can complete a task (Leavitt, 1951). Further

FIGURE 8.6

Small-Group Communication Networks

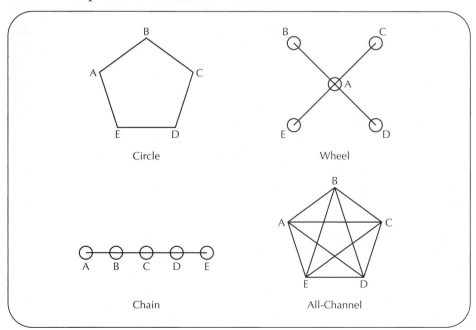

Source: W. Richard Scott, *Organizations: Rational, Natural, and Open Systems* (Englewood Cliffs, NJ: Prentice-Hall, 1981), p. 8.

investigations, however, reveal that centralized networks are not necessarily superior to decentralized networks:

> As tasks become more complex or ambiguous, decentralized net[works] are usually superior to centralized structures. . . . Formal hierarchies aid the performance of tasks requiring the efficient coordination of information and routine decision-making whereas they interfere with tasks presenting very complex or ambiguous problems. . . . Specifically, hierarchies impede work on the latter by stifling free interactions that can result in error-correction, by undermining the social support necessary to encourage all participants to propose solutions, and by reducing incentives for participants to search for solutions. (Scott, 1981, pp. 149–150)

This early research also yielded some interesting findings about small-group decision making. For example, when a group faces a routine task or a tight deadline, participation by and input from all members is not expected. In contrast, when a group faces more complex issues or problems, a more open dialogue promotes member satisfaction and better solutions.

However, many critics argued that the experimental small-group networks studied had little in common with actual groups in organizations (Farace, Monge, & Russell, 1977). In fact, research interest has recently turned toward what has been dubbed "bona fide groups" in organizations, groups that really function that way "in the wild." Bona fide groups have real histories and come together to solve real organizational and social problems. Early research suggests that these real embedded groups act in more contradictory and disorderly ways than were anticipated by laboratory studies (Sunwolf & Seibold, 1998).

Emergent Communication Networks

The most powerful groups within organizations are those that emerge from the formal and informal communication among people who work together. These groups are referred to as **emergent communication networks**.

The current focus on communication networks in organizations stems from a general acceptance of systems theories, which emphasize the connections between people and the relationships that constitute an organization. In terms of communication networks, researchers examine those relationships that emerge naturally within organizations as well as the groups and member roles associated with them (Rogers & Kincaid, 1981). Formal networks and emergent networks coexist in organizations, and each is best understood in the context of the other (Monge & Contractor, 2001; Monge & Eisenberg, 1987). For example, although new employees may rely on a copy of the formal organizational chart to understand reporting relationships and the structure of departments, over time they realize that the actual communication relationships among employees do not precisely mirror the organizational chart. Departments with no formal connections may nonetheless communicate in order to manage the workflow, and salespeople working on different product lines may share common experiences at lunchtime. A great deal can be learned about an organization's culture by identifying the discrepancies between informal emergent networks and the formal organizational chart.

Early research on emergent communication networks investigated the so-called organizational *grapevine*. The term dates to the Civil War, when telegraph wires strung through trees resembled grapevines (Daniels & Spiker, 1991). This term has since come to mean the persistent informal network in an organization, sometimes referred to disparagingly by management as the "rumor mill." In reality, most of the time the rumors are true; important information travels quickest through informal channels. Building on Chester Barnard's (1968) observations about the value of informal communication, Keith Davis (1953) argued against the standard party line, which encouraged managers to suppress the rumor mill, and instead supported the importance of such communication to the health of an organization, both as a source of information and for bolstering a sense of belonging. Subsequent research has shown that informal communication through the grapevine is as a rule more efficient and accurate than the formal dissemination of information (Hellweg, 1987).

☐ Analyzing Communication Networks

Analyses of communication networks are used to examine the structure of informal, emergent communication in organizations, reflecting the tendency of individuals to forge new linkages, that are separate from formal rules or boundaries. Informal communication in organizations is fluid and in a constant state of change. Whereas formal reorganizations may occur only infrequently, informal reorganizations occur continuously (Monge & Contractor, 2001). In studying emergent communication networks, we are concerned mainly with overall patterns of interaction, communication roles, and the content of communication.

Patterns of Interaction

As illustrated in the sample communication network shown in Figure 8.7, a number of informal groups or cliques emerge as a result of communication among people in organizations, both within and across departments or functions. Communication networks vary widely in density, which is determined by dividing the number of communication links (reported communication contacts) that exist among all organizational members by the number of possible links if everyone knew everyone else. For example, a professional association is a low-density network because communication among its members is infrequent, but the kitchen crew of a restaurant is a high-density network in which most or all members communicate regularly with one another. Similarly, formal hierarchies are less dense than more progressive organizations that encourage employee participation in decision making.

Research suggests that the density of organizational networks have considerable influence over whether other employees adopt a new idea or technology. In a study of elementary schools and administrations, it was found that personal relationships

FIGURE 8.7

A Sample Organizational Communication Network

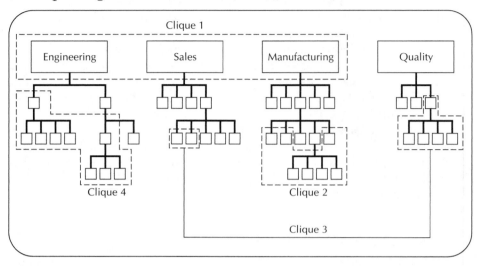

play a key role in the development and acceptance of new ideas when cliques form to focus on those ideas (Albrecht & Hall, 1991). These close connections help people overcome feelings of uncertainty and make them more likely to adapt to change.

The density of an organizational communication network can have some less obvious implications for organizational effectiveness. For example, we get less *new* information from people we work with every day than we do from people we know but contact less often. These infrequent contacts are called *weak ties*, and they can be very helpful for surfacing new perspectives and helpful people, as often happens in job hunting or recruiting (Granovetter, 1973). More recent research reveals that these same dynamics may apply globally; people in all cultures make use of their personal and professional networks in seeking new opportunities (Gao, 2005).

Some researchers use what they call a "network approach to participation" to redefine empowerment (Marshall & Stohl, 1993). According to this view, empowerment is a "process of developing key relationships in the organization in order to gain greater control over one's organizational life" (p. 141). An employee's personal communication network affects the experience of empowerment, involvement, and participation at work.

Extraorganizational networks — contacts from the industry or community — may be particularly important resources for employees in historically marginalized

EVERYDAY ORGANIZATIONAL COMMUNICATION

Networking on Campus: Communication, Identity, and Empowerment

As Bell and Nkomo (2001) and Parker's (2003) research indicates, *extraorganizational* networks benefit historically marginalized groups by providing mentors and support as well as a "collective identity" in professional settings. But such networking opportunities can begin even before one enters into his or her profession of choice. Most colleges and universities, for example, have developed identity-based groups—from LGBTQ coalitions to Muslim Students' Associations—to provide students with a space in which to congregate, share resources, and network with other students, faculty members, and professionals both on and off campus.

For example, at our home campus—Arizona State University—the Society of Mexican American Engineers and Scientists (MAES) defines their mission as follows:

> The purpose of MAES is to increase the number of Latinos in the academic and professional areas of Engineering and Science. We serve the needs of our members by sponsoring both academic and social programs as well as promoting academic and career development for students. MAES is dedicated to promoting our vision of developing Latino engineering and science students into leaders, both professionally and within the community. (MAES, 2006)

To achieve its goals, MAES invites professional speakers from the community and the university to speak to the group, giving the students an opportunity to network with other Latin American professionals who are established in their field. In return, the group gives back to the community by providing college students as mentors and role models who encourage and empower ". . . young students in need to attend college and achieve academic excellence" (2006). In addition, one of the objectives of MAES is to "[d]evelop a network with area schools to encourage minority students to enter engineering and science fields" thereby providing ASU students with peers and potential future colleagues at nearby institutions. (2006)

Consider what you have read thus far about networks as well as your own experience with networking on campus and answer the following questions:

DISCUSSION QUESTIONS

1. Are you a member of a student organization dedicated to the support and empowerment of a particular group whether social, cultural, religious, or even

(continued, Networking on Campus)

major-based (e.g., English or Business Honor Society)? If you are not, consider browsing through your university's Web site and taking a look at the variety of organizations available or speaking with a friend who is an active member.

2. If you are a member of such an organization, describe why your organization exists. In other words, what are the current conditions, within the university and beyond, that encouraged your group to form?

3. What are your organization's goals? How does your organization work to achieve those goals? And, do you anticipate that you will have a need for a group like this once you leave the university setting? If so, why?

4. What efforts does your group make to allow you to network and form ties with other students, faculty members, or outside professionals who support the organization's goals? How have you benefited from such opportunities? How might you potentially benefit from such networking in the future?

groups who have difficulty finding mentors and other supports in positions of power within the organizations. For example, networking and building informal coalitions and communities with other African Americans within and outside of their employing organization is a key strategy for upward mobility among African American women (Bell & Nkomo, 2001; Parker, 2003). Such networks serve as a means of maintaining a "collective identity" even "as they ascend the corporation with what might otherwise become an individualistic quest for success" (Bell & Nkomo, 2001, p. 183). That such networks often maintain an explicit attention to empowerment is evidenced by the recent gathering of African American members of corporate boards of directors, a group that is still woefully small in number. At their meeting, directors were reminded of their obligation to continue to bring up issues of diversity in their board meetings, otherwise issues of diversity, inclusion, and empowerment are not likely to be part of the boards' conversations. One member of the group commented, "This is a group of African Americans whom CEOs listen to. That's why developing this network is so important" (Cora, 2004, p. 43).

Communication Network Roles

Communication network roles — or the location individuals occupy in the flow of interaction — impact one's experience of work and degree of influence on others. Well-connected individuals in an organization tend to be the most influential and the least likely to leave (Brass, 1984). Four types of communication roles occur in networks: the isolate, group member, bridge, and liaison. Isolates have little contact with others in the organization; they work alone either by choice or because their

jobs require them to be structurally or geographically isolated from other employees (e.g., salespeople or service technicians who travel constantly). Group members
communicate mainly within an informal clique, which may at times involve communication with a departmental, professional, or demographic grouping (e.g., an
accounts receivable specialist or a member of an advertising team). Bridges (who
are also group members) have significant communication contact with at least one
member of another informal group (e.g., a human resources representative dedicated to serving a particular department), and liaisons have connections with two or
more cliques but are not exclusive members of any one group (e.g., mediators or facilitators who are not themselves part of a team; some senior managers specializing
in cross-functional initiatives like quality or strategy).

Recent developments in information technology have reduced the felt isolation of many jobs by connecting them through various forms of electronic communication. Research is mixed on whether these types of connections can substitute
for face-to-face contact, though some research does indicate that face-to-face is
still the preferred and most effective mode of communication for some tasks, including organizational socialization (Waldeck, Seibold, & Flanagin, 2005). In our
experience, some people are more likely to seek out and even thrive under relatively solitary conditions. Moreover, isolation within the organization does not
necessarily mean a lack of connection in the field or profession; in the new economy, a person's network of connections outside the organization (both personal
and professional) may be more important than internal organizational communication networks.

While we often think of networking as a means to develop and exploit one's
connections for personal gain, for some these networks are necessary strategies for
balancing work and family concerns. African American women have historically
formed communities of "othermothers" who help one another to care for children
and families. In contemporary culture, poor, working-class African American
women continue to develop networks in which they often act as "border guards"
who bridge boundaries between work and family, home and street. "In their roles as
border guards, these women employed collective forms of empowerment that included shared resources among families trying to keep their children and homes
safe in neighborhoods riddled with violence and drug use" (Parker, 2003, p. 268).
Networks are clearly instrumental both outside and within organizational life.

Within organizations, liaisons can be the dominant interpreters of the organizational culture. As key communicators with tremendous influence on the direction
of the company, they are able to transform any message into an interpretation that
is consistent with their beliefs and to pass that interpretation quickly throughout
the company (and at times to customers and the community). When organizational
improvement efforts fail, it is most often a result of the improper mobilization of
liaisons.

Any attempt to analyze communication network roles in an organization may
be a sensitive issue for employees, who do not always perceive their degree of communication contact with others in the same way. For example, a subordinate might

report having daily contact with a superior, whereas the superior may claim to have no communication with the subordinate. Differences in status or perception may also cause employees to respond in ways that reflect not actual but expected communication roles, reporting contact only with people they think they *ought* to communicate with at work. In addition, employees may be reluctant to participate in a network analysis because the results may reflect negatively on them. For example, in our analysis of network roles in a professional association, a department head who was identified by his subordinates as an isolate was subsequently dismissed from the organization. Consequently, it is critically important to collect and handle network analysis data with an awareness of the political implications of various findings. Network structures should not be shared with top management or the public without first considering the possible impact on employees who participated in the study.

Content of Communication Networks

Emergent communication networks develop around specific topics, or content areas, of communication (Farace, Monge, & Russell, 1977). Each content area is regarded as defining a separate network; for example, a bank may have a social network for communication about personal matters and a task network for discussion of work duties. An isolate in one network may be a bridge or a group member in another. We have all known people who are "well connected" when it comes to gossip but much less so with regard to business updates and company strategy.

Moreover, the identification of multiple types of communication content contributes to our understanding of the relationships between people in networks. For example, two people who communicate only about work are said to have a uniplex relationship, whereas people who communicate about two or more topics — say, personal issues, task issues, and new ideas — are said to have a multiplex relationship. Multiplex linkages have been identified as significant sources of social support and organizational innovation (Albrecht & Hall, 1991; Ray, 1987).

The content of communication networks takes on added significance when we consider it in terms of the sense-making process. In an attempt to extend the cultural approach to organizations, one of the authors of this textbook (Eisenberg) suggested that analysis of "semantic" networks (in which people hold similar interpretations of key organizational symbols or events) may be useful (Monge & Eisenberg, 1987). The same network measures may be applied (e.g., bridge, group member, isolate, and liaison), but in this case they would refer not to the presence or absence of communication, but to overlapping interpretations of key cultural symbols. Individuals who are in the mainstream with regard to employee values and beliefs would be group members; those holding radically different interpretations would be isolates. Measures of network density would also apply. In a dense semantic network, for example, there is shared meaning about major organizational issues. This approach has been successfully applied to the analysis of perceptions of organizational missions and value statements (Contractor, Eisenberg, & Monge, 1992; Peterson, 1995).

☐ Interorganizational Communication Networks

Employees communicate with co-workers within the organization as well as with customers, suppliers, and others in different organizations or institutions. In an advertising agency, for example, account managers interact with people from various newspapers and television stations, and in a university, the gifts and development staff communicates with alumni, accountants, attorneys, and local officials. Communication networks thus cross organizational boundaries.

Interorganizational communication networks are the enduring transactions, flows, and linkages that occur among or between organizations. Such networks vary in terms of their openness, density, and interdependence. Tightly coupled or highly interdependent interorganizational networks are sensitive to environmental jolts that affect whole industries (e.g., in the deregulated airline industry, a minor change introduced by one carrier, such as reduced fares, significantly affects all others).

As discussed in Chapter 4, open-systems theory assigns great significance to an organization's environment. Some researchers regard organizational environments as consisting mostly of networks of other organizations. The complexity of this network of interorganizational relations varies, and highly complex interorganizational environments require great vigilance and skill to manage. Put differently, an organization's environment is a kind of "nested box problem," where each network exists within a larger network, ranging from one's division, to one's industry, one's nation, and the world (Perrow, 1986).

Organizations participate in interorganizational communication networks in various ways. Two organizations are said to be vertically integrated when one builds parts or provides services that the other needs for its delivery of a product or service. For example, Pratt & Whitney manufactures aircraft engines for sale to Boeing. In contrast, two or more companies are horizontally integrated when their customers are passed from one to the other in the service cycle. An example of this is the connections between a cancer screening clinic, a hospital, and a hospice center.

One of the authors of this textbook (Eisenberg) developed a typology of interorganizational communication that is useful in sorting out different kinds of linkages (Eisenberg et al., 1985). Specifically, there are three types of network linkages for the exchange of materials and information: institutional, representative, and personal. An institutional linkage occurs without human communication, as in the automatic transfer of data between companies. A representative linkage exists when people from various organizations meet to negotiate a contract, plan a joint venture, and the like. A personal linkage occurs when members of two organizations communicate privately. However, it may be difficult to distinguish between personal and representative linkages when people meet informally without any intentions of discussing business but do discuss business with significant results. The various types of linkages may also change over time; for example, two companies planning to engage in a joint venture may initially host luncheons or dinners intended to make people more comfortable with each other personally. Later, representatives may be identified to work out the details of the plan, part of which may include the automatic transfer of data between the organizations.

Interestingly, one efficient way of sharing information across organizational lines is not through overt communication but by hiring employees from other companies. Ideas about management, marketing, structure, communication, and employee treatment are "imported" through personnel changes. In some cases, new employees who bring both their technical ability and their interpretive framework to organizations can help promote needed change. For instance, when Hughes Aircraft Company hired a former IBM executive to serve as its CEO, the company's emphasis shifted from engineering to business and financial management. In other cases, however, new employees' previous experience may become an obstacle to initiating change. For example, consulting companies that seek to hire people with extensive industry experience (which makes them more credible to clients) must also make sure that along with that expertise does not come a fixed set of beliefs about the right ways of solving problems.

In the contemporary economic environment, organizations are most likely to turn to strategic alliances—such as mergers, acquisitions, and joint ventures—to enhance their financial status and political power. Most companies recognize that they need to narrow the scope of their services by coordinating their activities with those of other organizations. This need is especially pronounced in industries that are highly specialized but serve a population that seeks a range of integrated services. For example, strategic alliances are common among highly specialized healthcare providers, and are increasingly seen in higher education, where universities can no longer afford to offer a full array of programs. Similarly, high-technology organizations are investing in joint research and development ventures to cut costs and improve the collective work of scientists.

Interorganizational networks are pervasive in the nonprofit sector as well. One excellent example is found in Andrews's (2000) study of the Hillsborough River Greenways Task Force in Tampa, Florida. The task force was formed by a unique combination of environmental activists, local scientists, land developers, phosphate miners and concerned citizens sharing a commitment to the health of the Hillsborough River. While the group had no official charter or authority, their diverse expertise spread across significant stakeholder groups and over time the group developed enormous informal influence on city and county policies.

Studies show clearly the advantages of interorganizational participation for organizations. A study of two hundred thirty private colleges over a sixteen-year period showed that "well-connected" schools were better able to learn from and adapt to changing environmental conditions (Kraatz, 1998). A ten-year study of more than four hundred hospitals in California showed that hospitals were more likely to adopt service innovations when they were linked to their peer institutions (Goes & Park, 1997). Smaller companies may be especially well served by interorganizational relations. Such partnerships (like the Kentucky wood manufacturers network) have been shown to be associated with more process improvements, enhanced company credibility, and access to important resources (Human & Provan, 1997).

While their potential benefits are clear, interorganizational communication networks can be difficult to manage. For example, scientists from one organization may be reluctant to share their best ideas with scientists from another organization. Formal interorganizational alliances are risky because they require a good deal of trust, a willingness to give up autonomy, and the juxtaposition of potentially incompatible organizational cultures. Many mergers and acquisitions in recent years have been problematic because the organizational partners brought different levels of formality and different attitudes toward employees to the alliance.

Like multidisciplinary groups, interorganizational communication networks are potential sites of dialogue. As interorganizational cooperation across organizational, industrial, and national boundaries increases, the challenges of communication will become greater. In particular, ways of promoting productive dialogue among diverse networks will become increasingly important.

☐ The Networked Society

Within only a few years, our understanding of what constitutes a network has changed considerably, from the connections among people within a single organization — such as a hospital, manufacturing plant, or school — to the connections among people in a global society. During this short time, we have seen tremendous growth both in network marketing and in computer networks on the Internet.

Global communication networks have been transformed by on-line communication. Significant changes in communication behaviors have been noted, especially in information seeking and relational development. For example, computer users post questions on Internet bulletin boards and receive responses within minutes from people around the world. In search of meaningful relationships, millions of computer users participate in thousands of virtual gathering places (currently dominated by MySpace and Facebook), sharing real or apparent disclosures in pursuit of intimacy.

Some critics mourn the demise of local communities, whereas others envision an electronic global village that provides people with instantaneous access to information and other people worldwide. With potentially disastrous consequences, terrorist organizations have turned to on-line communication as a means of recruiting and staying connected with new members.

◣ CREATIVITY AND CONSTRAINT IN TEAMS AND NETWORKS

Team-based organizations face the challenges of balancing creativity and constraint in group relationships and of productively dealing with diverse interpretations. The members of a newly formed team are typically anxious about their role in the group and struggle to find a voice for themselves in the context of the group. This can be a formidable challenge during the orientation phase of a team's development.

During the conflict and emergence stages, members attempt to articulate their perceptions creatively, but their efforts are heavily weighted with constraints (e.g., "We tried that, and it didn't work" or "Management will never take our proposal seriously"). Other constraints can be useful in promoting team effectiveness, such as meeting times and places, agendas, and problem-solving procedures. In general, however, team members' ability to function as a group depends on their skill in balancing the creative contributions of individual members with the constraints imposed by the group as a whole.

Networks both within and among organizations are notable for the speed with which creative new ideas can be diffused among large groups of people. Mostly independent of the usual constraints, such as formal positions and hierarchy, informal communication networks encourage innovation and collaboration. Nevertheless, over time networks may acquire a relatively stable structure that can act to constrain future communication. In some countries (particularly in Asia), informal connections among large corporations largely dictate the flow of business among these companies.

SUMMARY

Collaboration between and among employees and managers can occur in various ways and to varying degrees: Participation in organizations is both natural and desirable. The goal of increased participation brings with it paradoxes that can stop organizations from reaching other goals. These paradoxes are typically experienced as tensions by employees and managers, such as the tension an employee might feel about wanting more input into decision making, while dealing with the daily burdens of individual job responsibility in an already crowded workday. We recommend that such tensions be addressed rather than avoided if the goals of increased participation are to be achieved. The ideal of a democratic workplace is one in which organizations concern themselves with the interests of many different individuals and groups (not just the stockholders). The multiple stakeholder model promotes the type of participation necessary to achieve this ideal.

Teams and networks are now common organizational forms for collaborative work. The drive to organize in such a manner comes from the realization that no single individual — or pair of individuals — is sufficient to achieve complex goals. In team-based organizations employees from a variety of organizational functions serve as members of one or more working groups. These employees might work in one of several different types of teams, such as project teams to help coordinate the successful completion of a particular project; work teams to be responsible for a "whole" work process that delivers a product or service to a customer; quality improvement teams to improve customer satisfaction, and evaluate and improve team performance and reduce costs; or virtual teams to achieve goals and complete tasks across time and space. All types of teams, however, grow through five essential communicative elements: roles, norms, decision-making processes, management of conflict/consensus, and cultural diversity.

Communication networks, or groups of individuals who may be identified as sharing regular lines of communication, have emerged as a primary mode of organizing in the new economy. Networks are emergent, informal, and somewhat less interdependent than teams. They matter because regular contact between identifiable groups of people (whether they be scientists or political action groups) can play an important role in accessing information and in the quality and direction of decision making. In organizations, types of small-group networks include circle, wheel, chain, and all-channel. The more powerful emergent types of networks (grapevines, cliques, and loosely coupled networks) emerge from the formal and informal communication among people in organizations. Interorganizational types of networks include institutional, representative, and personal linkages. Network communication is affected by patterns of interaction, communication roles, and content areas.

Thanks in great part to advances in computer networks (e.g., the World Wide Web) our understanding of what constitutes a network has changed considerably. What was once a connection among people within a single organization (e.g., a school) is now a connection among people in an entirely global society. As advances in technology continue to expand (especially considering the growing popularity of networking Web sites such as Facebook and MySpace), we will see additional significant changes in communication behaviors, particularly in the areas of information seeking and relational development.

QUESTIONS FOR REVIEW AND DISCUSSION

1. What is meant by employee participation in decision making?

2. What are some of the paradoxes typically associated with the practical implementation of greater participation?

3. What is Deetz's ideal for democracy in the workplace? How does the multiple stakeholder model challenge accepted ideas about effective organizational communication?

4. List and explain the types of teams used in today's organizations. What are the advantages and disadvantages of taking a team-based approach to organizing?

5. What unique challenges are associated with virtual teams?

6. What is a communication role on a team? What types of roles are available to team members? Discuss the advantages and disadvantages of using a diverse array of roles in a team-based situation.

7. What are communication networks? What characteristics do communication networks share with organizational teams? How does a communication network differ from a team?

8. What are some examples of prominent interorganizational networks in your local community?

9. How do new network forms affect the way an organization thinks about growth and expansion? What effect does this new way of thinking have on the nature and challenge of competition between organizations?

KEY TERMS

CASE STUDY I

The Networked University

Like most social institutions, for most of their history universities have been associated with specific towns or locations, and it would be hard to conceive of them otherwise (e.g., how about moving the University of Southern California to Nevada, where the property taxes are lower?). At the same time, schools wishing to compete in a global marketplace have gradually expanded their offerings worldwide, establishing campuses in Europe, Asia, and elsewhere. And they offer a significant number of degrees on-line through distance education.

Still, most of these institutions continue to retain an attachment to a particular locale. Recently, private institutions like the University of Phoenix have emerged on the higher education scene without these preconceptions. They set up shop wherever potential customers (students) congregate, and they offer highly flexible degree programs that require very little in the way of physical presence in a classroom.

ASSIGNMENT

Imagine that you are the education reporter for the *New York Times*, and you are writing a feature article on the changing landscape of higher education in America.

1. Knowing what you do about organizational communication, what would you say are the main reasons for the emergence of these types of schools at this time in history?
2. What will be the main advantages and challenges of building a corporate network of schools like the University of Phoenix?
3. Finally, what should be the reaction of more traditional, place-oriented schools?

CASE STUDY II

The Networked Community

BACKGROUND

Founded in 1913, Fleeberville is an average American city of 1.5 million people with typical urban problems. The city is located on a large, spring-fed lake in a mountain setting just north of Atlanta, Georgia, and industrial pollution has over the years become a serious problem. Traffic on the two major highways gets worse every year, as does the rate of violent crime. The software companies that dominate the local economy are downsizing, and the remaining jobs require extensive technical expertise. The result has been an expanding underclass, much of which has been forced to seek public assistance. People with resources have increasingly isolated themselves from the city as a whole, and gated communities and private schools grow more numerous each year. Meanwhile, basic city services and public schools are in decline.

ASSIGNMENT

Imagine that you are an activist, community organizer, and communication expert who has recently decided to make Fleeberville your permanent home. You intend to put down roots, start a career, get married, and raise children there. However, for many reasons, you feel that the city must embark on a path of self-renewal.

You observe that many citizens seem to care about the city, but isolated efforts to improve things (e.g., clean up the lake, clothe the homeless, sponsor a school) don't appear to be very effective. Knowing what you do about systems, teams, networks, and organizing, how would you approach the problem of making Fleeberville a better place to live?

1. What actions would you begin with, and whom would you contact for help?
2. What patterns of communication would you encourage, and how ought they to change over time?
3. How would you deal with existing groups who feel uniquely responsible for determining the future direction of the city?
4. What teams and networks would you build to promote such a massive effort, and how would you prepare these groups for the challenges?
5. How would you evaluate the success or failure of your efforts?

CHAPTER 9

Communicating Leadership

In the lead essay for the international journal *Leadership*, prominent organizational scholars and coeditors David Collinson and Keith Grint (2005) write:

> Since the 1940s there has been an enormous outpouring of writing on leadership. Yet, there is little consensus on what counts as leadership, whether it can be taught, or even how effective it might be. . . . Leadership "research" has frequently been at best fragmented and at worst trivial, too often informed by the rather superficial ideas of management and academic consultants keen to peddle the latest, pre-packaged list of essential qualities deemed necessary for individual leaders and as the prescribed solution to all leadership dilemmas. (p. 5)

Despite this pessimistic assessment of the history of leadership research as well as the "best practices" models offered by leadership consultants, interest in articulating new ways of thinking about leadership continues to expand, and the stakes for finding and training effective leaders worldwide have never been higher. Failures in leadership span the globe and punctuate our present era. They include the various financial debacles of the late twentieth and early twenty-first centuries; failures of political leadership in a post-9/11 world to prevent war and insurrection; failures of federal, state, and local administrators and relief agency leadership to deal with unprecedented natural disasters in the United States; and a singular failure in moral leadership among the world's best-known and most-respected persons to offer a credible message of hope and unification capable of reaching diverse cultures worldwide.

In this chapter we provide some new thinking about leadership drawn from traditional and nontraditional sources. In part, this new thinking requires us to reframe what we mean by leadership as well as how we think about the role of communication in it. To guide us in our examination we will honor the advances made in leadership research that provide the basis for the bracing critique that began this chapter. We do so because without understanding the history of leadership research, we risk abandoning some useful insights that continue to serve us well. From that traditional foundation we move on the more innovative ways of thinking about leadership as communication and sense making, and the powerful role narrative and identity play in it as well as in everyday communication with employees.

◩ LAYING THE FOUNDATION: USEFUL INSIGHTS FROM PRIOR THEORETICAL FRAMES

In this section we detail the traits and styles of leadership and the situational and transformational approaches to leadership. We explore the implications of each approach for communication, along with its limitations.

☐ Trait Leadership

Trait theory is one of the earliest attempts to fashion a theory of leadership. It focused entirely on an individual's physical and social attributes. From the oral histories of the Peloponnesian wars (circa eighth century BCE) that chronicled the feats of warriors and goddesses through the profiling of more contemporary political icons (e.g., various U.S. presidents—Washington, Jefferson, Lincoln, T. Roosevelt, FDR, JFK, Reagan, etc.; world leaders from other regions—Golda Meir, Saddam Hussein, Evita Perón, Adolf Hitler, Desmond Tutu, Joseph Stalin, Winston Churchill, Mao Tse-tung, etc.); some recognized religious leaders (e.g., Gandhi, Jesus Christ, Buddha, Mohammed, Dalai Lama, etc.); and sports heroes (e.g., Lance Armstrong etc.) there continues to be a human fascination with the physical and behavioral characteristics of those who attain either greatness or infamy.

For this reason, it should come as no surprise that management researchers and theorists from the 1930s through the mid-1950s drew heavily on existing trait models to formulate the first profiles of great business leaders. Rather uncritically, these first efforts reflected the biases of the neo-European culture that generated them, so the traits of recognized leaders tended to be held by tall, blond, white males from upper-class or upper-middle-class families. When Hitler's rise to power in pre–World War II Germany emphasized the purported superiority of the (white) Aryan nation, the trait approach lost much of its appeal. Nonetheless, traits associated with great leaders (and great sports heroes) still capture a great deal of the public imagination and influence decision making. Candidates for the U.S. presidency, for example, are still expected to "look like leaders," which, as recently as the

2004 campaign, continues to be synonymous with "tall white male" in the public's imagination.

For scholars who understand the appeal of visual culture and its reliance on a commodity-based form of capitalism to sustain it, the appeal of trait theories of leadership transfers rather easily to traits associated with celebrity and popular culture stardom. In a striking critique, *New York Times* columnist Maureen Dowd (2005), exasperated by the fact that so many of the younger women she comes in contact with look alike, have the same hairstyles, wear the same fashions, and express themselves in a very similar celebrity-speak manner, commented that the triumph of feminine sameness was also the death of the feminist ideal. But this one-size-fits-all "picture of perfection" doesn't stop with fashion or even with plastic surgery. In a study of flight attendants, organizational scholar Alexandra Murphy (1998) pointed out that physical traits were still responsible for the selection, promotion, and retention of workers in the airline industry, particularly for female employees. In another well-known study, Angela Trethewey (1999) discussed the "disciplining" of the female body in the workplace and provided an analysis of how appearances at work are signs of power, authority, and privilege.

One insight we can gain from the trait approach to leadership is the fundamental idea that physical attractiveness is a key component—and an enduring one—of effective leadership. This reality was underscored years ago when those who listened to the Kennedy-Nixon presidential debates rated Nixon much more highly that those who saw the debate on television; much was written about Nixon's "five o'clock shadow" and "shifty eyes," which were contrasted with JFK's "boyish good looks." Despite the democratically dubious and clearly flawed social values that underscore it, ours is a world that more often than not gives a competitive edge to those of us who most closely resemble whatever physical and behavioral model of cultural attraction happens to be current.

☐ Leadership Style

Theories of leadership have also long been associated with issues of power and authority. Many years ago, Ralph White and Ronald Lippitt (1960) proposed that **leadership style** should be conceived of as a continuum from autocratic (boss-centered power and authority) to democratic (managers and subordinates share power and authority) to laissez-faire (subordinate-centered power and authority with little to no guidance from managers).

This leadership taxonomy reflected the world political climate during the time of its formation (circa post–World War II), right down to the language used to associate the "weak" French style (e.g., laissez-faire) with leadership that failed to defeat the Nazis in 1940. At the other end of the leadership continuum the terminology is equally suspect, as strong political leaders capable of bending nations to their will were well known—and, for good reason, often feared—throughout the world. It should be no surprise that the middle ground occupied by democratic leaders was the favored approach among post-war North American and European researchers. Democracy had triumphed over dictators and democratically elected leaders had also saved those countries whose own leaders had failed them. Why shouldn't this approach apply equally well to the workplace?

From the outset, one problem associated with the styles approach to leadership was its rigidity. What appeared as three distinct styles emerged as overlapping sets of behavior in practice. Effective leaders often displayed a dominant style, but were usually capable of behaving in other ways when the situation warranted. Moreover, the effectiveness of any given style depended on the consent of followers, who varied in their tolerance for different leadership styles (this remains very true today, where the styles appropriate to manufacturing work don't play as well with, for example, physicians or professors). Just as presidents seldom remain in office if they violate the trust or expectations of the electorate, so too do other leaders rise and fall with the success and relative satisfaction experienced by their subordinates.

Despite these problems, the styles approach to leadership continued to attract academic adherents and benefited from various keen theoretical refinements. For example, Robert Blake and Jane Mouton created "The Blake and Mouton Managerial Grid" (1964, 1985) as a by-product of the human relations and human resources movements (see Chapter 3). According to the Managerial Grid, there were two primary dimensions that defined appropriate choices of leadership style: concern for relationships (people) and concern for tasks (production). Figure 9.1 illustrates how those two key dimensions allow for five style-based options.

As with trait theory and the styles approach, this model closely fits the prevailing cultural and political climate of its time. Management is portrayed as a simple matter of balancing competing goals through rational decisions about people and tasks. Complicating factors such as race, class, gender, and ethnicity are all absent from this model. At the center of the grid is a yawning display of 1950s middle class suburban values, a preoccupation with avoiding conflict, and no clear role for communication processes in creating either productive relationships or completed tasks.

The five categories that inform the grid say as much about prevailing preferences for a class-based system for organizing as they do any enduring organizational reality (i.e., they are partisan). The top of the pecking order is divided into "Country Club Management" (for leaders more oriented toward "satisfying relationships") and "Team Management" (for those whose leadership role is defined by a group accomplishment of tasks because of "trust and respect"). At the bottom of the pecking order we find two choices as well: "Impoverished Management," whose language seems drawn from a caricatured view of the welfare state, pitted against a fascistic "Authority-Obedience" leader, with little or no concern for the value of human life.

Between these extremes we have the aptly named "Organization Man Management," a concept of leadership that balances a concern for others with a concern for the completion of tasks. The "Organization Man" reference is to a best-selling book by William H. Whyte Jr. that described a dominant North American culture

FIGURE 9.1

The Blake and Mouton Managerial Grid®

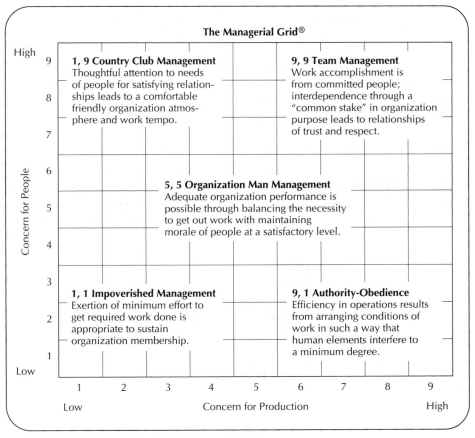

The Managerial Grid®

High

9 **1, 9 Country Club Management**
Thoughtful attention to needs of people for satisfying relationships leads to a comfortable friendly organization atmosphere and work tempo.

9, 9 Team Management
Work accomplishment is from committed people; interdependence through a "common stake" in organization purpose leads to relationships of trust and respect.

5, 5 Organization Man Management
Adequate organization performance is possible through balancing the necessity to get out work with maintaining morale of people at a satisfactory level.

1, 1 Impoverished Management
Exertion of minimum effort to get required work done is appropriate to sustain organization membership.

9, 1 Authority-Obedience
Efficiency in operations results from arranging conditions of work in such a way that human elements interfere to a minimum degree.

Concern for People

Low

1 2 3 4 5 6 7 8 9

Low   Concern for Production   High

Source: R. R. Blake and J. Srygley. *The Managerial Grid III: The Key to Leadership Excellence* (Houston, TX: Gulf Publishing Company, 1985).

of complacency in large organizations promoted by leaders more concerned with being liked than with being regarded for their good business sense. In Whyte's (1956) classic study, "good communications" was the ticket to a rewarding career because "the social ethic" (with its emphasis on fitting in, not standing out, and being well liked) had displaced the "Protestant ethic" of rugged individualism capable of independent judgment and a singular attention to the value of hard work and its positive effects on character.

☐ Situational Leadership

Situational leadership suggests that appropriate leadership emerges from behavior that is responsive to varied situations. The literature on leadership became more nuanced as systems theories began to suggest that the appropriate behavior in any situation was more a matter of reading and responding to contingencies than it was a fixed condition of traits or styles. In 1977, management theorists Paul Hersey and Kenneth Blanchard determined that the effectiveness of a leader had to do with the maturity of the group. They categorized four distinct styles of situational leadership based on a group's maturity: telling, selling, participating, and delegating. Figure 9.2 displays the concept. The more mature the group, the less direct authority

FIGURE 9.2

Situational Leadership Model

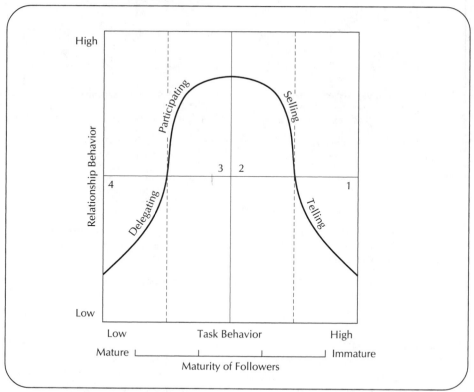

P. Hersey and K. Blanchard, *Management of Organizational Behavior: Utilizing Human Resources*, 3rd ed. (Englewood Cliffs, NJ: Prentice Hall, 1977).

(telling) or persuasion (selling) is required. Less direct supervision is also necessary. As groups become more mature, effective leaders participate more actively with the group, functioning at times as members or followers as the situation requires. In the most mature group settings, effective leaders delegate decision-making responsibilities to group members and empower them to create alternative ways and means to carry out tasks and evaluate performance (note the connection between levels of team empowerment in the previous chapter).

As appealing as the situational approach to leadership sounds, this approach ignores three things. First, it doesn't provide a way for organizations to identify persons for leadership who are flexible and adaptive in their orientation to others. More important, it also omits a method for identifying people who communicate effectively—and differently—in a variety of settings and with diverse others. Finally, this model for leadership omits a key skill: the ability to motivate and *inspire* others, not only to higher levels of performance but also to higher moral and ethical behavior.

☐ Transformational Leadership

Transformational leadership foregrounds organizational change and transformation as the essential task of effective leaders. Warren Bennis (1992) identified characteristics of such effective leaders for the global marketplace. This "new type of leader" is a **change agent**, one who seeks to lead an organization through an increasingly turbulent global business environment through the strategic use of communication.

The world of the late 1980s and early 1990s experienced a great deal of political, social, and economic change. The Cold War, which had dominated the global political stage since the end of World War II, ended with the tearing down of the Berlin wall in 1989 and the resignation of Soviet premier Mikhail Gorbachev on Christmas Day 1991. The U.S. economy was in flux, so much so that presidential candidate Bill Clinton's chief strategist, James Carville, made the mantra "it's the economy, stupid," the basis for Clinton's vision for change, a vision that led to a surprising victory in 1992. Organizations already rebounding from the massive restructuring that took place after the first Arab oil crisis and the sudden and unpredicted dominance of Japan in world manufacturing markets in the 1970s and 1980s were now learning how powerful the new information technologies — specifically the desktop computer—could be, as well as coming very quickly to understand how the Internet was changing the way business was done. And, after years of creating campaigns for ecological awareness, the Green movement in Europe and environmental advocates in North America finally began to see progress as world governments began to take seriously the negative consequences of carbon emissions, pollution, and the demise of the rain forests and the ominous potential for global warming. The time, the culture, and the economy seemed all ripe for change.

Bennis, of course, was not the only writer espousing a need for transformational leadership. Popular authors such as Tom Peters (1994) were lecturing to packed audiences about the power of transforming businesses through inspired leadership, empowerment of employees, and the strategic uses of new technologies. In the academy, researchers and theorists from a variety of fields were making a case for a new way of thinking about organizing. One such theorist, Margaret Wheatley (1992), used recent developments in theoretical physics to define some intriguing parameters for what she termed "the new science of leadership." In a bold extension of the democratic impulse, Wheatley's parameters encouraged leaders to think of themselves as stewards and employees at all levels to see themselves as stakeholders. She described the importance of thinking relationally rather than hierarchically and of conceiving of contexts as manifest through valued relationships rather than as something that exists in some rigid, impersonal organizational "structure." Her work continues to inspire leaders to look beyond traits, styles, and situations to fully acknowledge and embrace their enduring connection to their employees, society, and the world.

One leadership competency on which all writers can agree is on the importance of the leader's vision. Whether in politics, religion, social activism, education, or global business management, it is important for leaders to craft a credible and compelling view of the future, or **vision**, as well as cultivate an ability to communicate that future clearly and creatively to disparate others. Jim Collins and Jerry Porras (2002) offer this definition of a good vision:

> A well-conceived vision consists of two major components—*core ideology* and *envisioned future*. . . . A good vision builds on the interplay between these two complementary yin and yang forces: It defines "what we stand for and why we exist" and . . . "what we aspire to become, to achieve, [and] to create." (2002, p. 221)

To inspire a vision for change requires creating a language for that vision. Changing how we think requires changing how we speak because, as we learned from our discussion of Max Weber in Chapter 3, human beings are "suspended in webs of significance that we ourselves have spun" (cited in Geertz, 1973, p. 434). Those webs are constructed out of language, and the organizing practices we build are spun within them. Transformational leadership requires leaders to have a singular ability to communicate vision in a way that inspires others. For this reason, the new way of thinking about leadership truly began with a new way of valuing communication as the essential component of inspiration and change.

But understanding the role of communication in effective leadership is not the same as knowing how to do it, or doing it consistently over time in a range of challenging settings. The next turn in leadership studies moved from an emphasis on articulating a compelling vision to establishing behavioral habits that enact and reinforce that vision (i.e., "walking the talk"). Many of these habits are also communicative in nature.

◩ LEADERSHIP RECONSIDERED: EFFECTIVE LEADERSHIP HABITS

Contemporary authors who write on leadership suggest that great leaders possess a unique combination of habits: habits of mind, habits of character, and habits of authentic and compelling communicative performance. Understanding each of these sets of behavior helps inform our contemporary notion of leadership.

☐ Habits of Mind

Habits of mind are patterned ways of thinking that define how a person approaches issues and conceives of alternative ways of resolving or dealing with them. Robert E. Quinn, writing in the *Harvard Business Review* (2005), echoes the problems associated with leadership training when he observes:

> Nearly all corporate training programs and books on leadership are grounded in the assumption that we should study the behaviors of those who have been successful and teach people to emulate them. . . . But my colleagues and I have found that when leaders do their best work, they don't copy anyone. Instead, they draw on their own fundamental values and capabilities—operating in a frame of mind that is true to them yet, paradoxically, not their normal state of being. I call it the fundamental state of leadership. (2005, pp. 75–76)

Quinn goes on to elaborate the differences between a leader's "normal state of being" and the state of mind required to perform and communicate as a leader:

1. Move from being comfort-centered to being results centered. Ask: What results do you want to create?
2. Move from being externally directed to being more internally directed. Stop complying with others' expectations and clarify your core values. Increase your integrity, confidence, and authenticity.
3. Become less self-focused and more focused on others. Put the needs of the organization above your own.
4. Become more open to outside signals or stimuli, including those that require you to do things you are not comfortable doing. (p. 75)

Quinn's main point is that leadership is less a prescribed set of behaviors than it is a uniquely expansive mindset, one that is focused on the creation of possibility (see also Zander & Zander, 2002). This theme is echoed in recent work by Peter Senge and his colleagues at the Society for Organizational Learning in Cambridge, Massachusetts (Senge, Scharmer, Jaworski, & Flowers, 2005). Based on interviews with over 150 leaders in business, the arts, the martial arts, the military, politics, religion, and education and honed through examples taken from the experiences of the four co-authors over a two-year period of time, they posed the provocative question: "What would it take to shift the whole?" These authors (2005) then articulated a model that is composed of three habits of mind that feature the value of bringing together subjective and objective aspects of knowledge for leaders and others:

1. *Sensing*: The capacity to suspend, the courage to see freshly, seeing from the whole, seeing with the heart. Quieting the mind. Avoiding knee-jerk reactions to problems, or distancing yourself from the problem. Redirecting attention.
2. *Presencing*: Into the silence, reaching a state of clarity about what is emerging, an inner knowing that is quite the opposite of decision making. "What to do just becomes obvious." Presencing is seeing from the deepest source and becoming a vehicle for that source.
3. *Realizing*: Refers to the creative process, bringing something new into reality. This comes from a source that is deeper than the rational mind. "If you have to think in the martial arts, you're dead," says champion athlete Bryan Arthur (www.presence.net/roumiana.html). In the words of another interviewee, "It's almost as if I'm watching myself in action. I'm both engaged and simultaneously detached. When that happens, I know there will be magic." (Gotseva-Yordanova, 2006)

It would appear, then, that one mental habit of highly evolved leaders is the ability to enter a state of consciousness that goes beyond the limits of problem solving and enters the realm of the keenest sort of intuition. Yet, despite its counterrational tone and quasi-spiritual quality, this habit of mind is clearly focused on identifying future possibilities in the world and ridding oneself of the baggage associated with the past.

But is learning how to focus on possibility and the future really the best advice for leaders? Does ridding oneself of the baggage of the past improve one's effectiveness? British management theorist Annie Pye (2005) makes a very different argument. Using the work of systems theorist Karl Weick (see Chapter 4), she advances the idea that searching for the "Holy Grail" of leadership by focusing on future actions may be the wrong question to ask, or at least the wrong way to ask the question. Her comprehensive research with large organizations in the United Kingdom demonstrates that most of what we call "leading" on a daily basis is better conceived of as what Weick defined as *retrospective sense making*, or interpreting past events in a way that has important implications for the future. From Weick, she posits seven distinguishing characteristics of the activity that set sense making apart from other explanatory processes. Sense making is:

1. Grounded in identity construction
2. Retrospective
3. Enactive of sensible environments
4. Social
5. Ongoing
6. Focused on and by extracted cues
7. Driven by plausibility rather than accuracy (Weick, 1995, p. 17)

Drawing on Weick's famous statement "that people can only know what they are doing only after they have done it," Pye suggests that the "ongoing nature of experience means that retrospective sense may continue to be re-written" (Pye, 2005, p. 38; Weick, 1995, p. 49). From this perspective, leaders are uniquely adept at learning from their experiences by subjecting them—and the way they think about what they have done in the past—to critical scrutiny. Clearly, one implication of this way of thinking about leadership is that making sense of experience is less a matter of "truth" or representational accuracy than it is a matter of continuous editing and reframing. One habit of mind that is therefore essential for leaders is the ability to continuously learn from previous experiences. So it is that the ability to enter the state of mental awareness that marks effective leadership is one borne of a lifetime of cultivating the habit of mind that makes one's own lived experiences into a kind of critical and experiential database. We do not learn to become leaders by imitating others, but instead by learning lessons from our own personal experiences about how to face the future.

☐ Habits of Character

Jim Collins (2005), known for the idea of the "high-performance organization" and widely recognized for his studies of "visionary companies" that endure through turbulent times, echoes Quinn's views of the importance of internal states associated with what he terms "Level 5 Leadership" or the highest quality of leadership (p. 136). Yet for Collins, the essential component is only one part state of mind; it is also composed of ways of being in the world, or what we call **habits of character**. And, within those habits, we find that almost without fail the essence of a leader's character is not shameless self-promotion, or iconic bombast, or personal flamboyance, but simple modesty.

Collins's studies of eleven great companies helped him construct a hierarchy of learning experiences that prepare great leaders for modesty. These experiences begin with the identification of a "highly capable individual" who then advances to "contributing team member"; from success at the level of teamwork (which includes some leadership), the highly capable person evolves into a position where she or he can demonstrate skills as a "competent manager." "Effective leaders" emerge from successful managerial experiences (where success is also combined with lessons learned from failure). Collins labels Level 5 leaders as "Executives," and this is the only level where he found that rarest of human combinations: personal humility alongside professional will.

The importance of drive or professional will is widely understood as a key characteristic of success in the business world. Unfortunately, it is often confused with a "take no prisoners" mentality and a desire to succeed at all costs (recall the litany of recent ethics scandals recounted in Chapter 1). But those traits, while they may be found in leaders, are not what define success as a leader. Instead, professional will is generally made up of a strong drive to succeed based on a clear and compelling vision for the company, where a close connection exists between the image one has of oneself and one's professional identity. Ironically, individuals who rise to prominence through unrelenting personal ambition and a drive to succeed seldom achieve Level 5 leadership because they lack the corresponding essential quality of character: modesty. **Modesty**—personal humility about one's accomplishments and a profound commitment to the good of the company—is vital to leadership because it is inspiring.

The unique blending of professional will with personal humility is also found in the idea of "servant leadership" (Greenleaf, 1996). Beverly Alimo-Metcalfe and John Alban-Metcalfe (2005) provide an empirically field tested definition for the servant leader that is composed of the following qualities:

1. Valuing individuals (genuine concern for others' well-being and development)
2. Networking and achieving (inspirational communicator)
3. Enabling (empowers, delegates, develops potential)
4. Acting with integrity (consistent, honest, open)
5. Being accessible (approachable, in touch with others)
6. Being decisive (a risk taker)

Again, these habits of character are less learned or taught than they are cultivated through everyday disciplined thinking about the "work of the self" in a world of others. This principle is similar to what Bennis and Nanus (2003) call "management of self" and Senge (1995) calls "personal mastery"—the capacity for acquiring a critical appreciation of one's accomplishments in the context of a lifelong journey toward selfhood and the challenge of working with others to achieve a vision or create an imagined community. Such disciplined thinking views the evolving, questing, relating self as part of a much larger human project, and for this reason it carries with it an active commitment to the success of others as well as an appreciation for the privileges of education, race, class, gender, age, or simply being in the right place at the right time to succeed. Humility about one's accomplishments—regardless of what they are, or how grandiose they may seem to be—is the inevitable result of habits of mind and habits of character that are then realized fully in authentic communicative performance.

☐ Habits of Authentic Communicative Performance

From the outset, most leadership research has advanced the idea that effective leaders are skilled at **authentic communication**, in relating to others in a way that reflects their own deeply held values and beliefs. They are excellent communicators who have an ability to use language to influence and motivate others. This core idea has been key to every new approach to the subject of leadership since the ancient Greeks passed along this saying: "When Aschines speaks, the people say, 'How well he speaks,' but when Demosthenes speaks, the people say, 'Let's march against Philip!'" The ability to get others to willingly do what you ask of them, often with great personal sacrifice, is the mark of a great leader.

When we consider the power of the spoken word to inspire change, we may recall images from political and religious figures such as Martin Luther King Jr., speaking the famous words "I have a dream . . .," or John Fitzgerald Kennedy, who, during his inaugural address, said, "Ask not what your country can do for you, ask what you can do for your country." We may also think of former President Ronald Reagan, who combined a natural storytelling style with clear and compelling messages, and was known during his presidency as "the Great Communicator." We may think of Mary Kay Ash, visionary founder of Mary Kay Cosmetics, who found a way of combining traditional femininity, personal storytelling, and an entrepreneurial vision. We may think of former President Bill Clinton, who had both an encyclopedic knowledge of world history and literature as well as a charismatic quality that reportedly made people he spoke to feel as if they were the only person in the room and that their ideas were the most important ones on the table. And we may think of Oprah Winfrey, who provides a forum for talk about previously uncomfortable or publicly unspeakable topics, such as child abuse and molestation, racial inequality, obesity, and the importance of literacy worldwide. As an informal opinion leader operating in the public sphere, Winfrey uses her speaking platform as a change agent for issues of social justice. In all of these examples of leadership—as diverse in vision as they are in kind—the one common denominator is communication.

However, the term *communication* when applied to organizational settings can mean—and has meant—a lot of different things, as we have shown throughout this book. For example, during the scientific management era, effective communication meant top-down clarity and the cultivation of an authoritative style. The measure of communicative success was employees' strict adherence to orders given by the boss. This definition of good communication changed during the advent of the human relations and human resources eras, as researchers and managers learned that how employees felt they were being treated mattered to them. One lasting change from this era was a gradual new appreciation and behavioral focus on the importance of listening and responding skills, something unthinkable to authoritative, top-down managers engaged in what they believed were effective communication practices only a few years before.

Today the concept of leadership communication includes far more than success in the sender-receiver relationship. Giving clear instructions or listening to employees vent or even developing productive working relationships with others using a cell phone, a fax machine, or e-mail are merely the most-obvious aspects of effective communication for leaders. The concept of communication in the early twenty-first century reflects, as in the past, what has surfaced in our time as important indicators of cultural, social, economic, and political success. Because we live in a highly mediated world in a highly uncertain time, and because we have constructed a commodity-based capitalist system of economy that values the material as well as the symbolic dimensions of what is said or done, leadership today is ever-more dependent on the following:

- The ability to create, in straightforward if sometimes strategically ambiguous language, a clear and compelling *vision for the future* (Collins & Porras, 2002);
- The development of a *credible life story* that emphasizes the naturalness of the path you've taken to leadership despite having to overcome hardships and endure emotional pain while maintaining a core set of commonly held values (Benoit, 1997; Shamir, Dayan-Horesh, & Adler, 2005);
- The ability to *use language performatively* to inspire others to choose those desirable future actions and to work hard to help you obtain them (Deal & Kennedy, 1982; Pacanowsky & O'Donnell-Trujillo, 1983; Robbins, 1997).

A good leader is not only a visionary, but leads by example. This means being up to the daily challenges of organizing and decision making, but moreover it means showing others how much she or he enjoys being in charge of the ongoing action and is worthy of their trust and confidence. Good leaders today are, therefore, communicatively adept. They inspire others to work with them and for them through their humility and the power of their personal example.

◫ LEADING THE ORGANIZATION: COMMUNICATING WITH EMPLOYEES

One can get lost in the vast complexities of leadership theory and research, so it is helpful to remember some constant realities. All leadership has a communicative component and involves the purposeful exercise of influence over others. Moreover, this influence is independent of formal titles and reporting relationships and may extend in multiple directions within and between organizations. In this section, we discuss how leaders influence their employees through communication.

As we have seen throughout this book, organizational theories propose different approaches for leaders to communicate with their employees. In classical management theory, downward communication is emphasized; it is formal, precise, and work related. Human relations theory stresses supportive communication, while human resources theory emphasizes the need for supervisors to involve employees in decision making. The systems and cultural approaches make no specific prescriptions about communicating with employees, whereas critical theorists call for a radical leveling of power and authority among superiors and subordinates in which both are regarded as equally important to the organization. No matter what their perspective, however, contemporary observers agree that effective communication with employees on the part of leaders has at least four essential characteristics: It is open, supportive, motivating, and empowering.

☐ Openness

As a general rule, openness is a desirable goal in most supervisor-employee relationships (Redding, 1972). The parties in an **open communication** relationship "perceive the other interactant as a willing and receptive listener and refrain from responses that might be perceived as providing negative relational or disconfirming feedback" (Jablin, 1979, p. 1204). Openness has both verbal and nonverbal dimensions. Nonverbally, facial expression, eye gaze, tone, and the like contribute to degrees of open communication (Tjosvold, 1984).

Studies conducted by W. Charles Redding (1972) and his students at Purdue University revealed a positive correlation between a supervisor's open communication and employees' satisfaction with the relationship. The researchers identified five key components of an open communication relationship:

1. The most effective supervisors tend to emphasize the importance of communication in their relationships with employees. For example, they enjoy talking at meetings and conversing with subordinates, and they are skilled at explaining instructions and policies.
2. Effective supervisors are empathic listeners. They respond positively to employees' questions, listen to suggestions and complaints, and express a willingness to take fair and appropriate action when necessary.
3. Effective supervisors ask or persuade, rather than tell or demand.
4. Effective supervisors are sensitive to others' feelings. For instance, reprimands are made in private rather than in public work settings.
5. Effective supervisors share information with employees, including advance notices of impending changes and explanations about why the changes will be made.

In the 2004 book *Apollo, Challenger, and Columbia: The Decline of the Space Program (A Study in Organizational Communication)*, authors Phillip and Emily Tompkins examine the *Challenger* and *Columbia* disasters and find their cause to be in part due to the erosion of a culture of open communication and the loss of specific practices that ensured the exchange of ideas and information. Specifically, they describe the value of eminent scientist Wernher Von Braun's "Monday Notes" as a mechanism for both soliciting and responding to ideas on a regular basis. Von Braun required all of his lead engineers to submit written summaries of the progress and problems in their areas every Monday. He would read through the reports and make comments, then redistribute the entire package of notes (with his comments) to all of the submitters. In this way, he ensured regular communication across levels and departments. As Monday Notes were dropped and elements of shuttle design and manufacture were increasingly outsourced, communication was diminished and the safety of the program was put at risk (Tompkins & Tompkins, 2004). The Tompkinses' telling research on the history of NASA (and, specifically, the space shuttle program) underscores the value of open communication.

Other researchers suggest that openness plays a more complex role in the superior-subordinate relationship and that its effects are not always so easy to predict. Eisenberg argued that depending on the context, openness can have dramatically different outcomes (Eisenberg & Witten, 1987). For example, a supervisor may use openness in indiscreet or insincere ways or as a way to intimidate employees. Although supervisors should strive for open communication with employees in appropriate contexts, openness should not override other concerns, such as confidentiality and ethics. For example, it would be highly inappropriate for a supervisor to disclose reservations he or she may have about the performance of a colleague. Instead, the supervisor ought to share this information with the proper audience and in the proper context—that is, with his or her supervisor. Problems can arise when open communication is viewed ideologically and indiscriminately as a moral mandate for full and honest disclosure, without sensitivity to the communicative context of any given situation (Bochner, 1982; Eisenberg, 1984).

☐ Supportiveness

Research suggests that **supportive communication**—which emphasizes active listening and taking a real interest in employees—is even more useful to organizational leaders than openness. According to the **theory of leader-member exchange**, or LMX (Graen, 1976), supervisors typically divide their employees into two types and form very different relationships with members of each group. The two types of relationships are (1) in-group relationships, which are "characterized by high trust, mutual influence, support, and formal/informal rewards," and (2) out-group relationships, which are "characterized by . . . formal authority [and] low trust, support, and rewards" (Fairhurst & Chandler, 1989, pp. 215–216). In-group relationships develop over time, tend to be more trusting, and are characterized by a greater willingness by supervisors to delegate important tasks (Bauer & Green, 1996). In general, in-group relationships are associated with greater employee satisfaction, performance, agreement, and decision-making involvement as well as lower turnover rates than out-group relationships (Graen, Liden, & Hoel, 1982; Liden & Graen, 1980; Scandura, Graen, & Novak, 1986).

There is also evidence to suggest that having a positive in-group relationship with one's supervisor leads to better integration into important social networks (Sparrowe & Liden, 1997) as well as enhanced feelings of perceived organizational support, which in turn strengthen commitment and performance (Sparrowe & Liden, 1997; Wayne, Shore, & Liden, 1997). Communication researchers Gail Fairhurst and Theresa Chandler (1989) extended LMX theory in an examination of actual in-group and out-group conversations involving a warehouse supervisor and three subordinates. Their analysis reveals some consistency in the communication resources deployed by those in each type of relationship. The in-group relationship is characterized by influence by mutual persuasion (in which both parties challenge and disagree with each other frequently) and greater freedom of choice for subordinates. In contrast, the out-group relationship is marked by the supervisor's authority, a traditional chain of command, little freedom of choice for subordinates, and a disregard for their suggestions.

A more recent application of the leader-member exchange model to co-worker communication revealed how an employee's privileged relationship with a supervisor affected that employee's relationship with peers. In most cases, the employee's co-workers engaged in communication aimed at making sense of the preferential treatment, made judgments about the unfairness of the in-group relationship, and experienced a general erosion of trust in management (Sias & Jablin, 1995). Although the leader-member exchange distinction focuses on broad issues of trust and support, it does not prescribe open communication as the sole means for attaining supportive relationships. Instead, supervisory communication is viewed as an ongoing attempt to balance among multiple and competing relational, identity, and task goals (Dillard & Segrin, 1987; Eisenberg, 1984). Moreover, certain types of communication may ensure employee compliance but may also be demoralizing to employees. For example, a supervisor who insists on managing "by the book" despite employee extenuating circumstances (e.g., personal or medical emergencies) can create a negative work climate. Effective supervisors, in contrast, strive to communicate in ways that simultaneously show concern for the relationship, demonstrate respect for the individual, and promote task accomplishment.

☐ Motivation

Motivation can be defined as "the degree to which an individual is personally committed to expending effort in the accomplishment of a specified activity or goal" (Kreps, 1991, p. 154). Although various other factors contribute to employee motivation, our focus here is on how leaders encourage or discourage employee motivation through their communication. Their communication can function in two ways to motivate employees: Leaders can (1) provide information and feedback about employees' tasks, goals, performance, and future directions and (2) communicate encouragement, empathy, and concern. In both cases, however, the motivating effect comes from the manager's ability to endorse particular interpretations of organizational issues through communication (Sullivan, 1988). The four best-known theories of employee motivation involve goal setting, expectancy, equity, and compliance gaining.

Goal-Setting Theory

Goal-setting theory maintains that because employees' conscious objectives influence their performance, supervisors should assist employees in developing goals that are motivating (Locke & Latham, 1984). Some of the most important findings of this research are as follows:

1. Set clear and specific goals. Clear goals have a greater positive impact on performance than do general goals.
2. Set goals that are difficult but attainable. They will lead to higher performance than will easy goals.
3. Focus on participative rather than assigned goals.
4. Give frequent feedback about the goal-setting and work processes.

Although goal-setting theory is not a communication theory per se, most of these findings deal with communication. To be effective, goals must be clear and specific, must be developed through a dialogue with employees, and must be the subject of performance feedback. Feedback is especially important to employee motivation because it helps employees both to see how they're doing and how their efforts contribute to the success or failure of the company. Employees who receive such feedback from supervisors tend to be more satisfied, perform better, and are less likely to leave the company than those who do not receive feedback on their work (Jablin, 1979; Parsons, Herold, & Leatherwood, 1985).

Feedback on goals can take many forms, but to be effective must be timely, frequent, and specific. Annual performance reviews have been shown to be ineffective in influencing employee behavior (Ilgin & Knowlton, 1980). Such infrequent reviews encourage managers to focus on negative behavior that was noticed but not discussed throughout the year. Performance management should ideally be an ongoing, everyday conversation, since the best time to give feedback about employee performance is as soon as possible after it has occurred.

Not all supervisory feedback, of course, is negative. Tom Peters and Robert Waterman (1982) argue that successful managers give formal or informal recognition for a job well done. Management guru Ken Blanchard famously encouraged supervisors to "catch their employees doing something right." Generally speaking, positive feedback has been shown to encourage job satisfaction, identification, and commitment among employees (Larson, 1989).

Recently, some companies have made feedback part of certain jobs through the management of information systems. At Frito-Lay's snack food factory in California, for example, computer terminals are located in the packaging areas so that machine operators can access feedback on their daily performance, including the amount of raw material used, the number of hours an assembly line was not working due to repairs, and the number of person hours worked. According to one operator,

> People have more pride in their work now. We go to the computer at the end of the day and see how much we made or lost. If the numbers are good, we feel proud because we know we did it. If the numbers aren't good, we get with our team members and figure out what went wrong. Before, we seldom even saw the numbers. It's no wonder we weren't very interested in the business. (Grant, 1992, p. D7)

As this example shows, clear goals and immediate feedback are important in the increasingly popular shift from feedback from interpersonal communication to feedback from computer-accessed data.

Because many supervisors do not provide enough feedback, subordinates may actively seek it out (Ashford & Cummings, 1983). It is hard to do a job without knowing how you are doing. At the same time, it can be tricky to ask for feedback. Employees seeking feedback from a supervisor can be "faced with a conflict between the need to obtain useful information and the need to present a favorable image" (Morrison & Bies, 1991, p. 523). In a marked departure from times past, when seeking feedback was seen as a sign of weakness, effective performance today requires constant communication in all directions. Consequently, even when a supervisor does not provide sufficient feedback to an employee, the employee is making the right move in seeking it out.

Expectancy Theory

Expectancy theory makes three assumptions about employee behavior:

1. Employees perceive a relationship between a specific work behavior and some form of payoff or reward; that is, the behavior is viewed as instrumental to obtaining the reward.
2. Each reward or positive outcome is associated with a value (or valence, in the language of the theory) that reflects how much the individual wants the reward.
3. Employees develop expectations about their ability to perform the desired behavior successfully. (Vroom, 1964)

Employee motivation increases when outcome valences are positive, expectancies are high, and outcomes are clear. Under these circumstances, the employee desires the reward or outcome, feels capable of performing the desired behavior, and has a clear understanding of what will be rewarded as a result of that performance. For example, one resort manager who in the past had a serious employee absenteeism problem now bestows quarterly rewards of free weekend trips on employees who have records of perfect attendance for the three-month period. It's fair to say that everyone likes a free vacation, and that it is possible with some extra effort to have a perfect attendance record in most quarters. The existence of the program has been well communicated, and employees know what it takes to get the free trip. One could well argue that this manager's approach works because it meets all three criteria of expectancy theory.

Generally speaking, the expectancy model has been shown to benefit individuals and organizations by increasing employee motivation and improving the quality of the work life (Steers, 1981). In addition, because expectancy theory demands clear communication of performance outcomes, communication plays a key role in its successful implementation.

Equity Theory

In a different approach to employee motivation, **equity theory** examines the role of perceived inequities in the reward-to-work ratio (Altman, Valenzi, & Hodgetts, 1985). Employees who feel that they receive fewer rewards than their co-workers for performing comparable work are not likely to be motivated to perform their jobs well. Judgments of equity and perceptions of fairness are shaped by communication. In particular, the communication of superiors can affect subordinates' perceptions of equity. For example, a supervisor who takes the time to explain long-range plans for an employee's development helps the employee put present differences in position and salary into meaningful perspective.

Equity theory highlights the often subjective nature of employee performance evaluation and rewards. Although supervisors may strive to establish supportive relationships with employees, and organizations may be structured in ways that make identification and cooperation likely, employees may still lack motivation if they perceive themselves as underrewarded for their efforts.

Compliance-Gaining Theory

Compliance-gaining theory posits that leaders can effectively make use of informal communication strategies to motivate their employees. Supervisors who encourage employees with positive feedback are most likely to achieve task compliance and subordinate satisfaction (Daniels & Spiker, 1991). An investigation of the informal strategies used by superiors to influence subordinate behavior revealed that managers explain tasks or delegate assignments more often than they give orders (Keys & Case, 1990). They also tend to convey confidence, encouragement, or support in their attempts to influence employees, and to use reasoning and facts to suggest the merits of a new procedure or a desired behavior. In addition, managers often attempt to gain compliance by regularly soliciting employees' ideas (Keys & Case, 1990). However, these informal tactics of influence may be ineffective when dealing with chronically poor performers.

Current research on compliance-gaining tactics suggests that supervisors who rely on traditional lines of authority and punitive approaches are less effective motivators than supervisors who use a variety of influence tactics tailored to the needs and personalities of individual employees as well as to the specific goals involved. Indeed, setting clear goals, articulating ways of achieving them, and providing immediate feedback are an important part of the supervisor's job. From a communication perspective, conveying the right combination of these messages helps to motivate employees.

☐ Empowerment

Definitions of **empowerment** vary considerably from the sharing of power and decision making with employees through delegation, to enabling and motivating employees by building feelings of self-efficacy. The empowerment process enhances feelings of self-efficacy by identifying and removing conditions that foster employee powerlessness (Conger & Kanungo, 1988) (see Figure 9.3 on page 296). Furthermore, to feel empowered, an employee must also feel capable of performing the job and must possess the authority to decide how to do the job well (Chiles & Zorn, 1995).

Empowerment requires the manager to act more like a coach than a boss by listening to employees' concerns, avoiding close supervision, trusting employees to work within a framework of clear direction, and being responsive to employee feedback. An organization committed to empowerment encourages employees to take on ever-increasing responsibilities that utilize their knowledge and skills. A study of W. L. Gore & Associates (Pacanowsky, 1988), the company that invented GORE-TEX® fabric, identified six rules for empowering employees:

1. Distribute power and opportunity widely.
2. Maintain an open and decentralized communication system.
3. Use integrative problem solving to involve diverse groups and individuals.
4. Practice meeting challenges in an environment of trust.
5. Reward and recognize employees to encourage a high-performance ethic and self-responsibility.
6. Learn from organizational ambiguity, inconsistency, contradiction, and paradox.

Notice that these rules focus on providing the resources and opportunities for creating an environment in which subordinates become empowered by taking greater responsibility for their work.

Organizations (and departments within organizations) can vary with regard to their degree of empowerment (Ford & Fottler, 1995). Degree of empowerment is a direct result of how decision-making authority is defined. A distinction exists between the employee's control of job content (how the job gets done) versus job context (the conditions under which the job gets done, including goals, strategies, and standards). For example, it is increasingly common for line employees to have considerable say in the scheduling and tools they use to accomplish their work (job content) but still quite rare for them to have input into things like mission, strategy, and organizational structure (job context). What is of greatest importance is for managers and employees to maintain clear agreements about the expected degree of empowerment to avoid misunderstandings that can foster resentment and mistrust.

This section has provided you with some practical ideas, many of them long-established, about how one establishes positive influence with employees through openness, supportiveness, motivation, goal setting, and empowerment. The next section considers the negative consequences of organizational leaders who use their power to berate, belittle, and demean employees and subordinates.

EVERYDAY ORGANIZATIONAL COMMUNICATION

Zen and the Art of Basketball Leadership

In this chapter, we've tried to show that leaders can come out of any arena—politics, middle management, campus clubs, professional sports, and on and on. Consider the example of Phil Jackson, arguably the greatest head coach in the history of the National Basketball Association. He has the highest all-time playoff winning percentage. He coached Michael Jordan's Chicago Bulls to six NBA championships in the 1990s and won three consecutive titles with the L.A. Lakers in 2000, 2001, and 2002. His nine NBA championships as a coach place him at the top of the list, tied with Red Auerbach for the most all-time. And while his detractors point out that he's always benefited from having the best players (Michael Jordan, Scottie Pippen, Shaquille O'Neal, Kobe Bryant), no one can deny Jackson's leadership abilities. He manages egos brilliantly, connects with players on a personal level, and gets everyone to buy into his vision and play as a team.

Jackson takes a holistic approach to coaching. He's not only concerned with players' jump shots and rebounding skills, he also wants to influence their habits of mind, their sense of modesty, their character; in short, he wants to affect their overall psychological growth. Nicknamed the Zen Master, Jackson lectures on Buddhism, teaches his players meditation techniques, and talks at length about Native American spirituality. Like all great organizational leaders, he goes beyond the traditional player-coach (or supervisor-employee) relationship. By getting basketball superstars to link their work identity with their personal identity, Jackson has his players committing their entire selves—that's Phil Jackson's goal as a coach and as a leader. To win as a team, he believes players need to give their all.

To achieve his vision, Jackson needs to communicate his vision. Effective communication is the cornerstone of leadership, and few in basketball are better, more creative organizational communicators than Phil Jackson. He relates to players through books. He's given Nietzsche to Shaq and *To Kill a Mockingbird* to Bulls forward Horace Grant. Early in Kobe Bryant's career, Jackson gave the young star a copy of *Corelli's Mandolin*, a novel about a soldier sacrificing individual accomplishments for the benefit of his troops. Jackson's also been known to conduct practices in complete silence to bolster both his players' mindfulness and their nonverbal communication. And like any good L.A. resident, Jackson often uses film clips to communicate his message. When talking about teamwork, he'll show scenes from *The Green Mile*, where the prison guards work together as a unit. He'll screen frenetic *Three Stooges* shorts to show players how *not* to execute his triangle offense. And he'll dim the lights in the locker room and pop in *The Wizard of Oz*, underscoring his message that a title run requires heart, brains, and courage. The players love it—and they get the message. John Salley, who played for Jackson on the Lakers, said, "Phil makes it fun, entertaining as well as serious. We know when to laugh and giggle, and we know when to be serious. He makes sure we're not bored" (as cited in "Out of the Ordinary," 2000, para. 15).

By connecting with players in this way, Jackson is able to foster a supportive environment of in-group relationships. They respect him and he, in turn, trusts them to think on their own during games. His on-court style is quiet and detached. He doesn't employ the kind of sideline histrionics that other coaches use. When his team hits a bad spell, Jackson usually stays seated on the bench, sometimes even paring his nails (they don't call him the Zen Master for nothing). And he'll rarely call a timeout in situations like this. "Most coaches call timeouts immediately and kind of let the players rely on the coach," said Jerry Buss, the owner of the Lakers and Jackson's boss. "In Phil's case, I think he kind of says, 'You have to rely on yourself, because when it comes to crunch time, I'm not out there on the court with you'" (as cited in DuPree, 2002, para. 11).

Think of the great leaders in your life—the student assembly president who delegates responsibilities, the great professor who knows how to push students to their intellectual limits, the Army ROTC instructor who gets you to believe in yourself. Like Jackson, great leaders bolster confidence and trust their teams to do a great job on their own.

DISCUSSION QUESTIONS

1. In your own leadership capacities on campus—whether it be in sports, clubs, student government, Greek life, or anything else—what methods do you use to communicate your vision?
2. Who are the inspiring leaders in your life? What do they have in common? Do they share a similar vision or reveal uniform habits of mind and character?
3. Do you think these leadership models devalue the importance of peer influence? For example, is the influence of Michael Jordan on the Bulls overshadowed by all this emphasis on Phil Jackson? Who are some leaders that you think get too much credit for their team/organization/group's success?
4. In a team meeting before a playoff series with the Sacramento Kings, Jackson spliced images of Sacramento's white, shaved-headed, tattooed point guard with images of the neo-Nazi character played by Ed Norton in *American History X*. Did Jackson's motivational tactics cross the line? What ethical obligations do leaders have? Does it matter that Jackson's team won the series?

FIGURE 9.3

The Five Stages of the Empowerment Process

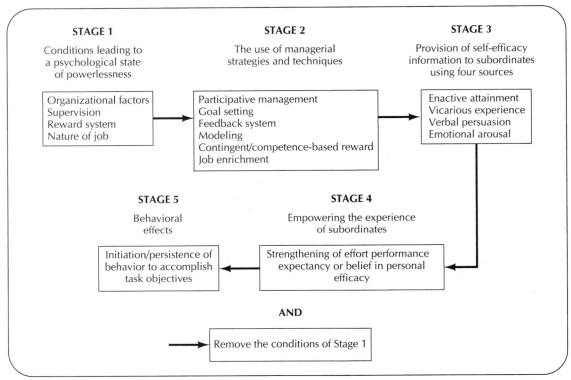

Source: Adapted from Jay Conger and Rabindra Kanungo, "The Empowerment Process: Integrating Theory and Practice," *Academy of Management Review* 13 (1988): 411–482.

◼ THE HIDDEN SIDE OF LEADERSHIP: BULLYING AND HARASSMENT

Theories of leadership have historically focused on the positive qualities associated with rising to the top of the organizational hierarchy. However, as we look around us, the chances are good that we notice that some leaders who have risen to positions of high prominence in the government, the military, the academy, the arts, and businesses are not pleasant people. Beyond some of the twentieth century's notorious murderers and political bullies—Adolf Hitler, Joseph Stalin, Pol Pot, or Saddam Hussein—there are also standout cases of women and men who have attained executive ranks by being emotionally and physically abusive to others.

☐ Bullying in the Workplace

Research suggests that emotionally abusive behavior in adults begins early in childhood development. Schoolyard bullies who develop an abusive skill set that gives them authority and power over others often find ways as adults to exercise their authority through incivility, abuses of power, and exerting extreme control over others at work (Hornstein, 2003; Tracy, Sandvik, & Alberts, 2006; Zellers & Tepper, 2002). This "dark side" of organizational leadership is not yet well documented but the best estimate is that one in six people complain of experiencing consistent mistreatment in the workplace (Meares, Oetzel, Torres, Derkacs, & Ginossar, 2004). Mistreatment is costly, not only to the individual on the receiving end, but to the organization because people who are bullied are neither happy nor productive workers (often they become depressed and anxious) and many choose to leave their jobs rather than put up with it.

What constitutes bullying behavior in the workplace? Robyn Mann, an Australian researcher who studies the subject, provides the following broad definition for **bullying**:

> Direct verbal communication such as name-calling, harsh criticism of outcomes, threats to job security, personal attack, supplying incorrect information and "dressing down." Indirect verbal communication such as gossip, slander and innuendo relayed to the individual. Non-verbal communication such as disparaging looks and noises, sarcastic/harsh tone of voice, offensive gestures, ignoring, "freezing out," physically standing over another with the intention of intimidating, and thrusting or throwing articles towards an individual. Manipulation of the working environment such as withholding needed information, setting unreasonable deadlines, excluding from critical meetings, changing work schedules unfairly, failing to give due credit and retarding opportunities for promotion or higher pay. (cited in Smith, 2005)

Why does bullying in the workplace persist when the majority of us would agree that it is unfair or unacceptable? There are two major reasons. First, bullies who are not held accountable for their behavior learn to repeat it (Smith, 2005). Second, people who are bullied often don't know how to tell their story of abuse to someone who can help them and often fear organizational inaction or, worse, retribution from the bully (Tracy, Lutgen-Sandvik, & Alberts, 2005). Furthermore, Pamela Sandvik (2003) suggests that bullies are both cultivated and rewarded in many organizational cultures. Some of the rewards are accrued unwittingly by managers and supervisors who perceive that results are more important than the means used to achieve them. But it is also true that aggressive organizational cultures—(e.g., Enron, Wal-Mart, World.com, The Trump Organization)—tend to reinforce the conditions that cultivate bullying as a norm: high expectations, strict loyalty to the boss, cronyism in hiring and promotion, secrecy about "what really goes on," and extreme measures taken to silence those who disagree, express criticism, or oppose actions. It is also true that bullying persists because employees who have been bullied often believe that complaining about it makes them seem weak and ineffectual.

Targets of mistreatment are often women and minorities (Meares et al., 2004). In one study by Gary Namie (2000), 23 percent of the targets of abusive behavior identified themselves as members of a minority group and 77 percent were female. In that same study, 81 percent of the abusers were bosses. These data suggest rather strongly that patterns of bullying often draw on and perpetuate larger social inequities.

☐ Harassment and Sexual Harassment

One of the most pervasive and problematic types of mistreatment in the workplace is **harassment**, a form of communicative behavior that degrades or humiliates people. Based on the federal Equal Employment Opportunity Commission (EEOC) guidelines, harassment includes:

- Slurs about sex, race, religion, ethnicity, or disabilities
- Offensive or derogatory remarks
- Verbal or physical conduct that creates an intimidating, hostile, or offensive work environment
- Creating conditions that interfere with the individual's work performance

One type of harassment that is prevalent in the workplace is sexual harassment. **Sexual harassment** refers to any verbal or nonverbal communication of a sexual nature that interferes with someone's work. According to the Civil Rights Act of 1964, additional legislation in Congress, and federal, state, and local court rulings, there are two forms of sexual harassment—quid pro quo and hostile work environment:

1. Quid pro quo ("this for that") harassment is based on the threat of retaliation or promise of workplace favoritism or promotion in exchange for dating or sexual favors. Recently, this principle has been interpreted to include suggestions and innuendoes as well as explicit quid pro quo comments.
2. Hostile work environment harassment is sexually explicit verbal or nonverbal communication that interferes with someone's work or is perceived as intimidating or offensive. It is important to note that the behavior doesn't have to be intentional to create or contribute to a hostile work environment. Offhand remarks or casual displays of sexually explicit materials count as harassment. So do remarks that the sender may think of as "compliments."

The EEOC maintains a comprehensive Web site charting the number of reported incidences of sexual harassment (see <http:www.eeoc.gov/stats/harass .html>). From this report it is clear that despite widespread availability of information about harassment and its consequences, there continue to be tens of thousands of cases annually. However, we also believe that continuing to provide information about sexual harassment has a positive effect on reducing the number of potential cases and making women and men more aware of what constitutes sexual harassment and what may be done about it in the workplace.

Effective Responses to Bullies, Harassers, and Bosses Who Mistreat Subordinates

Priscilla is a forty-year-old college senior studying communication at a large state university. She attends classes full time while helping out with her husband's business and caring for her elderly mother, who suffers from Alzheimer's disease. Despite the constraints on her personal time, her work at the university has been outstanding—she consistently receives high marks in her communication courses and two of her professors have urged her to seriously consider graduate studies.

In order to see if graduate school might be a suitable path, Priscilla registered for a faculty/student research project in health communication with Professor Layne. Though she had not previously studied with Professor Layne, several other students commented that she is a wonderful teacher and a great mentor. Priscilla eagerly began her research project, hoping to learn more about health communication and professional opportunities in the discipline. She even hoped that she might be able to secure a strong letter of recommendation from Professor Layne should she decide to pursue a graduate education!

Priscilla's experiences working with Professor Layne, however, did not turn out as she had hoped. Professor Layne was frequently too busy to meet with Priscilla about her research. She would fail to return e-mails and phone calls and would often cancel meetings, claiming to be "too busy." It seems, however, that Priscilla was the only one having this problem. The other students on the project (mostly traditionally college age juniors and seniors with strong interests in graduate studies) were able to establish positive relationships with the professor. Priscilla's situation worsened as the semester went on. When Professor Layne was finally able to find time in her schedule for meetings, she expected Priscilla to be available at 4:30 P.M. every Tuesday afternoon despite the fact that Priscilla could not arrange for the home-health-care worker to be with her mother during this time. Professor Layne began to suggest that Priscilla did not take her work seriously and, on occasion, would make comments that called into question Priscilla's intelligence and capability as a student. Hurt and confused, but bolstered by her previous academic success, Priscilla approached Professor Layne to discuss the prospect of graduate school, hoping to convince the professor of her sincere interest in academic study. Professor Layne, however, cut off the conversation noting that graduate school is for "serious students" who can make a "full-time commitment to study" without the influence of "outside concerns" (which Priscilla took to mean her mother). The final blow, however, was

(continued, Effective Responses)

Professor Layne's closing comment: "I'm just being honest and telling you how it is out there. Graduate school is for twenty-somethings. No one will hire a new faculty member who is pushing fifty."

We know that emotional narratives, like Priscilla's, are messy. Victims of workplace bullying, harassment, and mistreatment often remain silent. Consider Priscilla's situation: She may want to tell the department chair about her experiences with Professor Layne (especially since she now fears a low grade on her research project) but will anyone take her word over a generally respected, tenured professor? If no one believes her, will she risk angering Professor Layne and putting her grade in further jeopardy?

In a research study to investigate the characteristics of credible versus noncredible bullying narratives, Jess Alberts, Pamela Sandvik, and Sarah Tracy (2005) compared two real-world accounts with seventeen subjects. They found a clear pattern between stories of abusive behavior that were believed and those that were not. They found that credible narratives are marked by the following characteristics:

- They are linear. They have a clear beginning, middle, and end.
- They clearly identify the bully, speak as much or more about the bully as they do about the target, and provide details that paint the bully as the person who is clearly out of control and irrational.
- They "tell" about emotion, but the speaker himself/herself does not embody the emotion.
- They include details of quotations, times, places, and people.
- They include metaphors or stories to which other folks (who have not been bullied) may be able to relate.
- They include references to other people who have been bullied. (This shows that the problem is that of the bully and not necessarily of a lone problem employee/target.)
- They acknowledge small but not extremely damaging points of weakness in the target, and do so in a way in which the target is not cast as blameworthy.
- They anticipate and meet potential objections (e.g., "you're just a problem employee") through perspective talking (or considering the situation from various points of view).
- They indicate how the target has proactively met, managed, and tried to deal with the situation.
- They do not vividly expound on the harm the bullying has done to the target.

DISCUSSION QUESTIONS

1. Based on what you have read, how should Priscilla handle her situation with Professor Layne? Should she approach the department chair about the situation? Does she have an ethical obligation to do so?
2. If she does choose to bring another person into the situation, are there any steps that Priscilla should take before she initiates action?
3. How might Priscilla gain support and credibility for her case? Based on what you know of her situation and the research cited here, construct a believable narrative.

Sexual harassment suits occur between persons of the same sex as well as persons of the opposite sex. It has become so prevalent in the United States that most for-profit and nonprofit organizations, government agencies, and schools have implemented policies, mandatory seminars, and workshops to train employees in how to recognize harassment and prevent it. However, while sexual harassment is clearly recognized as a problem in the United States, it is not always viewed similarly in other countries and other cultures. Latin and Mediterranean cultures, for example, do not regulate physical contact or suggestive language usage in the workplace. As a result, cultural misunderstandings can and do take place. Once again, we see that our assumptions about the meanings of communicative acts are, in fact, culturally derived. Indeed, even the meanings for what constitutes sexual harassment vary across organizational cultures with different sense making practices (Dougherty & Smythe, 2004).

Women are usually the targets of sexual harassment by men because "as a group [women] have less formal and informal power than men in organizations, confront more obstacles on their path to developing organizational power, and have fewer opportunities to acquire organizational power through activities and alliances" (Bingham, 1991, p. 92). Commonplace in organizations, sexual harassment is the unacceptable behavior of men who cling to outdated notions of male-dominated leadership and organizational status quo. It is crucial to understand that sexual harassment is not a personal problem, rather, it is an organizational problem. It is management's responsibility to create a work climate that reinforces appropriate boundaries between employees (Cleveland & McNamara, 1996; Townsley & Geist-Martin, 2000).

In a special issue of the *Journal of Applied Communication Research* (Wood, 1992), a rich and complex assortment of firsthand accounts of sexual harassment on the job reveals a disturbing trend: Most often experienced initially by teenagers and students working a first job, sexual harassment may thereafter be accepted as normal or ordinary behavior. This may explain why many women tend to avoid reporting instances of sexual harassment to superiors, to underestimate their importance, or to be uncertain about identifying such behaviors (Clair, 1998). As a result, sexual harassment remains outside of mainstream communication in organizations, and women participate in both their own subjugation and the perpetuation of the male ideology.

In fact, male ideology has been cited as a major factor in the sudden reported increase in cases of male-on-male sexual harassment (Talbott, 2002). These cases demonstrate that "macho" male cultures contribute to hostile work environments for men as well as women, even in cases where no sexual favors are involved. In one particularly vivid case, a male sales manager for a Chevrolet dealership in Denver, Colorado, routinely grabbed the genitals of male salesmen to make them flinch, addressed them as "little girls" or "whores," and simulated masturbation when male employees talked. If a male employee failed to make a sale, he was asked "if he used tampons . . . or had to squat when he urinated" (p. 54). Even within a male-dominated car sales culture where being raunchy may have been accepted practice, the dealership was indicted, paid a $500,000 fine, and promised to implement sexual harassment training for all employees. The two managers who were the perpetrators of these actions were fired. Clearly, in the findings of the EEOC in this case, it was the organization's responsibility to create a positive working environment and the existence of a dominant male ideology was not an acceptable defense.

Dealing successfully with the problem of sexual harassment requires defining its characteristic behaviors more precisely. Once defined, this information can be used to raise employees' awareness and potentially change their abusive behavior. The following specific behaviors are considered sexual harassment:

- Inappropriate verbal comments, even those defended as compliments (e.g., "I wish my wife was as pretty as you")
- Inappropriate nonverbal gestures, such as outlining body parts or eyeing someone up and down
- Inappropriate visual displays or objects (e.g., posters or calendars depicting nude women or men)
- Terms of endearment (e.g., "sweetie," "dear," "honey")
- Inappropriate physical acts, such as patting, fondling, stroking, or standing in a doorway to obstruct someone's passage through it
- Asking for or implying that someone must submit to sexual advances as a basis for continued employment or advancement in the company

In addition, Tamaki (1991) outlines a series of strategies for dealing with sexual harassment: (1) Confront the harasser, (2) report the behavior to a supervisor or to the human resources department, (3) keep a written record of the offenses, and (4) confide in supportive colleagues, family members, and friends. If the harassment continues, the employee may request a formal investigation by the department of fair employment and housing or by the EEOC or the employee may file a lawsuit. Although the 1991 Anita Hill–Clarence Thomas hearings made the public aware of the difficulties of proving sexual harassment, legal awards for victims of sexual harassment at work are now quite common, especially when written records and support from others in the organization are provided as evidence.

Shereen Bingham (1991; Bingham & Battey, 2004) offers a communicative approach to collecting narratives and managing sexual harassment in the university or workplace. She argues that direct confrontation with a harasser is complicated by multiple risks, including losing a job, receiving an unfavorable recommendation, being demoted, losing interest in the job, and so on. Bingham suggests that various responses—assertive, nonassertive, and even aggressive—may be appropriate in certain circumstances. Most observers agree that assertiveness helps to confront a harasser in a direct but nonthreatening way. However, assertiveness may also be interpreted as a rejection of the other person, which practically speaking may cause the victim to "win the battle but lose the war." It may be more effective to temper assertiveness with "apparent" empathy when responding to a sexual advance.

Finally, the entrance of male-on-male sexual harassment cases has further complicated the concept of "hostile work environment" among legal scholars (Talbott, 2002). The idea was first introduced in the 1980s under the assumption that sexual jokes, vulgarity, and macho displays of dominance offended women because women are, as legal scholar Rosa Ehrenreich puts it, "uniquely vulnerable to men" (cited in Talbott, 2002, p. 55). However, as recent male-on-male harassment cases have documented, some men are clearly also vulnerable to other men and offended by coarse behavior. Another problem is that some men are victimized by male-on-male sexual harassment because they are gay, but sexual orientation is not covered by Title VII of the Civil Rights Act of 1964.

As law professor Deborah Zalesne argues, "[If] your *harasser* is gay, you stand a good chance of winning a same-sex harassment case. If *you* are gay, you lose" (cited in Talbott, 2002, p. 57). For these and other reasons, the theoretical framework of sexual harassment law is currently undergoing revisions on a case-by-case basis. In the meantime, some victims of sexual harassment have found that they can successfully bring charges under existing tort law, civil rights laws, and other federal and state statutes.

Sexual harassment is a crime. Organizational leaders should design educational programs for employees to help them understand sexual harassment, as well as offer strategies for dealing with it in particular situations. Workshops, films, and literature may be used to make employees more aware of the types of behavior that constitute sexual harassment in the workplace. Firms that operate with public monies are especially concerned with this issue. Responding effectively to sexual harassment requires paying close attention to ways of communicating appropriately at work.

Although we hate to end this chapter with bullying and harassment as the final thought on leadership, we would be remiss if we didn't include the "dark side" as a complement to otherwise noble, motivational, and exemplary models of leadership.

Moreover, we believe that it is important to offer you a full sampling of the types of experiences that employees encounter in the workplace. Some examples of leadership will be inspiring; others will be frustrating and ineffective. We hope that this chapter has challenged your ideas about the characteristics a great leader should have and how you might continue to evolve as a leader on your campus, in your current organizational affiliations, and in your future.

SUMMARY

Historically, new approaches to leadership have consistently reflected our culture and times. Ideas about what constitutes leadership emerged from an early belief that the traits associated with great leaders should be modeled by emulating the appearance, habits, and behaviors of persons who had attained leadership positions. This approach, which clearly favored successful white males in a time when white males were culturally dominant and rarely challenged for leadership roles by women or minorities, was augmented by studies that emphasized the style of leading, and specifically the style of communication, used by leaders. Limitations of this approach were revealed when newer studies demonstrated that the style of leadership selected depended on situations that often required creative, rather than established, ways of thinking and acting and that called for a repertoire of leadership styles rather than one consistent style. From these early attempts to find the secret of successful leadership emerged the transformational approach. This approach emphasized the communicative dimensions of effectiveness, particularly the ability to both articulate and lead with a vision that motivated others to attain closer personal identification with the company and inspired them to achieve higher performance goals as a result.

Recently, the story of leadership has turned the lens back on the self—on habits of mind, character, and authentic communication. While there is as yet no clear consensus on the details of these newer approaches, there is a pattern of recognizing lessons drawn from one's own experiences, the ability to create an empowering vision capable of inspiring others, the articulation of a credible life story that humanizes the trajectory taken to leadership, and—in our view, most important—the everyday ethics and authenticity of communication practices that demonstrate by personal example why trust and confidence in a leader is justified.

Leadership theory and practice has also been concerned with how leaders influence their employees through communication. Specific communicative strategies include open and supportive communication, where leaders are willing and receptive listeners who are highly trust-worthy and provide formal and informal rewards. Leaders also achieve effective communication through motivation (setting attainable and specific goals, offering and receiving feedback, offering clear outcomes and rewards, and empowering employees to develop a strong sense of self-efficacy).

Not all people who aspire to or attain leadership positions are inherently good. Bullies in the schoolyard often mature into bullies in the workplace, and unfortunately some of them rise to the top of the organizational chart because they intimidate and abuse others who themselves remain too frightened to speak out against them. Sexual harassment is a particularly insidious and illegal form of bullying that has significant negative consequences for individuals and organizations.

Leadership is vital to every organization. In our global economy, the diverse skills and understandings required for success have never been more demanding. At their core is the ability to communicate effectively and honestly with people who may not share your language or culture, as well as those who compete against you. While we can learn a great deal about how to meet those challenges from investigating the history of leadership research and exploring alternative approaches to leading, there will likely never be one approach that works in every situation. In our view, the central message of this book speaks directly to that challenge: Communication is how we learn to balance the ever-present and ever-shifting terrain of creativity and constraint in organizations. The more effective we learn to be as communicators, the more likely we will be viewed by others as leaders.

QUESTIONS FOR REVIEW AND DISCUSSION

1. Describe the progression of leadership thinking over the past one hundred years. What are the main changes that you observe, and how do these changes reflect important social and cultural changes?

2. Describe a situation where the careful selection of leaders is essential for public safety. Based on the leadership models you have just studied, what advice would you offer about how to best screen candidates for these positions?

3. Is transformational leadership and change agency critical in every type of organization? Are there any you can think of which require leaders mainly to maintain the status quo instead?

4. What do leaders do to empower employees? Do you think it is critical to communicate a sense of empowerment to all employees in every organization, or are there specific types of organizational settings for applying the empowerment principles that make more sense than others?

5. Look on the Web for examples of organizational vision statements. What makes for a compelling vision?

6. What kinds of life events are most likely to lead to the modesty and high level of self-examination that seems to characterize the greatest of leaders? By contrast, what events are likely to result in bullying or abusive leaders?

KEY TERMS

Authentic communication, p. 284
Bullying, p. 297
Change agent, p. 279
Compliance-gaining theory, p. 292
Empowerment, p. 292
Equity theory, p. 292
Expectancy theory, p. 291
Goal-setting theory, p. 289
Habits of character, p. 283
Habits of mind, p. 281
Harassment, p. 298
Leadership style, p. 275

Modesty, p. 284
Motivation, p. 289
Open communication, p. 287
Sexual Harassment, p. 298
Situational leadership, p. 278
Supportive communication, p. 288
Theory of leader-member exchange, p. 288
Trait theory, p. 274
Transformational leadership, p. 279
Vision, p. 280

The Stymied CEO

Paula Santoro is president and CEO of the Canyon Regional Health Care System in Utah. The system includes three large hospitals located in urban areas and a network of seventeen smaller medical clinics distributed throughout the more rural parts of the state. Santoro has both a PhD in nursing and an MBA, and is well-known for her assertive and principled style. A close colleague puts it this way: "You may not always agree with Paula, but you will always know where she stands. She wears her values on her sleeve."

From an outsider's perspective, Santoro's career has unfolded over thirty years in storybook fashion, as she has moved from floor nursing into the executive ranks, changing institutions only twice. Her most recent move was in 1999, when she went from COO of a hospital in Nebraska to become CEO of the Canyon system. When she arrived, the head of the Canyon human resources declared Paula to be "a real change to the organization, a breath of fresh air—but also a real departure from the past. We're all praying that she makes it."

And she has made it—sort of. Her first few years were an unqualified success, as the hospital system became more financially stable and Santoro enjoyed the new challenges that greeted her each morning. She worked hard to build an executive team that shared her passion and her values and felt that she had for the most part done so. But beginning a few years ago, things became a lot less enjoyable. Two high-profile malpractice lawsuits against the system, while ultimately settled, did much to damage public opinion. Government regulations increasingly place her in the position of having to choose the lesser of evils with regard to patient care, and the breakdown of insurance coverage has placed an inordinate strain on staff morale throughout all of the hospitals and clinics. She worries that her system is nowhere near prepared for the likely casualties that would result from bioterrorism, pandemic, or natural disaster. Just recently, the unrelenting stress has impacted her leadership team in the form of sudden departures by her medical chief of staff and her head of planning (the first to a smaller system in another state; the second to very early retirement).

Santoro attends leadership seminars and reads everything that comes out on the subject. She understands the need for visionary leadership based on enduring social values, and she feels clear about what matters to her. What is missing in her view is a plan for getting past the daily (and sometimes hourly) crises that occupy her time to a new way of working that would direct her time and energy into the formation and execution of a new vision. But all the while she wonders: Can it be done?

(continued, The Stymied CEO)

Assignment

1. Make a list of the full range of problems that Santoro is facing. Try to go beyond the ones that she identifies to other, deeper challenges that you can imagine underlying her current dilemma.
2. What unique resources can Santoro draw on to rise to the challenge she has crafted for herself? Where can she turn for help, strength, and practical advice?
3. Imagine that Santoro has hired you to serve as her "executive coach" for the next three years. What subjects would you identify to address with her early on? Is there a process that she could follow to "redirect her time and energy" and restore her sense of personal efficacy in the position? While there are no right answers, be as specific as you can in your suggestions.
4. What is the role of communication in addressing Santoro's leadership challenge?

CHAPTER 10

Organizational Alignment: Managing the Total Enterprise

For an organization or institution to succeed over time, senior managers and boards of directors must take a "bird's eye" view of the total enterprise, both to see what it looks like from the outside and to determine how it is perceived by various publics, partners, and competitors. Nevertheless, the temptation to not engage in this activity is great. Not only is it hard to find the time to speculate about the future when dealing with the crisis of the day, but honest talk about how others see the organization can be hard to take. Still, those possessing the discipline to engage in **strategic thinking**—making a conscious choice about organizational values, niche, and direction—invariably end up ahead of the game both financially and in terms of employee loyalty and morale.

But the game doesn't end there, of course, because no strategy works forever. Consumer tastes, market conditions, and countless other factors alter the organizational landscape on a daily, if not hourly, basis. What made sense yesterday may no longer make sense today. The only way of dealing with this dynamic environment is to encourage dialogue and learning—that is, to sponsor and stage regular conversations about the appropriateness of the current strategy and the possible alternatives.

This chapter begins with a detailed discussion of strategic positioning as a communication issue, followed by a description of strategic alignment, the process of bringing organizational systems in line with the strategy. Central to these systems is the management of human resources in all of its dimensions, from selection, to training, to individual and organizational development. The next section goes into more depth about these important details. The conclusion broadens our view by looking at organizational learning more generally, encompassing basic skills, technology, and morality.

But success begins with strategy. Contemporary organizations must position themselves effectively in the social and economic landscape. **Strategic positioning** involves selecting a strategy or purpose that distinguishes the organization from its competitors. In addition, the strategy must be effectively communicated to employees, who use it as a guide to decisions, and to customers, who use it to judge the company's image or reputation.

◨ POSITIONING THE ORGANIZATION

☐ Competitive Strategy

Strategy is of critical importance to the long-term success of a business. A **competitive strategy** is a clear statement of why customers should choose a company's products or services over those of competing companies. Simple descriptors such as *cheapest*, *fastest*, *most reliable*, *friendliest*, and *best quality* are typically used in the expression of a company strategy. In addition to communicating a strategy, however, a company must ensure that all aspects of its business reflect the strategy (cf., Day & Reibstein, 2004).

Despite the importance of strategy, few organizations actually have one, relying instead on their success with a particular product or service (typically introduced before the competition's product or service). However, contemporary organizations that lack a strategy are seriously at risk in today's highly competitive global market. Owners of brick and mortar movie theaters, for example, are seeing their business shrink as more customers choose to order movies on demand from their cable provider or use a movie mail service like NETFLIX. Fast-food restaurants like Checkers are struggling to carve out an identity in an industry saturated by giant brands like Subway and McDonald's.

As an example of how a competitive strategy works in practice, let's suppose that you own a new fast-food eatery that serves, among other foods, hamburgers stuffed with mashed potatoes. After your first six months in business, your customers are only beginning to warm up to the idea of stuffed burgers. However, as a local business owner, you have been invited to attend a reception hosted by the city's chamber of commerce, providing you with a unique opportunity to promote your fast-food business. You dress appropriately for the event and bring your business cards with you. More important, you prepare what you will say about your business to others at the reception, keeping in mind that it should take only about fifteen seconds to explain what you do and why your business is worthy of their attention. They, in turn, will be able to convey the same brief message to others later on, and it is your job to ensure that they want to do so. If you succeed in both respects—if your message is memorable and distinct—your company has a competitive strategy.

As competition continues to increase in today's business world and as the markets for products and services become more specialized, competitive strategies must adapt to these changes by targeting market niches and a narrower consumer audience (Day & Reibstein, 2004). In publishing and broadcasting, for example, both large and small companies now provide magazines and news programs that cover highly specific topics in order to target specific market segments. For example, few people know that the largest television station in Los Angeles in terms of viewership is the Spanish-language station. Very small companies sell specialty products like food or dietary supplements by mail or via the Internet. Similarly, following a trend called "narrowcasting," cable television companies typically offer a number of channels that focus exclusively on sports, comedy, news, women's issues, or home shopping programs. Large companies may pursue two or more strategies to target multiple market niches; for example, to appeal to an older, more affluent audience, MTV created its VH1 channel, Honda created its Acura model, and Gap introduced Banana Republic.

For communication specialists, crafting a competitive strategy involves close attention to message design. Thus, for instance, an effective strategy for your hypothetical potato-stuffed burger restaurant would likely focus on its uniqueness: "The only place in town with potato-stuffed burgers!" However, your strategy would be successful only if a niche market existed — or could be created — for your product. In the first case, pent-up demand can be identified for a product or service, so that its introduction is met with understanding and appreciation ("We've always needed a good coffee shop on this side of town"). In the second, niches can quite literally be created for novel products and services (e.g., bottled water, minivans, or venti nonfat decaf caramel mocha frappuccinos). The customer remarks, "I never knew I needed that until I saw it!"

A company that does not narrow its focus and attempts instead to target broad markets (e.g., "We serve potato-stuffed burgers, fresh-squeezed juices, and deli sandwiches at the lowest prices") is not likely to be able to serve the demands of all consumer markets or to distinguish itself as unique in any one market.

Developing a strategy for a new company often begins with the founder's intuition about the potential demand for a product or service. The next step is careful analyses of the target market, of the business environment (which includes potential customers, stakeholders, and community and government agencies), and of the existing competition. Termed **competitor analysis**, it is especially important in identifying whether a similar product or service is offered by other companies in nearby or remote locations or if any past attempts to offer the product or service have failed. In formulating a competitive strategy, then, the prospective business owner must consider not only the potential demand for a product or service, but also how the company's strategy will be received by various publics. A serious objection by any one group can threaten the survival of the business.

Put another way, strategy is a compelling story, a "teachable point of view" about where the company is going and how it will get there (Barry & Elmes, 1997;

Tichy, Prichett, & Cohen, 1998). The power of a strategy to motivate employees and to attract customers is largely dependent on whether the strategy makes for a compelling narrative. Moreover, company leaders no longer have a monopoly on telling their stories: The Internet in particular has encouraged the proliferation of "anti-sites" dedicated to trashing various businesses for poor quality, service, or community relations. This makes it even more challenging for companies to put forth a coherent story to the public.

☐ Types of Business Strategies

There are two basic types of business strategies: those that emphasize lowest cost and those that focus on differentiation (Porter, 1980; Walker, 2003).

Adopting a **lowest-cost** strategy involves a commitment to offering a product or service at the lowest-possible price. Examples include discount appliance stores, no-frills airlines, and manufacturers of generic products. These companies emphasize their lowest-cost products or services to target consumers motivated by that strategy. To reach that consumer market, however, the strategy must be communicated effectively. Among the disadvantages of a lowest-cost strategy is the need to reduce operating costs to maintain a cost advantage. In a competitive global market, it may be difficult for such companies to manage the high costs of labor and materials.

A more popular business strategy is **differentiation**, which involves highlighting the unique or special qualities of a company's product or service. For example, a company may be the most reliable, have the quickest delivery time, or offer the most comprehensive warranty service in the business. In the automobile industry, Volvo highlights safety (at least traditionally — they have been making some moves lately toward better styling), whereas BMW highlights performance. Differentiation is a highly communication-based strategy in that its success depends less on *actual* differences among competing products and more on the company's ability to create the *perception* of its product as unique in some way.

Developing a successful strategy can be as simple as noticing an unfilled niche in a particular market. For example, a physician might notice that a community's residents do not have access to medical care on weekends and may choose to address that need. The owner of a car rental company may respond to consumer demands for hourly rentals with a strategy that incorporates both daily and hourly rates. In most cases, however, developing a successful strategy is more difficult and complex because multiple businesses often compete within the same market (e.g., three Los Angeles supermarkets seeking to become the lowest-cost leader conduct ongoing comparison studies to support their claim).

Similarly, in the battle among leaders in the overnight package delivery business, various strategies are used to compete within the same market. Federal Express differentiates its service as being the most reliable, whereas the U.S. Postal Service emphasizes lowest cost. Although all of the major cellular phone companies claim to offer the highest quality service at the best price, their prices and levels of service are in reality quite similar. One of the reasons customer service levels are poor in the cell phone industry is the lack of real competition; recent lower-cost, broadband entrants like Vonage are sure to increase competitive pressure, which will result in better service throughout the industry.

Strategy is especially important in highly cost-sensitive industries with low brand loyalty, such as the airline industry. Following deregulation, relatively small airlines entered the marketplace and offered fares on major routes that were significantly less than the fares charged by major carriers. A fare war ensued; airfares continued to drop, but so did profits. Many of the small lowest-cost airlines failed, taking a few major carriers with them. The survivors, scrambling for a way to encourage brand loyalty, settled on frequent-flyer programs. Airfares increased, and the carriers developed differentiation strategies to entice consumers (e.g., "the most on-time departures" and "the best frequent flyer program").

In developing a differentiation strategy, a company chooses the most competitive aspect of its operation. This does not mean that the company is without other positive attributes, but it does mean that the company generally does not communicate them to the public as competitive advantages. At the department store Nordstrom, for instance, customer service is highlighted even though the company is also concerned with cost, quality, and other factors. More than any other attribute, Nordstrom believes its customer service is what most differentiates it from competitors.

Following is a comprehensive list of business strategies adopted by many familiar companies (Robert, 1993):

- Product- or service-driven companies, such as Boeing and Ritz-Carlton, strive to provide the highest-quality products or services in the business. They continually focus on how to improve their products or services as well as their work processes.
- Market-driven companies offer a wide range of products to a specific group of consumers. For example, Johnson & Johnson sells its products to doctors, nurses, patients, and parents. American Express Financial Advisors now targets affluent individuals and sells its ability to handle all of their financial needs. Companies like these must engage in ongoing market research and strive to cultivate consumer loyalty.
- Production-capacity-driven companies, such as airlines, make substantial investments in facilities and equipment and aim to have them running at full capacity at all times. They engage in market research to meet customers' needs and demands; they also offer special incentives (e.g., reduced fares or discounted vacation packages) to increase business during slack periods.
- Technology-driven companies, such as Apple Computer, 3M, Hughes Aircraft, Sony, Gore, Amgen, and DuPont, own or specialize in a unique technology. For example, DuPont invented nylon; the other companies on the list have each filed thousands of patents. Such companies invest a considerable amount of money in research and development.

- Sales- and marketing-driven companies, such as Mary Kay and Tupperware, provide a wide range of products or services to customers in unconventional ways, including door-to-door selling, home shopping club sales, and Internet sales.
- Distribution-driven companies, such as Wal-Mart, United Parcel Service, Home Shopping Network, and food wholesalers, and Internet-only businesses like Amazon and eBay, have unique ways of getting their products or services to the customer. Some may also push a variety of products through their distribution channels. Such companies strive to maintain a highly effective distribution system.

The overriding factor in strategy development is a keen awareness of the related industry as a whole as well as its potential for change or improvement. Before air travel was made possible, people crossed the oceans on ships. With the advent of passenger air travel, however, transportation companies offering ocean passage were threatened with obsolescence. Some of them survived by redefining their strategy: Instead of providing transportation, some changed their strategy to providing entertainment on cruise lines. Similarly, McDonald's, a leader in competitive strategy, is not in the food business. People go to McDonald's for comfort, security, predictability, and safety, which is for the most part reflected in the location and cleanliness of its restaurants and in its rigid standards for food worldwide. As recently as 2003, financial problems developed at least in part due to some franchisees losing sight of this strategy and allowing these factors to slip. It seems that when faced with the loss of cleanliness and predictability, people will happily buy better quality burgers elsewhere. Having closed hundreds of stores, McDonald's is now engaging in a worldwide campaign designed to convince customers that they will try harder to provide a positive, service-oriented environment.

☐ Strategy and the Business Life Cycle

Strategy changes as an organization progresses through what might be called the "stages of the business life cycle" (Kimberly & Miles, 1980). Strategic and communicative challenges also differ at each stage (Maug, 2001).

At "birth," a new company is concerned mainly with developing a strategy and finding a niche. The company secures financial backing and makes an initial foray into the marketplace.

In "childhood," the company's major challenge is managing its growth and development. In its pursuit of multiple opportunities, the growing organization may be distracted from its basic strategy or may lack the discipline needed to maintain a focus on its competitive advantage. Effective leadership can help counteract these problems.

When the company reaches "adolescence," it typically encounters stiff competition. As a result, the original strategy no longer functions as a competitive advantage, and the company must work to change or fine-tune it accordingly. This may require paying special attention to both internal communication (to streamline processes, cut costs, and develop new competencies) and external communication (to remind customers of why the company's product or service is superior to those of its competitors).

In the final phase of the business life cycle, "maturity," the company faces the difficult challenge of renewal — of letting go of the old business in favor of a new one, while also maintaining a position in the marketplace. The biggest success story of this sort in recent years has to be Abercrombie & Fitch, which almost overnight went from appealing to well-off, mature world travelers to fashion- and price-conscious teenagers! Efforts by JC Penney and Sears to upgrade their inventories and appeal to a broader market are other examples. Honda, which entered the world market in the 1970s with the tiny Honda Civic, is known for its strategic excellence. Since the 1970s, Honda has focused not on a particular product but on the customers who purchased the early Civics — baby boomers buying their first car. Transforming and upgrading its products to match those customers' needs, Honda introduced the Prelude and Accord as these young adults moved into their thirties, and the upscale Acura line as they moved into their forties and became more affluent. Honda's strategy is thus tied to satisfying a well-defined market segment.

The failure, or "death," rate in most industries is quite high. Failure can occur at any point in the life cycle, and in fact few start-up companies make it past their first two years, largely because they are undercapitalized. In recent years, many small businesses have either gone under or been sold to larger corporations because of the critical lack of available talent from which to choose.

◪ STRATEGIC ALIGNMENT

A company may communicate a strategy such as "environmentally friendly" or "superior customer service," but if customers and employees do not see evidence of the company's claim, the strategy will be unconvincing and ineffective. Therefore, in addition to communicating the strategy to various internal and external publics, the strategy must be reflected in various other aspects of the organization. **Strategic alignment**, then, refers to the process of modifying organizational systems and structures to support the competitive strategy. This may affect such areas as job design, levels of authority, job training, reward systems, and staffing, among many others.

In the absence of strategic alignment, a business can neither accomplish its strategy nor create the desired image. For example, a print shop that claims to have the lowest prices in town but pays its employees above-average wages is not likely to achieve success. Similarly, a company that claims to be responsive to customers would be unable to implement that strategy if its automated phone system did not give customers the option of speaking with a service representative directly.

Successful strategic alignment is difficult because it forces the company to consider the relationship between its strategy and its internal systems. In addition, strategic alignment is complicated by employees' reluctance to see themselves as part of a system and by managers' tendency to make decisions in isolation rather than based on the company's strategy. Companies that overcome these obstacles to strategic alignment, pursuing a carefully chosen strategy, are more likely to achieve success.

One model that is particularly helpful in thinking about strategic alignment is the original 7-S model, developed by members of the consulting firm McKinsey & Company (Figure 10.1). According to this model, strategic alignment involves the following seven factors:

- *Strategy*. Strategy provides a common purpose for all employees and stakeholders. It discriminates the company from its competitors.
- *Superordinate goals*. More specific than a company's mission statement, **superordinate goals** are those broad outcomes that everyone in the organization is motivated to achieve, such as attaining a particular percentage of market share or customer loyalty. To be effective, these goals must flow logically from the company's strategy. Some authors have argued that the best route is for firms to develop "big hairy audacious goals" (Collins & Porras, 1994).
- *Structure*. The formal reporting relationships as prescribed by the organizational chart should reflect the company's strategy and should symbolically represent the company's values. A team-based organization or an inverted chart with the customer at the top of the pyramid are two common examples of meaningful organizational structure.
- *Systems*. The flow of information through various media (e.g., telephones and computer systems and meetings), the formal systems of operation (e.g., management information systems), the informal operating procedures (e.g., cultural practices), and the informal connections among people (e.g., emergent networks) should all be aligned with the company's strategy. Systems are relevant to communication in that they deal with the distribution of information throughout a company. Certain strategies can be used only with certain types of systems. For example, a quality manufacturing strategy would require a control system to identify and correct defects immediately.
- *Staffing*. Here, the company's strategy is reflected in its hiring practices, in its job assignments, and in its workforce generally. Companies that promote from within and those that have technical as well as managerial career paths offer two examples of approaches to staffing that may support a specific competitive strategy.
- *Skills*. Employees' technical and interpersonal skills should be used in ways that promote the company's strategy. A company striving to differentiate itself as a leader in customer service would need employees with excellent interpersonal skills.

FIGURE 10.1

The Original 7-S Model of Strategic Alignment

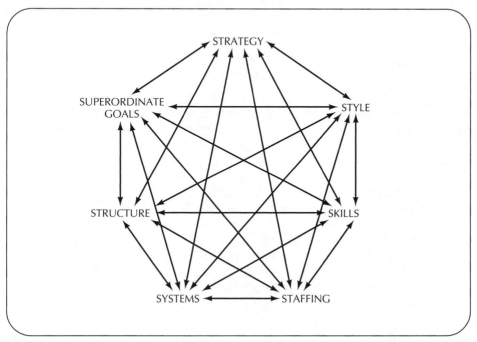

Source: R. D'Aveni, "Coping with Hypercompetition: Utilizing the New 7-S Model," *Academy of Management Executive* 9:3 (1995): 48.

- *Style.* Both management style and organizational culture (how a company perceives and treats its employees) can contribute to the success or failure of a business strategy. A company that strives to be competitive but that routinely permits its employees to miss deadlines is not likely to survive.

The strategic-alignment process is best approached by thinking of the organization as a communication system. In this way, we see how the information in each subsystem reflects and affects the whole organization. In an organization that is out of alignment, decisions in one subsystem (e.g., sales) are made without considering their potential effects on other subsystems. Over time, even the best organizations' systems usually drift out of alignment as internal functions become outdated and as external developments in technology and market demographics necessitate internal change. Employees are highly sensitive to misalignment; that is, if the company claims to promote trust and empowerment, employees are likely to voice their objections if their actual decision-making participation is limited. At Disneyland, for example, employees objected to what they perceived as inconsistencies between the company's strategy — "The happiest place on Earth" — and its poor treatment and compensation of employees (Smith & Eisenberg, 1987). More recently, employees across the financial services industry were shocked to learn that their firms' stated corporate values (e.g., ethics and integrity) apparently did not apply to the executive suite.

The strategic-alignment process begins with the development of a strategy, preferably one that focuses on reliable information about the future and aims to focus and invigorate the company. Once a strategy is developed, it must be translated into superordinate goals so that it can be communicated to all employees. Structure is examined next, to determine whether it supports the strategy. For example, in the process of transitioning from a government business to a commercial supplier, a major electronics company sought to become a customer-driven firm (unlike its competitors). However, the company's existing structure, characterized by vertical lines of expertise and authority and minimal cross-functional communication, would not support its new focus on customer relations. The company thus modified its structure by creating a centralized customer service office to act as an interface for customer communication, a repair center designed to meet customers' needs, and cross-functional teams to promote effective communication.

An analysis of systems typically occurs at this point in the strategic-alignment process. In our example, the electronics firm found that its existing voice-mail system kept customers on hold for too long, so it made changes to ensure that customers could reach a service representative within a reasonable amount of time. In addition, the company's past experience with military projects and lax schedules meant that group meetings would need to focus on addressing work issues more expediently. With the help of the human resources department, the company's chief decision-making groups worked together on creating a greater sense of urgency in its informal systems.

Staffing, skills, and style are the final considerations in strategic alignment. The electronics firm recruited employees with the technical and communication skills needed to enact the proposed strategy. Managers and employees in the customer service offices were trained in how to cultivate new customer-oriented styles of working and communication with openness and empathy. Employees who were less open to this change were reassigned to positions that were less visible to customers.

In most cases, strategic alignment is accomplished gradually; a management team focuses on each stage of the process before proceeding to the next stage. Sometimes, however, large-scale strategic alignment may be attempted, as in the case of **total quality management (TQM)**, a company-wide, comprehensive effort to create a culture of quality. In pursuing the strategy of total quality, a company may simultaneously redefine its objectives (superordinate goals), overhaul its organization (structure), fire managers from the "old school" (style), recruit new managers with skills better suited to the redefined structure (staffing), and train all employees in empowerment, teamwork, and other areas (skills).

However, as a large-scale intervention, total quality management is only occasionally successful. In addition to the difficulties associated with maintaining a focus amidst rapid change in multiple areas, employees tend to react negatively to change that is radical rather than gradual. They may become suspicious of the company's intentions, worry about losing their jobs, and be less willing to commit themselves to the program's success. Another problem associated with TQM occurs when a company focuses mainly on winning external recognition for its efforts. The Malcolm Baldrige National Quality Award, for example, is given by the U.S. government to companies for excellence in total quality management. Winning the award provides a company with excellent publicity and some powerful advertising copy. However, in the case of a Florida utility company that pursued TQM to win the award, its efforts led to internal havoc and a worse complaint record than that of several other Florida utilities (Sashkin, 1991). Moreover, winning the award may say more about *past* performance than the likelihood of future success. Motorola, the first recipient of the Baldrige award, has since struggled and hasn't had a market-changing invention for a decade (Jones, 2001).

Finally, strategic alignment is not just an issue for corporations and government agencies. Smaller not-for-profit companies and non-governmental organizations (NGOs) are also challenged to define their strategies in such a way that they send a consistent message and focus their efforts through alignment. A familiar example is environmental activist organizations like Greenpeace, which must be vigilant in communicating a clear and consistent focus both proactively and in response to external challenges.

◢ HUMAN RESOURCES

The shift from tangible local industries to global knowledge work has altered the essential elements of business. Whereas in the past enormous capital expenditures went into buildings and materials, today the two most critical parts of any successful business are people and technology. Increasingly, work can be done anywhere at anytime, and the work of an organization may even be done by people not on the payroll—outsourcers and subcontractors. Technology is addressed in the next section; this section deals with the human resources that are the core of any successful enterprise.

☐ Talent

Many chief executive officers are quick to minimize their role in their company's achievements and are anxious to celebrate the accomplishments of their *people*. This makes good sense. The primary role of the CEO and the senior management team (with some direction from the board of directors in the case of public and nonprofit companies) is to develop competitive strategy and communicate it in a way that fo-cuses and motivates the rest of the organization. Their other key role is to develop organizational systems (e.g., recruiting, reward, development, and communication) that support the acquisition and retention of talent.

When manufacturing was dominant and the machine model at its peak in America, hiring was done unsystematically, and nepotism (favoring one's relations) and other forms of favoritism were common. With the rise of bureaucracy in the mid-twentieth century, companies began to understand the importance of attract-ing and keeping good workers. They established personnel departments to provide a consistent focus on policies affecting employees. Shifting emphases toward em-ployee participation and innovation resulted in further transformation from per-sonnel departments to departments of human resources. As discussed in Chapter 3, the name itself reflects a willingness to see employees as having valuable knowledge that can serve as a resource for organizational success.

Over the past few decades, human resource management has grown into a credible and highly sophisticated discipline. Whereas in the past salaries, benefits, and training were treated as an afterthought and shaped by the opinions of line managers with little or no knowledge of research on attracting and developing tal-ent, today most large companies have a senior vice president of human resources who reports to the president or CEO and has input into strategic decisions. Recent developments have made the wisdom of this shift even more apparent. At a confer-ence of the five hundred fastest-growing companies in 1998, a large percentage of entrepreneur-founders were seen looking for people to buy their companies. The most common reason they gave for wanting to cash out was their inability to attract and retain sufficient talent.

Research shows that companies that treat people as their most important asset are also the most profitable. In one award-winning study of 968 companies across all industries, it was revealed that "a one standard deviation increase in the use of [high-performance practices] was associated with a 7.05 percent decrease in turn-over and, on a per employee basis, $27,044 more in sales and $18,641 and $3,814 more in market value and profits, respectively" (Huselid, 1995). When measuring the use of **high-performance practices** the researchers counted such things as self-managed teams, employee empowerment, pay for performance, extensive training, extensive information sharing, and a purposeful reduction in attention paid to sta-tus differences (Pfeffer & Veiga, 1999).

Companies in highly competitive industries are always seeking skilled employ-ees at all levels. Those that can afford to do so are trying new approaches, such as recruiting abroad, building employee housing, providing huge incentives to cur-rent employees who refer a new hire, and even hiring groups of friends. One pro-gressive firm, Warner-Lambert (now part of Pfizer), has a director of talent man-agement who defines her job as attracting the best and the brightest and then "protecting" them from the organization while they learn the culture and find their feet. Once they are integrated into the company, she sees her responsibility to "re-recruit" star performers to ensure that they don't leave to join the competition.

What we would consider progressive human resources management has many aspects, but three key components have everything to do with communication. These components are targeted selection, performance management, and training and development.

Targeted Selection

Particularly in times of low unemployment, there is a tendency to loosen job qualifications and to fill positions with anyone who seems minimally competent. Although this might get the company through the week, it is a losing strategy in the long run. The new employees are set up to fail, and fail they will, angering and alienating customers along the way. A much better approach is for senior management to have sufficient discipline to identify a unique competitive strategy and to define job qualifications in ways that support that strategy. Although this may seem obvious, it is difficult to pull off in practice: Think of all the companies you patronize as a customer whose mission is customer satisfaction but whose frontline employees lack the knowledge or the motivation to satisfy anyone! When jobs are created in a conscious way, each job comprises critical dimensions, such as word-processing skills, strategic thinking, oral communication, and tolerance for ambiguity. Successful organizations spend lots of time analyzing jobs to ensure that they support the company's strategy.

A good reason for careful job analysis and the identification of key job dimensions is that clear job descriptions communicate to everyone — managers, current job incumbents, and applicants — what is expected of them. **Targeted selection** is a systematic job-interview process through which selected company experts assess job candidates on the key dimensions of each job. At the end of a search process, the interviewers meet to pool their data and make an informed choice. Employees selected through targeted selection are, with few exceptions, immediately capable of making a contribution to the company's performance.

Performance Management

Just as key job dimensions are directly in support of company strategy, **performance management** is a name for any system that tracks and gives feedback to employees about how well they are accomplishing objectives tied to each of their key dimensions. For example, if skill in computer programming is a dimension, an objective might be to write three new programs without error each month. Managers and employees can track against these performance standards and record both the number of programs accomplished and the number of errors. Deviations from objectives can be easily brought to the surface and addressed.

It is this last step—using the performance-management system as a basis for an ongoing conversation with employees—that is both the heart of the system and the most difficult to achieve. When the system works, it can provide uncanny alignment between individual jobs at any level and organizational success in the aggregate. However, in the absence of any system, managers go by "gut feel" and in most cases play favorites based on personal relationships, not real productivity.

With a performance-management system in place, everyone knows what is expected of him or her, and performance is relatively public (at least to one's manager). A difficulty occurs, however, because most people avoid stressful communication situations that are potentially conflictual. This is why so many employees report that they are late in getting performance feedback, if they get any at all. The worst-case scenario occurs when cowardly managers leave employees a copy of their review with a note that says, "Call if you have any questions." This is unacceptable and defeats the purpose of performance management, which is designed to make both managers and employees accountable for open communication about results.

In the days before human resources departments, feedback on employee performance was either highly informal, annual, or nonexistent. Today's best thinking suggests that performance management is an ongoing conversation that every manager ought to have with employees, during which strategy is reinforced, objectives are reviewed, results are revealed, and gaps are examined. Failure to perform to standard can mean many things other than employee incompetence, including understaffing, inadequate tools, or poor planning. Quite often, it is the result of inadequate employee training and development.

Training and Development

In one form or another, employee **training and development**—formal and informal efforts to develop employee skill—has always been a function of management. Business people have long recognized that there are benefits to identifying the best practices in performing any given job and then communicating these practices systematically to employees. Even Frederick Taylor, inventor of the time-and-motion study, placed a heavy emphasis on training, inasmuch as scientific management could help identify the best ways of doing things that could (and should) be taught to everyone.

Training is much simpler when the job requirements stay roughly the same over a long period of time. What is challenging today is that the knowledge and skills to be taught are evolving at blinding speed, making last year's training potentially obsolete. For this reason, the notion of isolated training sessions has been replaced in almost every successful company with a focus on ongoing employee development and the facilitation of continuous learning.

There is further recognition that such development efforts cannot be "one size fits all." Employee-development programs are increasingly tailored to fit the interests, learning styles, locations, and even schedules of targeted employees. Like customers, employees want education that is "just in time, just for me." For this reason, companies are designing highly flexible and modular development centers or "corporate universities" that offer a dazzling array of learning opportunities through a range of media. The underlying idea is that the best time to teach someone something like Microsoft Excel or supervisory skills is when they most need to learn it.

Progressive companies tie training and development efforts to their performance-management systems. Job analysis shows the key dimensions in which an incumbent must excel to succeed at the job; performance management tracks how well the employee is doing along each dimension. A manager can use the performance-management conversation to coach employees about development opportunities in- or outside the company (much education is outsourced these days) that specifically target their areas of below-average performance. Senior managers can use summary performance data to target entire departments or regions for certain kinds of development, such as customer service or time-management training.

There is one last piece of the puzzle that, when applied, can turbocharge the whole human resources function. Tying employee performance to clearly defined rewards — compensation, benefits, advancement, recognition — rationalizes the system for employees. Rather than being busywork that has little to do with "my real job," the business of filling out tracking forms and meeting with managers to discuss performance becomes central to each employee's work life. Targeted selection ensures that people are hired who have a fighting chance of performing the needed functions; performance management tracks their success and provides specific feedback on where they must improve; training and development provide opportunities for continuous learning in those areas; and employees are rewarded for consistently doing the things that, by design, support the company's strategy.

Naturally, the best employees will get frustrated and quit if they lack appropriate tools to perform their jobs effectively. Interestingly, this problem is compounded in companies with performance-management systems because employees are acutely aware of their accountabilities and are given incentives for meeting their goals.

□ Organizational Development

Any progressive human resources practitioner will tell you that no amount of training can substitute for enterprise-wide efforts to transform and sustain a new kind of organizational culture. For this reason, the best and brightest HR professionals have over the years been drawn to the subfield of **organizational development (OD)**, which deals with the facilitation of strategic systems change. In practice, this usually amounted to senior management enlisting the help of their internal human resources staff — or hiring an external HR consultant — to assist in promoting a particularly challenging organizational change. The occasion for such an initiative varied from mergers to reorganization to downsizing.

EVERYDAY ORGANIZATIONAL COMMUNICATION

Human Resources in the Greek System

In this chapter, you're learning how companies use organizational systems to acquire and retain the best talent. Even if you've never worked for a company, you may already be familiar with the human resources model of employee management. College admissions departments seek to attract the best students and first-year deans work to ease those students' transition to college life. Varsity coaches sometimes recruit kids while they're still in high school and older team members mentor the rookies when they come to campus. And if you have Greek life at your school, you know that fraternities and sororities—just like Fortune 500 companies—require frequent replenishment of their talent. During rush and pledge terms, Pi Kappa Alpha, Gamma Phi Beta, and all the other fraternities and sororities use organizational systems like targeted selection, performance management, and training and development to attract, and then keep, new brothers and sisters.

Rush is the period of time, lasting anywhere from two days to two weeks, when fraternities and sororities seek to attract new members. Rush is, in part, an organized recruitment drive. Sororities and fraternities need to communicate to rushees why they should choose their house over others. Some houses will adopt a differentiation marketing strategy (telling the lacrosse players that "this is the lacrosse house"); other houses use a low-cost strategy ("Our sorority has the lowest dues"). Increasingly, Greek houses are using informational rush videos to better communicate the fraternity/sorority's message. And like a VP of human resources, most houses have a rush chair who acts as a liaison between the house and the rushees. A good deal of the rush chair's job is salesmanship—the rush chair must first "sell" rushees on the benefit of joining the Greek system and then convince potential members that their particular house is the best possible fit.

It's not all recruitment however. Since the Greek system has competitive entry, rush is also organized like a job interview. Rushees are not only choosing houses, houses are choosing them. Young men rushing a fraternity are expected to wear suits and come with a list of prepared questions. The principle of targeted selection is implemented. As Tom Hutchison, a member of Sigma Alpha Epsilon, explains, "We were supposed to replace ourselves. During rush, the athletes really concentrated on athletes, the charity guys looked for another charity guy, the party guy found a party guy. That way the house would always have a nice balance" (T. Hutchison, personal communication, May 2, 2006). Some sororities look to soften this job interview dynamic by organizing activities to structure the meet-and-greet. At Zoe Kazmierski's sorority, sisters and rushees sat down together and decorated ivy bags and painted terra cotta pots (Z. Kazmierski, personal communication, May 2, 2006). But still the goal was the same: to get to know the new girls and determine which ones would be the best fit, just as an HR director would do.

Once rush is over, members meet to pool their data and make an informed choice. Bids are given out and the hiring process begins. Once the rushees accept those bids, they become pledges. Pledges go through a period (usually either one school term or two) of performance management. Pledge educators (who are already established members of the fraternity or sorority) are supposed to track the pledges' development and communicate to the rest of the house how each person is doing. It's a performance management system based on the feedback model. In the worst cases, negative feedback takes the form of hazing, enforced drinking, or humiliating tasks. In the best cases, training and development is safe and progressive, and the communication goes back and forth. The pledges not only learn house songs and secret handshakes, they learn what it takes to live and communicate within a large organizational framework.

DISCUSSION QUESTIONS

1. Think about an organization you joined. What communication strategies were used to recruit you?
2. Again, consider any organizations to which you belong. Now that you're a member, do you find the recruitment message truthful? For example, does your college present itself in a way that accurately represents campus life?
3. Are there any everyday situations in which you feel you're on a job interview? What strategies do you use?

In every instance, the decision to involve an OD professional — many of whom have backgrounds in communication — reveals some important realities about the nature of strategic change in organizations and institutions. Having been involved in many of these initiatives ourselves, we will state these realities as three core "lessons" we have learned in approaching the strategic change process using a communication lens.

1. *People still want to be inspired.* Particularly in the wake of the old social contract, it is important to remember that people still look to work as a potential source of meaning in their lives, and a compelling vision or strategy can provide this. The flip side of this lesson is that you can't force people to change to meet a schedule — people enroll in a change when they are ready.

2. *People are more likely to support something they helped to create.* Another key principle of change management is that employees must be given sufficient information and opportunities for dialogue if one expects them to support the new direction. Much of what OD practitioners actually do is facilitate these conversations.

3. *Actions still speak louder than words.* The strategy can be inspiring and the dialogues far-reaching, but if the nonverbal behaviors of management conflict with the espoused direction, the change effort is dead in the water. This is the hardest part of alignment for an OD professional to address, since it implicates the judgment of senior management.

◪ ORGANIZATIONAL LEARNING

In our rapidly changing world, learning organizations have a distinct advantage. Composed of people who not only profit from past mistakes, but are also willing to question the assumptions that led to those mistakes, learning organizations are well-equipped to deal with continuous change (Marquardt, 2002; Senge, 2006; Steier, 1989).

☐ Learning Basic Skills

Most organizational practitioners, educators, and politicians agree that the U.S. educational system does a mediocre job of providing students with even the most basic job skills. The U.S. Labor Secretary's Commission on Achieving Necessary Skills identifies three foundational abilities and five learning areas as essential to success in the workplace (Table 10.1). One foundational ability is the ability to think, to reason, and to make decisions. This ability in turn supports each of the learning areas, such as the ability to troubleshoot and to work with advanced technologies. Other examples of specific details discussed in the commission's categories are creativity and learning how to learn, sociability, and skills in teamwork, negotiation, and giving and receiving feedback. In addition to negatively affecting people's quality of life, widespread deficits of basic skills pose a threat to the business world. Quality and customer service suffer in any industry that depends on an inadequately skilled workforce. In an attempt to address this problem, many food outlets have resorted to equipping cash registers with pictures of food items rather than monetary figures. Similarly, a growing number of manufacturing firms are redesigning complex, good-paying positions into simple, low-paying, dead-end jobs. The result is a downward spiral of quality, service, job skills, wages, and employee self-esteem.

One proposed solution to these serious problems is to establish workplace literacy programs designed to teach basic skills to employees. These programs, which are offered by private companies, public agencies, and corporations themselves, vary widely in their focus and intensity. For example, some programs focus on job-

TABLE 10.1

Necessary Workplace Skills

THE FOUNDATIONAL ABILITIES

Basic: Reading, writing, mathematics, speaking, and listening

Thinking: Creativity, making decisions, solving problems, seeing things in the mind's eye, knowing how to learn, reasoning

Personal qualities: Responsibility, self-esteem, sociability, self-management, and integrity

LEARNING AREAS

Resources: How to allocate time, money, materials, space, and staff

Interpersonal: How to work on teams, teach, serve customers, lead negotiations, and work well with people from culturally diverse backgrounds

Information: How to acquire and evaluate data, organize and maintain files, interpret and communicate, and use computers to acquire and process information

Systems: How to understand social, organizational, and technological systems; monitor and correct performance; and design improved systems

Technology: How to select equipment and tools, apply technology to specific tasks, and maintain and troubleshoot technologies

Source: U.S. Labor Secretary's Commission on Achieving Necessary Skills, June 1991.

related language skills, while others teach a broad array of basic skills that are useful in work and personal situations. In addition, the programs vary in length (from forty to four hundred hours). Some training programs are sensitive to employees' different needs; others make no such distinctions.

The most successful programs thus far are those initiated and taught by the companies themselves. At American Honda and General Motors, for instance, databases are used to match employees' level of education and skill with job opportunities. However, such programs are rare, and even when they do exist, they cannot adequately address the underlying problems in the U.S. educational system. "The share of the nation's economy invested . . . in education and training, children's programs, infrastructure, and civilian research and development has plummeted 40% since 1980. America ranks behind all its major competitors in each of these categories" (Tyson, 1991, p. D2). Although a tremendous amount of effort will be directed at teaching basic skills to employees of the twenty-first century, without major changes in the educational system and in the nation's spending priorities, those efforts will do little to solve the problem.

Taking a broader view, however, even skills training may not be sufficient in helping the unemployed and working poor to participate in an expanding economy. Social philosopher Earl Shorris (1997) has argued that it is not job skills but the ability to know about and reflect on questions central to all human existence, about life and death, right and wrong that is the genuine portal to a better life. To test this hypothesis, Shorris assembled a team of star college teachers (including some Nobel Prize winners) and began offering a course in the humanities to economically disadvantaged adults in New York City. The twenty-eight-week course, dubbed the Clemente Project, was sponsored by Bard College and included instruction in such topics as moral philosophy, art history, and American history. The results are encouraging. There is a big difference between teaching someone about specific business tasks and having them consider work behavior as it might have been seen by Aristotle. An old saying states, "If you give someone a fish, they eat for a day, but if you teach them to fish, they will never go hungry." The Clemente Project, now being tried in many cities around the country, is one attempt to teach "fishing" to the most disenfranchised members of our society. A recent example is the Prometheus Project at Valencia Community College (see <http://valenciacc.edu/clemente/> for more information).

However it is addressed, we must be sure to factor into our thinking about the future of work the "grotesque gap" that exists in income and living standards around the world. Consider this statement from the United Nations Human Development Report (July 12, 1999) on the problems with thinking of development solely in terms of financial markets:

> The richest nations of the world have 20% of the population, but 86% of the income, 91% of its Internet users, and 74% of its telephone users. . . . When the market goes too far in dominating social and political outcomes, the opportunities and rewards of globalization spread unequally and inequitably — concentrating power and wealth in a select group of people, nations, and corporations, marginalizing the others. The challenge is not to stop the expansion of global markets. The challenge is to find the rules and institutions for stronger governance . . . to preserve the advantage of global markets and competition but also to provide enough space for human, community, and environmental resources to ensure that globalization works for people, not just for profits. (Longworth, 1999, p. 16)

☐ Learning New Technologies

In the 1950s and 1960s, organizational researchers emphasized the importance of face-to-face communication between supervisors and employees and among coworkers. Although face-to-face interaction is still important in today's organizations, advances in communication technology — from e-mail to videoconferencing — have overcome some of the limits of face-to-face interaction, especially those associated with speed, geographic distance, and processing capacity. As a result, organizations can no longer function effectively without the use of some type of communication technology. Furthermore, implementing a new technology significantly affects work processes, employees' productivity and work life, and the character of interpersonal and power relationships.

Two broad categories of communication technology are available to organizations:

- **Computer-assisted communication technologies** include the various methods of image transmission, including facsimile (fax), videoconferencing, e-mail, voice mail, the Internet, and personal digital assistants. These are widely used both within organizations and with customers as part of the massive development of global electronic commerce (e-commerce).
- **Computer-assisted decision-aiding technologies** include on-line management information systems, group decision support systems, information retrieval database systems, and expert systems or programs that provide technical information. Traditionally used as tools internal to the organization, these technologies are now offered to customers as well.

Computer-assisted communication technologies are designed to enhance the speed of communication as well as the ability of people to communicate regardless of their geographic location. Most every reader of this textbook likely has experience with instant messaging (IM) as well as other forms of text messaging (SMS) that can be sent and received worldwide by computers, cell phones, and other devices. Text messaging has even developed its own vocabulary, an extension of the abbreviation process that began with e-mail (see Table 10.2).

Other popular computer-assisted communication technologies include voice mail, voice messaging, answering machines (sometimes connected to personal computers), audioconferencing, and cell phones. By far the most popular of the integrated personal devices is the BlackBerry, which continually forwards e-mail to users. PDA (personal digital assistant) technology is so addictive that even its adherents refer to these devices as "crackberries" and more than one business meeting has been disrupted by their overuse. In addition, health professionals report an increase in chronic hand injuries as a result of the proliferation of hand-held communication devices.

Computer-assisted decision-aiding technologies are designed primarily to provide easy access to hard-to-find information needed to make decisions. For example, a company may use market data accessed via an external database to decide whether it should introduce a new product. Internally, a sales manager may access information about last quarter's sales to decide whether the company's salespeople would benefit from a proposed training program. Information on virtually any topic is available on-line. Far from taking the place of humans, the systems that simply support decision making but leave final decisions to the user are more successful than systems that substitute machine decisions for human decisions or that significantly curtail the user's freedom of action.

TABLE 10.2

Learning the Language of Text Messaging

Anything	**NTHING**	Later	**L8R**	Thanks	**THX**
Are you OK	**RUOK?**	Love	**LUV**	Thank you	**THNQ**
Are	**R**	Happy/Smiley	**:-)**	To/too	**2**
Ate	**8**	Angry	**:-||**	To be	**2B**
Be	**B**	Very happy	**:-))**	Today	**2DAY**
Before	**B4**	Confused	**%-)**	Tomorrow	**2MORO**
Be seeing you	**BCNU**	Tonguetied	**:-&**	Want to	**WAN2**
Cutie	**QT**	Sad	**:-(**	What	**WOT**
Date	**D8**	Saintly	**O:-)**	Work	**WRK**
Dinner	**DNR**	Mate	**M8**	Why	**Y**
Easy	**EZ**	Please	**PLS**	You	**U**
Eh?	**A?**	Please call me	**PCM**	Laughing	**:-D**
Excellent	**XLNT**	Queue/cue	**Q**	Crying	**:'-(**
Fate	**F8**	Rate	**R8**	Surprised/shocked	**:-O**
For	**4**	See/sea	**C**	Screaming	**:-@**
For your information	**FYI**	See you later	**CU L8R**	Kiss	**:-***
Great	**GR8**	Speak	**SPK**	Pig	**:@)**
Late	**L8**	Tea	**T**	Clown	***:-)**

Source: <http://www.textmefree.com/text-abbreviation.html>

An especially useful decision-aiding program is the search engine or robot that permits computer users to direct a search for information based on their personal preferences. For instance, a whole family of search engines have been developed that work off user information about vacation preferences (e.g., location, price range, and other preferences) and have the computer shop for and book the trip (e.g., Travelocity, Hotwire, Orbitz). These search utilities significantly extend consumer reach by searching obscure and hard-to-find sources of needed information.

EFFECTS OF COMMUNICATION TECHNOLOGY

The potential effects of communication technology are multiple and varied. Contemporary observers usually support one of four major views on the subject: utopian, dystopian, neutral, and contingent.

From the **utopian view**, information technology serves to equalize power relationships at work by bridging time and space, thereby improving both productivity and work life. Proponents of this highly optimistic view see the computer as both encouraging employee voice and freeing employees to work anywhere, anytime. By contrast, the more pessimistic **dystopian view** sees communication technology as primarily benefiting an economic elite and—through the corporate colonization of the life world (Deetz, 1990)—progressively limiting our freedoms by bringing more of our personal lives under corporate surveillance and scrutiny.

Proponents of the dystopian view range from extremists, sometimes called "Luddites," who advocate a return to simpler times, to moderates, who suggest that a technology's consequences be considered. For example, many people today are frustrated with the overwhelming amount of information that has come with easier access to technology. In a survey of a diverse group of employees, respondents reported significant levels of overload due to the proliferation of electronic media. Indeed, the average Fortune 100 worker sends and receives 178 e-mail messages daily (Dunham, 1999). In contrast, there are those with little or no access to technology who, in the dystopian view, are fast becoming the have-nots in a growing "digital divide" (Dunham, 1999).

The **neutral view** of communication technology holds that it has no significant effects on human behavior and that people can be expected to behave in predictable ways whether they use a traditional telephone or a computer to communicate. Proponents of this view believe that the potential effects of technology on communication and behavior are exaggerated by utopians, dystopians, and others.

The **contingent view** of communication technology is best supported by research. From this view, the effect of a given innovation depends on the context or situation in which it is adopted. For example, the health hazards associated with video display terminals (VDTs)—which include radiation exposure, headaches, eyestrain, sleeplessness, anxiety, and repetitive-motion disorders—may be more the result of how an organization uses the technology (e.g., long working hours and poor design of workstations) than of the technology itself (Hamborg & Greif, 2002; Smith, Cohen, Stammerjohn, & Happ, 1981; Steelman & Klitzman, 1985).

The successful implementation of any communication technology takes into account the social and political aspects of the organizational environment in which it will be used. The "rational" use of communication technology is "subjective, retrospective, and influenced by information provided by others" (Fulk, Schmitz, & Steinfeld, 1990, p. 143). The authors of one study conclude,

> There is no such thing as pure technology. To understand technology, one must first understand social relationships. . . . Everything about the adoption and uses of media is social. . . . Logical expectations for the adoption and use of the new media are rarely met. The pragmatics of technological communication must always be understood in the context of motives, paradoxes, and contradictions of everyday life. (Contractor & Eisenberg, 1990, p. 143)

A good example of the relationship between technology and social context is the decision by some organizations to broadcast board meetings or senior executive updates to all employee computers via streaming video. If management/employee relationships are already strong, and if the broadcast is framed in such a way that

WHAT WOULD YOU DO?

Blogaholics

For some, computer-assisted technologies are addictive. We've discussed people who become highly dependent on their BlackBerrys; we've all heard stories of people who spend their free time browsing on eBay or text messaging friends. More recently, however, the discussion has turned to individuals who are addicted to posting journals and stories on personal Web logs, or *blogs*, for the entire world to see.

The *New York Times* examined this phenomenon in May 2004 in an article titled "For Some, the Blogging Never Ends." Let's take a look at a few excerpts to learn more:

- To celebrate four years of marriage, Richard Wiggins and his wife, Judy Matthews, recently spent a week in Key West, Florida. Early on the morning of their anniversary, Ms. Matthews heard her husband get up and go into the bathroom. He stayed there for a long time. "I didn't hear any water running, so I wondered what was going on," Ms. Matthews said. When she knocked on the door, she found him seated with his laptop balanced on his knees, typing into his Web log, a collection of observations about the technical world, over a wireless link. (para. 1–2)
- Jocelyn Wang, a twenty-seven-year-old marketing manager in Los Angeles, started her blog, a chronicle of whatever happens to pop into her head (www.jozjozjoz.com), eighteen months ago as an outlet for boredom. Now she spends at least four hours a day posting to her blog and reading other blogs. Ms. Wang's on-line journal is now her life. And the people she has met through the blog are a large part of her core of friends. "There is no real separation in my life," she said. Like Mr. Wiggins, Ms. Wang blogs while on vacation. She stays on floors at the Hotel Nikko in San Francisco with access to a free Internet connection. ("So I can blog," she explains.) (para. 28–30)
- Tony Pierce started his blog three years ago while in search of a distraction after breaking up with a girlfriend. "In three years I don't think I've missed a day," he said. . . . Where some frequent bloggers might label themselves merely ardent, Mr. Pierce is more realistic. "I wouldn't call it dedicated. I would call it a problem," he said. "If this were beer, I'd be an alcoholic." (para. 13–14)

Keep these examples in mind as you consider the questions below.

DISCUSSION QUESTIONS

1. Are you a blogger? If yes, how often do you post? If you are not a blogger, do you read others' blogs regularly? Why or why not?
2. Do you know someone whom you suspect is "addicted" to blogging? Why do you think this problem occurs?
3. In your opinion, when does an obsession with or addiction to technology become an ethical problem? Consider the examples from the *New York Times* article cited above or the "crackberry" mentioned earlier in this chapter.
4. In what ways do face-to-face communication and on-line communication through blogs differ? What are the advantages and disadvantages of both?
5. What advice would you give to the people who are featured in this news story?

---

employees are curious about new and relevant information that might be shared, the technology can be a smashing success. Alternatively, dropping such a broadcast into a secretive environment with no history of candid communication across levels will most likely lead at best to apathy and at worst to resentment and suspicion. It is important to keep in mind that the same technology may have radically different effects depending on the prevailing social context. Table 10.3 identifies six important considerations in the analysis of a communication technology.

☐ Synchronicity and Media Richness

Two particular aspects of communication technology are of special interest to communication scholars: synchronicity and media richness. **Synchronicity** refers to the capacity of a technology to allow for simultaneous two-way communication. For example, a telephone is synchronous, but an answering machine allows the telephone to become asynchronous. Similarly, while most e-mail is asynchronous, the proliferation of chat rooms on the Internet and instant and text messaging has created more possibilities for synchronicity. Both synchronous and asynchronous communication have their advantages. For instance, certain requests and work tasks are best approached via two-way communication, whereas other tasks may be well communicated and performed through asynchronous channels (e.g., when busy people leave messages for one another across time zones). However, asynchronous communication can lead people to make more contacts than they can reasonably handle (Gergen, 1991). This is why many people in high-status or high-visibility jobs sometimes avoid using voice-mail and e-mail systems.

TABLE 10.3

Six Concerns in the Analysis of Communication Technology

1. *Humans are agents.* Accept the fact that "humans are reflexively monitoring what goes on in a particular social system, that they are motivated by wants and aspirations, and that they have the power not to perform the prescription laid down by systems designers" (p. 312).

2. *Tacit knowledge should be respected.* "People know more about their lives than they can put into words. People do know how to handle practical affairs without being able to explain fully what they are really doing" (p. 312).

3. *Understanding is partial.* "There are always unacknowledged conditions for and unintended consequences of people's behavior" (p. 313).

4. *Technology is politically ambiguous.* Although a technology can be used to promote dialogue and to improve individual quality of life, the same technology can also be used to constrain, limit, and control.

5. *Informal communication must be acknowledged.* "Informal informing is an organizational fact. . . . It is necessary to understand how formal information is mediated through various more or less structured patterns of informing" (p. 313).

6. *Counterrational decision making should be acknowledged.* "The rational model is not a viable way of understanding the intricacies of modern business management. On the one hand it is questionable that decision-makers cognitively are able to cope with the complexity and amount of information needed to make rational decisions, and on the other hand, it is probable that all sorts of political and social pressures are called upon in everyday management" (pp. 313–314).

Source: Jan Mouritsen and Niels Bjorn-Andersen, "Understanding Third-Wave Information Systems," in C. Dunlop and R. Kling, eds., *Computerization and Controversy: Value Conflicts and Social Choices* (San Diego: Academic Press, 1991), pp. 308–320.

Media richness refers to the number of multiple channels of contact afforded by a communication medium (Daft & Lengel, 1984). Each channel roughly corresponds to one of our senses; consequently, face-to-face communication is classified as most rich because it simultaneously allows for speech, nonverbal communication, vision, smell, and touch. Using this definition, a letter would fall at the low end of the media richness scale, as it only allows for verbal exchange. Videoconferencing is a richer medium than telephone conferencing, but still falls short of face-to-face interaction. People are very often strategic when deciding how rich a medium to choose, depending on their goals. Most of us have on occasion left an uncomfortable message on someone's answering machine because we couldn't "face" their response.

☐ Secrecy and Privacy

The primary benefit of communication technology — the radical expansion of connections between people and institutions — is also its main liability. Every connection leaves traces that can be followed and exploited by others for personal gain. Issues of privacy, secrecy, and copyright in computer-aided interaction are currently being debated in courts around the world. In most companies, for example, managers have access to employees' e-mail messages. Major credit card companies follow consumer spending patterns very closely, including where transactions are made by clients. The effects of electronic surveillance on people's right to privacy is already a major issue.

As discussed in Chapter 6, we have witnessed an enormous increase in the computerized monitoring of employee productivity, wherein the frequency and speed of work are measured and stored by the computer and are reviewed by management. Most employers monitor their employees as a means of protecting themselves against possible litigation. According to the Privacy Rights Clearinghouse:

> A 2005 survey by the American Management Association found that three-fourths of employers monitor their employees' web site visits in order to prevent inappropriate surfing. And 65% use software to block connections to web sites deemed off limits for employees. About a third track keystrokes and time spent at the keyboard. Just over half of employers review and retain electronic mail messages. Over 80% of employers disclose their monitoring practices to employees. And most employers have established policies governing Internet use, including e-mail use (84%) and personal Internet use (81%). ("Employee Monitoring," 2006)

Employees' reactions have been mixed; although some employees consider electronic surveillance to be an invasion of their privacy, others believe that it is useful in giving good performers greater recognition for their efforts (Bell-Detienne, 1992).

☐ Mediated Interpersonal Communication

With the widespread use of telephones, fax machines, computers, and overnight delivery services, many interpersonal work relationships are routinely conducted by people who never actually meet face-to-face. The result is a new hybrid of social relationships that we call **mediated interpersonal communication**. Mediated forms of written communication are popular, particularly in international companies. For example, at Ryobi, a Japanese manufacturing firm with several U.S. subsidiaries, more money is spent on faxes than on any other form of communication. The same is true of many Asian-owned firms that operate in the United States, where culture demands strict adherence to procedures and an ongoing flow of information about work processes. However, at Sagem-Lucas, a French and British partnership with U.S. subsidiaries, appointed representatives are sent to the United States for several weeks to become acquainted with business colleagues and the local culture. The representatives report back to the company's headquarters in Europe, where their on-site observations become the topic of internal memos, faxes, and computer-based communication.

Similar patterns of mediated communication are found in U.S. companies. For many companies, real offices are being replaced by virtual ones (Gephart, 2002). A virtual office, with most of the usual functions of an office, can be literally anywhere the user can gain access to a high-speed or wireless Internet connection. Desktop computers, modems, and multiple phone lines serve communication needs, while productivity can be up to 20 percent higher than that of office-based workers, who are sometimes referred to as *non-distributed workers*. *Distributed workers* — those working in a virtual office — also tend to experience less job-related stress (Grantham, 1995).

Time will tell what new challenges and opportunities will arise in the transition to what has recently been called "nomadic" work (Bean & Eisenberg, 2006). As many of the logistical problems involving collaborative media and file transfer have been resolved, we can more productively turn our attention to the effect of such arrangements on social relationships and organizational culture. Research on e-mail usage reveals the tendency of users to feel less inhibited on-line and to say things that they would not in a face-to-face encounter. One would expect a similar dynamic to surface in distributed work. At the same time, the potential for outrageous emotional displays may be somewhat modulated by the increase in electronic surveillance (discussed in the previous section). As nearly everyone who works for a living comes to appreciate that their electronic communication is open to public scrutiny, we may see norms develop that encourage less, not more, intense or disclosive interaction.

Summary

Successful organizations have strategies. There are two general types of competitive strategy: lowest-cost and differentiation. To succeed, a company must select its strategy carefully and then purposefully align its systems and structures to reflect that strategy. Competitive strategies are only as good as how they are communicated. When employees truly understand the big picture, they are most likely to work in ways that support the overall direction of the firm.

Management of human resources has become a highly sophisticated discipline that addresses how companies can best attract and retain talented employees. Targeted selection is the general label for the conscious selection of employees with abilities that support the company strategy. Performance management is the system by which employee accomplishments are measured and discussed. Organizational development and training is made available to employees to support continuous learning. To be successful, a company's human resources function must be well integrated and become part of the corporate culture through its inclusion in regular conversations about results and improvement.

Learning has become the watchword for organizational effectiveness in the twenty-first century. The world changes so quickly that companies must continually be willing to question their assumptions about reality. Organizations and their employees must continually learn new skills and new technologies; some scholars even promote the idea of offering courses in the humanities to help promote lifelong critical thinking skills. Communication technology serves both to bring additional knowledge to the organization and to permit more and better connections among employees through computer-assisted communication technologies and computer-assisted decision-aiding technologies.

Technology is fundamentally changing every aspect of work and life, and scholars are mixed in their assessments of its benefits and detriments. Those who hold a utopian view believe the technology has had a positive effect on equalizing power relationships while those with a dystopian view are more pessimistic, believing that technology will continue to create a divide between the "haves" and "have nots" around the world. A neutral view of communication technology states that technology has no significant effect on human behavior — people will respond in predictable ways whether or not technology is involved. The contingent view is possibly the most realistic, noting that communication technology has advantages and disadvantages mainly derived from the way an individual or company chooses to utilize it. Regardless of which view one takes, it is clear that technology will continue to have a large-scale impact on individuals and companies, particularly in the areas of interpersonal communication and secrecy/privacy.

QUESTIONS FOR REVIEW AND DISCUSSION

1. Why is it important to take a "bird's eye" view of an organization in charting its future?

2. How do competitive strategies and competitor analysis work together to effectively position an organization? What role might the specific strategies we mentioned (lowest-cost and differentiation) play as well?

3. What happens to companies that are not consciously positioned in the marketplace, or to those whose employees are unaware of their companies' positioning?

4. Which elements of strategic alignment seem the most challenging, and why?

5. In what ways do human resources contribute to the successful implementation of company strategy? What are the roles of targeted selection, performance management, and training/development?

6. What are learning organizations and why are they at an advantage in today's competitive market?

7. What are the pros and cons of computer-assisted communication technology and computer-assisted decision-aiding technology? What view do you take of such technology — utopian, dystopian, neutral, or contingent? Why?

Key Terms

Competitive strategy, p. 310
Competitor analysis, p. 311
Computer-assisted communication technology, p. 329
Computer-assisted decision-aiding technology, p. 329
Contingent view (of communication technology), p. 331
Differentiation (strategy), p. 312
Dystopian view (of communication technology), p. 331
High-performance practices, p. 320
Lowest-cost (strategy), p. 312
Media richness, p. 334
Mediated interpersonal communication, p. 335

Neutral view (of communication technology), p. 331
Organizational development (OD), p. 323
Performance management, p. 321
Strategic alignment, p. 315
Strategic positioning, p. 310
Strategic thinking, p. 309
Superordinate goals, p. 316
Synchronicity, p. 333
Targeted selection, p. 321
Total quality management (TQM), p. 318
Training and development, p. 322
Utopian view (of communication technology), p. 330

Advertising and the American Way of Life

According to one study (Jhally, 1998), the average North American is exposed to more than 3,500 advertisements a day. Consider the number of commercial messages that you are bombarded with—everything from media images, Internet "banner ads," billboards, radio jingles, and print ads to designer labels on clothing. One effect of living in a media-rich environment is the increasing lack of public space available for noncommercial messages. Think about important public health information campaigns, antidrug messages, or open expressions of disagreement (or agreement) with public policies or governmental actions. Another effect is the increasingly visceral nature of the images and content of the advertisements themselves—more naked bodies, louder volumes, more "in your face" messages. According to Sut Jhally and his associates at the University of Massachusetts, Amherst, these two effects combine to squeeze out public dialogue about important issues related to global problems, such as the demise of the ecosystem.

Let's assume that you are director of Greenpeace, whose mission is to "use nonviolent, creative confrontation to expose global environmental problems, and force solutions for a green and peaceful future" and whose goal is to "ensure the ability of the Earth to nurture life in all its diversity" (<www.greenpeace.org/international/about/our-mission>). Your challenge is to develop a strategy for promoting public understanding and action regarding the relationship of unmonitored global capitalism and the rapid demise of the South American rain forests.

ASSIGNMENT

Using what you have read in this chapter about strategy, human resources, and technologies, as well as your experiences and knowledge of persuasive communication, answer these questions:

1. Describe what your strategy would be and how that strategy can help you align your resources and technologies to develop a successful campaign.
2. Think about how you would manage such an enterprise. What important questions and issues should you raise about the implementation of your business strategy? What human resources issues can you think of? What technology issues?
3. Using your strategy as a framework, develop ideas that can be translated into vivid images and powerful messages about the environment and that are capable of gaining the attention of audiences already overexposed to mediated messages. Come up with an advertising campaign capable of maximizing your strategy, resources, and technologies.

CASE STUDY II

Hacked Off

Computer hackers consistently pose threats to Internet users as well as to commercial, public, and governmental computer files and systems. By "hacking into" company or government files or by inserting computer viruses into these systems, hackers can do major harm in a very short period of time. One particularly noxious hacking venture involved the creation of "zombie" computers that flooded Internet sites with junk messages, effectively shutting them down for business for three days. Losses were estimated to be in the tens of millions of dollars.

One of the outcomes of computer hacking has been an increased need for security from such attacks. Some companies forbid employees from removing company computers or software from the premises, thus reducing the ability of some employees to work off-site or at home. In an unprecedented case in 1999, a former director of the Central Intelligence Agency was called on the carpet for taking his laptop home because it contained some secret and top secret files. Clearly, the rapid expansion of—and now dependence on—computer technologies in business and government has created unprecedented challenges to the management of organizations.

Balancing the legitimate needs of users with the legitimate rights of an organization to protect itself is a delicate activity. Based on your reading in this chapter as well as your own experiences, how would you go about establishing a fair and equitable policy about the use of technology in the workplace?

ASSIGNMENT

1. How should a business strategy be used to guide the development of a technology policy?
2. Would the 7-S model be useful in helping you develop such a policy? How?
3. What input should you seek in developing the particulars of such a policy?
4. How important do you think the language of the policy will be to its successful implementation?
5. What steps should you take to ensure the successful implementation of the policy?
6. How would you assess the effectiveness of the policy?

PART IV

APPLICATIONS

CHAPTER 11

Working with Integrity: Organizational Communication as Disciplined Practice

How should we think about and prepare for the future? What have you learned from this course that can be applied to your work life? The study of organizational communication theory can be a worthwhile pursuit in and of itself if you plan to become a university professor, but most students choose working lives outside of the academy. For them, the historical, cultural, and theoretical study of organizational communication is useful mainly as "equipment for living," which means that to be of value it must translate from theory to practice (Burke, 1989).

This chapter offers some help in making this translation. It is not our intention to provide a set of "right answers" about organizational communication—since these have a tendency to change—but to help you develop a more *conscious* approach to the choices you make about communicating in organizations, along with their likely consequences. Put another way, our primary aim is to encourage the practice of "mindfulness" that draws on what you have learned about communication for the purpose of living and working with integrity (Goodall & Goodall, 2002). Mindful communication practice offers productive and rewarding ways to balance the desire for individuality and creativity with organizational and social constraints.

▨ CONSCIOUS COMMUNICATION AND MINDFUL COMMUNICATION PRACTICES

☐ Mindful and Mindless Communication

While many people believe that communication is mostly a conscious activity, studies have demonstrated that this is not the case (for a comprehensive overview, see Langer, 1998; see also Motley, 1992). In fact, communication and cognition researchers believe that most of us behave mindlessly most of the time. This is because we rely on forms of talk that are easy to perform and whose likely outcomes are well known to us.

An advantage of being able to speak mindlessly is that the brain reserves energy for more challenging situations (King & Sawyer, 1998). The disadvantage is the tendency to get "locked into" rigid habits of mind. Physicist and dialogue theorist David Bohm (1980) underscores this tendency in his distinction between thinking and having thoughts. Most of the time, we mindlessly draw upon the stories we have been told throughout our lives to make sense of new situations (i.e., we "have thoughts"). The risk in doing this is that we will misapply what we believe we know. Alternatively, thinking involves genuine reflection on the nature of the situation and a conscious choice of appropriate frameworks. Unlike having thoughts, thinking implies a willingness to listen and be open to beliefs beyond what one already knows. Thinking is crucial in true collaboration and innovation, and is the essence of authentic dialogue (see Chapter 2).

Consider, for example, the following mindless exchange known as phatic communication:

"Hello, how are you?"

"Fine. And you?"

"Good. (Pause) So what's new?"

"Not much. And you?"

"Same old same old. (Pause) I have to get back to work."

"Yeah, me too."

"See you later—"

"Okay, see you later."

Phatic communication is a form of small talk that helps us appear social and gives the impression that we are interested in others. However, it also shows disregard for each other because nothing that is said really matters to either person. Regular reliance on these kinds of routines may prevent us from finding newer, more interesting, and ultimately more satisfying conversations at work.

A more elaborate form of mindless communication involves the use of a script. **Scripts** are routine exchanges of talk delivered in rote fashion, something like reading well-rehearsed lines in a play. We follow scripts at work when we engage in what we consider to be routine and unimportant interactions, such as selection and performance appraisals; dispute resolution sessions; and everyday conversations (i.e., "shooting the breeze") on well-known subjects with familiar co-workers. Scripts are played out automatically as if our communication is guided by formulas rather than by creative engagement or spontaneity.

Of course, mindless communication could never be eliminated entirely; all of us employ phatic communication and scripts much of the time. We are, however, concerned about how effective we can be in our work and home lives when we *rely too much* on these forms. Stephen Covey's *The 7 Habits of Highly Effective People* (1990) advocates that to be successful requires becoming more goal-oriented, focused, and strategic in our dealings with others. His prescriptions for success in the workplace prompt us to become more conscious of our communication and more reflective about the outcomes we wish to achieve.

☐ Becoming More Mindful

A **mindful** approach to organizational communication enables us to understand talk "as a mental and relational activity that is both purposeful and strategic" (Goodall & Goodall, 2006, p. 52). Elaine Langer (1998) found that when we become more conscious of our communication, we become more mindful and that when we become more mindful we will likely become more ethical as well. We will learn to recognize that we are responsible for our communication goals, our communication choices, and our performance relative to achieving them. We are less apt to act thoughtlessly toward others.

But how can people become more mindful, or what Weick and Sutcliffe (2001) describe as "heedful," in their communication? Research has shown that we "naturally" become more mindful under the following conditions:

- There is a conflict between perceived message goals.
- Undesirable consequences are expected from the use of a particular message strategy.
- There are time delays between messages and mental processing difficulties, such as interpreting the meaning or intention of the message.
- Communication situations are particularly troublesome or unique (Motley, 1992).

In other words, we naturally become more mindful when we sense danger, are confused, or perceive a negative outcome. When these things happen, we become more attuned to our surroundings, more alert, and more focused on the situation. We become more creative and rely less on scripts, or at the very least think carefully before selecting a course of action. We become conscious of how we are being perceived and attended to by others and we are more likely to interpret the messages of others meaningfully. Becoming more mindful in the workplace requires one to:

- Analyze communication situations and develop strategies for accomplishing goals informed by the organization's culture; power relations among participants; and differences in message interpretation derived from race, ethnicity, and gender.
- Think actively about possible communication choices (especially those that don't seem like choices!) as well as the potential organizational, relational, and personal outcomes of those choices.
- Adapt messages in a timely and thoughtful manner when seeking to inform, amuse, persuade, or otherwise influence listeners and audiences.
- Evaluate the feedback or responses we receive as an indication of how successful we were in accomplishing our purpose (Goodall & Goodall, 2006).

Mindful communication requires discipline and regular practice. It begins when we catch ourselves behaving mindlessly and decide to become more conscious of our interactions. It improves as we find that by not using phatic communication or scripts as much, we see new possibilities in our relationships with others. It provides us with a foundation for building trust and behaving authentically with others, which, in turn, encourages others to act with greater integrity toward us. And becoming more conscious as a communicator affords us one additional, crucial benefit: It promotes learning.

◪ CONSCIOUS INTEGRITY

Integrity is a mindful state of acting purposefully to fulfill the promises and commitments you make to others. It is a term that we associate with honesty, openness, commitment, and trust. It is also a term we associate with women and men who consciously make choices about treating others fairly and equitably, and who understand that in today's turbulent business and social environment those who lead have obligations to those who follow them as well as to the bottom line and stockholders.

There are some excellent examples of people who have done just that. *Time* magazine's "Person of the Year" for 2002 was, for the first time, shared by three brave women: Cynthia Cooper (WorldCom), Coleen Rowley (FBI), and Sherron Watkins (Enron). Each of them "blew the whistle" on unethical or irresponsible actions in her respective organization. Each risked her job and reputation to do what she believed was right for her co-workers and her company's stakeholders. In the case of Watkins, it also meant standing up for the interests of a nation. Each woman made a conscious choice to act in the best interests of others, regardless of the cost to themselves. Because these women were willing and able to speak up, their organizations were given a valuable opportunity to learn from past mistakes and create a better system going forward.

Another person who acted with integrity was Aaron Feuerstein, the owner of Massachusetts fabric maker Malden Mills. He chose to keep his three thousand employees on the payroll and rebuild his company after a devastating fire that destroyed three company buildings. Feuerstein, the grandson of the founder of the company, said that he never considered shutting down the business after the fire. He believed that his employees deserved to be treated well because without their dedication and hard work the company would not have grown. He made a conscious decision to honor his commitments to them even though it represented a huge personal loss for himself.

Our list could go on, but the point we are making is simple yet profound. Rather than being an abstract aspect of character, integrity is a core business principle that requires mindful, disciplined communication and considerable courage to enact (Beckett, 2005).

NEW LOGICS OF ORGANIZING

As we have hinted throughout this book, traditional organizational hierarchies are giving way to new alternative organizational forms. Philip Tompkins and Maryanne Wanca-Thibault (2001) provide an interesting account of the future prospects for organizational communication that underscores the importance of thinking through organizational issues in new ways. Their analysis suggests that one major accomplishment of organizational scholars has been the identification of key processes, relationships, issues, and challenges that define the basic facts of work: leadership and followership, structures and networks, the creation and interpretation of messages, communication media and channels for communication. Those basic facts — the basic grammar for organizational studies, if you will — are least likely to change.

What *has* changed is the underlying logic of organizing. More specifically, the "old" logic of organizational communication rested solidly on a seemingly bedrock principle that assumed hierarchies of all kinds were "givens." One consistent theme of this book has been the need for new, nonhierarchical, and empowering ways of thinking about communication in organizations. Another example of "old" logic that seemed incapable of change (even a generation ago) was the idea that the world of work revolved around men — and, in particular, white men. Our new understanding of (or logics for thinking about) diversity in the global workforce has caused dramatic changes in how we think about and perform communication at work. Time and space have collapsed, and new technologies have emerged that facilitate the operation of global organizations. And more than likely, the dominant organizational forms will change again (probably more than once) in your lifetime.

☐ Management as Poetry

One way to become more conscious of alternative logics is to rethink the ways in which we assume distinctions between and among categories. For example, Ian

Lennie in *Beyond Management* (1999) suggests that if we understand managing as "that activity of meaningfully organizing ourselves in everyday life," then we ought to consider poetry as fundamental to improving how we accomplish that in organizations (p. 1). He argues that **poetry** is a balancing of order and chaos made sensible through interpretation of language, and it is difficult *not* to see that same process of sense making as essential to managing an organization (Whyte, 1996). In so doing, we consciously alter the way we logically organize managerial tasks, seeing them less driven by a literal language and technical rationality and more driven by a language of story and metaphor.

☐ Communication as Discourse, Voice, and Performance

Three new metaphors — "discourse," "voice," and "performance" — are at the forefront of organizational thinking (Jablin & Putnam, 2001, p. xii). Each of these terms, when joined up with organizational communication, reveals new logics to guide both organizing and organizational research.

Discourse invites us to examine organizations as texts, and to bring to such examinations the well-developed logic of literary and conversation analyses. As we have seen in the Lennie example, thinking of what we say and do in a literary way opens up new possibilities for finding creative solutions to age-old organizational challenges (Fairhurst & Putnam, 2004).

Voice invites us to consider who has the right to speak in organizations and what a "chorus of diverse voices" or "singing solo" may mean in relation to the logics of power and suppression at work. Here again, by thinking creatively we broaden our understanding by bringing to it a new language of music.

Performance asks us to consider dramatic enactment as a new way of thinking about coordinated activities, storytelling, collaborative practices, and identity work in organizations (Lindemann, 2005; Pelias, 2003; Tracy, 2004; Whitney, 2006). We can also understand issues of identity as performances of self and teamwork or group work as an ensemble performance (Faber, 2002; Murphy, 2002). By employing the logic of dramatic enactment to understand life at work, new ideas may surface.

Viewing organizational communication through the lens of these metaphors puts us in a mindful state, makes us more aware of the language we use to represent and evoke organizational experiences, and prepares us for the likely changes in dominant organizational forms in our lives. Becoming more conscious of the language we use to represent and evoke organizational experiences will be a key factor in continuing to learn new ways to solve old problems. Acquiring sensitivity to language, and being able to think with it, only occurs when one is mindful.

MINDFULNESS, INTEGRITY, AND THE EXPERIENCE OF WORK

Throughout the previous chapters, we have detailed the factors that contribute to our experience of work in- and outside an organization. We discussed the organizational socialization process and how the tensions and sources of stress at work can lead to ill health, burnout, and a lack of commitment and loyalty to employers. We indicated that learning how to manage stress at work involves identification with the mission and values of the company; active involvement in decision making and feelings of empowerment; and the ability to balance home and work lives. All of these processes benefit from mindfulness and conscious communication.

We have also found it useful to incorporate the wisdom of the Dalai Lama into our thinking about work. In a widely circulated Internet message about achieving "Good Karma" in the new millennium, the Dalai Lama offered some practical advice that is useful to consider. Regardless of your spiritual orientation we feel his insights help put the experience of work into a broader experience of living well. Here are some excerpts from his statement "Instructions for Life in the New Millennium":

1. Take into account that great love and great achievements involve great risk.
2. When you lose, don't lose the lesson.
3. Follow the 3 *R*'s: *R*espect for the self; *R*espect for others; *R*esponsibility for all of your actions.
4. Not getting what you want is sometimes a wonderful stroke of luck.
5. Learn the rules so you can know how to break them.
6. Don't let a little dispute injure a great relationship.
7. When you realize you made a mistake, take immediate steps to correct it.
8. Spend some time alone each day.
9. Open your arms to change, but don't let go of your values.
10. Remember that silence is sometimes the best answer.
11. Live a good, honorable life. That way, when you get older and think back, you will be able to enjoy it a second time.
12. A loving atmosphere in your home is the foundation for your life.
13. Share your knowledge. It is a way of achieving immortality.
14. Be gentle with the earth.
15. Once a year go someplace you have never seen.
16. Judge your success by what you had to give up in order to get it.

Taken together, these recommendations underscore the importance of positive interpersonal relationships and openness to new experiences and to learning, personal growth, and happiness.

◪ CULTIVATING INTERPERSONAL INTEGRITY AND RELATIONAL MINDFULNESS

Whether your position inside or outside the company involves communicating with customers, clients, patrons, donors, bosses, employees, and/or peers, there is no doubt that interpersonal integrity and relational mindfulness form the core communication competencies in your workplace. In principle, this should be fairly easy to do — the bottom line for business relationships is DWYSYWD (Do What You Said You Would Do). In other words, follow through on your interpersonal commitments and make sure that others in your organization do the same.

However, this is easier said than done. Bruce Hyde (1995) asks his students to keep track of their verbal commitments over the course of a week, and to try to honor each one (which he calls "being your word"). The students are shocked by how often they fail to follow through on their commitments. In organizations, the question of follow-through is complicated by the fact that things and people change, and expectations for what is really promised by a slogan such as "provide the best customer service possible" is open to interpretation. Fortunately, understanding that conscious communication places a strong value on listening to others and trying to adapt your messages to them encourages all of us to become more mindful in our embodiment of organizational values, slogans, and commitments.

It is important to *establish expectations* and to *be mindful of boundaries* for relationships at work (Goodall & Goodall, 2006, pp. 179–181). This means applying what you have learned about organizational cultures as well as interpersonal relationships to your unique work environment. Each organization has evolved standards for communication practices among peers, subordinates, superiors, and customers that newcomers must acquire as part of the organizational socialization process. Learning the expectations and boundary standards will also help you behave ethically in all aspects of your job. Why? Because contrary to popular opinion when it comes to workplace communication, the ends *don't* justify the means. Behaving ethically means, as Gandhi put it, living with the profound understanding that "means are ends in the making."

Ethical behavior in the workplace is achieved on a solid foundation of core communication values. Communication is, after all, the primary means by which relational ends are attained. For example, in North American business cultures, the organizational values associated with ethical communication suggest that we should:

- Trust one another
- Treat each other with respect
- Recognize the value of each individual
- Keep your word
- Tell the truth; be honest with others

- Act with integrity
- Be open to change
- Risk failing in order to get better
- Learn; try new ideas (Harshman & Harshman, 1999, p. 30)

These values echo the timeless wisdom of the Dalai Lama. They are also reflected in the National Communication Association's Credo for Ethical Communication (1999) (see Table 11.1).

TABLE 11.1

NCA Credo for Ethical Communication

Questions of right and wrong arise whenever people communicate. Ethical communication is fundamental to responsible thinking, decision making, and the development of relationships and communities within and across contexts, cultures, channels, and media. Moreover, ethical communication enhances human worth and dignity by fostering truthfulness, fairness, responsibility, personal integrity, and respect for self and others. We believe that unethical communication threatens the quality of all communication and consequently the well-being of individuals and the society in which we live. Therefore, we, the members of the National Communication Association, endorse and are committed to practicing the following principles of ethical communication.

- We advocate truthfulness, accuracy, honesty, and reason as essential to the integrity of communication.
- We endorse freedom of expression, diversity of perspective, and tolerance of dissent to achieve the informed and responsible decision making fundamental to a civil society.
- We strive to understand and respect other communicators before evaluating and responding to their messages.
- We promote access to communication resources and opportunities as necessary to fulfill human potential and contribute to the well-being of families, communities, and society.
- We promote communication climates of caring and mutual understanding that respect the unique needs and characteristics of individual communicators.
- We condemn communication that degrades individuals and humanity through distortion, intimidation, coercion, and violence and through the expression of intolerance and hatred.
- We are committed to the courageous expression of personal convictions in pursuit of fairness and justice.
- We advocate sharing information, opinions, and feelings when facing significant choices while also respecting privacy and confidentiality.
- We accept responsibility for the short- and long-term consequences for our own communication and expect the same of others.

Source: <http://www.natcom.org/nca/Template2.asp?bid=514>

Contrary to popular opinion, then, ethical, effective communication is less about making others feel good than about a conscious commitment to speaking the truth in a constructive fashion. In many cases, we choose to avoid candid communication precisely because we are not emotionally prepared to handle the conflict that may ensue. Put another way, then, one predictable by-product of effective communication is conflict. Our goal in organizing, therefore, should not be to minimize conflict but to develop constructive ways of addressing it.

Behaving mindfully can help us work through conflict in constructive ways. From research done by Peter Kellett and Diana Dalton (2000), we learn that conscious communication in times of relational conflict teaches us to ask (and answer) the following questions:

- *Where does the conflict come from?* Who and what is producing the disagreement? Is there a history of disagreements between the communicators?
- *How is the conflict being managed?* Who avoids it, and who wants to engage in it? What goals are sought by the participants?
- *How do other people react to the conflict?* Is it perceived as "something new" or "nothing new"? What negative work-related consequences can be associated with the conflict? What personal consequences follow from it?
- *How does the conflict affect key organizational functions?* How does it influence productivity? How does it influence openness? Honesty? Learning? Dialogue?
- *How does the conflict manifest systemically in other organizational practices?* Are stress levels higher for those with similar conflicts? Are discussions routed around the key participants? Is there a loss of potentially important feedback? Are denial and blaming strategies spread to other conflicts? If the conflict is gender-, class-, or race-based, are other work relationships negatively impacted? If so, how?

In a global business environment, the idea of interpersonal effectiveness extends to global relational communities. The idea of a "global community" necessarily includes diversity, and with it come possibilities for distortion or misunderstanding based on a lack of a common or even a shared language, and vastly different beliefs about appropriate communication, face-saving, self-disclosure, and silence. This means that in addition to mastering the rules, boundaries, and expectations of *our own* organization's culture, it is vital to learn about the rules, boundaries, and expectations of *other nations'* business cultures.

One important idea to help you become more mindful of cultural differences is the distinction between individualist and collectivist cultures. **Individualist cultures,** such as the United States, revere the individual person and expect people "to make their own decisions, develop their own opinions, solve their own problems, have their own things, and, in general, learn to view the world from the point of view of the self" (Samovar, Jain, & Porter, 1998, pp. 73–74). Persons from individualist cultures value democratic relationships and distrust status and hierarchy as ways of informing how they should treat each other. By contrast, **collectivist cultures**, such as the dominant culture of China, revere the common good over self-interest, value group and family identity over individual achievement, and tend to respect vertical status hierarchies. These differences between individualist and collectivist cultures are so deep that they challenge our fundamental assumptions about communication. So what should we do to behave more mindfully, more consciously, when communicating in a global relational community?

Arthur Bell and Gary Williams (1999) suggest that mindful communication in a global business environment begins with the coproduction of a "transaction culture":

> When you and your own cultural background come into contact with persons of another culture, something new emerges—a middle ground, called a "**transaction culture**." In this new middle ground, sensitive and often unstated rules and understandings guide behavior. That is, if a member of Culture A interacts with a member of Culture B, neither the cultural rules of A nor those of B are the sole guide for behavior. Instead a mixed set of rules—middle Culture C—develops for the purposes of interaction. (pp. 452–453)

We discussed in Chapter 7 the nature of difference in the workplace and the ways that individuals can feel marginalized on the basis of gender, race, class, and intersecting identities. Indeed, behaving more mindfully, and communicating more consciously, helps us avoid giving offense to others as well as passively accepting it from others. It reinforces our perceptions of other's needs and sensitivities, and it helps us learn how to ask for, and to give, honest and productive feedback.

◨ THINKING TOGETHER: MINDFUL DIALOGUE

One of the most important lessons of living more mindfully and communicating more consciously at work is the idea of "thinking together" rather than "having thoughts individually" (Bohm, 1996). This is because when we think together we are truly engaging in a dialogic process.

In the West, dialogue is often depicted as a "peak experience" for humans (Goodall & Kellett, in press; Maslow, 1994). This is because it is experienced as a rare event between or among persons born to highly individualistic cultures. Our pride in "thinking for ourselves" is too often manifested as a *fear* of engaging the most intimate, deep, spiritual, or profound thoughts of others. We may confuse honest attempts at self-disclosure with a hidden desire to move a relationship to what may be perceived as an inappropriate level. Some of us may also believe that if we listen carefully to what others are really saying, we may be influenced to change our minds, something that people reared to be "self-sufficient" often avoid at any cost. Increasingly, one of the problems of democracy is that few people are willing to engage the ideas of others who differ from them.

Dialogue, as we have repeatedly observed, is based on a profound willingness and ability to engage differences without judgment (Hammond, Anderson, & Cissna, 2003). But it is also far more than that. It is also a cultivated, conscious ability to value the thoughts, passions, and actions of others who differ from us, and to work with those ideas, feelings, and behaviors in new ways. This is what Bohm means by "thinking together." The point of **mindful dialogue** is to produce thoughts that neither party in a relationship, nor any participant in a group, team, or network, could have produced alone.

As you studied in Chapter 8, the promise of groups, teams, and networks may only be fulfilled if the members of those collectivities learn together, speak and listen together, and move forward in new and creative ways. To accomplish such collective, dialogic action, each member must actively *choose to think together and to consciously suspend the judgmental self from the process.* Echoing the words of the Dalai Lama (but with an intentionally different spin), "judge your success by what you had to give up to get it." In this case, what "you had to give up" to become successful was the judgmental, egocentric self and an over-reliance on mindless communication.

▧ APPLYING WHAT YOU'VE LEARNED

As communication consultants, one of the best lessons we've learned about wrapping up an intervention is an activity called "What Will You Do Monday Morning?" Much of what you have read here mirrors what we offer our clients, inasmuch as we teach them a new vocabulary for addressing their problems and offer them tools for solving them. On Monday morning they return to their old jobs as newly minted organizational communicators, duly armed with new ways of thinking about, and thinking together about, issues as they arise at work.

Before we let them go we ask them to work together on one or more of the following four scenarios. Each scenario—or "caselet"—depicts a typical organizational dilemma and asks them to provide (1) an analysis of the situation based on what they have learned with us and (2) alternative plans to address or resolve the difficulty. Now that you have been educated to approach organizational life in a uniquely prepared way, we think this exercise will be valuable for you as well.

☐ King Dick

Richard is a senior vice president of technology for a large multinational firm specializing in athletic sportswear. Richard is a man driven by his own vision of perfection—to be the best at everything he does. This admirable motivation to succeed and competitive spirit has made him a local sports celebrity, with amateur awards and first-place trophies in golf, tennis, hockey, and billiards. It also has been a significant force in his meteoric rise from entry-level computer technician, at twenty-three, to senior vice president at the still youthful age of thirty-nine.

As he rose in the company, the company invested in him. At first they sponsored trips to management seminars, but as his strong motivation to "be the Man" led him further and further up the corporate ladder, they also provided Richard with access to the world's leading authorities on organizational leadership. Always, whether during retreats or seminars, Richard made a point of being heard, of proving that he was the one who had the answers and should, therefore, be in charge.

Moving up from middle management of computer resources into his first senior-level job as director of global networks, he confronted three new challenges. First, he had never operated as the leader of a group or of a network before. However, his track record of success in team sports combined with his stellar ratings in seminars marked him as capable of learning this aspect of his new job quickly. The second challenge was that his position was truly one that required constant contact with clients, customers, and support technicians in India, Ireland, Spain, France, Indonesia, and Mexico. Richard, like many North American men, does not speak any other languages, nor had he traveled extensively to any of those countries. The third challenge is harder to define. Richard is, as we said, a driven man, a competitor, and a consistent winner. He does not handle defeat well, probably because he has experienced it so rarely in his adult life. So when things don't exactly work out the way he planned, he explodes. In one recent meeting of his increasingly quiet, cowering managerial staff, he harshly interrupted a young woman, Tatiana, who was trying to explain why the backup systems failed a recent security test, with the question: "Do you want *me* to solve this problem *for* you? I can solve it, apparently unlike you or your half-witted staff, but I will guarantee you that neither you nor your half-witted staff will *enjoy* my solution. But you will all have to live with it. So, I ask you again, Tat, DO YOU WANT ME TO SOLVE THIS PROBLEM FOR YOU?"

You have been retained by Richard's company as an organizational communication and leadership consultant. Your job is to work with Richard to improve his leadership communication skills. It's Monday morning—what do you do?

☐ Miss Elizabeth

Elizabeth Peters is a woman in her mid-fifties with almost twenty years of seniority in a retail store that is part of a prominent national chain and is located in a suburban shopping mall in the southeastern United States. She is currently an assistant manager of the store after having been repeatedly turned down for promotion to store manager for reasons she associates with a sexist and racist superior in the regional corporate office. Her views of her manager are not shared by anyone who works with her, nor are they shared by his superiors at the corporate office.

Miss Elizabeth, as she demands to be called, is a technically proficient employee with a long list of customers, usually women "of a certain maturity" who can easily afford to spend large sums of money on clothing and accessories in the store. She guards her list of "preferred customers" and regularly hides new shipments from other sales associates so that she can provide them to her own customers. Partly for this reason, she also produces an annual level of sales far superior to anyone else's. A few years ago, when a former manager threatened to let her go because of her "uncooperative attitude," Miss Elizabeth made a few phone calls and had her manager removed instead. She clearly has friends in high places.

She is also a widow who lost her much older insurance broker husband to a heart attack. Prior to his passing the two of them were hailed as community leaders because of their wide-ranging charitable activities and support of the local community theater. In those days, she had been a leading actress and had previously been a beauty queen, and he had been an adoring theater-goer with no wife and deep pockets. When her husband died, she discovered that the life insurance policy he had written on himself barely paid off their splendid house in one of the better parts of town and did not insure a future for her without work. That is when she became an assistant manager, and that is when she used her contacts in the community to build her solid client list.

You have recently assumed the position of manager of the store. A week did not pass before each one of the sales associates had drawn you aside to complain about Miss Elizabeth. At first you sensed a conspiracy among the younger employees to get rid of Miss Elizabeth, and told them that you believed in giving every employee a fair chance to prove him- or herself. In staff meetings for the first month you couldn't help notice that Miss Elizabeth arrived late, left early, and mostly attended to her client list during your talks. When you asked her to perform a routine task, such as changing the clothes on a display or opening the store on a Saturday, she politely but firmly refused, suggesting that "perhaps this is the sort of task that ought to be assigned to someone with less seniority." At first you went along with her because she was, well, significantly older than you and because she seemed so confident that hers was the better way. This is your first management position and you have been out of college for only two years.

In short order you lose three valuable employees. They all clearly stated that they were leaving the store because they couldn't put up with Miss Elizabeth any longer. You called the regional corporate office and asked for advice from your mentor, who warned you that Miss Elizabeth was a legendary sales leader and that no matter what, you could not fire her. She advised that you needed to find some other way to solve your personnel problem. It's Monday morning—what do you do?

☐ Phone Rage

You are a customer service representative for a financial group whose clients are brokerage houses. It's a good job and pays well but has a downside. In this case, the downside is a client named Mr. Roberto Santini, Esquire, a senior stockbroker with a law degree and an MBA from Columbia University, a bachelor's from Princeton, and a war record from the Persian Gulf that includes a Silver Star and a Purple Heart. You know all of these things about Mr. Santini because he makes a point of dropping them into his phone conversations as if to repeatedly emphasize his superiority over you.

Mr. Santini is also very rich and powerful. His firm's account is vital to the success of your company and his happiness and relative satisfaction with the company is primarily *your* responsibility. Your co-workers often joke that you are, in fact, not a customer service rep, but "Santini's slave." You can't really deny it, but you would like to find a way to work with Mr. Santini on a somewhat more professional basis. If you can't, chances are very good that you will be forced to leave the company and, in the current economy, finding another job with what would only be a mediocre (if that) reference from your boss is unlikely.

And Santini, *Mr.* Santini, clearly understands this to be the case.

The phone rings, as it always does, ten minutes prior to the opening of your business day. But this is Mr. Santini, and Mr. Santini can call any time of the day or night and it is your job to deal with it.

"Hey, *jackass*, you there?" This is Mr. Santini's usual opening gambit. He never calls you by your name.

"Yes, Mr. Santini, I am here. And my name is Li." Inside, you seethe with anger. If your father knew someone talked to you like this, he would find the man and kill him. Which is precisely why you never mention this abuse at home.

"Yeah, *whatever*, jackass. So what do you have for me?" Santini's tone is visceral and bold, without a hint of respect.

So you run the numbers for him, just as you always do. From time to time he interrupts with some abrupt question, but by and large he just listens. Santini listens like other people speak—the absence of voice on his end of the phone feels like the presence of power. After you run the numbers for him, you ask, simply, "Will there be anything else, sir?"

Santini laughs. It is a dry laugh, full of menace. "You sound about the right age to enjoy this, jackass, so here's a fairy tale for you. Consider it a gift. Once upon a time, back when I was a tank commander on the second day of the Gulf War, we spotted a group of retreating enemy soldiers on the other side of a dune. They were scared shitless. So you know what I did?"

"No, Mr. Santini, what did you do?"

"I pointed my cannon at them and gave the order to fire." He paused, and the dry laugh came over the line again.

"Why did you *do* that, if they were retreating?"

"Because they were the enemy and because they were retreating," he said. "I never had any respect for a coward."

"Why are you telling me this?"

"Because, jackass, I think *you* are a coward, too."

There was a click and the line went silent.

You can't afford to lose this job, nor do you feel that you should have to be the one to back down in this situation. At the same time, you feel that you can't take much more of this abuse. After a long weekend of stewing in anger, it's Monday morning—what do you do?

☐ Whistle While You Work?

You are a public relations spokesperson for a major pharmaceutical company located in the northeastern United States. The company has made over-the-counter drugs for relief of headache pain and muscle aches for nearly thirty years. By and large, your relationship with the company has been very positive and you enjoy working as their spokesperson. You have applauded their efforts to provide free drugs to state nursing homes and day-care centers with tight budgets.

But recently something has come up that you feel isn't being handled correctly. Three teams of research scientists, in separate studies funded by this pharmaceutical firm, have discovered that people who take their best-selling pain reliever for prolonged periods of time often have "rebound syndrome"—that is, what the scientists are calling the propensity of the human brain to lose its natural ability to recognize pain signals as a result of exposure to the active ingredient in the pain reliever. For about a year the senior public relations officials have maneuvered around this issue by suggesting that the studies are "preliminary" and the findings "inconclusive."

But this is not what the research scientist in charge of one of the studies has told you in confidence. And you suspect he told you such sensitive information to impress you because he wants to date you. His claim is that the evidence is overwhelming but that the company is keeping it quiet because this would effectively end sales of this drug and seriously reduce profits for the foreseeable future.

It's Monday morning. What should you do?

Summary

Working with integrity is important to the well-being of individuals, organizations, society, and the planet. As we have shown in this concluding chapter, working with integrity means refusing to rely on old scripts and making informed choices about how you think, communicate, and act.

Working with integrity is primarily enabled by your willingness to learn how to think together and to discipline yourself to the habits and practices of mindful communication. In this way, working with integrity asks you to apply the lessons of balancing creativity and constraint through dialogue. It asks you to respect others and to respect yourself, to reach out to others while standing your ground. It asks you to live and work honorably, by accepting full responsibility for not only what you say and do, but for your human connection to the world outside your room and to people whom you have never met who nevertheless are now—and will always continue to be—affected by the choices you make, the decisions you reach, the words and actions you offer to the world.

Thank you for allowing us into your reading life. Thank you for inviting us into your ongoing conversation about communication, organizations, and the future we will make out of them.

QUESTIONS FOR REVIEW AND DISCUSSION

1. What aspects of your life do you consider to be the most scripted? Why?

2. Under what circumstances do you behave most mindfully? Think of situations in jobs or classes that required a great deal of mindfulness from employees and/or students. Did the expected degree of mindfulness cause any problems?

3. How might the four alternative metaphors — poetry, discourse, voice, and performance — be put to practical use by organizational leaders? What do these metaphors highlight that prior lenses for seeing organizations do not?

4. How do national cultures vary in their approach to communication and conflict?

5. What is the relationship between organizational communication and working with integrity?

KEY TERMS

Collectivist cultures, p. 353
Discourse, p. 348
Individualist cultures, p. 352
Integrity, p. 346
Mindful dialogue, p. 354
Mindfulness, p. 345

Performance, p. 348
Phatic communication, p. 344
Poetry, p. 348
Scripts, p. 344
Transaction culture, p. 353
Voice, p. 348

A Field Guide to Studying Organizational Communication

Many students enrolled in an organizational communication course are required to write a term paper. Usually, the paper involves applying concepts from the course to ongoing communication processes within an organization. In most cases, when presented with the requirement to write a paper of this sort, students ask for more specific guidelines—the practical how-tos—of studying organizational communication.

For this reason, we have prepared the following practical field guide to studying organizational communication. The use of the term *field guide* is intended to evoke an *ethnographic* approach to collecting data, analyzing it, and writing the paper. (For an extended discussion, see Goodall, 2000.) An ethnographic approach uses

- *Naturalistic observation* of everyday communication episodes and events as the primary source of data
- *Participant-observer interaction and interviews* to collect stories, accounts, and explanations for the events and episodes observed
- *A critical/historical framework* for developing key questions, problems, and issues to pursue through observations of and interactions with employees
- *A narrative format* for describing and analyzing the data

In short, what we describe is a way of doing field research in an organization for the purpose of finding and telling the story of one or more of its everyday communication practices.

▧ FINDING AN ORGANIZATION TO STUDY

One of the axioms of organizational ethnography is that you must *"know* where you are" (Goodall, 1994, p. 176). This means (in academic-speak) that all knowledge is *contextually derived;* it also means that it is a good idea to study an organization within the community in which you live. Why? Because chances are pretty good that access to the organization will be easier to acquire (e.g., friends and family members may work there, you may have had summer employment or an internship there, you may know someone who knows someone, etc.). Additionally, you will probably have a basic understanding of the history and role of the organization within the community, which will come in handy when you write the paper. If you are not a local and don't have personal contacts that can provide access to the organization for the purpose of conducting a communication study, ask your instructor for advice and guidance.

Approaching an organization for the purpose of doing a study is always problematic. Many for-profit companies and government agencies strictly limit access to employees and usually have no interest in allowing students from the local college or university to hang around observing people, interviewing employees and managers, and otherwise disrupting their work. Some companies even have regulations against it — and no company or agency is required to let you inside.

For these reasons, it is a good idea to develop a professional relationship with the organization you want to study before requesting permission to do a communication study. The more the people you contact trust you, the more they learn to see you as a serious person, the more likely it is that they will cooperate with your goals. To facilitate your professional relationship, we recommend the following:

- Write a one-page proposal detailing the purpose and time frame for your study, the methods of data collection that you plan to use, and the anticipated results. Your instructor can provide you with examples from prior student projects.
- Offer to provide the organization with a copy of your final paper. Agree that nothing you discover or write about will be disseminated to the public without prior written approval by the company.
- Always arrive at any appointment on time, dressed in a professional manner appropriate to the standards of the organization you want to study, with a prepared list of questions to ask and a way of recording or keeping notes of the interview.
- Never directly interfere with ongoing organizational work. Make your observations as unobtrusively as possible; schedule interviews for times convenient for the interviewees.

◼ FRAMING YOUR STUDY

To write a proposal for the study, you will first need to develop a research question and ground your study in the current research literature. These writing processes are called "framing a study" because, like placing a photograph within an appropriate frame, they allow you to place your *story* within a larger academic or professional *narrative*.

There are three major resources for locating information that might help you frame a study. First, as a student, you are part of a college or university that has resident experts in just about every aspect of life. Locate an instructor with research expertise in the general area that interests you. Arrange to interview her or him to find out what the current thinking is on the general topic you have selected. Be sure to ask what the two or three best articles are on the subject, and then go to your library and check them out. For example, let's assume you want to study the specific organizational practices associated with building and maintaining a learning organization. Chances are good that someone in the communication department or the business school will be able to help you find resources to frame a study of a learning organization.

The second resource is the library. Using the references provided in this book—as well as any additional ones provided by your instructor and local university experts in the subject area—you should be able to conduct library research on most topics relevant to organizational communication. If the library research process is unclear to you, contact your library for information about the research librarian most able to assist you with finding information about your topic.

A third resource is the Internet. By accessing on-line search engines like ProQuest and typing keywords, you can search a variety of databases for information. You may also join an Internet-based chat room or bulletin board where your topic is being discussed. Professional academic organizations typically sponsor such Internet activities and research sites. We recommend beginning your search by visiting the American Communication Association research site <http://www .americancomm.org/> or the National Communication Association research site <http://www.natcom.org>. You may also find relevant information by checking out the home pages of organizational communication scholars, who sometimes provide links to rich research resources relevant to their specialties.

After reading the available research on the general topic you plan to pursue, you should be able to articulate some of the questions that are of concern to scholars and professionals. Adapt these questions to the organization you plan to study and to the purpose of your paper.

Framing your study *before* you enter the organization for observations and interviews provides you with an important way to limit what you are looking at and asking questions about. You have to know what you are looking for in order to find it. However, as any ethnographer will tell you, surprises and setbacks will occur. You may find that the initial research question you posed doesn't really get at the meaning of the interactions you observe and participate in, or you may discover that you cannot complete all of the interviews you had planned. These are not necessarily problems, but they may be challenges. You may need to modify your research question. Settle for fewer interviews. Find other people to talk to. You may even need to reframe your study in light of what you find is *really* happening.

☒ TEN ASSUMPTIONS ABOUT DOING FIELD RESEARCH[1]

Organizational field researchers are interested in telling the stories that make up everyday organizational life. As such, they rarely are interested in issues typically associated with managerial notions of efficiency. For example, rather than asking how a particular routine can be streamlined or reengineered to improve the efficiency of an operation, field research asks how that particular routine came to be a routine and what it requires (mentally, morally, physically, culturally) of a person or group to accomplish it. Other characteristics of field research include:

1. Field research is *qualitative* in nature. The quality of it is largely dependent on the insights discovered by the researcher. By contrast, many worthwhile organizational studies are *quantitative*, which means that they derive their conclusions from facts that are amenable to statistical tabulation and analysis. Field research, being qualitative, derives insights from close observation of actual, ongoing, communication processes. Conclusions are generalizable; insights are contextual.

2. Field research begins from theoretical assumptions and conceptual underpinnings but is more generally dedicated to providing documentation for the *moral and ethical* knowledge of working. For this reason, many contemporary ethnographic studies of organizations focus on issues of power and strategic control, as well as on race, age, and gender.

3. Field research assumes that every organization is as unique as an individual human fingerprint. One way to think about this is that people are not understood as "types," and activities and practices are not reducible to "behaviors."

4. What people at work *say* and *do* are the substance of who they are (at work) and what your study should be about. By comparison, think of what you

---

[1]Some of the material contained in this section is adapted from a working paper developed by Michael E. Pacanowsky, "An Idiosyncratic Compilation of the Twenty-Seven Do's and Don'ts of Organizational Culture Research," unpublished paper, Department of Communication, University of Utah, 1986.

are studying as an exercise in observing and documenting a television sit-com about work. What is the setting? Who are the characters? Where do they come from? What are their dreams? What do they think about their jobs? About each other? What do they talk about? What clothes do they wear? And so on. You might want to practice your skills by observing and analyzing just such a television show.

5. Remember that you won't be watching a television show when you enter an organization. These aren't actors performing rehearsed scripts written by someone else. That is a major difference, and one that ultimately matters. You are studying ongoing life — *real* life. In real-life studies, expect a lot of empty spaces between the meaningful interactions. Don't expect conflicts to be solved in thirty minutes or less. People won't be as funny as they are on television, nor are they working out a predetermined theme. The theme, the thing you are studying, the story you are trying to find and tell about, emerges gradually from disparate places and people. *You* are the script-writer.

6. Don't neglect the places — the *contexts* — and their influences over the interaction. As Marshall Sahlins, a famous anthropologist, once put it, "A culture is the meaningful order of persons and things." Don't forget to observe *things*. Describe them. Ask people to comment on their meanings, *here*.

7. There is no such thing as "an organization." In real life, there are only "organization*s*," which means that every person you observe and talk to will have a slightly different take on what "reality" is. The farther you move away from a particular group of people who interact regularly and have tacitly agreed to see reality in similar ways, the more different and complex "reality" becomes.

8. You aren't going to find any one truth. At best, you will find many copresent and conflicting truths. That is why field researchers learn to think (and write) about life as a "plural present" (Goodall, 1991a, p. 320). If you doubt this statement, ask the same question three levels up the organization's ladder from where you are locating your study, and then three levels below it.

9. You are studying the *particulars* of human actions. Pay close attention to details. Nuances of speaking, of gesturing, of touching, of *not* saying something, all count. You are looking at what is said and done, what is given or foregrounded, but you are searching for what is unspoken, not done, withheld, and in the background, in the depths of shadows only the actors know.

10. Write down *everything* you observe and hear. You never know what will end up being important. Tape-record or videotape what you are allowed to record. Write out your notes and transcriptions the same day you take them (or else you lose 83 percent of the meaning), and write them out in story format. That is how, when, and where you will ultimately find the story line.

◫ HOW TO STUDY NATURALISTIC COMMUNICATION IN AN ORGANIZATION: A BASIC PROCESS OUTLINE WITH COMMENTARY[2]

We have found that it is very useful to instruct students to take field notes on their observations, interviews, conversations, and personal reflections on the meanings of people at work. Taking field notes is akin to keeping a diary, but instead of writing about your family and your love life, you write about your working life. In a notebook or on your computer, describe the events of your day, make theoretical and practical connections to what you are reading and thinking about, and try to use the writing process to help you figure out how to connect the dots that gradually emerge from your study.

To help you take field notes, here is a list of people and things, activities, symbols, and events that occur and have some meaning in most organizations. This list may help you isolate field note entries and organize your research.

- Begin in the parking lot. Begin early. Watch the cars file in, and note where they park. Make notes on the kinds of vehicles that individuals drive. At lunchtime, observe who drives the gang from work, and where they go. If possible, join in on their lunch conversations. Watch when they leave work in the afternoon or late evening. Who leaves last? Why?
- Phone the public relations department, and ask for a company tour. Explain that you are doing research on similar types of companies in the area. Listen carefully to what the official version of the company is during the tour, and collect as much written documentation as possible. These resources will become important to you later.
- Research the financial standing of the company if it is publicly held. How is it doing? How does it compare to other companies in the industry? Do a keyword search for the local newspapers in your library to see what kinds of stories have appeared about the company and about its people in the past year or so. These details can become useful as a way of understanding the evolving context of the interaction.
- Make a chart of all the people (or the department) you plan to include in your study, and note their organizational relationships to one another. Ask yourself how your understanding of organizational hierarchies may inform what you are observing.

---

[2]The following outline will not apply equally to all organizations or be appropriate for all classes in organizational communication. Some advisories provided here will fit the place you want to study; some won't. We recommend limiting your study to a particular work group, team, or department, but your instructor may want a larger-scale study. Depending on your instructor's preferences, you may also want to conduct a quantitative study, in which case all of the information in this appendix may help you create material from which you develop hypotheses to test via surveys or experiments.

Using what you have read in this book about classical theories of organization and communication, what kind of organization would you say this is? Do you see Frederick Taylor or Abraham Maslow lurking about? Is this more like a Theory X or a Theory Y company? Are elements of all of the classical theories evident here? If not, why not? If so, what does this suggest to you about theories of organizing or about this place?

Now think about this group or department as a system or as part of a system. Draw or describe the group's interactions accordingly. Think about the organization of feedback among members of the group. Think about access to and distribution of information. Listen to their accounts of "how things are around here," and see if Karl Weick's "retrospective sense making" helps you understand them. Keep applying ideas from what you read to what you are seeing, hearing, and attending to.

Now do the same sort of thing with your knowledge of organizational cultures, by assuming that these people are part of a culture. They *are* part of a culture, so this shouldn't be too difficult.

Ask questions about leadership and power. Who is in charge here — *really* in charge? How do you know that? What is it about this person's communication, manner, style, or attitude that conveys this to the people here? Perhaps there is no one leader. How is leadership shared? What does that mean, in terms of exchanges of talk, every day? In either case, how are individuals' control needs being met? How are they negotiated? What conflicts exist? How do you know this? What happens to inform your evaluations and your judgments?

- Using what you have learned about the study of power, how would you describe its uses and abuses in this locale? Is power linked to gender? To race? To age? To beauty? Are there different forms and expressions of power? Is power related to expertise? If so, how? If not, what is it related to?

- Given that all organizations exist within a global economic structure and have dealt with issues of reorganization, downsizing, team-based organizing, flattening hierarchies, information technologies, and other concepts associated with the rise of the postmodern, what *stories* are told here about all of that? Are there heroes and heroines? Villains? Legendary mistakes? Bits of good fortune? What do these people talk about when they talk about the future? Are there active company training programs? What do people say about them? Are they preparing for a lifetime of employment with this company?

- You want to find as much as you can about each individual's personal experience of work. See what you can observe, discover, or otherwise find out about the organizational socialization process, about signs of organizational identification, satisfaction, and burnout. How do individuals deal with differences that make a difference in the workplace? (See Chapter 7.) How do people negotiate the work/life balance? What stressors do people routinely deal with? How do they deal with them? Is there any difference between what they say and what you observe? What can this mean?

- How are work groups, teams, and networks organized in this organization? What systems of problem solving and decision making are employed? What is the influence of information technology on their operation and functions? What have you learned from reading about groups, teams, and networks that seems to apply directly to what happens here? What doesn't apply? For example, do you find evidence for the concept of team learning or interorganizational networks?

- You want to attune yourself to the ways in which the overall vision, mission, and core values of the organization play out in everyday discourse and interactions. Are the workers familiar enough with the organization's vision, mission, and values to talk openly about them? Do they try to consciously apply them to their everyday work habits? Where are the deviations? Why are there deviations? Are the deviations a sign of resistance or perhaps only of ignorance? How does this group or department handle crises? How do individual members' identities figure into the image of the firm?

- Trace the uses of technology in this organization. Are there stories about the introduction of new technologies? What lessons were learned about technology that are practiced today? How are the members of this department preparing themselves for continuing demands for technological skill and knowledge? How has the availability of laptop computers, cell phones, pagers, and the like changed their working and personal lives? How do they feel about this?

- What is the role of communication consulting and training in this group or department? Is there an overall company plan for training and development, or is it left up to the individual workers? What kinds of issues or problems are managed by the group or department, and what kinds of issues or problems require the assistance of a professional consultant? How satisfied are the employees with past consulting interventions? What stories do they tell? How do the members describe the future of this company or agency? Do their metaphors suggest particular scenarios?

- Remember, you are studying everyday communication in this organization. How are you defining *communication* for the purposes of your study? What counts as communication? What doesn't? How valuable is our definition in your study? Can you see communication as the moment-to-moment working out of the tensions between individuals' desire for creativity and the organization's need for constraint (order)? When you examine your field notes with this definition in mind, what is accounted for? What is left out?

- If you are still having trouble deciding how to tell this story, go back over your notes and look carefully at the metaphors used by employees and managers. Many organizational scholars believe that people live and interpret their lives through the linguistic lenses of their daily metaphors. What metaphors do you find in their talk? What metaphors do you see in their actions and activities? What does the presence of these particular metaphors suggest are their binary opposites? Are the binary opposites places where you can also make sense of the unsaid, the unspoken, the covered up, or the neglected?

- When you write your account, include as many particulars — reports of conversations and observations of actions, clothes, cars, and gestures — as you can. These are your primary sources of evidence for the case that you are making. Remember that it is a case that *you* are making. You are ultimately responsible for what you say. Your views will not necessarily be the views of the people you have observed, of your instructor, or of the authors of this textbook. Write what you have lived through, what you have experienced, in the course of doing your research.

- Make sure you follow the style guide (APA, MLA, Chicago, Turabian, etc.) appropriate to your instructor's requirements.

▨ TYPICAL ORGANIZATION OF A PAPER BASED ON FIELD STUDY METHODS

Research reports typically follow an established pattern. Below we offer one you can use to organize your paper.

Title page
  Title of the paper
  Your name, class, and instructor
  Date
  Academic integrity statement (optional)

Abstract
  Brief description of the purposes of the study and its conclusions

Introduction
  Narrative orientation to the company, team, or department studied
  Statement about the specific purpose of the study
  Literature review (focusing on the specific topic area)
  Research questions
  Description of method chosen to answer the questions

Body
  Narrative account of the organization's communication organized *linearly* over time from initial observations through final conclusions and *topically* by communication issue or question raised
  Analysis and interpretation of the field study via research questions

Conclusion
   Review of the study, purpose, method, and major insights
   Link or contribution of this study to current literature on the topic
   Conclusion and suggestions for future research

References

Good luck! Studying and writing about organizations and communication can be an interesting and rewarding activity. It allows you to really work with concepts, apply them to ongoing processes of communicating and organizing, and find meaning in otherwise everyday occurrences. It will enrich your educational experience.

References

Acker, J. (1990). Hierarchies, jobs, bodies: A theory of gendered organization. *Gender & Society*, *4*, 139–148.

Adams, J. (1980). Interorganizational processes and organizational boundary activities. In L. L. Cummings & B. Staw (Eds.), *Research in organizational behavior* (Vol. 2, pp. 321–355). Greenwich, CT: JAI Press.

Adorno, T., & Horkheimer, M. (1972). *Dialectic of enlightenment*. New York: Herder and Herder.

Ahrne, G. (1990). *Agency and organization*. London: Sage.

Alberts, J., Lutgen-Sandvik, P., & Tracy, S. (2005). Escalated incivility: Analyzing workplace bullying as a communication phenomenon. Paper presented at the annual meeting of the International Communication Association, New York.

Alberts, J., Lutgen-Sandvik, P., & Tracy, S. (in press). Is it really that bad? A metaphorical analysis exploring the emotional pain of workplace bullying. *Management Communication Quarterly*.

Albrecht, K. (1992). *The only thing that matters: Bringing the power of the customer into the center of your business*. New York: HarperBusiness.

Albrecht, T., & Adelman, M. (1987). *Communicating social support*. Beverly Hills, CA: Sage.

Albrecht, T., & Hall, B. (1991). Facilitating talk about new ideas: The role of personal relationships in organizational innovation. *Communication Monographs*, *58*, 273–288.

Alimo-Metcalfe, B., & Alban-Metcalfe, J. (2005). Leadership: Time for a new direction? *Leadership*, *1*, 51–71.

Allen, B. (2000). "Learning the ropes": A Black feminist standpoint analysis. In P. Buzzanell (Ed.), *Rethinking organizational & managerial communication from feminist perspectives* (pp. 177–208). Thousand Oaks, CA: Sage.

Allen, B. (2003). *Difference matters: Communicating social identity*. Long Grove, IL: Waveland.

Allen, B. (2005). Social constructionism. In S. May & D. Mumby (Eds.), *Engaging organizational communication theory and research: Multiple perspectives* (pp. 35–54). Thousand Oaks, CA: Sage.

Altman, S., Valenzi, E., & Hodgetts, R. (1985). *Organizational behavior: Theory and practice*. New York: Academic Press.

Alvesson, M. (1993). *Cultural perspectives on organizations*. New York: Cambridge University Press.

Alvesson, M., & Wilmott, H. (2002). Identity regulation as organizational control: Producing the appropriate individual. *Journal of Management Studies*, *39*, 619–644.

American Anti-Slavery Group. (2005). Slavery around the world. Retrieved January 25, 2006, from http://www.iabolish.com/slavery_today/primer/map.html

Anderson, J. (1987). *Communication research: Issues and methods*. New York: McGraw-Hill.

Anderson, R., Cissna, K., & Arnett, R. (1994). *The reach of dialogue*. Cresskill, NJ: Hampton Press.

Andrews, L. (2000). *The Hillsborough River Greenways Taskforce: An ethnographic study of collaboration for the love of a river*. Unpublished doctoral dissertation, University of South Florida, Tampa, FL.

Annie, P. (2005). Leadership and organizing: Sensemaking and organizing in action. *Leadership, 1*, 31–49.

Arena, M., & Arrigo, B. (2005). Social psychology, terrorism, and identity: A preliminary re-examination of theory, culture, self, and society. *Behavioral Sciences and the Law, 23*, 485–506.

Argyris, C. (1957). *Personality and organization*. New York: Harper & Row.

Argyris, C., & Schon, D. (1978). *Organizational learning: A theory of action perspective*. Reading, MA: Addison-Wesley.

Armstrong, N. (2005, June). Resistance through risk: Women and cervical cancer screening. *Health, Risk & Society, 7*, 161–176.

Arquilla, J., & Ronfeldt, D. (1997). *In Athena's camp: Preparing for conflict in the Information Age*. Santa Monica, CA: Rand Corporation.

Arquilla, J., & Ronfeldt, D. (2001). *Networks and netwars: The future of terror, crime, and militancy*. Santa Monica, CA: Rand Corporation.

Ashcraft, K. (1999). Managing maternity leave: A qualititative analysis of temporary executive succession. *Administrative Science Quarterly, 44*, 240–280.

Ashcraft, K. (2000). Empowering "professional" relationships: Organizational communication meets feminist practice. *Management Communication Quarterly, 13*, 347–392.

Ashcraft, K. (2001). Organized dissonance: Feminist bureaucracy as hybrid form. *Academy of Management Journal, 44*, 1301–1322.

Ashcraft, K. (2004). Gender, discourse, and organization: Framing a shifting relationship. In D. Grant, C. Hardy, C. Oswick, & L. Putnam (Eds.), *The Sage handbook of organizational discourse* (pp. 275–291). London: Sage.

Ashcraft, K. (2005). Feminist organizational communication studies: Engaging gender in public and private. In S. May & D. Mumby (Eds.), *Engaging organizational communication theory and research: Multiple perspectives* (pp. 141–170). Thousand Oaks, CA: Sage.

Ashcraft, K., & Allen, B. (2003). The racial foundation of organizational communication. *Communication Theory, 13*, 5–38.

Ashcraft, K., & Flores, L. (2003). "Slaves with white collars": Persistent performances of masculinity in crisis. *Text and Performance Quarterly, 23*, 1–29.

Ashcraft, K., & Mumby, D. (2004). *Reworking gender: A feminist communicology of organization*. Thousand Oaks, CA: Sage.

Ashcraft, K., & Pacanowsky, M. (1996). "A woman's worst enemy": Reflections on a narrative of organizational life and female identity. *Journal of Applied Communication Research, 24*, 217–239.

Ashcraft, K., & Trethewey, A. (2004). Developing tension: An agenda for applied research on the "organization of irrationality." *Journal of Applied Communication Research, 32*, 171–181.

Ashford, S., & Cummings, L. (1983). Feedback as an individual resource: Personal strategies of creating information. *Organizational Behavior and Human Performance, 32*, 370–398.

Ashforth, B., & Kreiner, G. (1999). How can you do it? Dirty work and the challenge of constructing a positive identity. *Academy of Management Review, 24*, 413–434.

Atkouf, O. (1992). Management and theories of organizations in the 1990's: Toward a critical radical humanism? *Academy of Management Review, 17,* 407–431.

Atwood, M. (1990). *Adolescent socialization into work environments.* Unpublished master's thesis, University of Southern California, Los Angeles.

Axley, S. (1984). Managerial and organizational communication in terms of the conduit metaphor. *Academy of Management Review, 9,* 428–437.

Baba, M. (1999). Dangerous liaisons: Trust, distrust, and information technology in American work organizations. *Human Organization, 58*(3), 331–346.

Babcock, L., & Laschever, S. (2003). *Women don't ask: Negotiation and the gender divide.* Princeton, NJ: Princeton University Press.

Baker, B. (1991, October 6). Safety risks: The price of productivity. *Los Angeles Times,* pp. 35–36.

Bakhtin, M. (1981). *The dialogic imagination* (C. Emerson & M. Holquist, Trans.). Austin: University of Texas Press.

Bakhtin, M. (1984). *Problems of Dostoevsky's poetics.* (C. Emerson, Ed. & Trans.). Minneapolis: University of Minnesota Press.

Bakhtin, M. (1986). *Speech genres and other late essays* (C. Emerson, Trans.). Minneapolis: University of Minnesota Press.

Bales, K. (2000). *Disposable people.* Berkeley: University of California Press.

Banks, A., & Banks, S. (1998). *Fiction and social research: By ice or fire.* Lanham, MD: Alta Mira.

Banta, M. (1993). *Taylored lives: Narrative productions in the age of Taylor, Veblen, and Ford.* Chicago: University of Chicago Press.

Bantz, C. (1993). *Understanding organizations: Interpreting organizational communication cultures.* Columbia: University of South Carolina Press.

Barabasi, A. (2002). *Linked: The new science of networks.* Cambridge, MA: Perseus.

Barbaro, M. (2005, October 24). Wal-Mart to expand health plan for workers. *New York Times.* Retrieved February 11, 2006, from http://www.nytimes.com/2005/10/24/business/24mart.html

Barge, K., & Little, M. (2002). Dialogical wisdom, communicative practice, and organizational life. *Communication Theory, 12*(4), 375–397.

Barker, J. (1993). Tightening the iron cage: Concertive control in self-managing teams. *Administrative Science Quarterly, 38,* 408–437.

Barker, J. (1999). *The discipline of teamwork: Participation and concertive control.* Thousand Oaks, CA: Sage.

Barker, J., & Cheney, G. (1994). The concept and practices of discipline in contemporary organizational life. *Communication Monographs, 61,* 19–43.

Barker, J., & Tompkins, P. (1994). Identification in the self-managing organization: Characteristics of target and tenure. *Human Communication Research, 21,* 223–240.

Barley, S. (1983). Semiotics and the study of occupational and organizational culture. *Administrative Science Quarterly, 23,* 393–413.

Barnard, C. (1968). *The functions of the executive.* Cambridge, MA: Harvard University Press. (Original work published 1938)

Barnet, R., & Cavanagh, J. (1994). *Global dreams.* New York: Simon & Schuster.

Barnlund, D. (1994). *Communicative styles of Japanese and Americans.* Belmont, CA: Wadsworth.

Barrett, F. (1998). Creativity and improvisation in jazz and organizations: Implications for organizational learning. *Organizational Science, 9,* 605–622.

Barry, D., & Elmes, M. (1997). Strategy retold: Toward a narrative view of strategic discourse. *Academy of Management Review, 22,* 429–452.

Bartlett, C., & Ghoshal, S. (1994, November–December). Changing the role of top management: Beyond strategy to purpose. *Harvard Business Review,* 79–88.

Bash, D., Mirian, A., & Newman, L. (2005, November). Americas summit protest turns violent. Retrieved January 12, 2006, from http://www.cnn.com/2005/WORLD/americas/11/04/bush.summit/

Bastien, D., & Hostager, T. (1988). Jazz as a process of organizational innovation. *Communication Research*, *15*, 582–602.

Bateson, G. (1972). *Steps to an ecology of mind*. New York: Ballantine.

Bauer, T., & Green, S. (1996). Development of leader member exchange: A longitudinal test. *Academy of Management Journal*, *39*, 1538–1567.

Baxter, L. A., & DeGooyer, D. H., Jr. (2001). Perceived aesthetic characteristics of interpersonal conversations. *Southern Communication Journal*, *67*, 1–18.

Baxter, L. A., & Montgomery, B. (1996). *Relating: Dialogues and dialectics*. New York: Guilford.

Bean, C. & Eisenberg, E. (2006). Employee sense-making in the transition to nomadic work. *Journal of Organizational Change Management*, 19, 210–222.

Beato, C. V. (2004, February 18). Progress review: Occupational safety and health. *Healthy People 2010*. Retrieved March 10, 2006 from http://www.healthypeople.gov/data/2010prog/focus20/default.htm

Beckett, R. (2005). Communication ethics: Principle and practice. *Journal of Communication Management*, 9, 41–52.

Bell, A. H., & Williams, G. G. (1999). *Intercultural business*. Hauppauge, NY: Barron's.

Bell, E., & Forbes, L. (1994). Office folklore in the academic paperwork empire: The interstitial space of gendered (con)texts. *Text and Performance Quarterly*, *38*, 181–196.

Bell, E., & Nkomo, S. (2001). *Our separate ways: Black and White women and the struggle for professional identity*. Boston: Harvard Business School Press.

Bellah, R., Madsen, R., Sullivan, W., Swidler, A., & Tipton, S. (1985). *Habits of the heart*. Berkeley: University of California Press.

Bell-Detienne, K. (1992). *The control factor: An empirical investigation of employees' reaction to control in an organizational work environment*. Unpublished doctoral dissertation, University of Southern California, Los Angeles.

Bendix, R. (1956). *Work and authority in industry*. New York: Wiley.

Benne, K., & Sheats, P. (1948). Functional roles of group members. *Journal of Social Issues*, *4*, 41–49.

Bennis, W. (1998). *On becoming a leader*. London: Arrow.

Bennis, W., & Nanus, B. (2003). *Leaders: Strategies for taking charge*. New York: HarperCollins.

Benoit, P. (1997). *Telling the success story: Acclaiming and disclaiming discourse*. Albany: SUNY Press.

Berger, P., & Luckmann, T. (1967). *The social construction of reality*. Garden City, NY: Anchor.

Berlo, D. (1960). *The process of communication*. New York: Holt.

Bhabha, H. (1990). Dissemination: Time, narrative, and the modern nation. In H. Bhabha (Ed.), *Nation and narration* (pp. 291–322). London: Routledge.

Bingham, S. (1991). Communication strategies for managing sexual harassment in organizations: Understanding message options and their effects. *Journal of Applied Communication Research*, *19*, 88–115.

Bingham, S., & Battey, K. (2005). Communication of social support to sexual harassment victims: Professors' responses to a student's narrative of unwanted sexual attention. *Communication Studies*, *56*, 131–155.

Blair, C., Brown, J., & Baxter, L. (1995). Disciplining the feminine. *Quarterly Journal of Speech*, *81*, 1–24.

Blake, R., & Mouton, J. (1964). *The managerial grid*. Houston, TX: Gulf.

Blake, R., & Mouton, J. (1985). *The managerial grid III: The key to leadership excellence*. Houston, TX: Gulf.

Block, P. (1993). *Stewardship*. San Francisco: Berrett-Koehler.

Blumer, H. (1969). *Symbolic interactionism: Perspective and method*. Englewood Cliffs, NJ: Prentice Hall.

Bochner, A. (1982). The functions of human communication in interpersonal bonding. In C. Arnold & J. Waite-Bowser (Eds.), *Handbook of rhetorical and communication theory* (pp. 544–621). Boston: Allyn and Bacon.

Bohm, D. (1980). *Wholeness and the implicate order*. London: Ark.

Bohm, D. (1996). *On dialogue*. New York: Routledge.

Boje, D. (1991). The storytelling organization: A study of story performance in an office-supply firm. *Administrative Science Quarterly, 36*, 106–126.

Boje, D. (1995). Stories of the storytelling organization: A postmodern analysis of Disney in "Tamara-Land." *Academy of Management Journal, 38*, 997–1035.

Boland, R., & Hoffman, R. (1983). Humor in a machine shop. In L. Pondy, P. Frost, G. Morgan, & T. Dandridge (Eds.), *Organizational symbolism* (pp. 187–198). Greenwich, CT: JAI Press.

Brandenburger, A., & Nalebuff, B. (1996). *Co-opetition*. New York: Doubleday.

Brannan, M. (2005). Effects of communication trainings on medical student performance. *Gender, Work & Organization, 12*(5), 420–439.

Brass, D. (1984). Being in the right place: A structural analysis of individual influence in an organization. *Administrative Science Quarterly, 29*, 518–539.

Braverman, H. (1974). *Labor and monopoly capital: The degradation of work in the twentieth century*. New York: Monthly Review Press.

Brett, J. M., & Okumura, T. (1998). Inter- and intracultural negotiation: U.S. and Japanese negotiators. *Academy of Management Journal, 41*, 495–510.

Brewis, J., Hampton, M., & Linstead, S. (1997). Unpacking Priscilla: Subjectivity and identity in the organization of gendered appearance. *Human Relations, 50*, 1275–1304.

Browning, L. (1992a). Lists and stories as organizational communication. *Communication Theory, 2*, 281–302.

Browning, L. (1992b, May). *Reasons for success at Motorola*. Paper presented at the applied communication pre-conference of the International Communication Association, Miami.

Browning, L., & Shetler, J. (2000). *Sematech: Saving the U.S. semiconductor industry*. College Station: Texas A & M University Press.

Bruni, A., Gherardi, S., & Poggio, B. (2004). Doing gender, doing entrepreneurship: An ethnographic account of intertwined practices. *Gender, Work & Organization, 11*, 406–429.

Brzezinski, M. (2002, June 23). The re-engineering of the drug business. *New York Times Magazine*, pp. 24–29, 46, 54–55.

Buckley, W. (1967). *Sociology and modern systems theory*. Englewood Cliffs, NJ: Prentice Hall.

Bullis, C. (1999). Forum on organizational socialization research. *Communication Monographs, 66*, 368–373.

Bullis, C., & Bach, B. (1989). Socialization turning points: An examination of change in organizational identification. *Western Journal of Speech Communication, 53*, 273–293.

Bullis, C., & Glaser, H. (1992). Bureaucratic discourse and the Goddess: Towards an ecofeminist critique and rearticulation. *Journal of Organizational Change Management, 5*, 50–60.

Bullis, C., & Stout, K. R. (2000). Organizational socialization: A feminist standpoint approach. In P. Buzzanell (Ed.), *Rethinking organizational & managerial communication from feminist perspectives* (pp. 47–75). Thousand Oaks, CA: Sage.

Bullis, C., & Tompkins, P. (1989). The forest ranger revisited: A study of control practices and identification. *Communication Monographs, 56*, 287–306.

Burke, K. (1966). *Language as symbolic action*. Berkeley: University of California Press.

Burke, K. (1969). *A rhetoric of motives*. Berkeley: University of California Press.

Burke, K. (1989). *On symbols and society*. Chicago: University of Chicago Press.

Burke, R., Weir, T., & Duwors, R., Jr. (1979). Type A behavior of administrators and wives' reports of marital satisfaction and well-being. *Journal of Applied Psychology, 64,* 57–65.

Burrell, G. (1988). Modernism, postmodernism, and organizational analysis 2: The contribution of Michel Foucault. *Organization Studies, 9,* 221–235.

Burrell, N. A., Buzzanell, P., & McMillan, J. (1992). Feminine tensions in conflict situations as revealed by metaphoric analyses. *Management Communication Quarterly, 6,* 115–149.

Butler, J. (1988). Performative acts and gender constitution: An essay in phenomenology and feminist theory. *Theater Journal, 40,* 519–531.

Buzzanell, P. (2000a). Dialoguing. . . . In P. Buzzanell (Ed.), *Rethinking organizational & managerial communication from feminist perspectives* (pp. 257–264). Thousand Oaks, CA: Sage.

Buzzanell, P. (2000b). The promise and practice of the new career and social contract: Illusions exposed and suggestions for reform. In P. Buzzanell (Ed.), *Rethinking organizational & managerial communication from feminist perspectives* (pp. 209–235). Thousand Oaks, CA: Sage.

Buzzanell, P. (2000c). *Rethinking organizational & managerial communication from feminist perspectives* (pp. 3–23). Thousand Oaks, CA: Sage.

Buzzanell, P., & Liu, M. (2005). Struggling with maternity leave policies and practices: A poststructuralist feminist analysis of gendered organizing. *Journal of Applied Communication Research, 33,* 1–25.

Calas, M., & Smircich, L. (1996). From "the woman's" point of view: Feminist approaches to organization studies. In S. Clegg, C. Hardy, & W. Nord (Eds.), *Handbook of organization studies* (pp. 218–257). London: Sage.

Calder, B. (1977). An attribution theory of leadership. In B. Staw & G. Salancik (Eds.), *New directions in organizational behavior*. Chicago: St. Clair Press.

Calvert, L., & Ramsey, V. (1992). Bringing women's voices to research on women in management: A feminist perspective. *Journal of Management Inquiry, 1,* 79–88.

Campbell, J., & Campbell, R. (1988). *Productivity in organizations*. San Francisco: Jossey-Bass.

Canary, D., & Hause, K. (1993). Is there any reason to study sex differences in communication? *Communication Quarterly, 41,* 129–144.

Carbaugh, D. (1995). *Are Americans really superficial? Notes on Finnish and American cultures in linguistic action*. Unpublished manuscript, University of Massachusetts at Amherst.

Carey, J. (1992). *Sexual harassment in the workplace*. New York: Practicing Law Institute.

Carlone, D., & Taylor, B. (1998). Organizational communication and cultural studies. *Communication Theory, 8,* 337–367.

Cartwright, D. (1977). Risk taking by individuals and groups: An assessment of research employing choice dilemmas. *Journal of Personality and Social Psychology, 85,* 361–378.

Cavallo, K., & Brienza, D. (2001). Emotional competence and leadership excellence at Johnson & Johnson. Message posted to http://www.eiconsortium.org

Chan, A., & Garrick, J. (2003). The moral "technologies" of knowledge management. *Information Communication & Society, 6,* 291–306.

Chandler, C., & Ingrassia, P. (1991, April 11). Shifting gears. *The Wall Street Journal*, p. 1.

Cheney, G. (1983). The rhetoric of identification and the study of organizational communication. *Quarterly Journal of Speech, 69,* 143–158.

Cheney, G. (1995). Democracy in the workplace: Theory and practice from the perspective of communication. *Journal of Applied Communication Research, 23,* 167–200.

Chiles, A., & Zorn, T. (1995). Empowerment in organizations: Employees' perceptions of the influences on empowerment. *Journal of Applied Communication Research, 23,* 1–25.

Chung, V. (2000). Men in nursing. MinorityNurse.com. Retrieved March 3, 2006, from http://www.minoritynurse.com/features/nurse_emp/08-30-00c.html

Clair, R. (1993). The use of framing devices to sequester organizational narratives: Hegemony and harassment. *Communication Monographs, 60,* 113–136.

Clair, R. (1996). The political nature of the colloquialism "a real job": Implications for organizational socialization. *Communication Monographs, 63,* 249–267.

Clair, R. (1998). *Organizing silence: A world of possibilities.* Albany: SUNY Press.

Clair, R. (Ed.). (2003). *Expressions of ethnography: Novel approaches to qualitative methods.* Albany: SUNY Press.

Clegg, S. (1989). *Frameworks of power.* Newbury Park, CA: Sage.

Clegg, S. (1990). *Modern organizations.* Newbury Park, CA: Sage.

Cleveland, J., & McNamara, K. (1996). Understanding sexual harassment. In M. Stockdale (Ed.), *Sexual harassment in the workplace* (pp. 217–240). Newbury Park, CA: Sage.

Clifford, J. (1992). Traveling cultures. In L. Grossberg, C. Nelson, & P. Treichler (Eds.), *Cultural studies* (pp. 96–116). New York: Routledge.

Clifford, J., & Marcus, G. (1985). *Writing culture: The poetics and politics of ethnography.* Berkeley: University of California Press.

Cohen, H. (1985). The development of research in speech communication: An historical perspective. In T. Benson (Ed.), *Speech communication in the 20th century* (pp. 282–298). Carbondale: Southern Illinois University Press.

Cohen, R. (2002, September 22). Discounting teens. *New York Times Magazine,* p. 26.

Collins, J. (2005). Level 5 leadership: The triumph of humility and fierce resolve. *Harvard Business Review, 83,* 136–147.

Collins, J., & Porras, J. (1994). *Built to last: Successful habits of visionary companies.* New York: HarperCollins.

Collins, J., & Porras, J. (1996). Building your company's vision. *Harvard Business Review, 74,* 65–78.

Collins, J., & Porras, J. (2002). *Built to last: Successful habits of visionary companies.* New York: HarperCollins.

Collinson, D. (1992). *Managing the shopfloor: Subjectivity, masculinity and workplace culture.* Berlin, Germany: Walter de Gruyter.

Collinson, D. (1999). "Surviving the rigs": Safety and surveillance and North Sea oil installations. *Organization Studies, 20,* 579–600.

Collinson, D. (2002). Managing humour. *Journal of Management Studies, 39,* 269–288.

Collinson, D., & Grint, K. (2005). Leadership. *Leadership, 1,* 1–10.

Coltrane, S. (2000). Research on household labor: Modeling and measuring the social embeddedness of routine family work. *Journal of Marriage and Family, 62,* 1208–1233.

Conger, J., & Kanungo, R. (1988). The empowerment process: Integrating theory and practice. *Academy of Management Review, 13,* 471–482.

Conlin, M. (1999, September 20). 9 to 5 isn't working anymore. *Business Week, 94,* 98.

Conquergood, D. (1991). Rethinking ethnography: Towards a critical cultural politics. *Communication Monographs, 58,* 179–194.

Conquergood, D. (1992). Ethnography, rhetoric, and performance. *Quarterly Journal of Speech, 78,* 80–97.

Conrad, C. (1983). Organizational power: Faces and symbolic forms. In L. Putnam & M. Pacanowsky (Eds.), *Communication and organizations* (pp. 173–194). Beverly Hills, CA: Sage.

Conrad, C. (1988). Work songs, hegemony, and illusions of self. *Critical Studies in Mass Communication, 5,* 179–201.

Conrad, C. (1991). Communication in conflict: Style-strategy relationships. *Communication Monographs, 58,* 135–155.

Conrad, C., & Poole, M. S. (Eds.). (1997). Communication in the age of the disposable worker. *Communication Research, 24,* 581–592.

Contractor, N. (1992). Self-organizing systems perspective in the study of organizational communication. In B. Kovacic (Ed.), *Organizational communication: New perspectives.* Albany: SUNY Press.

Contractor, N., & Eisenberg, E. (1990). Communication networks and the new media in organizations. In J. Fulk & C. Steinfeld (Eds.), *Organizations and communication technology* (pp. 143–172). Newbury Park, CA: Sage.

Contractor, N., Eisenberg, E., & Monge, P. (1992). *Antecedents and outcomes of interpretive diversity in organizations.* Unpublished manuscript, University of Illinois, Urbana.

Contractor, N., & Seibold, D. (1992). *Theoretical frameworks for the study of structuring processes in group decision support systems.* Unpublished manuscript, University of Illinois, Urbana.

Cooke, B., Mills, A., & Kelley, E. (2005). Situating Maslow in Cold War America: A recontextualization of management theory. *Group & Organization Management, 30,* 129–152.

Cooper, C. J. (1984). Executive stress: A ten country comparison. *Human Resource Management, 23,* 395–407.

Cooper, R. K. (2002). *The other 90%: How to unlock your vast untapped potential for leadership and life.* New York: Three Rivers Press.

Coopman, S. (2001). Democracy, performance, and outcomes in interdisciplinary health care teams. *Journal of Business Communication, 38,* 261–284.

Cooren, F. (2004). The communicative achievement of collective minding: Analysis of board meeting excerpts. *Management Communication Quarterly, 17,* 517–551.

Cora, D. (2004, October 10). Finally in the director's chair. *Fortune, 150,* 42–44.

Corman, S. (2006). Using activity focus networks to pressure terrorist organizations. *Computational and Mathematical Organizational Theory, 12,* 35–49.

Covey, S. (1990). *The 7 habits of highly effective people.* New York: Simon & Schuster.

Craig, R. (1999). Communication theory as a field. *Communication Theory, 9,* 119–161.

Csikszentmihalyi, M. (1990). *Flow: The psychology of optimal experience.* New York: Harper & Row.

Curves. (2006). Retrieved January 20, 2006, from http://www.curves.com

Daft, R., & Lengel, R. (1984). Information richness: A new approach to managerial information processing and organizational design. In B. Staw & L. Cummings (Eds.), *Research in organizational behaviors* (Vol. 6, pp. 191–233). Greenwich, CT: JAI Press.

Dalton, M., Ernst, C., Deal, J., & Leslie, J. (2002). *Success for the new global manager: How to work across distances, countries and cultures.* San Francisco: Jossey-Bass.

Daniels, T., & Spiker, B. (1991). *Perspectives on organizational communication.* Dubuque, IA: Brown.

Dansereau, F., & Markham, S. (1987). Superior-subordinate communication: Multiple levels of analysis. In F. Jablin, L. Putnam, K. Roberts, & L. Porter (Eds.), *Handbook of organizational communication* (pp. 343–388). Beverly Hills, CA: Sage.

D'Aveni, R. (1995). Coping with hypercompetition: Utilizing the new 7-S model. *Academy of Management Executive, 9*(3), 45–57.

Davis, J., Schoorman, F., & Donaldson, L. (1997). Toward a stewardship theory of management. *Academy of Management Review, 22,* 20–47.

Davis, K. (1953). Management communication and the grapevine. *Harvard Business Review, 31,* 43–49.

Davis, K. (1972). *Human behavior at work*. New York: McGraw-Hill.

Davis, S., & Davidson, B. (1992). *2020 vision*. New York: Fireside Press.

Day, G. S. & Reibstein, D. J. (1997). *Dynamic Competitive Advantage*. New York: Wiley.

Deal, T., & Kennedy, A. (1982). *Corporate cultures: The rites and rituals of corporate life*. Reading, MA: Addison-Wesley.

De Certeau, M. (1984). *The practice of everyday life*. Berkeley: University of California Press.

Deetz, S. (1992). *Democracy in an age of corporate colonization*. Albany: SUNY Press.

Deetz, S. (1995). *Transforming communication, transforming business*. Cresskill, NJ: Hampton Press.

Deetz, S. (2005). Critical theory. In S. May & D. Mumby (Eds.), *Engaging organizational communication theory and research* (pp. 85–112). Thousand Oaks, CA: Sage.

Deetz, S. (2006). Critical theory. In E. Griffin (Ed.), *Conversations with the communication theorists* [CD-ROM]. Boston: McGraw-Hill.

Deetz, S., & Kersten, A. (1983). Critical models of interpretive research. In L. Putnam & M. Pacanowsky (Eds.), *Communication and organizations: An interpretive approach*. Beverly Hills, CA: Sage.

Deetz, S., Tracy, S., & Simpson, J. (2000). *Leading organizations through transitions*. Thousand Oaks, CA: Sage.

Dentzer, S. (1995, May 22). The death of the middleman. *U.S. News & World Report*, p. 56.

Derrida, J. (1972). Structure, sign, and play in the discourse of the human sciences. In R. Macksay & E. Donato (Eds.), *The structuralist controversy: The language of criticism and the science of man*. Baltimore: Johns Hopkins University Press.

DeSantis, A., & Hane, A. (2004, November). *Greek sex: Understanding conceptions of gender and sexuality in fraternities and sororities*. Paper presented at the annual convention of the National Communication Association, Chicago.

Dessler, G. (1982). *Organization and management*. Reston, VA: Reston.

Dillard, J., & Miller, K. (1988). Intimate relationships in task environments. In S. Duck (Ed.), *Handbook of personal relationships* (pp. 449–465). New York: Wiley.

Dillard, J., & Segrin, C. (1987). *Intimate relationships in organizations: Relational types, illicitness, and power*. Paper presented at the annual conference of the International Communication Association, Montreal, Canada.

Dixon, L. (2004). A case study of an intercultural health care visit: An African American woman and her white male physician. *Women and Language*, *27*, 45–52.

Dixon, T. (1996). Mary Parker Follett and community. *Australian Journal of Communication*, *23*, 68–83.

Donnellon, A., Gray, B., & Bougon, M. (1986). Communication, meaning, and organized action. *Administrative Science Quarterly*, *31*, 43–55.

Dooley, K., Corman, S., & McPhee, R. (2002). A knowledge directory for identifying experts and areas of expertise. *Human Systems Management*, *21*, 217–228.

Dougherty, D., & Smythe, D. (2004). Sensemaking, organizational culture, and sexual harassment. *Journal of Applied Communication Research*, *32*, 293–317.

Dowd, M. (2005, October 30). What's a modern girl to do? *New York Times*. Retrieved January 14, 2006, from http://www.nytimes.com/2005/10/30/magazine/30feminism/html

Drucker, P. (1957). *The landmarks of tomorrow*. New York: Harper & Row.

Drucker, P. (1974). *Management: Tasks, responsibilities, practices*. New York: Harper & Row.

Drucker, P. (1992a). *Managing for the future: The 1990s and beyond*. New York: Truman Talley Books/Dutton.

Drucker, P. (1992b, February 11). There's more than one kind of team. *The Wall Street Journal*, p. 16.

Drucker, P. (1993). *Management*. New York: Harper & Row.

Drucker, P. (1996). Introduction. In *Mary Parker Follett: Prophet of management*. Cambridge, MA: Harvard Business School Press.

Dunham, R. (1999, August 2). Across America: A troubling digital divide. *Business Week, 40*.

Dykstra, K. (2006). Quick profile fixes. *Match.com*. Retrieved January 30, 2006, from http://www.match.com/magazine

Edley, P. (2001). Technology, employed mothers, and corporate colonization of the lifeworld: A gendered paradox of work and family balance. *Women and Language, 24*, 27–35.

Ehrenreich, B. (2001). *Nickel and dimed: On (not) getting by in America*. New York: Holt.

Ehrenreich, B. (2005). *Bait and switch: The (futile) pursuit of the American Dream*. New York: Metropolitan Books.

Einstein, A. (1961). *Relativity: The special and general theory*. New York: Bonanza Books. (Original work published 1921)

Eisenberg, E. (1984). Ambiguity as strategy in organizational communication. *Communication Monographs, 51*, 227–242.

Eisenberg, E. (1986). Meaning and interpretation in organizations. *Quarterly Journal of Speech, 72*, 88–98.

Eisenberg, E. (1990). Jamming: Transcendence through organizing. *Communication Research, 17*, 139–164.

Eisenberg, E. (1995). A communication perspective on interorganizational cooperation and inner-city education. In L. Rigsby, M. Reynolds, & M. Wang (Eds.), *School-community connections* (pp. 101–120). San Francisco: Jossey-Bass.

Eisenberg, E. (1998). Flirting with meaning. *Journal of Language and Social Psychology, 17*, 97–108.

Eisenberg, E. (2001). Building a mystery: Toward a new theory of communication and identity. *Journal of Communication, 51*, 534–552.

Eisenberg, E., Baglia, J., & Pynes, J. (2006). Transforming emergency medicine through narrative: Qualitative action research at a community hospital. *Health Communication, 19*, 197–208.

Eisenberg, E., & Eschenfelder, B. (in press). In L. Frey & K. Cissna (Eds.), *Handbook of applied communication*. Thousand Oaks, CA: Sage.

Eisenberg, E., Farace, R., Monge, P., Bettinghaus, E., Kurchner-Hawkins, R., Miller, K., et al. (1985). Communication linkages in interorganizational systems: Review and synthesis. In B. Dervin & M. Voight (Eds.), *Progress in communication sciences* (Vol. 6, pp. 231–258). Norwood, NJ: Ablex.

Eisenberg, E., Monge, P., & Farace, R. V. (1984). Co-orientation on communication rules in managerial dyads. *Human Communication Research, 11*, 261–271.

Eisenberg, E., Monge, P., & Miller, K. (1983). Involvement in communication networks as a predictor of organizational commitment. *Human Communication Research, 10*, 179–201.

Eisenberg, E., Murphy, A., & Andrews, L. (1998). Openness and decision-making in the search for a university provost. *Communication Monographs, 65*, 1–23.

Eisenberg, E., Murphy, A., Sutcliffe, K., Wears, R., Schenkel, S., Perry, S., et al. (2005). Communication in emergency medicine: Implications for patient safety. *Communication Monographs, 72*, 390–413.

Eisenberg, E., & Riley, P. (2001). A communication approach to organizational culture. In L. Putnam & F. Jablin (Eds.), *New handbook of organizational communication*. Newbury Park, CA: Sage.

Eisenberg, E., & Weller-Gregory, K. (2000). *Ethics of the urgent organization*. Unpublished manuscript, University of South Florida, Tampa.

Eisenberg, E., & Witten, M. (1987). Reconsidering openness in organizational communication. *Academy of Management Review, 12,* 418–426.

Eliot, T. S. (1949). *Notes toward the definition of culture.* New York: Harcourt, Brace.

Ellis, C. (2002). Shattered lives: Making sense of September 11 and its aftermath. *Journal of Contemporary Ethnography, 31,* 375–410.

Ellingson, L. L. & Buzzanell, P. M. (1999). Listening to women's narratives of breast cancer treatment: A feminist approach to patient satisfaction with physician-patient communication. *Health Communication, 11,* 153–183.

Emerson, C. (1983). Bakhtin and Vygotsky on internalization of language. *Quarterly Newsletter of the Laboratory of Comparative Human Cognition, 5,* 9–13.

Emery, F., & Trist, E. (1965). The causal texture of organizational environments. *Human Relations, 18,* 21–32.

Erez, M., & Earley, P. (1993). *Culture, self-identity, and work.* New York: Oxford University Press.

Erickson, R. (2005). Why emotion work matters: Sex, gender, and the division of household labor. *Journal of Marriage and Family, 67,* 337–351.

Evans, P., & Wolf, B. (2005). Collaboration rules. *Harvard Business Review, 83,* 96–104.

Evered, R., & Tannenbaum, R. (1992). A dialog on dialog. *Journal of Management Inquiry, 1,* 43–55.

Faber, B. (2002). *Community action and organizational change: Image, narrative, identity.* Carbondale: Southern Illinois University Press.

Fairhurst, G., & Chandler, T. (1989). Social structure in leader-member interaction. *Communication Monographs, 56,* 215–239.

Fairhurst, G., Green, S., & Snavely, B. (1984). Face support in controlling poor performance. *Human Communications Research, 11,* 272–295.

Fairhurst, G., & Putnam, L. (2004). Organizations as discursive constructions. *Communication Theory, 14,* 5–26.

Fairhurst, G., & Sarr, R. (1996). *The art of framing: Managing the language of leadership.* San Francisco: Jossey-Bass.

Farace, R., Monge, P., & Russell, H. (1977). *Communicating and organizing.* Reading, MA: Addison-Wesley.

Farrell, A., & Geist-Martin, P. (2005). Communicating social health: Perceptions of wellness at work. *Management Communication Quarterly, 18,* 543–592.

Fayol, H. (1949). *General and industrial management.* London: Pitman.

Feldman, M., & March, J. (1981). Information in organizations as signal and symbol. *Administrative Science Quarterly, 26,* 171–186.

Feldman, S. (1991). The meaning of ambiguity: Learning from stories and metaphors. In P. Frost, L. Moore, M. Louis, C. Lundberg, & J. Martin (Eds.), *Reframing organizational culture* (pp. 145–156). Newbury Park, CA: Sage.

Ferguson, K. (1984). *The feminist case against bureaucracy.* Philadelphia: Temple University Press.

Fiedler, F. (1967). *A theory of leadership effectiveness.* New York: McGraw-Hill.

Fine, M., & Buzzanell, P. (2000). Walking the high wire: Leadership theorizing, daily acts, and tensions. In P. Buzzanell (Ed.), *Rethinking organizational & managerial communication from feminist perspectives* (pp. 128–156). Thousand Oaks, CA: Sage.

Fisher, A. (1980). *Small group decision making* (2nd ed.). New York: McGraw-Hill.

Fisher, R., & Ury, W. (1981). *Getting to yes.* New York: Penguin.

Flamm, M. (2003). Trafficking of women and children in Southeast Asia. *United Nations Chronicle, 15*(2). Retrieved December 7, 2005, from http://www.heritage.org/Research/Economy/bg1757.cfm

Flanagan, C. (2004, March). How serfdom saved the women's movement. *Atlantic Monthly*, *293*(2), 109–128.

Flanagin, A., & Waldeck, J. (2004). Technology use and organizational newcomer socialization. *Journal of Business Communication, 41*, 137–165.

Fleming, P. (2005). Metaphors of resistance. *Management Communication Quarterly, 19*, 45–66.

Fleming, P., & Spicer, A. (2003). Working at a cynical distance: Implications for power, subjectivity and resistance. *Organization, 10*, 157–179.

Ford, R., & Fottler, M. (1995). Empowerment: A matter of degree. *Academy of Management Executive, 9*, 21–31.

Foucault, M. (1972). *The archaeology of knowledge*. London: Tavistock.

Foucault, M. (1979). *The birth of the prison*. Harmondsworth, England: Penguin.

Fox, M. (1994). *The reinvention of work*. San Francisco: HarperCollins.

Franklin, B. (1970). *The complete Poor Richard almanacs published by Benjamin Franklin*. Barre, MA: Imprint Society.

Franz, C., & Jin, K. (1995). The structure of group conflict in a collaborative work group during information systems development. *Journal of Applied Communication Research, 23*, 108–122.

Freeman, S. (1990). *Managing lives: Corporate women and social change*. Amherst: University of Massachusetts Press.

Freire, P. (1968). *Pedagogy of the oppressed*. Berkeley: University of California Press.

French, R., & Raven, B. (1968). The bases of social power. In D. Cartwright & A. Zander (Eds.), *Group dynamics* (pp. 601–623). New York: Harper & Row.

Friedman, M. (1992). *Dialogue and the human image*. Newbury Park, CA: Sage.

Friedman, T. (2002, August 13). India's leaders think twice about war with Pakistan thanks to GE. *St. Petersburg Times*, p. 8A.

Friedman, T. (2005). *The world is flat: A brief history of the twenty-first century*. New York: Farrar, Straus & Giroux.

Frost, P., Moore, L., Louis, M., Lundberg, C., & Martin, J. (1991). *Reframing organizational culture*. Newbury Park, CA: Sage.

Fulk, J., & DeSanctis, G. (1995). Electronic communication and changing organizational forms. *Organization Science, 6*(4), 337–349.

Fulk, J., & Mani, S. (1986). Distortion of communication in hierarchical relationships. *Communication yearbook* (Vol. 9, pp. 483–510). Newbury Park, CA: Sage.

Fulk, J., Schmitz, J., & Steinfeld, C. (1990). A social influence model of technology use. In J. Fulk & C. Steinfeld (Eds.), *Organizational and communication technology* (pp. 143–172). Newbury Park, CA: Sage.

Gabarro, J., & Kotter, J. (1993). Managing your boss. *Harvard Business Review, 58*, 92–100.

Gabriel, Y. (1999). Beyond happy families: A critical reevaluation of the control-resistance-identity triangle. *Human Relations, 52*, 179–203.

Galbraith, J. (1973). *Designing complex organizations*. Reading, MA: Addison-Wesley.

Ganesh, S., Zoller, H., & Cheney, G. (2005). Transforming resistance, broadening our boundaries: Critical organizational communication meets globalization from below. *Communication Monographs, 72*, 169–191.

Gao, J. (2006). Organized international asylum-seeker networks: Formation and utilization by Chinese students. *International Migration Review, 40*, 294–317.

Gardner, H. (1996). *Leading minds: An anatomy of leadership*. New York: Basic Books.

Garfield, C. (1992). *Business in the ecological age* [Audiotape]. San Francisco: Berrett-Koehler.

Garfield, C. (1999, September/October). Peak performances and organizational transformation: An interview with Charles Garfield. *Educom Review, 34*.

Gates, B. (1999). *Business at the speed of thought*. New York: Time Warner.

Geertz, C. (1973). *The interpretation of cultures*. New York: Basic Books.

Geist, P. (1995). Negotiating whose order? Communicating to negotiate identities and revise organizational structures. In A. Nicotera (Ed.), *Conflict and organizations: Communicative processes* (pp. 45–64). Albany: SUNY Press.

Geist, P., & Dreyer, J. (1993). The demise of dialogue: A critique of medical encounter ideology. *Western Journal of Communication, 57*, 233–246.

Gendron, G. (1999). Seizing opportunities for meaning. *Inc., 21*, 87.

Gephart, R. P. (2002). Introduction to the brave new workplace: Organizational behavior in the electronic age. *Journal of Organizational Behavior, 23*, 327–344.

Gergen, K. (1991). *The saturated self*. New York: Basic Books.

Gersick, C. (1991). Revolutionary change theories: A multi-level explanation of the punctuated equilibrium paradigm. *Academy of Management Review, 16*, 10–36.

Gibson, D., & Rogers, E. (in press). *Synergy on trial: Texas high tech and the MCC*. Newbury Park, CA: Sage.

Gibson, J., & Hodgetts, R. (1986). *Organizational communication: A managerial perspective*. New York: Academic Press.

Gibson, M., & Papa, M. (2000). The mud, blood and beer guys: Organizational osmosis in blue-collar work groups. *Journal of Applied Communication Research, 28*, 68–88.

Giddens, A. (1979). *Central problems in social theory*. London: Hutchinson.

Giddens, A. (1984). *The constitution of society: Outline of the theory of structuration*. Berkeley: University of California Press.

Gillespie, S. (2001). The politics of breathing: Asthmatic Medicaid patients under managed care. *Journal of Applied Communication Research, 29*, 97–116.

Gitlin, T. (1987). *The sixties: Years of hope, days of rage*. New York: Bantam.

Glaser, H., & Bullis, C. (1992, November). *Ecofeminism and organizational communication*. Paper presented at the annual meeting of the Speech Communication Association, Chicago.

Gleick, J. (2000). *Faster: The acceleration of just about everything*. New York: Vintage Books.

Gluesing, J. (1998). Building connections and balancing power in global teams: Toward a reconceptualization of culture as composite. *Anthropology of Work Review XVIII*(2/3), 18–30.

Goes, J., & Park, S. (1997). Interorganizational links and innovation: The case of hospital services. *Academy of Management Journal, 40*, 673–696.

Goffman, E. (1959). *The presentation of self in everyday life*. New York: Doubleday.

Goleman, D. (1995). *Emotional intelligence*. New York: Bantam.

Goodall, H. L. (1984). The status of communication studies in organizational contexts: One rhetorician's lament after a year-long odyssey. *Communication Quarterly, 32*, 133–147.

Goodall, H. L. (1989). *Casing a promised land*. Carbondale: Southern Illinois University Press.

Goodall, H. L. (1990a). Interpretive contexts for decision-making: Toward an understanding of the physical, economic, dramatic, and hierarchical interplays of language in groups. In G. M. Phillips (Ed.), *Teaching how to work in groups* (pp. 197–224). Norwood, NJ: Ablex.

Goodall, H. L. (1990b). A theatre of motives and the "meaningful order of persons and things." In J. Anderson (Ed.), *Communication yearbook* (Vol. 13, pp. 69–94). Newbury Park, CA: Sage.

Goodall, H. L. (1991a). *Living in the rock 'n' roll mystery*. Carbondale: Southern Illinois University Press.

Goodall, H. L. (1991b). *Unchained melodies: Toward a poetics of organizing*. Blair Hart lecture on communication, University of Arkansas, Fayetteville.

Goodall, H. L. (1994). *Casing a promised land: The autobiography of an organizational detective as cultural ethnographer* (Rev. ed.). Carbondale: Southern Illinois University Press.

Goodall, H. L., Jr. (1995). Work-hate narratives. In R. Whillock & D. Slayden (Eds.), *Hate speech*. Thousand Oaks, CA: Sage.

Goodall, H. L., Jr. (1996). *Divine signs: Connecting spirit to community*. Carbondale: Southern Illinois University Press.

Goodall, H. L., Jr. (2000). *Writing the new ethnography*. Newbury Park, CA: Alta Mira Press.

Goodall, H. L., Jr. (2002). Fieldnotes from our war zone: Living in America during the aftermath of September 11. *Qualitative Inquiry*, *8*, 203–218.

Goodall, H. L., Jr. (2003). What is interpretive ethnography? An eclectic's tale. In R. Clair (Ed.), *Expressions of ethnography: Novel approaches to qualitative methods* (pp. 55–64). Albany: SUNY Press.

Goodall, H. L., Jr. (2004). Narrative ethnography and applied communication research. *Journal of Applied Communication Research*, *32*, 185–194.

Goodall, H. L., Jr., & Goodall, S. (2002). *Communicating in professional contexts: Skills, ethics, and technologies*. Belmont, CA: Wadsworth/Thomson Learning.

Goodall, H. L., Jr., & Goodall, S. (2006). *Communicating in professional contexts: Skills, ethics, and technologies* (2nd ed.). Belmont, CA: Wadsworth/Thomson Learning.

Goodall, H. L., Jr., & Kellett, P. M. (2003). Dialectical tensions and dialogic moments as pathways to peak experiences. In R. Anderson, L. Baxter, and K. Cissna (Eds.), *Dialogic approaches to communication* (pp. 159–174). Thousand Oaks, CA: Sage.

Goodall, H. L., Jr., & Kellett, P. M. (2004). Dialectical tensions and dialogic moments as pathways to peak experiences. In R. Anderson, L. Baxter, and K. Cissna (Eds.), *Dialogue: Theorizing difference in communication studies* (pp. 159–174). Thousand Oaks, CA: Sage.

Goodbody, J. (2005, February/March). Conference documentation: PPP in Ireland and Northern Ireland. *Strategic Communication Management*, *9*, 18–21.

Goodier, B., & Eisenberg, E. (2006). Seeking the spirit: Communication and the (re)development of a "spiritual" organization. *Communication Studies*, *57*, 47–65.

Google. (2006). Working at Google. Retrieved May 2, 2006, from http://www.google.com/intl/en/jobs/working.html

Gotseva-Yordanova, R. Review: A double bill with Peter Senge et al.: Society for Organizational Learning's Foundation of Leadership program and presencing. Retrieved February 8, 2006, from http://www.presence.net/roumiana.html

Graen, G. (1976). Role making processes within complex organizations. In M. Dunnette (Ed.), *Handbook of industrial and organizational psychology* (pp. 1201–1245). Chicago: Rand McNally.

Graen, G., Liden, R., & Hoel, W. (1982). Role of leadership in the employee withdrawal process. *Journal of Applied Psychology*, *67*, 868–872.

Graham, P. (1997). *Mary Parker Follett—Prophet of management*. Cambridge, MA: Harvard Business School Press.

Gramsci, A. (1971). *Selections from the prison notebooks*. London: Lawrence & Wishart.

Granovetter, M. (1973). The strength of weak ties. *American Journal of Sociology*, *78*, 1360–1380.

Grant, L. (1992, May 3). Breaking the mold: Companies struggle to reinvent themselves. *Los Angeles Times*, pp. D1, D16.

Grantham, C. (1999). *The future of work: The promise of the new digital work society*. New York: McGraw-Hill.

Greenblatt, S. (1990). Culture. In F. Lentricchia & T. McLaughlin (Eds.), *Critical terms for literary study* (pp. 225–232). Chicago: University of Chicago Press.

Greenleaf, R. (1998). *The power of servant leadership*. San Francisco: Berrett-Koehler.

Grossberg, L. (1991). Review of theories of human communication. *Communication Theory*, *1*, 171–176.

Grossberg, L. (2002). Postscript. *Communication Theory, 12*, 367–370.

Grossman, H., & Chester, N. (1990). *The experience and meaning of work in women's lives.* Hillsdale, NJ: Erlbaum.

A gym for the non-lycra crowd? The pluses—and minuses—of Curves for women. (2004, February). *Health and Nutrition Letter.* Retrieved January 20, 2006, from http://www.healthletter.tufts.edu

Haas, T., & Deetz, S. (2000). Between the generalized and the concrete other: Approaching organizational ethics from feminist perspectives. In P. Buzzanell (Ed.), *Rethinking organizational & managerial communication from feminist perspectives* (pp. 24–46). Thousand Oaks, CA: Sage.

Habermas, J. (1972). *Knowledge and human interests.* London: Heinemann Educational Books.

Hackman, R., & Oldham, G. (1975). Development of the Job Diagnostic Survey. *Journal of Applied Psychology, 60*, 159–170.

Hackman, R., & Oldham, G. (1980). *Work redesign.* Reading, MA: Addison-Wesley.

Hackman, R., & Suttle, J. (1977). *Improving life at work: Behavioral science approaches to organizational change.* Santa Monica, CA: Goodyear.

Hafner, K., & Gnatek, T. (2004, May 27). For some, the blogging never stops. *New York Times.* Retrieved May 15, 2006, from http://tech2.nytimes.com/mem/technology

Hall, D. (1986). *Career development in organizations.* San Francisco: Jossey-Bass.

Hall, D. (1996). Protean careers of the 21st century. *Academy of Management Executive, 10*, 8–16.

Hall, E. T. (1973). *The silent language.* New York: Anchor.

Hall, K., & Savery, L. (1987). Stress management. *Management Decision, 25*, 29–35.

Hamborg, K., & Greif, S. (1996). *Handbook of Work and Health Psychology.* Chichester, UK: John Wiley & Sons.

Hammond, S., Anderson, R., & Cissna, K. (2003). The problematics of dialogue and power. In P. Kalfleisch (Ed.), *Communication yearbook* (Vol. 27, pp. 125–157). Mahwah, NJ: Erlbaum.

Handy, C. (1994). *The age of paradox.* Cambridge, MA: Harvard University Press.

Haraway, D. (1991). Simians, cyborgs, and women. New York: Routledge.

Hardin, G. (1968, December 13). The tragedy of the commons. *Science, 162*, 1243–1248.

Harrigan, B. (1977). *Games mother never taught you: Corporate gamesmanship for women.* New York: Warner.

Harrison, T. (1985). Communication and participative decision-making: An exploratory study. *Personnel Psychology, 38*, 93–116.

Harrison, T. (1994). Communication and interdependence in democratic organizations. In S. Deetz (Ed.), *Communication yearbook* (Vol. 17, pp. 247–274). Newbury Park, CA: Sage.

Harshman, E., & Harshman, C. (1999). Communicating with employees: Building on an ethical foundation. *Journal of Business Ethics, 19*, 3–11.

Hart, R., & Burks, D. (1972). Rhetorical sensitivity and social interaction. *Speech Monographs, 39*, 75–91.

Harter, L. (2004). Masculinity(s), the agrarian frontier myth, and cooperative ways of organizing: Contradictions and tensions in the experience and enactment of democracy. *Journal of Applied Communication Research, 32*, 89–118.

Hatch, M. (1993). The dynamics of organizational culture. *Academy of Management Review, 18*, 657–693.

Hatch, M. (1999). Exploring the empty spaces of organizing: How improvisational jazz helps redescribe organizational structure. *Organization Studies, 20*, 75–100.

Hawken, P. (1994). *The ecology of commerce.* New York: HarperBusiness.

Hawking, S. (1988). *A brief history of time.* New York: Bantam.

Heald, M., Contractor, N., Koehlt, L., & Wasserman, S. (1998). Formal and emergent predictors of coworkers' perceptual congruence on an organization's social structure. *Human Communication Research, 24,* 536–563.

Helgeson, S. (1990). *The female advantage: Women's ways of leadership.* New York: Doubleday.

Hellweg, S. (1987). Organizational grapevines: A state of the art review. In B. Dervin & M. Voight (Eds.), *Progress in the communication sciences* (Vol. 8). Norwood, NJ: Ablex.

Hersey, P., & Blanchard, K. (1977). *Management of organizational behavior: Utilizing human resources* (3rd ed.). Englewood Cliffs, NJ: Prentice Hall.

Herzberg, F. (1966). *Work and the nature of man.* New York: HarperCollins.

Hess, J. (1993). Assimilating newcomers into an organization: A cultural perspective. *Journal of Applied Communication Research, 21,* 189–210.

Hirokawa, R., & Rost, K. (1992). Effective group decision making in organizations. *Management Communication Quarterly, 5,* 267–388.

Hirschman, A. (1970). *Exit, voice, and loyalty.* Cambridge, MA: Harvard University Press.

Hochschild, A. (1979). Emotion work, feeling rules and social structure. *American Journal of Sociology, 85,* 551–575.

Hochschild, A. (1983). *The managed heart: Commercialization of human feeling.* Berkeley: University of California Press.

Hochschild, A. (1989). *Second shift: Working parents and the revolution at home.* New York: Viking.

Hochschild, A. (1993). Preface. In S. Fineman (Ed.), *Emotion in organizations.* Newbury Park, CA: Sage.

Hochschild, A. (1997). *The time bind.* New York: Holt.

Hofstede, G. (1983). National cultures in four dimensions. *International Studies of Management and Organization, 13,* 46–74.

Hofstede, G. (1995). *Culture and organizations: Software of the mind.* New York: McGraw-Hill.

Hollander, E., & Offerman, L. (1990). Power and leadership in organizations. *American Psychologist, 45,* 179–189.

Holmer Nadesan, M. (1996). Organizational identity and space of action. *Organization Studies, 17,* 49–81.

Holzer, H. (1996). *What employers want: Job prospects for less educated workers.* New York: Russell Sage Foundation.

Homans, G. (1961). *Social behavior: Its elementary forms.* New York: Harcourt, Brace.

Hornstein, H. A. (1996). *Brutal bosses and their prey: How to identify and overcome abuse in the workplace.* New York: Riverhead Books.

Howard, R., & Sawyer, R. (2003). *Defeating terrorism: Shaping the new security environment.* Boston: McGraw-Hill.

Hughes, C. (2004). Class and other identifications of managerial careers: The case of the lemon dress. *Gender, Work & Organization, 11,* 526–543.

Human, S., & Provan, K. (1997). An emergent theory of structure and outcomes in small-firm strategic manufacturing networks. *Academy of Management Journal, 40,* 368–403.

Hunger, R., & Stern, L. (1976). Assessment of the functionality of subordinate goals in reducing conflict. *Academy of Management Journal, 16,* 591–605.

Hurst, D. (1992). Thoroughly modern—Mary Parker Follett. *Business Quarterly, 56,* 55–59.

Huselid, M. (1995). The impact of human resource management practices on turnover, productivity, and corporate financial performance. *Academy of Management Journal, 38,* 635–673.

Hyde, R. B. (1994). Listening authentically: A Heideggerian perspective on interpersonal communication. In K. Carter and M. Presnell (Eds.), *Interpretive approaches to interpersonal communication* (pp. 179–195). Albany: SUNY Press.

Ilgin, D., & Knowlton, W., Jr. (1980). Performance attributional effects on feedback from supervisors. *Organizational Behavior and Human Performance, 25*, 441–456.

Infante, D., Trebing, J., Sheperd, P., & Seeds, D. (1984). The relationship of argumentativeness to verbal aggression. *Southern Speech Communication Journal, 50*, 67–77.

Isaacs, W. (1993, Fall). Taking flight: Dialogue, collaborative thinking, and organizational learning. *Organizational Dynamics, 22*(2), 24–39.

Isaacs, W. (1999). *Dialogue*. New York: Doubleday/Currency.

Israel, B., House, J., Schurman, S., Heaney, C., & Mero, R. (1989). The relation of personal resources, participation, influence, interpersonal relationships, and coping strategies to occupational stress, job strains and health: A multivariate analysis. *Work and Stress, 3*, 163–194.

Ivancevich, J., & Matteson, M. (1980). *Stress and work: A managerial perspective*. Glenview, IL: Scott Foresman.

Iverson, J., & McPhee, R. (2002). Knowledge management in communities of practice. *Management Communication Quarterly, 16*, 259–266.

Jablin, F. (1979). Superior-subordinate communication: The state of the art. *Psychological Bulletin, 86*, 1201–1222.

Jablin, F. (1985). Task/work relationships: A life-span perspective. In M. Knapp & G. Miller (Eds.), *Handbook of interpersonal communication* (pp. 615–654). Newbury Park, CA: Sage.

Jablin, F. (1987). Organizational entry, assimilation, and exit. In F. Jablin, L. Putnam, K. Roberts, & L. Porter (Eds.), *Handbook of organizational communication* (pp. 679–740). Newbury Park, CA: Sage.

Jablin, F., & Putnam, L. (2001). *The new handbook of organizational communication*. Thousand Oaks, CA: Sage.

Jackson, M. (1989). *Paths toward a clearing*. Bloomington: Indiana University Press.

Jackson, S. (1983). Participation in decision-making as a strategy for reducing job-related strain. *Journal of Applied Psychology, 68*, 3–19.

Jacobson, R. (1992). Colleges face new pressure to increase faculty productivity. *Chronicle of Higher Education, 38*(32), 1, 16.

Janis, I. (1971). *Victims of groupthink* (2nd ed.). Boston: Houghton Mifflin.

Jantsch, E. (1980). *The self organizing universe*. Oxford: Pergamon Press.

Jassawalla, A., & Sashittal, H. (1999). Building collaborative cross-functional new product teams. *Academy of Management Executive, 13*, 50–63.

Jencks, C. (1977). *The language of postmodern architecture*. New York: Pantheon.

Jhally, S. (1998). *Representation in media* [Film]. (Available from Media Education Foundation, Amherst, MA)

Jobs, S. (2005, June 12). Commencement address presented at Stanford University. Retrieved March 22, 2006, from http://news-service.stanford.edu/news/2005/june15/jobs-061505.html

Johnson, B. (1977). *Communication: The process of organizing*. Boston: Allyn and Bacon.

Johnson, D. (1993). *Circles of learning*. Edina, MN: Interaction Books.

Jones, B. (1972, June). Sex in the office. *National Times*, 12.

Jones, E., Jr. (1973, July/August). What it's like to be a black manager. *Harvard Business Review*.

Jones, S. (2001). Employee rights, employee responsibilities and knowledge sharing in intelligent organization. *Employee Responsibility and Rights, 14*, 69–78.

Jorgenson, J. (2002). Engineering selves: Negotiating gender and identity in technical work. *Management Communication Quarterly, 15*(3), 350–380.

Jorgenson, J., Gregory, K., & Goodier, B. (1998). Working the boundaries: The enfamilied self in the traditional organization. *Human Systems, 8*, 3–4, 139–151.

Jovanovic, S. (in press). Difficult conversations as moral imperative: Negotiating ethnic identities during war. *Communication Quarterly*.

Kane, T., Schaefer, B., & Fraser, A. (2004, May 13). Myths and realities: The false crisis of outsourcing. Retrieved December 7, 2005, from http://www.heritage.org/Research/Economy/bg1757.cfm.

Kanter, R. M. (1977). *Men and women of the corporation*. New York: Basic Books.

Kanter, R. M. (1989, November/December). The new managerial work. *Harvard Business Review*, *67*, 85–92.

Karasek, R. (1979). Job demands, job decisions, latitude and mental strain: Implications for job redesign. *Administrative Science Quarterly*, *24*, 285–308.

Katz, D., & Kahn, R. (1966). *The social psychology of organizations*. New York: Wiley.

Keeley, M. (1980). Organizational analogy: A comparison of organismic and social contract models. *Administrative Science Quarterly*, *25*, 337–362.

Kellett, P. M. (1999). Dialogue and dialectics in organizational change: The case of a mission-based transformation. *Southern Communication Journal*, *64*, 211–231.

Kellett, P. M., & Dalton, D. G. (2000). *Managing conflict in a negotiated world: A narrative approach to achieving dialogue and change*. Thousand Oaks, CA: Sage.

Kelly, J. (1992). *Scientific management, job redesign, and work performance*. London: Academic Press.

Kerr, S. (2001). Boundaryless. In W. Bennis, G. Spreitzer, & T. Cummings (Eds.), *The future of leadership* (pp. 59–66). San Francisco: Jossey-Bass.

Keys, B., & Case, T. (1990). How to become an influential manager. *Academy of Management Executive*, *4*, 38–50.

Kiechel, W. (1994, April 4). A manager's career in the new economy. *Fortune*, 68–72.

Kiesler, C. (1971). *The psychology of commitment*. New York: Academic Press.

Kilmann, R., & Thomas, K. (1975). Interpersonal conflict handling behavior as a reflection of Jungian personality dimensions. *Psychological Reports*, *37*, 971–980.

Kim, C., & Tamborini, T. (2006). The continuing significance of race in the occupational attainment of whites and blacks: A segmented labor market analysis. *Sociological Inquiry*, *76*, 23–51.

Kimberly, J., & Miles, R. (1980). *The organizational life cycle*. San Francisco: Jossey-Bass.

King, P., & Sawyer, C. (1998). Mindfulness, mindlessness, and communication instruction. *Communication Education*, *47*, 326–338.

Kinsella, W. (1999). Discourse, power, and knowledge in the management of big science. *Management Communication Quarterly*, *13*, 171.

Kipnis, D., & Schmidt, S. (1982). *Profile of organizational influence strategies*. San Diego: University Associates.

Kipnis, D., Schmidt, S., & Braxton-Brown, G. (1990). The hidden costs of persistence. In M. Cody & M. McLaughlin (Eds.), *The psychology of tactical communication*. Philadelphia: Multilingual Matters.

Kipnis, D., Schmidt, S., & Wilkinson, I. (1980). Intraorganizational influence tactics: Explorations in getting one's way. *Journal of Applied Psychology*, *65*, 440–452.

Kirby, E., Golden, A., Medved, C., Jorgenson, J., & Buzzanell, P. (2003). An organizational communication challenge to the discourse of work and family research: From problematics to empowerment. In P. Kalbfleish (Ed.), *Communication yearbook* (Vol. 27, pp. 1–44). Mahwah, NJ: Erlbaum.

Kirby, E., & Krone, K. (2002). "The policy exists but you can't really use it": Communication and the structuration of work-family policies. *Journal of Applied Communication Research*, *30*, 50–77.

Kobasa, S., Maddi, S., & Kahn, S. (1982). Hardiness and health: A prospective study. *Journal of Personality and Social Psychology, 42,* 168–177.

Kotter, J. (1995). *The new rules.* New York: Free Press.

Kotter, J., & Heskett, J. (1992). *Corporate culture and performance.* New York: Free Press.

Kraatz, M. (1998). Learning by association? Interorganizational networks and adaptation to environmental change. *Academy of Management Journal, 41,* 621–643.

Kramer, M., & Miller, V. (1999). In response to criticisms of organizational socialization research. *Communication Monographs, 66,* 358–367.

Kreps, G. (1991). *Organizational communication: Theory and practice* (2nd ed.). New York: Longman.

Krippendorff, K. (1985, June). *On the ethics of constructing communication.* Presidential address of the International Communication Association, Honolulu, HI.

Krivonos, P. (1982). Distortion of subordinate to superior communication in organizational settings. *Central States Speech Journal, 33,* 345–352.

Krizek, R. (2003). Ethnography as the excavation of personal narrative. In R. Clair (Ed.), *Expressions of ethnography: Novel approaches to qualitative methods* (pp. 141–152). Albany: SUNY Press.

Kunda, G. (1993). *Engineering culture: Control and commitment in a high-tech corporation.* Philadelphia: Temple University Press.

Laine-Timmerman, L. (1999). *The emotional experience of floor nursing.* Unpublished doctoral dissertation, University of South Florida, Tampa.

Laing, R. D. (1965). *The divided self.* Harmondsworth, England: Penguin.

Lair, D., Sullivan, K., & Cheney, G. (2005). Marketization and the recasting of the professional self: The rhetoric and ethics of personal branding. *Management Communication Quarterly, 18,* 307–343.

Langer, E. (1998). *The power of mindful learning.* New York: Perseus Publishing.

Langewiesche, W. (2002). *American ground: Unbuilding the World Trade Center.* Boston: North Point Press.

Larkey, P. (1984). The management of attention. In P. Larkey & L. Sproull (Eds.), *Advances in information processing in organizations* (Vol. I). Greenwich, CT: JAI Press.

Larson, G., & Tompkins, P. (2005). Ambivalence and resistance: A study of management in a concertive control system. *Communication Monographs, 72,* 1–21.

Larson, J., Jr. (1989). The dynamic interplay between employees: Feedback-seeking strategies and supervisors' delivery of performance feedback. *Academy of Management Review, 14,* 408–422.

Lawler, E., III. (1986). *High involvement management.* San Francisco: Jossey-Bass.

Lawler, E., III, & Finegold, D. (2000). Individualizing the organization: Past, present, and future. *Organizational Dynamics, 29,* 1–15.

Lawrence, P., & Lorsch, J. (1967). *Organization and environment: Mapping differentiation and integration.* Boston: Graduate School of Business Administration, Harvard University.

Leavitt, H. (1951). Some effects of certain communication patterns on group performance. *Journal of Abnormal and Social Psychology, 46,* 38–50.

Leidner, R. (1993). *Fast food, fast talk: Service work and the routinization of everyday life.* Berkeley: University of California Press.

Lennie, I. (1999). *Beyond management.* London: Sage.

LeVine, S. (1984). *The flight from ambiguity.* Chicago: University of Chicago Press.

Lewin, R. (1997, November 29). Ecosystems as a metaphor for business. *New Scientist, 156,* 30–34.

Lewis, M. (2000, March). The artist in the gray flannel pajamas. *New York Times Magazine*, p. 45.

Liden, R., & Graen, G. (1980). Generalizability of the vertical dyad linkage model of leadership. *Academy of Management Journal, 23*, 451–465.

Likert, R. (1961). *New patterns of management.* New York: McGraw-Hill.

Lindemann, K. (2005). Live(s) online: Narrative performance, presence, and community in livejournal.com. *Text and Performance Quarterly, 25*, 354–372.

Locke, E., & Latham, G. (1984). *Goal setting: A motivational technique that really works!* Englewood Cliffs, NJ: Prentice Hall.

Loher, B., Noe, R., Moeller, N., & Fitzgerald, M. (1985). A meta-analysis of the relation of job characteristics to job satisfaction. *Journal of Applied Psychology, 70*, 280–289.

Longworth, R. C. (1998). *Global squeeze: The coming crisis for first world nations.* New York: McGraw-Hill.

Louis, M. (1980). Surprise and sense-making: What newcomers experience in entering unfamiliar organizational settings. *Administrative Science Quarterly, 23*, 225–251.

Luhmann, A. D., & Albrecht, T. L. (1990, May). *The impact of supportive communication and personal control on job stress and performance.* Paper presented at the International Communication Association, Chicago.

Lukes, S. (1986). *Power.* New York: New York University Press.

Lunneborg, D. (1990). *Women changing work.* New York: Greenwood Press.

Lutgen-Sandvik, P. (2003). The communicative cycle of employee emotional abuse. *Management Communication Quarterly, 16*, 471–502.

Lyotard, J. F. (1984). *The postmodern condition: A report on knowledge* (G. Bennington & B. Massumi, Trans.). Minneapolis: University of Minnesota Press.

March, J., & Olsen, J. (1976). *Ambiguity and choice in organizations.* Bergen, Norway: Universitetsforlaget.

March, J., & Simon, H. (1958). *Organizations.* New York: Wiley.

Marcus, G., & Fischer, M. (1986). *Anthropology as cultural critique.* Chicago: University of Chicago Press.

Markham, A. (1998). *Life online.* Newbury Park, CA: Alta Mira Press.

Marshall, A., & Stohl, C. (1993). Participating as participation: A network approach. *Communication Monographs, 60*, 137–157.

Marshall, J. (1984). *Women managers: Travelers in a male world.* New York: Wiley.

Marshall, J. (1989). Revisioning career concepts: A feminist invitation. In M. Arthur, D. Hall, & B. Lawrence (Eds.), *Handbook of career theory* (pp. 275–291). Cambridge, England: Cambridge University Press.

Marshall, K. (1993). Viewing organizational communication from a feminist perspective: A critique and some offerings. In S. Deetz (Ed.), *Communication yearbook* (Vol. 16, pp. 122–141). Newbury Park, CA: Sage.

Martin, D. (2004). Humor in middle management: Women negotiating the paradoxes of organizational life. *Journal of Applied Communication Research, 32*, 147–170.

Martin, J. (1985). Can organizational culture be managed? In P. Frost, L. Moore, M. Louis, C. Lundberg, & J. Martin (Eds.), *Organizational culture* (pp. 95–98). Beverly Hills, CA: Sage.

Martin, J. (1990). Rethinking feminist organizations. *Gender & Society, 4*, 182–206.

Martin, J. (1992). *Cultures in organizations: Three perspectives.* New York: Oxford University Press.

Martin, J. (1994). The organization of exclusion: Institutionalization of sex inequality, gendered faculty jobs and gendered knowledge in organizational theory and research. *Organization, 1*, 401–431.

Martin, J., Feldman, M., Hatch, M., & Sitkin, S. (1983). The uniqueness paradox in organizational stories. *Administrative Science Quarterly, 28*, 438–453.

Martin, J., & Nakayama, T. (1999). Thinking dialectically about culture and communication. *Communication Theory, 9*, 1–25.

Marquardt, M. J. (2002). *Building the learning organization: Mastering the five elements for corporate learning.* Mountain View, CA: Davies-Black Publishing.

Maruyama, M. (1963). The second cybernetics: Deviation amplifying mutual cause processes. *American Scientist, 51*, 164–179.

Maruyama, M. (1994). *Mindscapes in management: Use of individual differences in multicultural management.* Sudbury, MA: Dartmouth Publishing.

Maslach, C. (1982). *Burnout: The cost of caring.* Englewood Cliffs, NJ: Prentice-Hall.

Maslow, A. (1965). *Eupsychian management.* Homewood, IL: Irwin.

Maslow, A. (1994). *Religions, values, and peak experiences.* New York: Viking Press.

Mattson, M., Clair, R., Sanger, P. A. C., & Kunkel, A. (2000). A feminist reframing of stress: Rose's story. In P. Buzzanell (Ed.), *Rethinking organizational & managerial communication from feminist perspectives* (pp. 157–176). Thousand Oaks, CA: Sage.

Maug, E. (2001). Ownership structure and the lifecycle of the firm: A theory of the decision to go public. *European Finance Review, 5*, 167–200.

May, S. (1988, May). *The modernist monologue in organizational communication research: The text, the subject, and the audience.* Paper presented at the annual convention of the International Communication Association, San Francisco.

May, S. (2000). *Silencing the feminine in managerial discourse.* Unpublished manuscript, University of North Carolina at Chapel Hill.

Mayo, E. (1945). *The social problems of industrial civilization.* Cambridge, MA: Graduate School of Business Administration, Harvard University.

McDonald, P. (1988). The Los Angeles Olympic Organizing Committee: Developing organizational culture in the short run. *Public Administration Quarterly, 10*, 189–205.

McGregor, D. (1960). *The human side of enterprise.* New York: McGraw-Hill.

McLarney, C., & Rhyno, S. (1999). Mary Parker Follett: Visionary leadership and strategic management. *Women in Management Review, 14*, 292–302.

McLuhan, M. (1964). *Understanding media: The extensions of man.* New York: McGraw-Hill.

McPhee, R. (1985). Formal structures and organizational communication. In R. McPhee & P. Tompkins (Eds.), *Organizational communication: Traditional themes and new directions* (pp. 149–177). Beverly Hills, CA: Sage.

McPhee, R., & Corman, S. (1995). An activity based theory of communication networks in organizations, applied to the case of a local church. *Communication Monographs, 62*, 132–151.

McPhee, R., & Poole, M. S. (2001). Organizational structures and configurations. In F. Jablin & L. Putnam (Eds.), *The new handbook of organizational communication: Advances in theory, research, and methods* (pp. 503–543). Thousand Oaks, CA: Sage.

Mead, G. (1991, May 30). The new old capitalism: Long hours, low wages. *Rolling Stone, 27*(3).

Mead, G. H. (1934). *Mind, self, and society.* Chicago: University of Chicago Press.

Meares, M., Oetzel, J., Torres, A., Derkacs, D., & Ginossar, T. (2004). Employee mistreatment and muted voices in the culturally diverse workplace. *Journal of Applied Communication Research, 32*, 4–27.

Medved, C., & Kirby, E. (2005). Family CEOs: A feminist analysis of corporate mothering discourses. *Management Communication Quarterly, 18*, 307–343.

Meyer, G. (1995). *Executive blues.* San Francisco: Franklin Square Press.

Meyer, J., & Rowan, B. (1977). Institutionalized organizations: Formal structure as myth and ceremony. *American Journal of Sociology, 83*, 340–363.

Meyerson, D. (1991). "Normal" ambiguity? Glimpse of an occupational culture. In P. Frost, L. Moore, M. Louis, C. Lundberg, & J. Martin (Eds.), *Reframing organizational culture* (pp. 131–144). Newbury Park, CA: Sage.

Miller, D., & Form, W. (1951). *Industrial sociology: An introduction to the sociology of work relations*. New York: Harper.

Miller, J. G. (1978). *Living systems*. New York: McGraw-Hill.

Miller, K. (1995). *Organizational communication: Approaches and processes*. Belmont, CA: Wadsworth.

Miller, K. (2003). *Organizational communication: Approaches and processes* (3rd ed.). Belmont, CA: Wadsworth.

Miller, K., Ellis, B., Zook, E., & Lyles, J. (1990). An integrated model of communication, stress, and burnout in the workplace. *Communication Research, 17*, 300–326.

Miller, K., & Monge, P. (1986). Participation, satisfaction, and productivity: A meta-analytic review. *Academy of Management Journal, 29*, 727–753.

Miller, K., Stiff, J., & Ellis, B. (1988). Communication and empathy as precursors to burnout among human service workers. *Communication Monographs, 55*, 250–265.

Miller, V., & Jablin, F. (1991). Information seeking during organizational entry: Influences, tactics, and a model of the process. *Academy of Management Review, 16*, 92–120.

Millions forced into slavery. (2002, May 27). BBC News. Retrieved December 7, 2005, from http://news.bbc.co.uk/1/hi/world/2010401.stm

Minh-Ha, T. (1991). *When the moon waxes red: Representation, gender, and cultural politics*. New York: Routledge.

Mitchell, T., & Scott, W. (1990). America's problems and needed reforms: Confronting the ethic of personal advantage. *The Executive, 4*, 23–35.

Mitroff, I., & Kilmann, R. (1975). Stories managers tell: A new tool for organizational problem-solving. *Management Review, 64*, 18–28.

Mohan, M. (1993). *Organizational communication and cultural vision*. Albany, NY: SUNY Press.

Monge, P., Bachman, S., Dillard, J., & Eisenberg, E. (1982). Communicator competence in the workplace: Model testing and scale development. In M. Burgoon (Ed.), *Communication yearbook* (Vol. 5, pp. 505–528). New Brunswick, NJ: Transaction.

Monge, P., & Contractor, N. (2001). Emergence of communication networks. In F. Jablin & L. Putnam (Eds.), *The new handbook of organizational communication* (pp. 440–502). Thousand Oaks, CA: Sage.

Monge, P., Cozzens, M., & Contractor, N. (1992). Communication and motivational predictors of the dynamics of organizational innovations. *Organization Science, 3*, 250–274.

Monge, P., & Eisenberg, E. (1987). Emergent communication networks. In F. Jablin, L. Putnam, K. Roberts, & L. Porter (Eds.), *Handbook of organizational communication* (pp. 204–342). Beverly Hills, CA: Sage.

Monge, P., & Fulk, J. (1995, May). *Global network organizations*. Paper presented at the annual meeting of the International Communication Association, Albuquerque, NM.

Morgan, G. (1986). *Images of organization*. Newbury Park, CA: Sage.

Morrison, E., & Bies, R. (1991). Impression management in the feedback-seeking process: A literature review and research agenda. *Academy of Management Review, 16*, 522–541.

Moskowitz, M., & Townsend, C. (1991, October). The 85 best companies for working mothers. *Working Mother*, 29–64.

Motley, M. (1992). Mindfulness in solving communicators' dilemmas. *Communication Monographs, 59*, 306–317.

Mouritsen, J., & Bjorn-Andersen, N. (1991). Understanding third-wave information systems. In C. Dunlop & R. Kling (Eds.), *Computerization and controversy: Value conflicts and social choices* (pp. 308–320). San Diego, CA: Academic Press.

Moxley, R. (1994, September). *Foundations of leadership.* Paper presented at the Center for Creative Leadership, Greensboro, NC.

Moyers, B. (1989). *A world of ideas.* New York: Doubleday.

Mumby, D. (1987). The political function of narratives in organizations. *Communication Monographs, 54,* 113–127.

Mumby, D. (1988). *Communication and power in the organization: Discourse, ideology, and domination.* Norwood, NJ: Ablex.

Mumby, D. (1993). *Narrative and social control.* Newbury Park, CA: Sage.

Mumby, D. (2000). Communication, organization, and the public sphere: A feminist perspective. In P. Buzzanell (Ed.), *Rethinking organizational & managerial communication from feminist perspectives* (pp. 3–23). Thousand Oaks, CA: Sage.

Mumby, D. (2005). Theorizing resistance in organization studies: A dialectical approach. *Management Communication Quarterly, 19,* 19–44.

Mumby, D., & Putnam, L. (1993). The politics of emotion: A feminist reading of bounded rationality. *Academy of Management Review, 17,* 465–486.

Mumby, D., & Stohl, C. (1996). Disciplining organizational communication studies. *Management Communication Quarterly, 10,* 465–486.

Murphy, A. (1998). Hidden transcripts of flight attendant resistance. *Management Communication Quarterly, 11,* 499–535.

Murphy, A. (1999). Managing "nowhere": The changing organizational performance of air travel. *Dissertation Abstracts, 59*(11-A), 4012.

Murphy, A. (2001). The flight attendant dilemma: An analysis of communication and sensemaking during in-flight emergencies. *Journal of Applied Communication Research, 29,* 30–53.

Murphy, A. (2002). Struggling for organizational voice. *Management Communication Quarterly, 15*(4), 626–631.

Murphy, A. (2003). The dialectical gaze. *Journal of Contemporary Ethnography, 32,* 305–336.

Murphy, D. (1999, May 30). A new attitude. *San Francisco Examiner,* pp. J1–J2.

Myerson, D. (2003). *Tempered radicals: How people use difference to inspire change at work.* Cambridge, MA: Harvard Business School Press.

Nadesan, M., & Trethewey, A. (2000). Enterprising subjects: Gendered strategies of success. *Text and Performance Quarterly, 20,* 1–28.

Namie, G. (2000, September). U.S. hostile workplace survey 2000. Retrieved September 17, 2003, from http://bullyinginstitute.org/home/twd/bb/res/bullinst.pdf

National Commission on Terrorist Attacks. *The 9/11 Commission Report.* Washington, DC: U.S. Government Printing Office.

National Communication Association. (1999, September). Credo. *Spectra,* p. 4.

Neale, M. A., & Bazerman, M. H. (1985). The effects of framing and negotiator overconfidence on bargaining behaviors and outcomes. *Academy of Management Journal, 28,* 34–49.

Nicotera, A., Clinkscales, M., & Walker, F. (in press). *Understanding organizations through culture and structure: Relational and other lessons from the African-American organization.* New York: Erlbaum.

Noer, D. (1995). *Healing the wounds: Overcoming the trauma of layoffs and revitalizing downsized organizations.* San Francisco: Jossey-Bass.

Nomaguchi, K., & Bianchi, S. (2004). Exercise time: Gender differences in the effects of marriage, parenthood and employment. *Journal of Marriage and Family*, *66*, 413–430.

Ochs, E., Smith, R., & Taylor, C. (1989). Detective stories at dinnertime: Problem solving through co-narration. *Cultural Dynamics*, *2*, 238–257.

Ogden, C., & Richards, I. (1936). *The meaning of meaning.* New York: Harcourt, Brace.

Oldenburg, R. (1999). *The great good place.* New York: Marlowe.

Oldham, G., & Rotchford, N. (1983). Relationships between office characteristics and employee reactions: A study of the physical environment. *Administrative Science Quarterly*, *28*, 542–556.

100 best corporate citizens for 2005. (2005, Spring). *Business ethics.* Retrieved April 12, 2006, from http://www.business-ethics.com/whats_new/100best.html

Orbe, M. P. (1998). *Constructing co-cultural theory: An explication of culture, power, and communication.* Thousand Oaks, CA: Sage.

Orbe, M. P. (2004). Negotiating multiple identities within multiple frames: An analysis of first-generation college students. *Communication Education*, *53*, 131–149.

Ortner, S. (1980). Theory in anthropology since the sixties. *Journal for the Comparative Study of Society and History*, 126–166.

Osborn, J., Moran, L., Musselwhite, E., & Zenger, J. (1990). *Self-directed work teams.* Homewood, IL: Business One Irwin.

Ouchi, W. (1981). *Theory Z.* Reading, MA: Addison-Wesley.

Ouchi, W., & Wilkins, A. (1985). Organizational culture. *Annual Review of Sociology*, *11*, 457–483.

Oxfam America. (2006). Retrieved January 20, 2006, from http://www.oxfamamerica.org

Pacanowsky, M. (1988). Communication in the empowering organization. In J. Anderson (Ed.), *Communication yearbook* (Vol. 11, pp. 356–379). Newbury Park, CA: Sage.

Pacanowsky, M., & O'Donnell-Trujillo, N. (1983). Organizational communication as cultural performance. *Communication Monographs*, *50*, 126–147.

Papa, M. (1989). Communicator competence and employee performance with new technology: A case study. *The Southern Communication Journal*, *55*, 87–101.

Papa, M. (1990). Communication network patterns and employee performance with new technology. *Communication Research*, *17*, 344–368.

Papa, M., Auwal, M., & Singhal, A. (1997). Organizing for social change within concertive control systems. *Communication Monographs*, *64*, 219–249.

Parker, P. (1997). *African American women executives within dominant culture organizations: An examination of leadership socialization, communication strategies, and leadership behavior.* Unpublished doctoral dissertation, University of Texas, Austin.

Parker, P. (2003). Control, resistance, and empowerment in raced, gendered, and classed contexts: The case of the African American woman. In P. Kalbfleisch, (Ed.), *Communication yearbook* (Vol. 27, pp. 257–291). London: Lawrence Erlbaum Associates.

Parks, M. (1982). Ideology in interpersonal communication: Off the couch and into the world. In M. Burgoon (Ed.), *Communication yearbook* (Vol. 5, pp. 79–108). New Brunswick, NJ: Transaction.

Parsons, C., Herold, D., & Leatherwood, M. (1985). Turnover during initial employment: A longitudinal study of the role of causal attributions. *Journal of Applied Psychology*, *70*, 337–341.

Parsons, T. (1951). *The social system.* New York: Free Press of Glencoe.

Pearson, A. (2003). *I don't know how she does it: The life of Kate Reddy, working mother.* New York: Knopf.

Pelias, R. (2003). *Methodology of the heart.* Carbondale: Southern Illinois University Press.

Pendele, G. (1999, June 9). A man in a woman's world. *The Times*. Retrieved January 5, 2006, from http://www.timesonline.co.uk

Pennsylvania State University. (2006, January 5). A brief Penn State history. Retrieved January 15, 2006, from http://www.psu.edu/ur/about/history/historyshort.html

Peppers, D., & Rogers, M. (1996). *The one to one future*. New York: Doubleday/Currency.

Perrons, D. (2003). The new economy and the work-life balance: Conceptual explorations and a case study of new media. *Gender, Work & Organization, 10*, 65–93.

Perrow, C. (1986). *Complex organizations: A critical essay* (3rd ed.). New York: Random House.

Peters, T. (1987). *Thriving on chaos*. New York: Knopf.

Peters, T. (1994a). *Liberation management*. New York: Ballantine.

Peters, T. (1994b). *The pursuit of wow*. New York: Vintage.

Peters, T., & Waterman, R. (1982). *In search of excellence*. New York: Harper & Row.

Peterson, L. (1995, November). *The influence of sharing a semantic link on social support in work relationships at a hospital*. Paper presented at the annual meeting of the Speech Communication Association, San Antonio, TX.

Peterson, L., & Albrecht, T. (1999). Where gender/power/politics collide: Deconstructing organizational maternity leave policy. *Journal of Management Inquiry, 8*, 168–181.

Pettigrew, A. (1979). On studying organizational cultures. *Administrative Science Quarterly, 24*, 570–581.

Pfeffer, J., & Sutton, R. (1999, May/June). The smart talk trap. *Harvard Business Review, 77*, 134–142.

Pfeffer, J., & Veiga, J. (1999). Putting people first for organizational success. *Academy of Management Executive, 13*, 37–48.

Phillips, G. (1991). *Communication incompetencies: A theory of training oral performance behavior*. Carbondale: Southern Illinois University Press.

Phillips, K. (2002). *Wealth and democracy: A political history of the American rich*. New York: Broadway Books.

Pinchot, G., & Pinchot, E. (1993). *The end of bureaucracy and the rise of the intelligent organization*. San Francisco: Berrett-Koehler.

Pine, B. J., Gilmore, J., & Pine, B. J., II. (1999). *The experience economy*. Cambridge, MA: Harvard Business School Press.

Poole, M. S. (1983). Decision development in small groups II: A study of multiple sequences in decision making. *Communication Monographs, 50*, 321–341.

Poole, M. S. (1996, February). *A turn of the wheel: The case for a renewal of systems inquiry in organizational communication research*. Paper presented at the Conference on Organizational Communication and Change, Austin, TX.

Poole, M. S. (in press). Organizational challenges for the new forms. In G. DeSanctis & J. Fulk (Eds.), *Shaping organizational form: Communication, connection, and community*. Thousand Oaks, CA: Sage.

Poole, M. S., & DeSanctis, G. (1990). Understanding the use of group decision support systems: The theory of adaptive structuration. In J. Fulk & C. Steinfeld (Eds.), *Organizations and communication technology* (pp. 173–193). Newbury Park, CA: Sage.

Poole, M. S., & Roth, J. (1989). Decision development in small groups V: Test of a contingency model. *Human Communication Research, 15*, 549–589.

Porter, L. (2003). *Organizational influence processes*. New York: M. E. Sharpe.

Porter, M. (1980). *Competitive strategy: Techniques for analyzing industries and competitors*. New York: Free Press.

Prigogine, I. (1980). *From being to becoming*. San Francisco: Freeman.

Pritchard, R., Jones, S., Roth, P., & Steubing, K. (1988). Effects of group feedback, goal setting, and incentives on organizational productivity. *Journal of Applied Psychology, 73,* 337–358.

Putnam, L. (1982). Paradigms for organizational communication research: An overview and synthesis. *Western Journal of Speech Communication, 46,* 192–206.

Putnam, L. (1985). Contradictions and paradoxes in organizations. In L. Thayer (Ed.), *Organization and communication: Emerging perspectives* (pp. 151–167). Norwood, NJ: Ablex.

Putnam, L. (1995). Formal negotiations: The productive side of organizational conflict. In A. Nicotera (Ed.), *Conflict and organizations: Communication processes* (pp. 183–200). Albany: SUNY Press.

Putnam, L., & Fairhurst, G. (2001). Discourse analysis in organizations: Issues and concerns. In F. Jablin & G. Fairhurst (Eds.), *The new handbook of organizational communication* (pp. 78–136). Thousand Oaks, CA: Sage.

Putnam, L., & Kolb, D. M. (2000). Rethinking negotiation: Feminist views of communication and exchange. In P. Buzzanell (Ed.), *Rethinking organizational & managerial communication from feminist perspectives* (pp. 76–106). Thousand Oaks, CA: Sage.

Putnam, L., & Pacanowsky, M. (1983). *Communication and organizations: An interpretive approach.* Beverly Hills, CA: Sage.

Putnam, L., & Poole, M. S. (1987). Conflict and negotiation. In F. Jablin, L. Putnam, K. Roberts, & L. Porter (Eds.), *Handbook of organizational communication* (pp. 549–599). Newbury Park, CA: Sage.

Pynchon, T. (1973). *Gravity's rainbow.* New York: Viking.

Quick, J., & Quick, J. (1984). *Organizational stress and preventative management.* New York: McGraw-Hill.

Quinn, R. (1977). Coping with Cupid: The formation, impact, and management of romantic relationships in organizations. *Administrative Science Quarterly, 22,* 30–45.

Quinn, R. (2005). Moments of greatness: Entering the fundamental state of leadership. *Harvard Business Review, 83,* 74–83.

Raban, J. (1991). *Hunting mister heartbreak: A discovery of America.* San Francisco: HarperCollins.

Rabinow, P., & Sullivan, W. (1986). *Interpretive social science — A second look.* Berkeley: University of California Press.

Rafaeli, A., & Sutton, R. (1987). The expression of emotion as part of the work role. *Academy of Management Review, 12,* 23–37.

Rawlins, W. K. (1994). Being there and growing apart: Sustaining friendships during adulthood. In D. Canary & L. Stafford (Eds.), *Communication and relational maintenance* (pp. 275–296). San Diego, CA: Academic Press.

Ray, E. (1987). Supportive relationships and occupational stress in the workplace. In T. Albrecht & M. Adelman (Eds.), *Communicating social support* (pp. 172–191). Newbury Park, CA: Sage.

Reardon, K. (1997). Dysfunctional communication patterns in the workplace: Closing the gap between men and women. In D. Dunn (Ed.), *Workplace/women's place: An anthology* (pp. 165–180). Los Angeles: Roxbury.

Redding, W. C. (1972). *Communication within the organization.* New York: Industrial Communications Council.

Redding, W. C. (1985). Rocking boats, blowing whistles, teaching speech communication. *Communication Education, 34,* 245–258.

Redding, W. C. (1991). *Unethical messages in the organizational context.* Paper presented at the Annual Convention of the International Communication Association, Chicago.

Reuther, C., & Fairhurst, G. T. (2000). Chaos theory and the glass ceiling. In P. Buzzanell (Ed.), *Rethinking organizational & managerial communication from feminist perspectives* (pp. 236–256). Thousand Oaks, CA: Sage.

Rice, R. E., & Aydin, C. (1990). Social worlds, information systems and intraorganizational boundaries. In D. Henderson (Ed.), *Proceedings of the American Society for Information Science* (Vol. 27, pp. 256–260). Medford, NJ: Learned Information.

Richards, I. (1936). *The philosophy of rhetoric.* New York and London: Oxford University Press.

Richmond, V., Davis, L., Saylor, K., & McCroskey, J. (1984). Power strategies in organizations: Communication techniques and messages. *Human Communication Research, 11,* 85–108.

Richmond, V., & McCroskey, J. (1979). Management communication style, tolerance for disagreement, and innovativeness as predictors of employee satisfaction: A comparison of single-factor, two-factor, and multiple-factor approaches. In D. Nimmo (Ed.), *Communication yearbook* (Vol. 3, pp. 359–374). New Brunswick, NJ: Transaction.

Rider, A. (1992, September 15). Wishful thinking. *Los Angeles Times Magazine,* p. 10.

Rifkin, J. (1995). *The end of work.* New York: Tarcher/Putnam.

Rifkin, J. (1999). *The biotech century.* New York: Tarcher.

Riley, P., & Eisenberg, E. (1992). *The ACE model of management.* (Unpublished working paper). University of Southern California, Los Angeles.

Robbins, A. (1997). *Unleashing the Power Within.* New York: Free Press.

Robert, M. (1993). *Strategy: Pure and simple.* New York: McGraw-Hill.

Roberts, K., & O'Reilly, C. (1974). Failures in upward communication: Three possible culprits. *Academy of Management Journal, 17,* 205–215.

Robertson, J. (1985). *Future work: Jobs, self-employment, and leisure after the industrial age.* New York: Universe Books.

Robin & Associates. (2002). A better workplace: Dealing with difficult people. Retrieved from http://www.abetterworkplace.com

Rogers, E., & Kincaid, D. (1981). *Communication networks: Toward a new paradigm for research.* New York: Free Press.

Ronfeldt, D., and Arquilla, J. Networks, netwars, and the fight for the future. *First Monday, 6*(10). Retrieved March 3, 2006, from http://firstmonday.org/issues/issue6_10/ronfeldt/index.html

Rose, D. (1989). *Patterns of American culture.* Philadelphia: University of Pennsylvania Press.

Rose, H. (1983). Hand, brain, and heart: A feminist epistemology for the natural sciences. *Signs, 9,* 81.

Rosen, M. (1985). Breakfast at Spiro's: Dramaturgy and dominance. *Journal of Management, 11,* 31–48.

Rosenberg, T. (2002, August 18). The free-trade fix. *New York Times Magazine,* pp. 28–33, 50, 74–75.

Rosener, J. (1990). Ways women lead. *Harvard Business Review, 68,* 119–125.

Rosenfeld, L., Richman, J., & May, S. (2004). Information adequacy, job satisfaction and organizational culture in a dispersed-network organization. *Journal of Applied Communication Research, 32,* 28–54.

Rounds, J. (1984). Information and ambiguity in organizational change. *Advances in information processing in organizations, 1,* 111–141.

Roy, D. (1960). Banana time: Job satisfaction and informal interaction. *Human Organization, 18,* 156–180.

Rummler, G., & Brache, A. (1991). *Managing the white space in your organizational chart.* New York: Free Press.

Rushing, J. (1993). Power, Other, and Spirit in cultural texts. *Western Journal of Communication, 57*, 159–168.

Sackmann, S. (1991). *Cultural knowledge in organizations.* Newbury Park, CA: Sage.

Sahlins, M. (1976). *Culture and practical reason.* Chicago: University of Chicago Press.

Said, E. (1978). *Orientalism.* New York: Pantheon.

Said, E. (1984). *The world, the text, and the critic.* Cambridge, MA: Harvard University Press.

Sailer, H., Schlachter, J., & Edwards, M. (1982, July/August). Stress: Causes, consequences, and coping strategies. *Personnel, 59*, 35–48.

Sala, F., Druskat, V., & Mount, G. (2005). *Linking emotional intelligence and performance at work: Current research with individuals and groups.* New York: Erlbaum.

Samovar, L., Jain, N., & Porter, R. (1998). *Understanding intercultural communication.* New York: Wadsworth.

Sample, S. (2001). *A contrarian's guide to leadership.* San Francisco: Jossey-Bass.

Sashkin, M. (1991). *Total quality management.* Brentwood, MD: International Graphics.

Saul, S. (2005, November 28). Gimme an Rx! Cheerleaders pep up drug sales. *New York Times.* Retrieved March 3, 2006, from http://www.nytimes.com

Scandura, T., Graen, G., & Novak, M. (1986). When managers decide not to decide autocratically. *Journal of Applied Psychology, 71*, 1–6.

Schaef, A. W., & Fassel, D. (1988). *The addictive organization.* San Francisco: Harper & Row.

Schaubroeck, J., & Merritt, D. (1997). Divergent effects of job control on coping with work stressors: The key role of self-efficacy. *Academy of Management Journal, 40*, 738–754.

Scheibel, D. (1996). Appropriating bodies: Organizing ideology and cultural practice in medical school. *Journal of Applied Communication Research, 24*, 310–331.

Scheibel, D. (2003). "Reality ends here": Graffiti as an artifact. In R. Clair (Ed.), *Expressions of ethnography: Novel approaches to qualitative methods* (pp. 219–230). Albany: SUNY Press.

Schein, E. (1969). *Process consultation: Its role in organizational development.* Reading, MA: Addison-Wesley.

Schein, E. (1988). *Organizational culture and leadership: A dynamic view.* San Francisco: Jossey-Bass.

Schein, E. (1991). The role of the founder in the creation of organizational culture. In P. Frost, L. Moore, & M. Louis (Eds.), *Reframing organizational culture* (pp. 14–25). Newbury Park, CA: Sage.

Schor, J. (1998). *The overspent American: Upscaling, downshifting, and the new consumer.* New York: Basic Books.

Schuler, R., & Jackson, S. (1986). Managing stress through PHRM practices: An uncertainty interpretation. *Research in Personnel and Human Resource Management, 4*, 183–224.

Schwartzman, H. (1993). *Ethnography in organizations.* Newbury Park, CA: Sage.

Scott, C. (2005). *The discursive organization of risk and safety: How firefighters manage occupational hazards.* Unpublished doctoral dissertation, Arizona State University.

Scott, C., Corman, S., & Cheney, G. (1998). Development of a structurational model of identification in an organization. *Communication Theory, 8*, 298–336.

Scott, J. (1990). *Domination and the arts of resistance: Hidden transcripts.* New Haven, CT: Yale University Press.

Scott, W. R. (1981). *Organizations: Rational, natural, and open systems.* Englewood Cliffs, NJ: Prentice Hall.

Selznick, P. (1948). Foundations of the theory of organizations. *American Sociological Review, 13*, 25–35.

Selznick, P. (1957). *Leadership in administration.* New York: Harper & Row.

Senge, P. (1990). *The fifth discipline: The art and practice of the learning organization*. New York: Doubleday/Currency.

Senge, P. (1994). *The fifth discipline: The art and practice of the learning organization*. New York: Doubleday/Currency.

Senge, P., Roberts, C., Ross, R., Smith, B., & Kleiner, A. (1994). *The fifth discipline fieldbook*. New York: Doubleday/Currency.

Senge, P., Scharmer, C., Jaworski, J., & Flowers, B. (2004). *Presence: Human purpose and the field of the future*. Cambridge, MA: Society for Organizational Learning.

Senge, P., Scharmer, C., Jaworski, J., & Flowers, B. (2005). *Presence: An exploration of profound change in people, organizations, and society*. New York: Penguin.

Shamir, B., Dayan-Horesh, H., & Adler, D. (2005). Leading by biography: Towards a life-story approach to the study of leadership. *Leadership, 1*, 13–29.

Shipler, D. (2004). *The working poor: Invisible in America*. New York: Vintage.

Shockley-Zalabak, P. (1991). *Fundamentals of organizational communication*. New York: Longman.

Shockley-Zalabak, P. (2002). Protean places: Teams across time and space. *Journal of Applied Communication Research, 30*(3), 231–250.

Shockley-Zalabak, P., & Morley, D. (1994). Creating a culture. *Human Communication Research, 20*, 334–355.

Shome, R., & Hegde, R. S. (2002). Postcolonial approaches to communication: Charting the terrain, engaging the intersections. *Communication Theory, 12*, 249–270.

Shorris, E. (1984). *Scenes from corporate life: The politics of middle management*. New York: Penguin.

Shorris, E. (1997). *New American blues*. New York: Norton.

Shuler, S. (2000, November). *Breaking through the glass ceiling without breaking a nail: Portrayal of women executives in the popular business press*. Paper presented at the annual convention of the National Communication Association, Seattle, WA.

Shuter, R., & Turner, L. H. (1997). African American and European American women in the workplace: Perceptions of conflict communication. *Management Communication Quarterly, 11*, 74–96.

Sias, P., & Jablin, F. (1995). Differential superior-subordinate relations, perceptions of fairness, and coworker communication. *Human Communication Research, 22*, 5–38.

Silverstein, S. (1992, January 1). Sabbaticals are costly for women. *Los Angeles Times*, p. D1.

Simon, H. (1957). *Administrative behavior* (3rd ed.). New York: Free Press.

Sivard, R. (1983). *World military and social expenditures 1983*. Washington, DC: World Priorities.

Sloan, A. (2002, January 21). Who killed Enron? *Newsweek*, pp. 18–24.

Small, A. (1905). *General sociology*. Chicago: University of Chicago Press.

Smircich, L., & Calas, M. (1987). Organizational culture: A critical assessment. In F. Jablin, L. Putnam, K. Roberts, & L. Porter (Eds.), *Handbook of organizational communication* (pp. 228–263). Newbury Park, CA: Sage.

Smith, A. (1898). *Wealth of nations*. London: Routledge.

Smith, D. (1972). Communication research and the idea of process. *Speech Monographs, 39*, 174–182.

Smith, F., & Keyton, J. (2001). Organizational storytelling: Metaphors for relational power and identity struggles. *Management Communication Quarterly, 15*, 149–182.

Smith, H. (1982). *Beyond the postmodern mind*. New York: Crossroad.

Smith, H. (1995, May). *The three faces of capitalism*. Public Broadcasting System.

Smith, M., Cohen, B., Stammerjohn, V., & Happ, A. (1981). An investigation of health complaints and job stress in video display operations. *Human Factors, 23*, 387–400.

Smith, P. (2005, February 11). Bullies incorporated. *Sydney Morning Herald*. Retrieved March 14, 2006, from http://www.smh.com.au/news/Management-Focus/Bullies-incorporated/2005/02/14/1108229910089.html

Smith, R., & Eisenberg, E. (1987). Conflict at Disneyland: A root metaphor analysis. *Communication Monographs, 54*, 367–380.

Society for Human Resource Management. (2002). *Benefits survey*. Alexandria, VA: Society for Human Resource Management.

Somervell, D., & Toynbee, A. (1947). *A study of history*. New York: Oxford University Press.

Sotirin, P. (2000). "All they do is bitch bitch bitch": Political and interactional features of women's office talk. *Women's Studies in Communication, 23*, 19–25.

Southwest Airlines. (1988, January). The mission of Southwest Airlines. Retrieved January 16, 2006, from http://www.southwest.com/about_swa/mision.html

Sparrowe, R., & Liden, E. (1997). Process and structure in leader member exchange. *Academy of Management Review, 22*, 522–552.

Speech Communication Association. (1991). *Pathways to careers in communication*. Annandale, VA: Author.

Spellers, R. (1998). Happy to be nappy: Embracing an Afrocentric aesthetic of beauty. In J. Martin, T. Nakayama, & L. Flores (Eds.), *Readings in cultural contexts* (pp. 70–78). Mountain View, CA: Mayfield.

Spradlin, A. (1998). The price of "passing." *Management Communication Quarterly, 11*, 598–606.

Spretnak, C. (1991). *States of grace*. San Francisco: HarperCollins.

Staimer, M. (1992). U.S. workers get little vacation. *USA Today*, A1.

Stalk, G. (1998). Time: The next source of competitive advantage. In R. Gupta (Ed.), *Managerial excellence* (pp. 171–192). Cambridge, MA: Harvard Business School Press.

Stallybrass, P., & White, A. (1986). *The politics and poetics of transgression*. Ithaca, NY: Cornell University Press.

Steelman, J., & Klitzman, S. (1985). *The VDT: Hazardous to your health*. Ithaca, NY: Cornell University Press.

Steers, R. (1977). Antecedents and outcomes of organizational commitment. *Administrative Science Quarterly, 22*, 46–56.

Steers, R. (1981). *Introduction to organizational behavior*. Santa Monica, CA: Goodyear.

Steier, F. (1989). Toward a radical and ecological constructivist approach to family communication. *Journal of Applied Communication Research, 17*, 1–26.

Steier, F., & Smith, K. (1992). The cybernetics of cybernetics and the organization of organization. In L. Thayer (Ed.), *Organization-communication: Emerging perspectives*. Norwood, NJ: Ablex.

Stewart, J. (2000, April). *The practice of dialogue*. Grazier Lecture, Department of Communication, University of South Florida, Tampa.

Stewart, T. (1991, August 12). GE keeps those ideas coming. *Fortune, 40*(8).

Stewart, T. (1998, September 7). The cunning plots of leadership. *Fortune*, 165.

Stiglitz, J. E. (2002). *Globalization and its discontents*. New York: Norton.

Stohl, C., & Cheney, G. (2001). Participatory processes/paradoxical practices: Communication and the dilemmas of organizational democracy. *Management Communication Quarterly, 14*, 349–407.

Stoller, P. (1989). *The taste of ethnographic things*. Philadelphia: University of Pennsylvania Press.

Stork, D., Wilson, F., Wicks, A., Sproull, J., & Vena, J. (2005). *The new workforce reality: Insights for today, implications for tomorrow*. Boston: Simmons School of Management and Bright Horizons Family Solutions.

Strine, M. (1991). Critical theory and "organic" intellectuals: Reframing the work of cultural critique. *Communication Monographs, 58*, 195–201.

Sullivan, J. (1988). Three roles of language in motivation theory. *Academy of Management Review, 13*, 104–115.

Sunwolf, & Seibold, D. R. (1998). Jurors' intuitive rules for deliberation: A structurational approach to the study of communication in jury decision making. *Communication Monographs, 65*, 282–307.

Talbott, M. (2002, October 13). When men taunt men, is it sexual harassment? *New York Times Magazine*, pp. 52–57, 82, 84, 95.

Tamaki, J. (1991, October 10). Sexual harassment in the workplace. *Los Angeles Times*, p. D2.

Tannen, D. (1990). *You just don't understand: Men and women in conversation*. New York: Ballantine.

Taylor, B. C. (1990). Reminiscences of Los Alamos: Narrative, critical theory and the organizational subject. *Western Journal of Speech Communication, 54*, 395–419.

Taylor, C. (1991). *The ethics of authenticity*. Cambridge, MA: Harvard University Press.

Taylor, F. (1913). *The principles of scientific management*. New York: Harper.

Taylor, F. (1947). *Scientific management*. New York: Harper & Brothers.

Therborn, G. (1980). *The ideology of power and the power of ideology*. London: Verso.

Thomas, J. (1993). *Doing critical ethnography*. Newbury Park, CA: Sage.

Thomas, L. (1975). *The lives of a cell*. New York: Penguin.

Thompson, J. (1967). *Organizations in action*. New York: McGraw-Hill.

Tichy, N., Pritchett, P., & Cohen, E. (1998). *The leadership engine*. New York: Pritchett.

Tjosvold, D. (1984). Effects of leader warmth and directiveness on subordinate performance on a subsequent task. *Journal of Applied Psychology, 69*, 422–427.

Tjosvold, D., & Tjosvold, M. (1991). *Leading the team organization*. New York: Lexington.

Tompkins, P. (1984). Functions of communication in organizations. In C. Arnold & J. Bowers (Eds.), *Handbook of rhetorical and communication theory*. Boston: Allyn and Bacon.

Tompkins, P. (1987). Translating organizational theory: Symbolism over substance. In F. Jablin, L. Putnam, K. Roberts, & L. Porter (Eds.), *Handbook of organizational communication* (pp. 70–96). Newbury Park, CA: Sage.

Tompkins, P., & Cheney, G. (1985). Communication and unobtrusive control in contemporary organizations. In R. McPhee & P. Tompkins (Eds.), *Organizational communication: Traditional themes and new directions* (pp. 179–210). Beverly Hills, CA: Sage.

Tompkins, P., & Tompkins, E. (2004). Apollo, Challenger, *and* Columbia: *The decline of the space program*. Los Angeles: Roxbury.

Tompkins, P., & Wanca-Thibault, M. (2001). Organizational communication: Prelude and prospects. In F. Jablin & L. Putnam (Eds.), *The new handbook of organizational communication* (pp. xvii–xxxi). Thousand Oaks, CA: Sage.

Torbert, W. (1991). *The power of balance*. Newbury Park, CA: Sage.

Townsley, N., & Geist, P. (2000). The discursive enactment of hegemony: Sexual harassment and academic organizing. *Western Journal of Communication, 64*, 190–217.

Townsley, N., & Stohl, C. (2003). Contracting corporate social responsibility: Swedish expansion in global temporary agency work. *Management Communication Quarterly, 16*, 599–605.

Tracy, K., & Eisenberg, E. (1991). Giving criticism: A multiple goals case study. *Research on Language and Social Interaction, 24*, 37–70.

Tracy, S. (2000). Becoming a character for commerce: Emotion labor, self subordination and discursive construction of identity in a total institution. *Management Communication Quarterly, 14*(1), 90–128.

Tracy, S. (2003). Watching the watchers: Making sense of emotional constructions behind bars. In R. Clair (Ed.), *Expressions of ethnography: Novel approaches to qualitative methods* (pp. 153–158). Albany: SUNY Press.

Tracy, S. (2004). The construction of correctional officers: Layers of emotionality behind bars. *Qualitative Inquiry, 10*, 509–533.

Tracy, S. (2005). Locking up emotion: Moving beyond dissonance for understanding emotion labor discomfort. *Communication Monographs, 72*, 261–283.

Tracy, S., Alberts, J., & Lutgen-Sandvik, P. (2005, November). *Why define myself as a low-status organizational victim? The challenges of telling stories about workplace bullying.* Paper presented at the annual convention of the National Communication Association, Boston, MA.

Tracy, S., Lutgen-Sandvik, P., & Alberts, J. (in press). Is it really that bad? A metaphorical analysis exploring the emotional pain of workplace bullying. *Management Communication Quarterly.*

Tracy, S., & Tracy, K. (1998). Emotion labor at 911. *Journal of Applied Communication Research, 26*, 390–411.

Tracy, S., & Trethewey, A. (2005). Fracturing the real-self ↔ fake-self dichotomy: Moving toward "crystallized" organizational discourses and identities. *Communication Theory, 15*, 168–195.

Trethewey, A. (1997). Resistance, identity, and empowerment. *Communication Monographs, 64*, 281–301.

Trethewey, A. (1999a). Disciplined bodies: Women's embodied identities at work. *Organization Studies, 20*, 423–450.

Trethewey, A. (1999b). Isn't it ironic: Using irony to explore the contradictions of organizational life. *Western Journal of Communication, 63*, 140–167.

Trethewey, A. (2000). Revisioning control: A feminist critique of disciplined bodies. In P. Buzzanell (Ed.), *Rethinking organizational & managerial communication from feminist perspectives* (pp. 107–127). Thousand Oaks, CA: Sage.

Trethewey, A. (2001). Reproducing and resisting the master narrative of decline: Midlife professional women's experience of aging. *Management Communication Quarterly, 15*, 183–226.

Trethewey, A. (2004). Sexuality, eros and pedagogy: Desiring laughter in the classroom. *Women and Language, 27*, 35–41.

Trethewey, A., & Corman, S. (2001). Anticipating K-Commerce: E-Commerce, knowledge management and organizational communication. *Management Communication Quarterly, 14*, 619–628.

Triece, M. (1999). The practical true woman: Reconciling women and work in popular mail-order magazines. *Critical Studies in Mass Communication, 16*, 42–62.

Trist, E. (1981). *The evolution of socio-technical systems.* (Occasional Paper No. 2). Toronto: Quality of Work Life Centre.

Turnage, J. (1990). The challenge of new workplace technology for psychology. *American Psychologist, 45*, 171–178.

Turner, P. (2003). Telling the story of birth. In R. Clair (Ed.), *Expressions of ethnography: Novel approaches to qualitative methods* (pp. 55–64). Albany: SUNY Press.

Turner, V. (1982). *From ritual to theatre: The human seriousness of play.* New York: Performing Arts Journal Publications.

Tyler, M. (2004). Managing between the sheets: Lifestyle magazines and the management of sexuality in everyday life. *Sexualities, 7*, 81–106.

Tyson, L. (1991, November 10). U.S. needs new spending priorities. *Los Angeles Times*, p. D2.

UNCG Undergraduate Bulletin. (2002–2003). Greensboro, NC: University of North Carolina Greensboro.

U.S. Bureau of Labor Statistics. Home page. Retrieved August 2006 from http://stats.bls .gov/

U.S. Department of Homeland Security. (n.d.). SAFECOM. Retrieved March 30, 2006, from http://www.safecomprogram.gov/SAFECOM/about/default.htm

U.S. Department of Labor. Secretary's Commission on Achieving Necessary Skills. (1991). Retrieved May 15, 2006, from http://wdr.doleta.gov/SCANS/whatwork/whatwork.pdf

Van Maanen, J. (1979). *Qualitative methodology*. Beverly Hills, CA: Sage.

Van Maanen, J. (1988). *Tales of the field: On writing ethnography*. Chicago: University of Chicago Press.

Van Maanen, J. (1991). The smile factory: Work at Disneyland. In P. Frost, L. Moore, & M. Louis (Eds.), *Reframing organizational culture* (pp. 58–76). Newbury Park, CA: Sage.

Varner, I., & Beamer, L. (1995). *Intercultural communication in the global workplace*. Chicago: Irwin.

Victor, D. A. (1994). *International business communication*. New York: HarperCollins.

von Bertalanffy, L. (1968). *General systems theory*. New York: George Braziller.

Vroom, V. (1964). *Work and motivation*. New York: Wiley.

Waldeck, J., Seibold, D., & Flanagin, A. (2005). Organizational assimilation and technology use. *Communication Monographs, 72,* 161–183.

Waldera, L. (1988). *The effects of influence strategy, influence objective, and leader member exchange on upward influence*. Unpublished doctoral dissertation, George Washington University, Washington, DC.

Waldron, V. (1991). Achieving communication goals in superior-subordinate relationships: The multi-functionality of upward maintenance tactics. *Communication Monographs, 58,* 289–306.

Ward, J., & Winstanley, D. (2004). Sexuality and the city: Exploring the experience of minority sexual identity through storytelling. *Culture and Organization, 10,* 219–236.

Warren, E., & Tyagi, A. (2003). *The two-income trap: Why middle-class fathers and mothers are going broke*. New York: Basic Books.

Watkins, L., & Johnston, L. (2000). Screening job applicants: The impact of physical attractiveness and application quality. *International Journal of Selection and Assessment, 8,* 76–96.

Watzlawick, P., Beavin, J., & Jackson, D. (1967). *The pragmatics of human communication: A study of interactional patterns, pathologies, and paradoxes*. New York: Norton.

Wayne, S., Shore, L., & Liden, R. (1997). Perceived organizational support and leader member exchange. *Academy of Management Journal, 40,* 82–111.

Weedon, C. (1997). *Feminist practice and poststructuralist theory* (2nd ed.). Oxford, England: Basil Blackwell.

Weick, K. (1976). Educational organizations as loosely coupled systems. *Administrative Science Quarterly, 21,* 1–19.

Weick, K. (1979). *The social psychology of organizing* (2nd ed.). Reading, MA: Addison-Wesley.

Weick, K. (1980). The management of eloquence. *Executive, 6,* 18–21.

Weick, K. (1990). The collapse of sensemaking in organizations: The Mann Gulch disaster. *Administrative Science Quarterly, 38,* 628–652.

Weick, K. (1995). *Sensemaking in organizations*. Newbury Park, CA: Sage.

Weick, K., & Roberts, K. (1993). Collective mind in organizations: Heedful interrelating on flight decks. *Administrative Science Quarterly, 38,* 357–381.

Weick, K., & Sutcliffe, K. (2001). *Managing the unexpected: Assuring high performance in an age of complexity*. San Francisco: Jossey-Bass.

Weick, K., Sutcliffe, K., & Obstfeld, D. (1999). Organizing for high reliability: Processes of collective mindfulness. *Research in Organizational Behavior, 21,* 81–123.

Wellins, R., Byham, W., & Wilson, J. (1991). *Empowered teams*. San Francisco: Jossey-Bass.

Wenberg, J., & Wilmot, W. (1973). *The personal communication process*. New York: Wiley.

Wentworth, W. (1980). *Context and understanding*. New York: Elsevier.

Wesley, J. (2003). Exotic dancing and the negotiation of identity: The multiple uses of body technologies. *Journal of Contemporary Ethnography, 32*, 643–669.

West, C., & Zimmerman, D. (1987). Doing gender. *Gender & Society, 1*, 125–151.

Wheatley, E. (2005). Discipline and resistance: Order and disorder in a cardiac rehabilitation clinic. *Qualitative Health Research, 15*(4), 438–459.

Wheatley, M. (1992). *Leadership and the new science*. San Francisco: Berrett-Koehler.

White, R., & Lippitt, R. (1960). *Autocracy and democracy: An experimental inquiry*. New York: Harper & Brothers.

White workplace frustrates many Blacks. (1995, October 30). *Tampa Tribune*, p. 122.

Whitney, E. (2006) Capitalizing on camp: Greed and the queer marketplace. *Text and Performance Quarterly, 26*, 36–46.

Whyte, D. (1996). *The heart aroused*. New York: Bantam Doubleday.

Whyte, W. (1948). *Human relations in the restaurant industry*. New York: McGraw-Hill.

Whyte, W. (1956). *The organization man*. New York: Simon & Schuster.

Whyte, W. (1969). *Organizational behavior: Theory and application*. Homewood, IL: Irwin.

Wilkins, A. (1984). The creation of company cultures: The role of stories and human resource systems. *Human Resource Management, 23*, 41–60.

Wilkinson, L. (1995, May). How to build scenarios. *Wired*, 4–81.

Williams, M. (1977). *The new executive woman: A guide to business success*. New York: New American Library.

Wilson, G., & Goodall, H. L. (1991). *Interviewing in context*. New York: McGraw-Hill.

Witte, G. (2004, September 20). An income gap widens, uncertainty spreads. *The Washington Post*. Retrieved April 10, 2006, from http://www.washingtonpost.com/wp-dyn/articles/A34235-2004Sep19_2.html

Wood, J. (1992). Telling our stories: Narratives as a basis for theorizing sexual harassment. *Journal of Applied Communication Research, 20*, 349–362.

Yale University. (2006). Home page. Retrieved January 5, 2006, from http://www.yale.edu

Yankelovich, D. (1999). *The magic of dialogue*. New York: Simon & Schuster.

Yedidia, M., Gillespie, C., Kachur, E., Schwartz, M., Ockene, J., Chepaitis, A., et al. (2003). Effect of communications training on medical student performance. *Journal of the American Medical Association, 290*, 1157–1165.

Zander, B., Zander, R. S. (2000). *The art of possibility*. Boston, MA: Harvard Business School Press.

Zedeck, S., & Mosier, K. (1990). Work in the family and employing organization. *American Psychologist, 45*, 240–251.

Zeithaml, V., Parasuraman, A., & Berry, L. (1990). *Delivering quality service: Balancing customer perceptions and expectations*. New York: Free Press.

Zellars, K. L., Tepper, B. J., & Duffy, M. K. (2002). Abusive supervision and subordinates' organizational citizenship behavior. *Journal of Applied Psychology, 87*, 1068–1076.

Zoller, H. (2003). Health on the line: Identity and disciplinary control in employees' occupational health and safety discourse. *Journal of Applied Communication Research, 33*, 118–139.

Acknowledgments

Page 48: R. Evered and B. Tannenbaum, excerpts from "A Dialog on Dialog" from *Journal of Management Inquiry* 1, 1992. Copyright © 1992 by Sage Publications, Inc. Reprinted with the permission of Sage Publications, Inc.

Figure 3.1: Gareth Morgan, "Organization Chart Illustrating the Principles of Classical Management Theory and Bureaucratic Organization" from *Images of Organization*. Copyright © 1986 by Sage Publications, Inc. Reprinted with the permission of Sage Publications, Inc.

Pages 79–80: Mary Truscott, excerpt from *Brats: Children of the American Military Speak Out*. Copyright © 1989 by Mary Truscott. Reprinted with the permission of Dutton, a division of Penguin Group (USA) Inc.

Page 83: Charles Perrow, excerpt from *Complex Organizations: A Critical Essay*, 3e. Copyright © 1986 by Charles Perrow. Reprinted with the permission of The McGraw-Hill Companies.

Table 3.1: Charles Perrow, "Summary of Historical and Cultural Influences on the Classical Management and Human Relations Approaches to Organizations and Communication" from *Complex Organizations: A Critical Essay*, 3e. Copyright © 1986 by Charles Perrow. Reprinted with the permission of The McGraw-Hill Companies.

Figure 3.4: Abraham Maslow, "Maslow's Hierarchy of Needs" from *Motivation and Personality* 3e. Copyright 1954 by Abraham Maslow. Reprinted with the permission of Pearson Education, Inc., Upper Saddle River, New Jersey.

Page 89: Douglas McGregor, six principles of "Theory Y" from *The Human Side of Enterprise*. Copyright © 1960 by Douglas McGregor. Reprinted with the permission of The McGraw-Hill Companies.

Page 91: Earl Shorris, excerpts from "The Politics of Middle Management" from *The Oppressed Middle: Politics of Middle Management: Scenes from a Corporate Life* (Garden City, New York: Anchor/Doubleday, 1981). Copyright © 1981 by Earl Shorris. Reprinted with the permission of the author.

Pages 103, 105: Ludwig von Bertalanffy, excerpt from *General Systems Theory*. Copyright © 1968 by Ludwig von Bertalanffy. Reprinted with the permission of George Braziller, Inc.

Table 4.1: Ludwig von Bertalanffy, "The Hierarchy of General Systems Theory" from *General Systems Theory*. Copyright © 1968 by Ludwig von Bertalanffy. Reprinted with the permission of George Braziller, Inc.

Figure 4.1: Karl Weick, "Weick's Model of Organizing" from *The Social Psychology of Organizing*. Copyright © 1979 by Karl Weick. Reprinted with the permission of The McGraw-Hill Companies.

Pages 115–16: Karl Weick, "Seven Properties of Sensemaking" from *Sensemaking in Organizations*. Copyright © 1996 by Sage Publications, Inc. Reprinted with the permission of Sage Publications, Inc.

Page 119, What Would You Do?: Reprinted with the permission of Sandra Goodall.

Page 167: Randy Cohen, excerpt from "The Ethicist" in *The New York Times Magazine*, September 22, 2002. Copyright © 2002 by Randy Cohen. Reprinted with permission.

Table 6.1: A. Trethewey and S. Corman, "Ethical Dimensions of Knowledge Management Applications" from "Anticipating K-Commerce, E-Commerce, Knowledge Management, and Organizations

Communication" in *Management Communication Quarterly 14*, 2001. Copyright © 2001 by Sage Publications, Inc. Reprinted with the permission of Sage Publications, Inc.

Figure 6.1: E. Bell and L. C. Forbes, "Cartoons as Micropractices of Resistance" from "Office Folklore in the Academic Paperwork Empire: The Interstitial Space of Gendered (Con)texts" in *Text and Performance Quarterly 38*, 1994: 181–196. Reprinted with the permission of the author and Taylor & Francis.

Pages 193–94, Case Study I: Reprinted with the permission of Clifton Scott.

Table 7.1: Adapted from K. L. Ashcroft, "Gender, Discourse and Organization: Framing a Shifting Relationship" from *The Sage Handbook of Organizational Discourse*, edited by D. Grant, C. Hardy, C. Oswick, and L. Putnam. Copyright © 2005 by Sage Publications Ltd. Adapted by permission.

Pages 228–29, Case Study: Adapted from S. Saul, "Gimme an Rx! Cheerleaders Pep Up Drug Sales" in *The New York Times*, November 28, 2005. Copyright © 2005 by The New York Times Company. Adapted with permission.

Table 8.1: Adapted from Cynthia Stohl and George Cheney, "Participatory Processes/Paradoxical Practices: Communication and the Dilemmas of Organizational Democracy" in *Management Communication Quarterly 14*, 2001: 349–407. Copyright © 2001 by Sage Publications, Inc. Adapted with permission of Sage Publications, Inc.

Figure 8.1: Stanley Deetz, "Multiple Stakeholder Model of the Corporation in Society" from *Transforming Communication, Transforming Business* (Cresskill, New Jersey: Hampton Press, 1995), p. 50. Reprinted with the permission of the publisher.

Figure 8.2: Richard Wellins, William Byham, and Jeanne Wilson, "The Empowerment Continuum of Work Teams" from *Empowered Teams*. Reprinted with the permission of Jossey-Bass Publishers.

Table 8.2: J. Goodbody, "Critical Success Factors for Global Virtual Teams" from *Strategic Communication Management 9*, no. 2, February/March 2005, www.melcrum.com/link/scm. Reprinted with permission.

Pages 251–52, 254: Peter Senge et al., excerpts (approximately 55 words) from *The Fifth Discipline Fieldbook*. Copyright © 1994 by Peter M. Senge, Art Kleiner, Charlotte Roberts, Richard B. Ross, and Bryan J. Smith. Reprinted with the permission of Doubleday, a division of Random House, Inc.

Figure 8.3: Peter Senge et al., "Balancing Inquiry and Advocacy" from *The Fifth Discipline Fieldbook*. Copyright © 1994 by Peter M. Senge, Art Kleiner, Charlotte Roberts, Richard B. Ross, and Bryan J. Smith. Reprinted with the permission of Doubleday, a division of Random House, Inc.

Figure 8.4: Peter Senge et al., "The Ladder of Inference" from *The Fifth Discipline Fieldbook*. Copyright © 1994 by Peter M. Senge, Art Kleiner, Charlotte Roberts, Richard B. Ross, and Bryan J. Smith. Reprinted with the permission of Doubleday, a division of Random House, Inc.

Figure 8.5: Peter Senge et al., "The Evolution of Dialogue" from *The Fifth Discipline Fieldbook*. Copyright © 1994 by Peter M. Senge, Art Kleiner, Charlotte Roberts, Richard B. Ross, and Bryan J. Smith. Reprinted with the permission of Doubleday, a division of Random House, Inc.

Page 257: W. Richard Scott, excerpts from *Organizations: Rational, Natural, and Open Systems*. Copyright © 1981. Reprinted with the permission of Pearson Education, Upper Saddle River, NJ.

Figure 8.6: W. Richard Scott, "Small-Group Communication Networks" from *Organizations: Rational, Natural, and Open Systems*. (Englewood Cliffs, New Jersey: Prentice-Hall, 1981), p. 8. Copyright © 1981. Reprinted with the permission of Pearson Education, Upper Saddle River, NJ.

Figure 9.1: Robert R. Blake and Jane Srygley Mouton, "The Blake and Mouton Managerial Grid" from *The Managerial Grid III: The Key to Leadership Excellence* (Houston: Gulf Publishing Company, 1985), p. 12. Reprinted with permission.

Figure 9.2: P. Hersey and K. Blanchard, "Situational Leadership Model" from *Management of Organizational Behavior: Utilizing Human Resources* 3e. Reprinted with the permission of the Center for Leadership Studies.

Figure 9.3: "The Five Stages of the Empowerment Process." Copyright © 1988 by the Academy of Management (NY). Adapted with the permission of the Academy of Management via Copyright Clearance Center.

Page 297: Paul Smith, excerpt from "Bullies Incorporated" from *MIS Australia*, February 2005. Reprinted with the permission of the author.

Figure 10.1: R. D'Aveni, "The Original 7-S Model of Strategic Alignment" from "Coping with Hypercompetition: Utilizing the New 7-S Model" in *Academy of Management Executive 9*, no. 3, 1995: 48. Copyright © 1995 by The Academy of Management. Reprinted with the permission of the Academy of Management.

Table 10.2: "Learning the Language of Text Messaging." Copyright © 2006 by Steve Nash Ltd. Reprinted with permission.

Pages 332–33: Katie Hafner, excerpt from "For Some, the Blogging Never Stops" in *The New York Times*, May 24, 2004: G1. Copyright © 2004 by The New York Times Company. Reprinted with permission.

Table 11-1: "NCA Credo for Ethical Communication." Reprinted with the permission of the National Communication Association.

Author Index

Subject Index